Politics of Impunity

Series Editors: Victoria M. Basham and Sarah Bulmer

The Critical Military Studies series welcomes original thinking on the ways in which military power works within different societies and geopolitical arenas.

Militaries are central to the production and dissemination of force globally, but the enduring legacies of military intervention are increasingly apparent at the societal and personal bodily levels as well, demonstrating that violence and war-making function on multiple scales. At the same time, the notion that violence is an appropriate response to wider social and political problems transcends militaries: from private security to seemingly 'non-military' settings such as fitness training and schooling, the legitimisation and normalisation of authoritarianism and military power occurs in various sites. This series seeks original, high-quality manuscripts and edited volumes that engage with such questions of how militaries, militarism and militarisation assemble and disassemble worlds touched and shaped by violence in these multiple ways. It will showcase innovative and interdisciplinary work that engages critically with the operation and effects of military power and provokes original questions for researchers and students alike.

Available Titles:

Resisting Militarism: Direct Action and the Politics of Subversion
Chris Rossdale

Making War on Bodies: Militarisation, Aesthetics and Embodiment in International Politics
Catherine Baker

Disordered Violence: How Gender, Race and Heteronormativity Structure Terrorism
Caron Gentry

Sex and the Nazi Soldier: Violent, Commercial and Consensual Contacts during the War in the Soviet Union, 1941–1945
Regina Mühlhäuser (translated by Jessica Spengler)

The Military-Peace Complex: Gender and Materiality in Afghanistan
Hannah Partis-Jennings

Politics of Impunity: Torture, the Armed Forces and the Failure of Transitional Justice in Brazil
Henrique Tavares Furtado

Forthcoming:

Inhabiting No-Man's-Land: Army Wives, Gender and Militarisation
Alexandra Hyde

Poetic Prosthetics: Contemporary Soldier Writing and the Limping Back from War
Ron Ben-Tovim

Conscientious Objection in Turkey: A Socio-legal Analysis of the Right to Refuse Military Service
Demet Caltekin

War and Militarisation: The British, Canadian and Dutch Invasion of Southern Afghanistan
Paul Dixon

Beyond the Wire: The Cultural Politics of Veteran Narratives
Nick Caddick

Politics of Impunity

Torture, the Armed Forces and the
Failure of Transitional Justice in Brazil

HENRIQUE TAVARES FURTADO

EDINBURGH
University Press

Edinburgh University Press is one of the leading university presses in the UK. We publish academic books and journals in our selected subject areas across the humanities and social sciences, combining cutting-edge scholarship with high editorial and production values to produce academic works of lasting importance. For more information visit our website: edinburghuniversitypress.com

Edinburgh University Press Ltd
The Tun – Holyrood Road
12(2f) Jackson's Entry
Edinburgh EH8 8PJ

First published in hardback by Edinburgh University Press 2022

Typeset in 10.5/13 ITC Giovanni Std by
IDSUK (DataConnection) Ltd, and
printed and bound by CPI Group (UK) Ltd,
Croydon, CR0 4YY

A CIP record for this book is available from the British Library

ISBN 978 1 4744 9150 1 (hardback)
ISBN 978 1 4744 9151 8 (paperback)
ISBN 978 1 4744 9152 5 (webready PDF)
ISBN 978 1 4744 9153 2 (epub)

CONTENTS

LIST OF FIGURES AND TABLES

Figures

Table

ACKNOWLEDGEMENTS

This project could not have been completed without the editors of the series Advances in Critical Military Studies, Sarah Bulmer and Victoria Basham. I thank you and the editorial board for the belief you showed in my work and for your incredibly encouraging, thorough and helpful feedback. I am also indebted to my editors Gillian Leslie, Sarah Foyle and Ersev Ersoy for their help and support during the different stages of production; a very special thanks goes to Camilla Rockwood for her patience and thorough engagement with the text. I extend my gratitude to Andreja Zevnik, Maja Zehfuss, Kimberly Hutchings, Japhy Wilson, Charlotte Heath-Kelly and Maria Mälksoo, who all read previous versions of this manuscript. Your comments and guidance have always enriched my work and pushed the boundaries of my research. I also remember fondly the many cups of coffee and pints we shared over the years. You have made me a better researcher and writer, but more importantly, a happier person.

I also thank the interviewees and the staff of the Memorial da Resistência de São Paulo who agreed to take part in the decade-long research that preceded the writing of this book. In particular, I am grateful to Julia Gumieri and Marilia Bonas for having spared me their time. I have always been and will forever remain inspired by your commitment to opposing past and present forms of authoritarianism.

I would like to thank the Public Archives of the State of São Paulo for allowing me to reprint the photos of the Memorial da Resistência. The material in Chapter 4 is adapted from Furtado, Henrique Tavares, 'The Memory of Militarism and the Value of Resistance: an Analysis of the Resistance Memorial of São Paulo', *Critical Military Studies* 6, no. 34 (2020), 376–96, and is reproduced with permission.

Lastly, I thank my family for the love and care you have given me during the past couple of years. I have a big family, so brace yourselves: my mother and father Alda and Henrique, my aunts Fátima, Letícia and Neuza, my uncle Manoel, my cousins Ná and Jú and my in-laws Lotta and Berth. I think we can all agree that things have been challenging lately, and I would not have made it without you. I especially thank my wife Emmy and my baby boy Victor (one day you will hate that I referred to you as 'baby boy', but today is not that day). I write for a living and yet I cannot put into words what you mean to me. I guess 'everything' would be a good start. It does not quite cover it, but it would be a start. I love you two, dearly. Thank you for being so patient.

PS: I am terribly sorry to inform you, Victor, but under current international law it remains illegal for a child to support a football team other than his father's. If you do not believe me, ask your godfather Gabriel.

LIST OF ABBREVIATIONS

ALN	Ação Libertadora Nacional (National Liberation Action)
Amnesty Commission	Comissão de Anistia do Ministério da Justiça (Amnesty Commission of the Ministry of Justice)
ANC	African National Congress
AV	Ala Vermelha do Partido Comunista (Red Wing)
CAVR	Comissão de Acolhimento, Verdade e Reconciliação (Commission of Reception, Truth and Reconciliation)
CBA	Comitê Brasileiro pela Anistia (Brazilian Amnesty Committee)
CCC	Comando de Caça aos Comunistas (Command of Communist Manhunting)
CCV	Comissão Camponesa da Verdade (Peasant's Truth Commission)
CEH	Comisión para el Esclarecimiento Histórico (Commission for Historical Clarification)
CEMDP	Comissão Especial sobre os Mortos e Desaparecidos Políticos (Special Commission on Political Deaths and Disappearances)
CENIMAR	Centro de Informações da Marinha (Navy Information Centre)
CIE	Centro de Informacões do Exército (Army Information Centre)

CISA	Centro de Informacões de Seguranca da Aeronáutica (Air Force Centre of Information and Security)
CJP	Comissão de Justiça e Paz (Commission of Peace and Justice)
CNV	Comissão Nacional da Verdade (National Truth Commission)
CNVJ	Commission Nationale de Vérité et de Justice (National Truth and Justice Commission)
CNVR	Comisión Nacional de Verdad y Reconciliación (National Truth and Reconciliation Commission)
COLINA	Comandos de Libertação Nacional (National Liberation Commands)
Comissão Arns	Comissão de Defesa dos Direitos Humanos Dom Paulo Evaristo Arns (Arns Commission for Human Rights Defence)
CONADEP	Comisión Nacional sobre la Desaparición de Personas (National Commission on the Disappearance of Persons)
CVES	Comisión de la Verdad para El Salvador (Commission on the Truth for El Salvador)
DOI-CODI	Destacamento de Operações de Informação – Centro de Operações de Defesa Interna (Deployment Group for Intelligence Operations – Centre of Operations of Internal Defence)
DOPS	Departamento de Ordem Política e Social (Department of Political and Social Order)
ESG	Escola Superior de Guerra (Superior War College)
FORGA	Forças Guerrilheiras do Araguaia (Araguaia Guerrilla Forces)
GVHRs	Gross Violations of Human Rights
HRAs	Human Rights Activists
IACHR	Inter-American Commission on Human Rights
IACtHR	Inter-American Court of Human Rights
ICTJ	International Center for Transitional Justice
IJTJ	International Journal of Transitional Justice
IDASA	Institute for a Democratic Alternative for South Africa

IEVE	Instituto de Estudo da Violência do Estado (Institute for the Study of State Violence)
ISER	Instituto de Estudos da Religião (Institute of Religion Studies)
LSN	Lei de Segurança Nacional (National Security Law)
MR-8	Movimento Revolucionário 8 de Outubro (Revolutionary Movement 8 October)
MRT	Movimento Revolucionário Tiradentes (Tiradentes Revolutionary Movement)
OAB	Ordem dos Advogados do Brasil (Brazilian Order of Attorneys)
OBAN	Operação Bandeirantes (Operation Bandeirantes)
PCB	Partido Comunista Brasileiro (Brazilian Communist Party)
PCdoB	Partido Comunista do Brasil (Communist Party of Brazil)
PNDH-3	Terceiro Programa Nacional de Direitos Humanos (Third National Programme of Human Rights)
POLOP	Organização Revolucionária Marxista (Revolutionary Marxist Organisation)
PTB	Partido Trabalhista Brasileiro (Brazilian Labour Party)
RM-SP	Resistance Memorial of São Paulo
SNI	Serviço Nacional de Informação (National Information Service)
TRC	Truth and Reconciliation Commission of South Africa
UDHR	Universal Declaration of Human Rights
UN	United Nations
UNDP	United Nations Development Programme
VAR-Palmares	Vanguarda Armada Revolucionária Palmares (Palmares Revolutionary Armed Vanguard)
VHRs	Violations of Human Rights

Introduction: Hope in the Violent Land

Transitional justice follows a simple script. The promotion of account-ability in the wake of systematic violence is supposed to take a given society from a state of 'madness' (ravaged by violence, authoritarianism and intractable divisions) into a future of 'hope' (a promised time when violence, authoritarianism or impunity never happen again).[1] Efforts towards reconciliation and truth-seeking are meant to contribute to the goal of overcoming 'cultures of impunity' and vicious 'cycles of violence'.

In Brazil, 18 November 2011 conveyed this sense of hope like no other day. This date marked the long-awaited creation of the Comissão Nacional da Verdade (National Truth Commission, CNV) in a country affected by the unwillingness to investigate gross violations of human rights (GVHRs) committed by agents of state in the recent past. Like other countries in the Southern Cone of Latin America, Brazil had endured a brutal civic-military dictatorship during the Cold War. The dictator-ship instituted an authoritarian regime that lasted for twenty-one years (1964–85) and was responsible for 70,000 cases of political persecution, 20,000 cases of torture, 10,000 cases of forced exile and hundreds of deaths and forced disappearances.[2] But unlike other countries such as Argentina, Chile, Germany and South Africa, the process of re-democrati-sation in Brazil witnessed no meaningful efforts towards accountability, no criminal trials and no official truth-seeking policies. The transition rested on a blanket amnesty, decreed in 1979 and respected ever since. Brazil was a latecomer to the global boom of transitional justice. The creation of the CNV during the presidency of Dilma Rousseff, herself a survivor of the military regime and a member of the Workers' Party, was powerfully symbolic of a new era when, at last, *a esperança tinha vencido o medo* (hope had beaten fear).[3]

Or was it? Most stories about transitions begin with a clear ending: the moment war turns into peace, authoritarianism into democracy, political enmity into civil disagreement. The moment conflict in its various forms stops, and efforts towards remembrance, redressing and coming to terms begin. This was allegedly the case with Germany in the post-1945 era, with Argentina in 1984, with Chile in 1990 and South Africa five years later. Arguably, time moved on in those places, bringing an aftermath to violence, authoritarianism and conflict. Democracy was restored – or first implemented – and the crimes of the past (the Holocaust, *la guerra sucia*, apartheid) came to a halt. This was never the case with Brazil. More than half a century after the 1964 coup, the country still struggles with the absence of a proper 'aftermath' to a certain regime of fear.

In a painful sense, there was no aftermath for survivors and relatives of victims of the dictatorship. There usually is not, when it comes to forced disappearances. Due to the very nature of their traumatic experience – never knowing how, when or if their loved ones have died – survivors and relatives never experience a sense of closure, let alone a feeling of justice. The legal impediments enacted by the outgoing regime in Brazil added further layers of cruelty to their pain. After the end of the *anos de chumbo* (Years of Lead) and before the beginning of re-democratisation, the blanket amnesty (Law 6.683/1979) significantly constrained the possibilities for reckoning. The amnesty law protected perpetrators of political violence from future litigation and unofficially imposed an enduring silence about the past. The archives of the political police remained closed for a decade, authorities continued to deny the existence of cases of torture or dismissed them as unimportant, and the military kept commemorating their horrendous crimes as part of a dirty but justifiable war effort against international communism.

There is also a more literal sense to the absence of an aftermath in Brazil – a sense that allegedly sets it apart from other transitions in the Southern Cone, meaning, quite simply, that there was no proper end to violence, fear and insecurity. On the contrary, the 'pacification' of state terrorists, the relative demilitarisation of the state and the national pact of reconciliation were followed by a shocking rise in the level of violence.[4] The assessment by the Political Terror Scale (PTS) dataset illustrates the daunting reality of a place that does not fit into the general script of transitions to democracy. If, following the apex of the dictatorship, authorities resorted to 'extensive political imprisonment' and 'political murders and brutality', five years into the democratic regime 'terror' was 'expanded to the whole population'.[5] From the early 1980s to the late 1990s, the country witnessed a 209 per cent increase in homicide rates.[6] This meant that no fewer than 229,266 individuals were intentionally assassinated during the re-democratisation,[7] more than twenty times the number of the highest estimates of disappearances during the military regime. The excitement with the prospects of the new republic was tempered by the realisation, one massacre after another, that the military had stepped away from government, but they had never left the front. In 1992, 111 inmates were shot dead by the riot police in a detention centre in São Paulo (the Carandiru massacre).[8] In July 1993, eight homeless children were murdered by a death squad in Rio (the Candelária church massacre); in August, twenty-one residents of a local favela were killed in similar conditions (the Vigário Geral massacre); and between July and August, sixteen Yanomamis were assassinated on the border with Venezuela (the Yanomami massacre).[9] In 1996, nineteen members of the landless movement were gunned down during the occupation of a plantation-like estate in the north-east (the Eldorado dos Carajás massacre).[10] The Brazilian state was not only unwilling to provide respite for those traumatised by the military regime, it was effectively manufacturing new traumatic experiences at an industrial pace. In the mid-1990s, members of Médecins Sans Frontières concluded that 90 per cent of residents of the favelas they visited in Rio de Janeiro showed signs of post-traumatic stress disorder.[11]

Between 2003 and 2011, millions of Brazilians were immersed in an atmosphere of hope. The election of Rousseff's predecessor and mentor, the working-class leader Lula da Silva, was followed by a sustained period of socio-economic gains. During the Workers' Party years, the economy grew 4.5 per cent a year on average (2006–10),[12] social benefits were expanded to almost 40 million individuals, house ownership and further education were subsidised,[13] and affirmative action programmes were introduced in public universities.[14] Crowning the decade's achievements, Brazil gained the right to host the 2014 World Cup and the 2016 Olympics. The hopeful atmosphere created a widespread feeling that things were finally changing; that Brazilian society was on the verge of overcoming its historical malaises. The creation of a truth commission under the presidency of a survivor of torture added another layer to the general atmosphere: the hope that the country's 'culture of impunity' and 'cycle of violence' would soon come to an end.

But hope and fear can coexist in a strange harmony. Although there has been some fluctuation over the years, these frightening homicide figures have continued to increase. At the turn of the century, Brazil had metrics of violence that, given their specific proportions, could be compared to those of famous international conflicts and warzones. From

2003 to 2011, during the years of hope, 449,985 Brazilians were killed; a number 2.24 times higher than the number of disappearances of the Guatemalan Civil War, and 1.5 times higher than the overall casualties of the Iraq War (2003–11).[15] In 2014 alone, the figure of 60,000 violent deaths equalled the number of US soldiers lost during the entire Vietnam War (if we count from 1979, they surpass the number of dead Vietnamese combatants by half a million).[16] In 2016, the 61,283 violent deaths witnessed in Brazil were comparable to the nuclear bombing of Nagasaki in 1945.[17] Most commentators ran out of comparable cases when the figures surpassed 63,000 violent deaths in 2017, painfully stating the normalisation of death in the land of fear.[18] In absolute terms, no 'peaceful' and 'reconciled' democracy has been more lethal than the Brazilian democracy.[19]

Violence in the present also bears a stark similarity with the violence of the past. One of the most worrying features in this scenario is the fact that the state continues to kill. In the context of an ever-growing feeling of insecurity,[20] the perpetration of abuses and wrongdoing by the militarised police forces has been a constant routine.[21] Almost three decades after the end of the dictatorship, the practices of torture, extrajudicial executions and forced disappearances are still a normalised part of everyday policing, disproportionately (not to say almost exclusively) targeting Brazil's black precariat.[22] State killing continues to be justified with reference to new 'wars' (e.g., the war on drugs, the war on organised crime) and new projects of 'pacification' (the 2014 World Cup, the 2016 Olympics). This form of 'quasi-official' brutality – never truly acknowledged, but near institutionalised violence – feeds on what Chevigny called the 'populism of fear' of those who stand behind the extremist position that 'bandido bom é bandido morto' (a good thug is a dead thug).[23] This position continues to enjoy the support of the upper/middle classes, who preach state-sanctioned murder as a public security policy from behind the walls of private gated condominiums.[24] The far-right leader Jair Bolsonaro is the latest and most unfortunate child of this grotesque death cult.

Meanwhile, state killing produces more victims, more mothers without their children, more traces of bodies who simply vanish. Between the 12th and 21st of May 2006, 505 civilians were assassinated by the gendarmerie and members of a death squad in return for a large-scale prison rebellion organised by a crime faction in São Paulo (which resulted in the deaths of fifty-nine state agents).[25] The 'crimes of May' sparked the formation of the 'mothers of May', a group of organised family members who demand proper measures of accountability and whose name, fruit of an uncanny coincidence, evokes the symbology of the Argentine Madres de Plaza de Mayo. In 2013, the forced disappearance of Amarildo de Souza at the hands of officers from a pacifying unit in the Rocinha favela in Rio sparked international outrage.[26] In 2018, it was the brutal death of Marielle Franco, a socialist/LGBT leader who opposed the militarisation of policing, that shocked the world. Franco and her driver Anderson Gomes were gunned down by two militiamen on their way home from a roundtable about the empowerment of black women.[27] Those are only a few examples of the cases of which we have become aware. Since the year the amnesty law was implemented, 1,345 political leaders have been assassinated.[28] In 2017 alone, 82,000 disappearances were registered.[29] There is a much larger, more terrifying and under-reported reality in which, over the past eighteen years, agents of the Brazilian state were responsible for at least 26,858 deaths during 'legal interventions or warlike operations'.[30] This is a level of lethality on average 4.6 times higher than that of the US police forces, to name a more visible case.[31] From the perspective of the groups at the margins of Brazilian society, those usually victimised by police brutality, state terror never came to an end.

The normalisation of death in Brazil contributed to the dissemination of a particular trope, blaming present-day violence on the absence of transitional justice initiatives during the re-democratisation. For decades, experts and politicians, human rights activists (HRAs), survivors and transitional justice scholars/practitioners have described Brazil as the quintessential case of a 'culture of impunity'.[32] In their view, the country provides a clear-cut case where amnesty for perpetrators in the post-authoritarian scenario and the forced amnesia concerning GVHRs has paved the way for the banalisation of abuses. According to this reasoning, the regime of silence and forgetfulness[33] instituted by the 1979 amnesty law undermined the process of democratisation, which was left as 'incomplete'.[34] Incapable of coming to terms with its past, of assimilating properly liberal, democratic values and of punishing those who committed wrongdoing, Brazil had turned into an 'ugly' democracy: a place where misuses of state authority are normal and atrocities are committed with impunity.[35] All such descriptions concur as to the purpose of transitional justice in the country, framing its implementation as a matter of urgency. In the words of staff members of the CNV, accountability was needed in order to 'excise the enduring metastasis of the dictatorship'.[36]

The Failure of Transitional Justice

Transitional justice might follow a simple script, but reality hardly ever does. Overcoming a series of difficulties, and after a period of hard but impressive work, the CNV released its final report on 10 December 2014 (Human Rights Day) during the 50th anniversary of the military coup. The powerful symbology of Rousseff's reception of the report was hard to miss. The deliverance of truth to the survivor of torture turned president was taken as a historical moment towards the 'closing of the books of the past', to use transitional justice jargon. But the date could easily mark the end of the years of hope. In the space of four years, the promising atmosphere brought by a decade of Workers' Party government had developed into something else entirely. The involvement of the Workers' Party in a massive corruption scandal resurrected old anti-communist tropes of the past with a newly found ferocity. The president who attempted to 'close the books' of the dictatorship was controversially impeached for a supposed attempt to 'cook the books', masking a robust budget deficit to support her re-election. Amidst a deep economic crisis and a growing anti-political atmosphere, Jair Bolsonaro, a neo-fascist leader with alleged ties to local militia groups, supporter of the military regime and apologist for torture, was elected president.

This book is part of the effort to understand what went wrong. It is written as general advice against the temptation to see the present crisis as confirmation of old assumptions about violence, militarism and justice. The analysis is particularly critical of explanations of the rise of *Bolsonarismo* as a 'return of the repressed', or the natural consequence of the failure of transitional justice in the country. On the contrary, the analysis that follows argues that the brand of militarism behind *Bolsonarismo* was never 'repressed', in a Freudian register or otherwise, and that, if transitional justice mechanisms have failed, the discourse of transitional justice has been very successful in Brazil and elsewhere. The manuscript's main contribution lies in scrutinising the Brazilian case, about which surprisingly little has been written, and using it as the basis for a theory of processes of accountability that pushes beyond the boundaries of (re)current debates regarding the implementation of justice after mass atrocities.

The suggestion that impunity for GVHRs works like a cancer, growing and metastasising to the rest of the social body if left unchecked, leading to 'cultures of impunity', is neither new nor specific to Brazil. The expression 'cultures of impunity' is a central part of the transitional justice vocabulary, popularised after 1993 as the scholarship and practice of transitional justice was mainstreamed across the world.[37] Ever since, scholars have continuously warned us of the dangers of leaving past historical traumas unaddressed for too long.[38] Wherever they were implemented, truth commissions, special courts and reparation programmes mobilised the slogans 'Never again!' or 'Enough!'; the promises that societies ravaged by conflict and authoritarianism could transcend a legacy of violence and fully develop into 'mature' liberal democracies through measures of accountability.

The Brazilian case presents a new development in terms of timing. Transitional justice was called upon to resolve the public security crisis in Brazil while the field was experiencing a crisis of its own. After a swift and impressive rise at the turn of the millennium, the scholarship and practice of transitional justice was now faced with growing scepticism. The slogans that once captivated entire societies and global audiences no longer seemed to enjoy the same unquestionable appeal that they enjoyed in the 1990s. The past fifteen years have witnessed the growth of a body of literature that, while adhering to humanitarian principles, was more critical of processes of transitional justice. Distancing themselves from earlier works, scholars were more aware of the limitations, complexities and political undertones of ideas such as truth, justice and reconciliation.[39] Some were very critical of the field's excessive legalism and unwavering faith in the powers of accountability and liberalisation.[40] The critique came from the perceived flaws and failures of truth commissions and courts, reparations and processes of reconciliation that, contrary to expectations, were incapable of putting an end to violence in societies in Latin America, Africa and Southeast Asia.

The biggest theme holding this wave of criticism together was the concept of violence. Most works argued that transitional justice initiatives had excessively focused on violations of civil and political rights (e.g. torture, forced disappearances and extrajudicial executions) while overlooking historical violations of social and economic rights (e.g. unequal patterns of land distribution, structural racism, gender gaps).[41] The joint diagnosis was that interventions failed because they stuck to legalistic principles (the framing of justice as criminal accountability) and a rather narrow understanding of violence, characteristic of the liberal peace paradigm.[42] Both posed unnecessary hindrances to peacebuilding because of their tendency to eschew a deep analysis of the root causes of conflict, and the relationship between violence and underdevelopment.[43]

This critical wave developed with time, changing in quality. While the first works criticised the exclusion of structural forms of violence from transitional justice's agenda, particularly focusing on specific cases, a growing number of voices is now calling for a reconfiguration of the whole theoretical edifice and practices of transitional justice. The latest development of this critique is the concept of transformative justice. Drawing considerable attention in recent years,[44] this concept encapsulates the need to move beyond legalistic principles, top-down approaches, one-size-fits-all formulae and narrow ideas of what counts as violence. Instead, a transformative approach 'emphasizes local agency and resources, the prioritization of process rather than preconceived outcomes and the challenging of unequal and intersecting power relationships and structures of exclusion at both the local and the global level'.[45] The bottom line is that only a new practice of transitional justice, reimagined towards the promotion of transformative change, will be capable of bringing a self-sustaining peace to societies ravaged by conflict and authoritarianism.

The Missing Link: Violence and Militarism

The intersection between the Brazilian crisis (the paradox of growing levels of violence amidst democratisation) and the crisis of transitional justice (the growing scepticism about the promise of 'never again') provides an opportunity to push the boundaries of critique, investigating the deeper political dimensions of transitional justice. The history of almost-continuous GVHRs in Brazil is disturbing, not only in the sense conveyed by its gruesome figures, but also in the sense of disturbing the legalistic and liberal assumptions of transitional justice. The fact that a stable democracy that 'has not been involved in any armed conflicts since 1946'[46] can still endure the losses of one (American) Vietnam War per year is certainly a challenge for the clean-cut distinctions of advocates of the liberal peace. It brings into question assumptions regarding war, militarism and political repression that have been central to projects of pacification and to eurocentric narratives of civility. The very argument about 'cultures of impunity', constantly evoked by transitional justice experts, is an attempt to explain a situation that seems unexplainable or paradoxical: the existence of a liberal democracy that seems to be as dangerous to the lives of its citizens as an atomic bomb. An investigation of the structure of this argument, revealing its main assumptions and political consequences in the Brazilian context, is also an investigation of the core principles and political effects of transitional justice initiatives. A close look at the ways in which the idea of Brazil as a 'culture of impunity' affects our understanding of violence in the country can shed a much-needed light into the future of transitional justice.

New ideas, such as transformative justice, are a sign that the critique of transitional justice has reached a crossroads. What is at stake in recent debates is, quite simply, whether we can throw the bathwater away and save the baby; whether transitional justice as an enterprise and an aspiration can be saved from its own flaws and failures; whether the critiques of the past fifteen years point towards an end to the field, or towards a new beginning. This book was written with this central dilemma in mind. My intention is to propose an answer by drawing lessons from the challenges, the shortcomings, but most importantly, the often unacknowledged successes of the implementation of transitional justice in Brazil.

The investigation that follows centres on the main culprit of the crisis of transitional justice: the concept of violence. Violence, as it were, is a complex matter. Almost every work on violence begins by emphasising the concept's polysemic nature, pointing out the overwhelming profusion of things that could be called 'violent'.[47] The interdisciplinary literature on what we could loosely call 'violence studies' is pervaded by laments about the lack of deep theorisations concerning important aspects of the phenomenon.[48] As it turns out, the 'essence' of violence as a social and political phenomenon remains elusive. But we can discern, in this overwhelming abundance, a bifurcation in ways of making sense of violence. On one hand, and most commonly, the phenomenon of violence can be treated as a visible act. It is read as an individual or collective action that represents a direct, physical offense against another individual or group. This form of violence represents an instrumental action,[49] and it is based on particular reasons that can be seen as political or non-political,[50] justified or illegitimate,[51] and rational or emotional.[52] Most of the violence I have described concerning the crisis of public security in Brazil fits in this category. Mistreatments, homicides and GVHRs are all visible forms of violence, even when perpetrated covertly. They are visible because they express a sense in which the phenomenon of violence originates in an individual source that carries an indivisible responsibility, which poses crucial consequences for the question of accountability and the problematic of impunity. Visible violence is a form of violence that, in the words of Étienne Balibar, possesses a clearly identifiable face: the face of perpetrators of violent acts.[53]

As the critique of transitional justice suggests, this is not the only recognisable form of violence. Over the last two centuries a number of critical scholars have suggested different ways of thinking about violence beyond its visible face, as a phenomenon that involves an invisible or concealed facet, subjected to hidden dynamics. In transitional justice and the wider field of peace and conflict research, this sense of invisibility is often conveyed by reference to Galtung's concept of structural violence, as impediments to the realisations of the full potential of human beings.[54] For him, violence is not necessarily or primarily an act; it does not involve only a physical wound. While traditional approaches see the effects of violence in terms of body counts and homicide rates, Galtung's structural violence is expressed in terms of differentials in development indicators (such as life expectancy).[55] But, however influential his thesis may be, it is not exhaustive of other theorisations of invisible violence. If we are to seriously scrutinise transitional justice's narrow conceptualisation of violence, we ought to include more (and more radical) qualifiers to the concept of violence such as constitutive,[56] psychopathological,[57] symbolic,[58] objective,[59] ultra-objective,[60] patriarchal,[61] epistemic,[62] metaphysical,[63] modern/colonial[64] and necropolitical.[65] Importantly, transitional justice scholars have engaged relatively little, if at all, with scholars for whom violence is not only structural but *structuring of contemporary social relations*. These radical theorisations of violence situate it at the very basis of a given political order, as a language that frames certain bodies as 'violatable', inscribing in them the processes of differentiation that sustain the contemporary capitalist world.[66] This violence does not originate from the rule of generals, but from the general forms of racialised, patriarchal and class-based exclusion that are co-constitutive of our everyday lives. This violence is invisible because it has no identifiable face,[67] meaning it cannot be blamed on any individual/indivisible source without a certain loss of meaning. It is inescapably political because it does not render itself easily translatable into matters of accountability or the terminology of violation; it does not refer to instances or structures of wrongdoing, but to the essential wrong that founds the political order.[68]

The investigation of violence in the context of post-conflict and post-authoritarian societies (if we can ever speak of such constructs, to begin with) also leads to the interrogation of the equally elusive concepts of militarism and militarisation. As Anna Stavrianakis and Jan Selby contend, after enjoying a period of burgeoning intellectual production during the late Cold War, the study of militarism suffered a relative decline in the discipline of international relations after the 1990s.[69] The original concerns with the glorification of belligerent values,[70] the question of civilian oversight of the armed forces,[71] the pace of the arms race and the risk of mutually assured destruction[72] eventually gave way to the new concerns of the new millennium: the apparently changing nature of warfare in a globalised world, the dynamics and root causes of the so-called 'state failure' and the new requirements of human security. An important critical turn in the subfield of security studies also attributed a certain heuristic privilege to the study of processes securitisation – or the social construction of threat and danger – over what was seen as an outdated and excessively rigid focus on military institutions and state capabilities. All of these tendencies coalesced into evaluations of the 'war on terror' after September 11th, 2001, which, for better or worse, have nearly monopolised the attention of critical scholarship in international relations.

It is interesting to contrast Stavrianakis' and Selby's claims about the levels of interest in the study of militarism in international relations with scholars working in a different context. For example, both Martin Shaw and Peter Feaver state that sociological and comparativist interest in the concept enjoyed a revival in the 2000s.[73] Feaver goes as far as to speak of a renaissance in the field of civil-military studies,[74] a claim disputed by Thomas Bruneau and José Olmeda, who complain about the lack of theoretical sophistication in a field still very much dominated by the problematic of civilian oversight.[75] Curiously, and at times contradictorily, social scientists have both lamented that attention to militarism is waning[76] and cherished that the study of militarism is booming.[77] Such claims are, by their very nature, difficult to assess. Issues ranging from specific disciplinary foci to the trouble (or some would say the blessing) of conceptual fluidity could affect the diagnosis. As it were, like the concept of violence, militarism has been applied to numerous phenomena. Since the heyday of the study of militarism in the 1980s, there has been no single, undisputed definition of the term, and the first comprehensive typologies of its different uses only began to appear recently.[78]

What happens if we ask the same question about transitional justice? Regardless of the fluidity of meanings, most uses of the concept of militarism evoke the element of *war-making* and, more importantly for the purposes of the present work, 'the preparation for, and conduct of, organized political violence'.[79] Arguably, a field of scholarship and practice meant to design interventions for societies dealing with the legacy of violence in the wake of military regimes/conflicts would have something to say about the nature of militarism. Yet, a quick search on the webpage of the field's main journal, *The International Journal of Transitional Justice* (*IJTJ*), surveying the academic production between 2007 and 2021, reveals a startling paradox. Out of a total universe of 500 outputs published in the journal within the timeframe, around 300 articles appear in a search for the entries 'military' and 'armed forces',[80] but only fifty-three articles appear if we search for the entries 'militarism' or 'militarisation'.[81] Out of the fifty-three, only nine outputs actually contain the word 'militarism' in their full text, but none of them mention it more than once or elaborate on what militarism actually means. A similar search on the website of the biggest think thank/consultancy in the field, the International Centre for Transitional Justice (ICTJ), yields similar results;

we find 1,320 items of news and publications for the entry 'military',[82] twenty-nine for the entry 'militarisation'[83] and a meagre seven results for 'militarism'.[84] The Lexis library database shows around 1,602 results for 'transitional justice', out of which 367 mention 'armed forces' but only twenty the term 'militarism'.[85]

Obviously, this simple exercise is not meant to produce an exhaustive account – website search functions are, after all, imperfect measures of engagement – but mostly an illustration of a persistent and worrisome imbalance: the startling paradox that transitional justice's focus on the aftermath of military regimes and armed conflicts has generated little to marginal engagement with theorisations of the phenomenon of militarism itself. Once again, the fate of militarism in transitional justice shows uncanny similarities with the study of violence. The relative scarcity of references to militarism in the field's journals echoes Hannah Arendt's famous 1969 remarks concerning the absence of an entry for 'violence' in the *Encyclopaedia of the Social Sciences*. For Arendt, this absence showed 'to what an extent violence and its arbitrariness were taken for granted and therefore neglected'[86] by the very professionals who investigated 'the enormous role violence has always played in human affairs'.[87] As will become clear in the course of this book, the phenomenon of militarism has been largely taken for granted in the field of transitional justice. Even the recent critique of violence seems to have missed its importance. Arendt's judgement on the reasons for such neglect could be easily paraphrased and applied to transitional justice scholarship: perhaps 'no one questions or examines what is obvious to all'.[88]

There is, of course, a notable exception to the rule. Almost all of the nine works that reference militarism in the *IJTJ* are written from a gender-aware or feminist perspective.[89] This is not a coincidence. Feminists – always pushing the boundaries of our traditional understandings of the *political* and of *violence* – have long been at the forefront of the study of militarism and anti-militarist practice. Their ethos and practice of enquiring into pervasive effects of violence, something Rita Segato defined as the act of bringing violence to the realm of nameable things,[90] presents a natural starting point for an investigation of militarism itself. Feminist scholarship in critical security studies pioneered the field of critical military studies (CMS), with an important research agenda to take 'military power as a question, rather than taking it for granted'.[91] CMS work has revealed how the most diverse aspects of the lives and bodies of men and women across the world are dragged into, moulded and coerced by the preparation for, and justification of, warfare. Problematising simple oppositions between militarism and liberalism, the field has exposed the manifold processes that render large-scale killing normal, or even desirable, especially in so-called liberal, 'peaceful' societies.[92] An engagement with CMS has the potential to address the gap between an empirical focus on the effects of militarised violence and a theoretical understanding of militarism in transitional justice. On the other hand, transitional justice's marked, if mostly empirical, decades-long expertise on the problematic of bearing witness to atrocities (from a victim-centric perspective) is invaluable to CMS scholars working on remembrance and wartime testimonies, more often than not from the perspective of the perpetrators.[93] Moreover, while transitional justice scholarship has, rightly or wrongly, exhibited a predilection for case studies in the Global South, the study of militarism has been criticised for an excessive focus on the Global North.[94] For these reasons, more engagement between the fields is warranted.

This book is a call to close this gap, searching for the missing links between violence and the phenomenon of militarism in the context of struggles for accountability. It contributes both to the critique of violence in transitional justice and to recent debates regarding the relevance and significance of the concept of militarisation in the study of organised political violence. CMS has seen a lively discussion in recent years involving the use of the concept of militarisation (denoting a gradual extension of militarism) *vis-à-vis* the concept of security[95] and the burgeoning use of the adjective 'martial', as pertaining to all things 'of war'.[96] The analysis here shares, to a certain extent, Alison Howell's provocative critique of the uses of the concept of militarisation, by showcasing how transitional justice processes both rely on and actively sell 'the hope that military encroachment on an otherwise un-militarized past can be reversed'.[97] The following analysis shows a certain resonance between Howell's critique and the work of scholars and activists in the Global South, who have been trying to make sense of state terror for the past fifty years. The manuscript shares Howell's understanding, and that of other critics of the concept of militarisation, that (political) violence is a constitutive element of the modern world.

But a caveat must be added. While I certainly welcome a perspective that 'dispenses with the before/after temporality of "militarization"',[98] it is with great discomfort that I see the call to dispense with 'the assumed separation between [. . .] war and peace'.[99] As the following chapters make clear, the talk of blurring the boundaries between war and peace – so insidious in certain types of contemporary critical theory[100] – echoes the writings of the military strategists in the Southern Cone behind the implementation of counterinsurgency practices in the 1970s. They, too, understood war and peace as two indistinct zones, a vision inherited by French theories of colonial warfare so avidly consumed and implemented in Argentina and Brazil. They, too, spoke of their reign of terror and torture in terms of a 'dirty war', a fantastical war waged in the absence of an opposing army. This is obviously not to suggest an absurd and false symmetry between critiques of militarisation and doctrines of counterinsurgency. Militarism and anti-militarism are far from the same, but sometimes end up speaking strikingly similar languages. This book urges the field to pay closer attention to this fact.

In the following chapters, whenever the term 'civic-military' appears, it does so to highlight the essential collusion (and not a supposed collision) between the 'civil' and the 'military' faces of state terror, treated as two sides of the same coin. But the analysis pushes beyond the view that *all forms of militarism – understood as the normalisation of political violence – can be read through the lenses of warfare*. It explores the hypothesis, hardly ever pursued in the war-centric analysis of critical security studies and the CMS literature, that militarism might be about something else entirely. The Brazilian case is intriguing in part because it shows how militarism might exist, survive and even thrive *in the absence of, and disconnected from, any large-scale processes of preparation for warfare*. Instead of treating the concept of war as an a priori principle of the study of political violence,[101] the manuscript proposes to take the idea of 'war-making' – present in most definitions of militarism – to its last consequences. It proposes an understanding of 'war' as part of the 'mythology' and symbolism of social control; not so much as an external phenomenon that needs to be justified and for which society needs preparation, but as the very 'lenses', the very language through which experiences of violence are finally rendered intelligible in the contemporary world.

Conditions of Implementation vs Conditions of Possibility

This book builds on the existing critique of transitional justice, but sets itself apart from it, in questioning four of its central assumptions: (1) that transitional justice has failed; (2) that transitional justice needs saving; (3) that the field's legalism and narrow understanding of violence are simple flaws to be amended by a new approach; and (4) that transitional justice lacks economic considerations. In order to address the current dilemma and to suggest a future for critique in the field, the book proposes a new reading of transitional justice scholarship and practice based on a methodological shift: a step away from the *conditions of implementation* of justice in post-conflict or post-authoritarian scenarios, towards an analysis of its *conditions of possibility*. The core argument is heavily indebted to Foucault's work, post-Marxist scholarship and a (decolonial) feminist ethos of critique as well as previous attempts to apply critical theory to the problematic of accountability.[102]

The central argument here is that critiques of transitional justice that remain focused on questions of implementation are bound to repeat the field's mistakes, falling into what I call the politics of impunity: the depoliticisation of radical conceptions of violence via their reduction to visible violations. No matter how many transformational concepts of justice scholars formulate, no matter how many genealogies of the field are written, we will all still be discussing which interventions are best suited to implement the end of violence and conflict. Instead, I contend that a truly critical stance needs to take Foucault's work to its radical conclusion, addressing a different set of questions related to the conditions of possibility of justice in the wake of atrocities. Questions such as when, and under which conditions, scholars and practitioners began to think that violence and conflict could ever end. By operating this apparently simple but significant change of perspective, the manuscript reveals how, far from failing, the discourse of transitional justice has been extremely successful, from its inception to the present days, in Brazil and elsewhere.

The analysis that follows is unapologetically critical. It assumes that transitional justice interventions are not only constituted as responses to the legacy of systematic violence but are in themselves productive of the reality they seek to redress. Take the example of truth commissions, the temporary bodies mandated to investigate past abuses, concluding with a report.[103] This final report is supposed to narrate a violent past in an objective and dispassionate manner. Yet, reports actively identify what is particularly atrocious about the past, situating events into a larger historical and political context.[104] They produce a specific storyline that has 'a beginning and an end'[105] and is preceded by a process of editing. As sites where historical and national narratives are reproduced and legitimised,[106] they not only remember a traumatic past but also paint a particular view of the present. Because they essentially speak of systematic wrongdoing – most prominently, acts of state terror – they provide an important source of information regarding which forms of violence are regarded as 'violations' and which experiences are considered 'traumatic'. As important channels for remembrance in the aftermath, they are supposed to resist illiberal regimes of silence and 'allow survivors a voice'.[107] But, above all else, truth commission reports are sites where violence is represented through the use of a specific language for the purpose of creating a credible promise of justice, non-recurrence and demilitarisation.

One thing needs clarification here. Truth commissions are neither essentially biased nor part of an elaborate 'lawfare'. To suggest so would be to give credence to the facile and dangerous cries of fascists around the world. They are simply given an almost impossible job. Representations of the past cannot bridge the fact that 'it is impossible to remember everything'.[108] Most legislators acknowledge this impediment by adding 'as complete a picture of the past as possible' to the mandates of truth commissions, but this can only mitigate the issue. The same practices that seek to represent the past and do justice to its memory are also practices that conceal and omit the complexity of the past. Representational practices are always, to some extent, unrepresentative, and always part of a process of interpretation and 'copy-editing', as objective and as dispassionate as they might be. They constitute a process wherein a complex reality is filtered down to a neat and singular outcome. In the case of narratives about the past, this outcome is a coherent storyline. What enables these stories to work – what makes them meaningful and credible – is the 'exclusions and breaks'[109] they perform. It is what they do not say, what they avoid, and what they forget: what they deem unessential or secondary about their central tale. Representational practices can make 'sense of experience through synthesising perceptions, emotions and meanings',[110] but this process leaves behind a trace of silences and things unsaid.[111] This essential limitation is not a failure of representation. On the contrary, it provides the conditions under which something becomes representable. Metaphorically speaking, the traces of silence and the things left unsaid by representational practices work like the frames of a painting, the limits delimiting its boundaries, separating it from what it is not.

A focus on their conditions of possibility fundamentally changes our perception of transitional justice processes. This book argues that far from neglecting economic concerns, transitional justice is based on a what I call an *economy of anti-impunity* that tends towards the depoliticisation of critiques of violence by accommodating them into a structure of blame and attribution of responsibility. It argues that far from constituting a mistake, the absence of radical critiques of violence in the field represents the logical and practical conditions without which there could be no convincing promise of 'never again'. The manuscript explains truth commissions, criminal tribunals and reparation programmes as parts of a historically situated set of ideologically embedded *disciplines*; that is, the conjunction between a body of knowledge and codes of conduct centred on an ideological point of misrecognition: the representation of violence as an *intentional, cyclical, and exceptional phenomenon*. This set of disciplines is ideological not in the sense that it is politically biased towards legalism, but because it produces forms of subjectivity (subjection to particular rules) and codes of conduct that reproduce the *conditions of production* of contemporary capitalism. I argue that representations of violence in a liberal humanitarian frame (as visible violations) are part of a *post-conflictual economy of signification* – the circulation of narratives and symbols, the production and extraction of 'values' performed by a certain language (set of equivalences and differences) – that create (objectify) what we call the post-conflictual state. This economy defines (1) the limits of what counted as violence in the past, (2) the modes of acceptable political resistance in the present and (3) the possibilities of justice in the future. And it is exactly by setting rather conservative limits on the ideas of resistance and justice that the *ideological* underpinning of transitional justice succeeds in safeguarding the basis of the present, unequal order.

This book uses the Brazilian case to illustrate this theoretical development, focusing on an analysis of two recent transitional justice interventions in Brazil: the Memorial da Resistência de São Paulo (Resistance Memorial, RM-SP) and, to a greater extent, the CNV. Specifically, it discusses how the history of transitional justice in Brazil reveals the workings of a historical discipline. I provide an in-depth analysis of the permanent exhibition of the RM-SP based on two fieldwork trips to the memorial in 2014 and 2018, and an extensive narrative analysis of the documents produced by the CNV over a period of two years (2012–14): the final report, eight other auxiliary reports and 400 press releases. This data is backed up by an auxiliary data set comprising eight semi-structured and unstructured interviews with members of the truth commission, former state ministers, ex-political prisoners, relatives of the disappeared and HRAs, conducted between 2014 and 2018. The outcome of this analysis offers a new reading of transitional justice's so-called flaws and failures. In the Brazilian context, these 'flaws' are explained as the constitutive elements of a discipline that works precisely by controlling *what counts as violence, what must be resisted* and *who can be held accountable*. The idea that transitional justice is in crisis and that its interventions have systematically failed seems to stem from a profound misunderstanding of what transitional justice actually does.

Chapter Outline

The first chapter provides a historical account of transitional justice's 'punishment vs impunity' debates, from the prehistory of transitional justice in the 1970s to the formation of a 'common language of justice' at the turn of the century. First, the chapter recounts the rise of a global, anti-impunity movement during the Cold War, focusing in particular on the resistance to authoritarianism in the Southern Cone. Second, the chapter moves on to the last decades of the twentieth century (1980s–1990s). It recounts how the strategies of accountability devised by HRAs and politicians in South America and South Africa reached global notoriety and, in particular, how a series of initiatives that were the fruit of political compromises were mainstreamed and disseminated globally as transitional justice. The chapter describes the early days of the discipline as permeated by attempts to dissociate calls for criminal accountability from the ideas of forgiveness and responsibility, leading to the opposition between retributive and restorative justice. It then explains how the rise of a restorative agenda (based on a therapeutic approach to reconciliation) set into motion an internal struggle to retrieve the wholesome meaning of justice as it was envisioned by the anti-impunity movement in the 1970s. Finally, the chapter clarifies how the efforts of scholars and practitioners to reconnect the ideas of truth, memory and justice led to a new development at the turn of the century (1990–2010): the creation of a 'common language of justice'.

Chapter 2 develops the sense in which the present of transitional justice was constituted by a certain rupture, moving away from concerns with the *conditions of implementations* of justice in the aftermath of violence towards a deep investigation of the *conditions of possibility* of the discipline. Inspired by the works of Foucault and drawing insights from Žižek, this chapter begins to sketch out a critical genealogy of transitional justice as a historical discipline: a body of knowledge that possesses a disciplinary function, in other words, that exercises a form of power over individuals, moulding their conduct and behaviour. The chapter identifies the emergence of this new discipline of justice around the end of the Cold War (1989) and the end of 'Dirty Wars' in the Global South (1980s–1990s), the so-called 'end of history' defined by claims that alternatives to liberal capitalist development had disappeared. The analysis focuses on the productive facet of this new discipline, arguing that criminal trials, truth commissions and reparation programmes are not merely reactive responses to the end of conflict and authoritarianism, but active instruments that produce a *post-conflictual* reality where violence has either ended or can end: a new object of analysis and field of intervention for the emerging discipline. The chapter argues that this post-conflictual reality is built upon what Žižek defines as a symptom: a fundamental misrecognition of violence as an *intentional, cyclical and exceptional phenomenon*. The chapter argues that it is this misrecognition that sustains the possibility of the post-conflict, exactly by excluding (repressing) other, more fundamental forms of violence.

Chapter 3 offers a historical account of the Brazilian case. Working as a bridge between the theoretical and empirical contributions of the manuscript, it traces the historical changes and ruptures of ideas about violence and justice produced by the emergence of the anti-impunity movement in Brazil (1970–9). The chapter explains the atmosphere of radicalisation that preceded the 1964 coup. It describes the explosive rise of far-right anti-communism across society, the effects of the Cuban Revolution in the imaginary of the radical left and the adoption of French theories of counterinsurgency by the armed forces. The chapter recounts the overthrowing of Goulart's labour administration in 1964 and the ensuing Years of Lead (1968–79), when torture, extrajudicial executions and forced disappearances became institutionalised. It then moves on to show how the gruesome actions of the military unintentionally paved the way for a new form of democratic resistance. The violent repression of political dissidents, the repression of strikes, the deterioration of wages, the expansion of censorship to the most banal dimensions of everyday life united various societal grievances (the struggles of survivors, family members, workers, legal practitioners, feminists) around the amnesty movement in the mid-1970s. The chapter then shows the tensions within the anti-impunity movement, focusing on the necessity of portraying the movement as a non-partisan force and of separating the specific demands of transitional justice from other demands of social justice. Fundamentally, the chapter connects the prehistory of the discipline in Brazil to the twofold disappearances that characterised the political transition: the *disappearances* of the bodies of political dissidents, and the *declared disappearance* of their political project of radical change, their ideas about the complexity of violence and their understanding of justice. The chapter argues that these declared disappearances are part of the constitutive or essential exclusions and silences upon which the idea of a post-conflictual reality is based.

Praises to the CNV aside, the truth commission was not the first effort of accountability in Brazil. It was preceded by two reparation commissions (1995 and 2001) the institution of a public memorial (2008), a conviction in the Inter-American Court of Human Rights (IACtHR) and the implementation of a new national plan on human rights (both in 2010). Chapter 4 investigates this 'prehistory' of official truth-seeking in the country, focusing on the relationship between transitional justice practices and processes of memorialisation. The chapter is written from the perspective of the RM-SP, an institution whose history was shaped by the different turns that the question of historical accountability took from the early 1990s until the 2010s. The central objective here is to analyse how the memory of political violence in the past, and the narratives of transitional justice, are affected by the (neo)liberal times; how they express the concern of a society in crisis, torn between the *liberal* defence of democratic principles and the reorganisation of social relations according to the *neoliberal* market. Against the usual narrative that transitional justice overlooks the economic sphere, the chapter reveals the similarities between the 'common language of justice' and what it defines as the language of (neo)liberalism: the set of equivalences and differences between concepts, practices and experiences that constitutes the frame through which the past is represented and communicated to present audiences. Drawing insights from the works of Baudrillard, Žižek and Rancière, the chapter analyses the effects of this language on the representational practices of the permanent exhibition of the RM-SP. It argues that transitional justice initiatives can promote a depoliticised memory of resistance in two ways: by confusing the values of past political struggles with present-day values, and by equating the practice of resistance with the defence of the (neo)liberal order.

Chapter 5 introduces the first part of my analysis of the CNV (2012–14), focusing on the implementation of truth-seeking and analysing the mandate, composition and size of the truth commission. The text assesses two instances where the CNV was accused of failing to deliver justice: the failure to give survivors a voice, based on the lukewarm relations between the CNV and local activists, and the failure to bring about reconciliation, given the armed forces' refusal to accept the conclusions of the final report. The central argument of this chapter is to redirect responsibility for these failures away from the members of the truth commission and to dispute claims that truth-seeking was mishandled. Instead, the chapter argues that both 'failures' were a direct result of the CNV's acceptance of the global, common language of justice with a specific theory of accountability defined by technocratic methods and contradictory demands. The objective is to connect the problems of implementation faced by the CNV to problems at the heart of the conditions of possibility of the discipline of transitional justice.

Chapter 6 provides the second part of my analysis of the CNV, focusing on the final report, published on 10 December 2014. The chapter looks at the twenty-nine policy recommendations proposed by the CNV in order to solve the paradox of democratisation and the Brazilian 'culture of impunity'. It divides the recommendations into five interrelated themes of punishment, demilitarisation, re-education, restitution and protection. Inspired by Foucault's analytics of power and Rancière's critique of political philosophy (in particular his views on accountability), the chapter analyses the ways in which these themes are based on the *economy of anti-impunity*: a set of assumptions about power and policies of redress that grossly simplify the question of responsibility in post-authoritarian scenarios. The chapter argues that the themes convey a *market model of accountability*, assuming that power is a commodity, that political violence comes out of misuses of this commodity, and that policies of redress must simply redistribute rights across society. It links this model of accountability to a certain *fetishism of responsibility*: the excessive focus on perpetrators of GVHRs in the reports of truth commissions in detriments of wider social relations that constituted officers as state terrorists. The chapter argues that the attribution of responsibility for wrongdoing in the final report is akin to a process of *enclosure of blame*: the fencing off of responsibility around an individual and indivisible source of blame for the violent past (the military and the military dictatorship). This process of enclosure excludes other potentially culpable sectors of society, such as business elites, but most importantly it renders responsibility a matter of discrete units. The enclosure of blame operates by hiding the relational face of violence and naturalising forms of violence that are structuring of Brazil's unequal order.

The book's conclusion investigates the troubled years that followed the release of the CNV's final report. From 2014 to 2018, the atmosphere of hope in Brazil quickly deteriorated. Economic growth was halted by the effects of the global financial crisis and a massive corruption scandal devastated the credibility of the Workers' Party. Two years after creating a truth commission, Rousseff was impeached for crimes of responsibility, in a controversial process that many denounced as a new coup. Having just taken the first steps towards historical accountability, the country witnessed a virulent explosion of patriarchal militarism, the rise of historical revisionism and the return of old anti-communist tropes. In 2018, Jair Bolsonaro, a far-right leader, torture apologist and devout supporter of the dictatorship with suspected links to local militia groups, was elected president. The conclusion disputes interpretations of the rise of *Bolsonarismo* as a return of past authoritarianism, allegedly repressed by the delay in the promotion of transitional justice, emphasising the need for a new theory of accountability after mass atrocities. The book ends by discussing how the present Covid-19 crisis requires an urgent rethinking of the meaning and practice of anti-impunity.

Notes

1. The words 'hope' and 'madness' allude to the report of the Salvadoran truth commission. See United Nations, 'From Madness to Hope'.
2. Arquidiocese de São Paulo, *Brasil: Nunca Mais*; Instituto de Estudos da Violência, *Dossiê dos Mortos e Desaparecidos Poléticos a partir de 1964*; Comissão Especial sobre Mortos e Desaparecidos Políticos, *Direito à Memória e à Verdade: Comissão Especial sobre Mortos e Desaparecidos Políticos*; Maria José Coelho and Vera Rotta, *Caravanas da Anistia: O Brasil Pede Perdão*; Secretaria de Direitos Humanos da Presidência da República, *Programa Nacional de Direitos Humanos (PNDH -3)*.
3. *A esperança venceu/vencerá o medo* (Hope has beaten/will beat fear) is a slogan commonly used by the Workers' Party.
4. Adorno, 'Monopólio Estatal da Violência na Sociedade Brasileira Contemporânea'; Adorno, 'Insegurança versus Direitos Humanos'; Adorno, 'Exclusão Socioeconômica e Violência Urbana'; Cardia, Adorno and Poleto, 'Homicide Rates and Human Rights Violations'; Pinheiro, 'Notas sobre o Futuro da Violência na Cidade Democrática'; Waiselfisz, *Mapa da Violencia*.
5. Gibney et al., 'Database: The Political Terror Scale 1976–2015'.
6. Adorno, 'Exclusão Socioeconômica e Violência Urbana', p. 92.
7. Waiselfisz, *Mapa da Violencia*, p. 27.
8. Amnesty International, 'Brazil: "They Treat Us Like Animals"', 2001.
9. Panizza and Brito, 'The Politics of Human Rights in Democratic Brazil'.
10. Adorno, 'Insegurança versus Direitos Humanos', p. 31.
11. Cardia, 'Exposição à Violência'.
12. Carvalho, *Valsa Brasileira*.
13. Pereira, 'Continuity Is Not Lack of Change'.
14. Kent and Wade, 'Genetics against Race'.
15. The numbers are still impressive even if we only take into account the state of São Paulo, whose population is roughly similar to Iraq's. During the same period of time, the number of intentional killings in São Paulo accounted for around 60 per cent of the number of civilian deaths during the Iraq War. See CEH, 'Guatemala: Memory of Silence'; Waiselfisz, *Mapa da Violencia*; IBC, 'Database: Iraq Body Count'.
16. Fórum Brasileiro de Segurança Pública, *Anuário do Fórum Brasileiro de Segurança Pública – 2015*.
17. Fórum Brasileiro de Segurança Pública, *Anuário do Fórum Brasileiro de Segurança Pública – 2017*.
18. Fórum Brasileiro de Segurança Pública, *Anuário do Fórum Brasileiro de Segurança Pública – 2018*.
19. Fórum Brasileiro de Segurança Pública, *Anuário do Fórum Brasileiro de Segurança Pública – 2015*.
20. Adorno, 'Insegurança versus Direitos Humanos'; Cardia, Adorno and Poleto, 'Homicide Rates and Human Rights Violations'; Misse, 'Violência, Ciminalidade e Mais-Valia'.

21. Panizza and Brito, 'The Politics of Human Rights in Democratic Brazil'; Pereira, 'An Ugly Democracy'.
22. Amnesty International, 'Brazil: "They Treat Us Like Animals"'; Human Rights Watch, *World Report 2015*; Poets, 'The Securitization of Citizenship in a "Segregated City"'; Zaluar, 'Um Debate Disperso'; Vargas and Alves, 'Geographies of Death'.
23. Fórum Brasileiro de Segurança Pública, *Anuário do Fórum Brasileiro de Segurança Pública – 2015*; Chevigny, 'The Populism of Fear'.
24. Caldeira, *City of Walls*.
25. 'Crimes de Maio Causaram 564 Mortes em 2006; Entenda o Caso'.
26. 'Onde Está Amarildo? Saiba quem é o Pedreiro que Desapareceu na Rocinha'; 'Where's Amarildo? How the Disappearance of a Construction Worker Taken from His Home by Police Has Sparked Protests in Brazil'.
27. 'Marielle Franco: Brazil's Favelas Mourn the Death of a Champion'.
28. 'País Tem pelo menos 194 Assassinatos de Políticos ou Ativistas Sociais em 5 Anos'.
29. Fórum Brasileiro de Segurança Pública, *Anuário do Fórum Brasileiro de Segurança Pública – 2018*.
30. Fórum Brasileiro de Segurança Pública, *Anuário do Fórum Brasileiro de Segurança Pública – 2015*.
31. Ibid.
32. Abrão et al., 'Educação e Anistia Política'; Genro and Abrão, 'Memória Histórica, Justiça de Transição e Democracia Sem Fim'; Heloisa Amelia Greco, '50 Anos do Golpe Militar/35 Anos da Lei de Anistia'.
33. Greco, '50 Anos do Golpe Militar/35 Anos da Lei de Anistia'; Schneider, 'Impunity in Post-Authoritarian Brazil'.
34. Zaluar, 'Democratizacao Inacabada'; Garcia, 'Not Yet a Democracy'.
35. Pereira, 'An Ugly Democracy?'
36. Dias, 'Precisamos Extirpar as Metástases Da Ditadura'.
37. Arthur, 'How "Transitions" Reshaped Human Rights'; Eagle, 'A Genealogy of the Criminal Turn in Human Rights'.
38. LaCapra, *Representing the Holocaust*; Schwan, 'Political Consequences of Silenced Guilt'; Leys, *Trauma: A Genealogy*; Schick, 'Acting Out and Working Through'; Bickford, 'Unofficial Truth Projects'; Goldman, 'History and Action'; Orentlicher, 'Settling Accounts'.
39. Weinstein, 'Editorial Note: The Myth of Closure, the Illusion of Reconciliation'; Doxtader, 'A Critique of Law's Violence yet (Never) to Come'; Moon, *Narrating Political Reconciliation*; Humphrey, 'From Terror to Trauma'; Renner, 'The Local Roots of the Global Politics of Reconciliation'.
40. Nagy, 'Transitional Justice as Global Project'; Miller, '(Re)Distributing Transition'; Laplante, 'Transitional Justice and Peace Building'; Andrieu, 'Civilizing Peacebuilding'; Fourlas, 'No Future without Transition'; McEvoy, 'Beyond Legalism'.
41. Miller, '(Re)Distributing Transition'; Schmid and Nolan, '"Do No Harm"? Exploring the Scope of Economic and Social Rights in Transitional Justice';

Dancy and Wiebelhaus-Brahm, 'Bridge to Human Development or Vehicle of Inequality?'; Björkdahl and Selimovic, 'Gendered Justice Gaps in Bosnia-Herzegovina'; Björkdahl and Selimovic, 'Gendering Agency in Transitional Justice'; Evans, 'Structural Violence, Socioeconomic Rights, and Transformative Justice'.

42. Richmond, 'The Problem of Peace'.

43. Mani, 'Balancing Peace with Justice in the Aftermath of Violent Conflict'; Mani, 'Rebuilding an Inclusive Political Community After War'; Sharp, 'Development, Human Rights and Transitional Justice'.

44. Gready and Robins, 'From Transitional to Transformative Justice'; Galliher, 'Transformative Justice'; Lambourne and Carreon, 'Engendering Transitional Justice'; Balasco, 'Locating Transformative Justice'; Walker, 'Transformative Reparations?'; Balint, Evans and McMillan, 'Rethinking Transitional Justice'; Sharp, *Rethinking Transitional Justice for the Twenty-First Century*.

45. Gready and Robins, 'From Transitional to Transformative Justice', p. 2.

46. UCDP, 'Database: Uppsala Conflict Data Program (UCDP)'.

47. Collins, *Violence: A Micro-Sociological Theory*; Galtung, 'Violence, Peace, and Peace Research'; Wieviorka, *Violence: A New Approach*; Martuccelli, 'Reflexões sobre a Violência na Condição Moderna'; Lee and Stanko (eds), *Researching Violence*; Bufacchi, 'Two Concepts of Violence'.

48. Arendt, *On Violence*; Malešević, *The Sociology of War and Violence*; Clastres, *Archéologie de la violence*.

49. Arendt, *On Violence*.

50. Wieviorka, *Violence: A New Approach*.

51. Agamben, Fabbri and Fay, 'On the Limits of Violence'.

52. Collins, *Violence: A Micro-Sociological Theory*.

53. Balibar, *Politics and the Other Scene*.

54. Galtung, 'Violence, Peace, and Peace Research'.

55. Galtung and Hoivik, 'Structural and Direct Violence'.

56. Benjamin, 'Critique of Violence'.

57. Fanon, *The Wretched of the Earth*.

58. Bourdieu and Wacquant, *An Invitation to Reflexive Sociology*.

59. Žižek, 'The Obscenity of Human Rights'.

60. Balibar, *Politics and the Other Scene*.

61. Segato, *Las estructuras elementares de la violencia*; Segato, *La guerra contra las mujeres*.

62. Spivak, 'Can the Subaltern Speak?'

63. Derrida, *Writing and Difference*.

64. Maldonado-Torres, *Against War*.

65. Mbembe, *Necropolitics*.

66. Segato, *La guerra contra las mujeres*.

67. Balibar, *Politics and the Other Scene*.

68. Rancière, *Disagreement*.

69. Stavrianakis and Selby, 'Militarism and International Relations in the Twenty-First Century'.

70. Vagts, *A History of Militarism*.
71. Huntington, *The Soldier and the State*.
72. Thompson, 'Notes on Exterminism, the Last Stage of Civilization'.
73. Shaw, 'Twenty-First Century Militarism'.
74. Feaver, 'Civil-Military Relations'.
75. Olmeda, 'Escape from Huntington's Labyrinth'; Bruneau, 'Impediments to the Accurate Conceptualization of Civil–Military Relations'.
76. Diamint, 'A New Militarism in Latin America'.
77. Brooks, 'Integrating the Civil-Military Relations Subfield'; Mabee and Vucetic, 'Varieties of Militarism'.
78. Definitions of militarism may associate it with a set of values and practices glorifying war, the ethos of the military profession, any actual increase in military spending and operational capacity or, in institutionalist terms, the interference of the military in the domain of public society. See Mabee and Vucetic, 'Varieties of Militarism'; Joana and Mérand, 'The Varieties of Liberal Militarism'; Stavrianakis and Selby, 'Militarism and International Relations in the Twenty-First Century'.
79. Stavrianakis and Selby, 'Militarism and International Relations in the Twenty-First Century', p. 3.
80. 'Military', <https://academic.oup.com/ijtj/search-results?q=military&allJournals=1&fl_SiteID=5176&page=1&qb=%7B%22q%22:%22military%22%7D>; 'Armed Forces', <https://academic.oup.com/ijtj/search-results?page=1&q=armed forces&fl_SiteID=5176&SearchSourceType=1&allJournals=1>.
81. 'Militarism', <https://academic.oup.com/ijtj/search-results?page=1&q=militarism&fl_SiteID=5176&SearchSourceType=1&allJournals=1.>
82. 'Military', <https://www.ictj.org/search-results?search=military>.
83. 'Militarization', <https://www.ictj.org/search-results?search=militarization>.
84. 'Militarism', <https://www.ictj.org/search-results?search=militarism>.
85. 'Transitional Justice AND Armed Forces', <https://www.lexisnexis.com/uk/legal/search/journalssubmitForm.do#0%7C%7CCOMMON-DATE,D,H,$PSEUDOLOSK,A,H%7C%7C%7C%7Carmed forces>; 'Transitional Justice AND Militarism', <https://www.lexisnexis.com/uk/legal/auth/checkbrowser.do?t=1622894545819&bhcp=1&bhhash=1#0%7C%7CCOMMON-DATE,D,H,$PSEUDOLOSK,A,H%7C%7C%7C%7Cmilitarism>.
86. Arendt, *On Violence*, p. 8.
87. Ibid. p. 8.
88. Ibid. p. 8.
89. Clark, 'Transitional Justice as Recognition'; Ashe, 'Sexuality and Gender Identity in Transitional Societies'; Rosser, 'Depoliticised Speech and Sexed Visibility'; Boesten, 'Analyzing Rape Regimes at the Interface of War and Peace in Peru'; Simić and Daly, '"One Pair of Shoes, One Life"'.
90. Segato, *La guerra contra las mujeres*.
91. Basham, Belkin and Gifkins, 'What Is Critical Military Studies?'.

92. Basham, 'Raising an Army'; Shaw, 'Twenty-First Century Militarism'; Eastwood, 'Rethinking Militarism as Ideology'; Ferguson, 'The Sublime Object of Militarism'; Åhäll, 'The Dance of Militarisation'; Howell, 'Forget "Militarization"'; Welland, 'Militarised Violences, Basic Training, and the Myths of Asexuality and Discipline'; Segal, 'Gender, War and Militarism'; Basham and Catignani, 'War Is Where the Hearth Is'; Rossdale, *Resisting Militarism*.

93. Basham, 'Gender, Race, Militarism and Remembrance'; Welland, 'Violence and the Contemporary Soldiering Body'; Åhäll, 'The Dance of Militarisation'; Reeves and Heath-Kelly, 'Curating Conflict'; Sylvester, 'Curating and Re-Curating the American War in Vietnam'.

94. Barkawi and Laffey, 'The Postcolonial Moment in Security Studies'; Baaz and Verweijen, 'Confronting the Colonial'.

95. Wibben, 'Why We Need to Study (US) Militarism'; Stavrianakis and Stern, 'Militarism and Security'.

96. Howell, 'Forget "Militarization"'; MacKenzie et al., 'Can We Really "Forget" Militarization?'.

97. Howell, 'Forget "Militarization"', p. 120.

98. Ibid. p. 121.

99. Ibid. p. 121.

100. Ior a critique of this assumption in contemporary post-colonial/decolonial thought see Furtado, 'Confronting the Gated Community'.

101. I take the expression from Nisha Shah's insightful comments in MacKenzie et al., 'Can We Really "Forget" Militarization?'.

102. For a few commendable examples see Moon, *Narrating Political Reconciliation*; Humphrey, *The Politics of Atrocity and Reconciliation*; Norval, 'Memory, Identity and the (Im)possibility of Reconciliation; Doxtader, 'A Critique of Law's Violence yet (Never) to Come'.

103. Hayner, *Unspeakable Truths*.

104. Leebaw, *Judging State-Sponsored Violence*; Moon, 'Narrating Political Reconciliation'.

105. Misztal, *Theories of Social Remembering*, p. 10.

106. Wilson, *The Politics of Truth and Reconciliation in South Africa*.

107. Edkins, *Trauma and the Memory of Politics*, p. 18.

108. Zehfuss, *Wounds of Memory*, p. 157.

109. Spaulding, 'Resistance, Countermemory, Justice', p. 140.

110. Humphrey, 'From Terror to Trauma', p. 10.

111. Foucault, *History of Madness*.

CHAPTER 1

The 'Common Language' of Justice

To punish or to forgive perpetrators of mass atrocity? This question was, for a long time, described as the central dilemma of transitional justice.[1] Since the beginnings of the field in the late twentieth century (1980s–1990s), the dilemma has been there, animating the writings of advocates of criminal accountability and the counter-arguments of those in favour of alternative forms of justice.[2] But things have changed. The difficult choice between punishment and reconciliation does not seem to hold sway in the twenty-first century.[3] Nowadays, it is widely accepted within transitional justice circles that responses to systematic violence require multifaceted, complex approaches involving both punishment and forgiveness; that truth commissions are no longer replacements for trials; that reconciliation cannot be based on blanket or bargained amnesties. The dilemma, we are told, belongs to history.[4]

The purpose of this chapter is to provide an introductory account of the historical transformation of the punishment vs impunity debates, from an intractable choice between punishment and forgiveness in the wake of mass atrocities to the present-day synthesis. Its central objective is to trace and explain the developments of the twenty-first-century 'common language of justice' that works as the guiding principle of transitional or post-conflict justice. Avoiding the temptation to treat the punishment vs impunity debates as a technocratic question, I address the debates from the perspective of political struggles that first inspired the scholarship and practice of transitional justice. This is done in hope of reconnecting the ideas and policies that scholars have exhaustively discussed on paper to the political commitments they invite in practice; to the politics that first stimulated the emergence of transitional justice but were later obfuscated as the practice was mainstreamed into a set of global responses to systematic violence. Furthermore, as an exercise of historical contextualisation, this chapter provides the first step towards a new, critically inspired reading of transitional justice.

The chapter begins by investigating the appearance of a global anti-impunity movement in the context of democratic transitions in the Global South (roughly from the 1970s to the 1990s). It is hard to over-state the importance of this 'movement' in the process of institution-alisation of transitional justice. At first, a transnational, disjointed and heterogeneous alliance between activists, intellectuals, legal practitioners and policymakers worked in a support capacity to direct and indirect victims of state terror. Later, after achieving global notoriety, some of the same individuals would help to devise and legitimise the toolbox of transitional justice measures as a set of global policies to be imple-mented in the wake of atrocities.

The first section emphasises the intrinsic links between the anti-impunity movement and the struggles of family members in the South-ern Cone of Latin America in the late 1970s. Much of the methods, the language and the pathos later used by defenders of criminal account-ability were in fact inspired by South American movements such as the Madres de La Plaza de Mayo in Argentina, or the Feminist Movement for Amnesty in Brazil. The section draws attention to a central argument within the anti-impunity movement: the fact that the tripartite demands of truth (knowledge), memory (acknowledgement) and justice (crimi-nal accountability) were historically articulated as *inalienable demands* of survivors and family members. The second section investigates the emer-gence of the idea of reconciliation as an alternative form of justice in the 1990s, focusing on the Chilean and South African truth and reconcilia-tion commissions. It distinguishes between different paradigms of rec-onciliation as they appeared across the South Atlantic, drawing attention to the uncomfortable resonance that the policy of forgiveness enjoyed among supporters of state terror. The final section investigates how the 'tug-of war' between retributive and restorative justice was finally tran-scended in the new millennium, when transitional justice was institu-tionalised as part of a global peacebuilding project.

The Anti-Impunity Movement

Humanitarian activism during the Cold War is usually portrayed in the literature of transitional justice as a humble practice of 'naming and shaming'.[5] The story is simple: faced with the unlikelihood of criminal prosecutions in authoritarian settings (due to the lethargy, impotence or unwillingness of local judiciaries), survivors of state terror were limited to making public, locally and overseas, the atrocities they endured.[6] This process involved disclosing patterns of violations 'to the light of international scrutiny'[7] as part of a campaign 'lobbying for policy change'.[8] Although not without its merits, this common representation provides a rather crude picture of what was at stake at the time, especially in the Southern Cone. In fact, 'naming and shaming' is too vague and simplistic a term to capture the complexity of movements such as the Madres and the Abuelas de la Plaza de Mayo in Argentina, the Feminist Movement for Amnesty in Brazil or the Association of Family Members of the Detained and Disappeared (AFDD) in Chile. More than pro-democracy 'lobbyists', these were complex social movements that opened new forms of resistance to authoritarianism, refused to accept the official version of the past and, in many senses, re-signified the role of women in politics.[9] Most importantly, activists in the Southern Cone gave a fundamental contribution to the anti-impunity movement by making the word *impunity* synonymous with the words *silence* and *forgetfulness*.

The Southern Cone experienced the brutal reality of state terrorism during the Cold War. Once in power, military dictatorships sought to pacify social conflicts and exert control over their respective populations via the dissemination of fear.[10] Inspired by doctrines preaching the radicalisation of counterinsurgency responses to the perceived threat of communist subversion, military juntas made the annihilation of dissidents a central state policy. This decision had significant consequences for South American societies. The coups that were meant to protect the core values of 'Western civilisation' left a shocking record of abuses. In all countries, thousands were arbitrarily incarcerated, tortured and exiled. Legal and extra-legal executions were not uncommon, albeit the quantity and quality of violence varied from case to case. Between 36,000 and 74,000 individuals were politically persecuted in Brazil;[11] 20 per cent of the Uruguayan population was incarcerated;[12] almost 40,000 were imprisoned and tortured in Chile;[13] and 30,000 people were 'disappeared' in Argentina.[14]

The infamous disappearances became paradigmatic of the distorted logic of state terror. In the course of the 1970s, state-led violence moved away from overt and explosive acts of violence to silent, covert operations that left no trace. The dissemination of forced disappearances as a method of counterinsurgency posed a form of violence that left no body, had no end and, for all official purposes, had never actually happened. In the eyes of the military, disappearing with the bodies of political dissidents had the double 'benefit' of reducing the political cost from international naming and shaming and strengthening the fear and terror within clandestine organisations and society at large. But the macabre practice also had an unintended effect.

Disappearances did not just affect those whose mortal remains vanished; they also robbed their family members of a much-needed closure. Forced disappearances produced three absences: 'the absence of a body, the absence of a moment of grief, and the absence of a grave'.[15] As every action faces a reaction, the dissemination of disappearances paved the way for the emergence of new movements of resistance spearheaded by the families of victims. They opened the space for the politicisation of relatives' grief. In denying family members a moment of mourning that would otherwise remain limited to a small circle of individuals, the military unintentionally transformed the loss of a loved one into a collective issue, a problem no longer of the family but of the authorities, society and even the international community. In Brazil, from 1973 onwards, there was no longer any 'news of casualties, dead bodies, death certificates'[16] that could suggest the end of someone's life and the beginning of another's mourning. In Argentina, by 1977, the mothers of those disappeared by the state forces were gathering around the Plaza de Mayo (May Square) in downtown Buenos Aires, asking for information, questioning the authorities and seeking the support of the foreign press.[17] They kept on demonstrating, waving the banner of *aparición con vida*, demanding their loved ones be returned to them alive, just as they were taken.[18]

The struggles of family members and survivors enjoyed the vital support of human rights organisations (many with religious links) and liberal professionals. The Asamblea Permanente por los Derechos Humanos (APDH) in Argentina, the Servicio Paz y Justicia (SERPAJ) in Argentina and Uruguay, the Vicaría de la Solidaridad in Chile, and the Comissão de Justiça e Paz (CJP) in Brazil all made profound contributions to the efforts of truth-seeking.[19] Journalists, such as Robert Cox from the newspaper *Buenos Aires Herald*, kept on publicising the struggle of the Madres despite state censorship and real risks to his life. Likewise, legal practitioners in Brazil were representing the wives, daughters and mothers of victims of state-led violence in court cases at least a decade before the authoritarian regime ended.[20] Human rights activists and organisations could mobilise their connections with organisations based in the Global North, such as the World Council of Churches (1948), Amnesty International (1961) and Human Rights Watch (1978).[21] With the support of renowned intellectuals such as Bertrand Russell and Jean-Paul Sartre, exiles gathered in unofficial tribunals denouncing the crimes of the Latin American military as crimes against humanity.[22]

The anti-impunity alliance between survivors, exiles, legal professionals, intellectuals and NGOs was very successful in terms of promoting
regime change. Their relentless effort to denounce the crimes of state terror was instrumental in corroding the basis of legitimacy of local dictatorships and preparing the ground for transitions to democracy. But
as far as demands for accountability go, the results were mixed. In the
cases of Brazil, Chile and Uruguay, where the military remained strong
and conservatives remained in power, impediments to legal prosecutions
remained.[23] Pinochet's regime passed an amnesty law in 1978, when the
state of exception ended. In 1979, the Brazilian military followed suit and
in 1986 it was the Uruguayans' turn. In this context, the anti-impunity
movement was forced to work around the institutionalisation of impunity and the official silence in the post-transitional scene. Relatives of the
disappeared would find new committees in search of their whereabouts;[24]
public servants purged by the military coups demanded reparations.[25]
Individual victims also continued to pursue civil legal action against the
state.[26] Following their specific agendas, activists kept compiling lists with
names of individuals persecuted, murdered or disappeared by the forces
of political repression, and also with the names of perpetrators enjoying
impunity. Released in unauthorised and constantly updated reports or
simply leaked to the press, these lists offered the first, rudimentary picture
of state terror.

As forms of unofficial truth-seeking the lists of perpetrators had one
problem. State authorities easily dismissed them as mere 'inventions',
or allegations lacking objective proof. The Madres were stigmatised as
locas (crazy) by the Argentine junta, while others had to endure the extra
trauma of being questioned on their motives and the more or less veiled
suggestions that they were liars. Therefore, the central goals of the anti-
impunity movement became to search for credible (meaning objective)
evidence of atrocities: the sort of evidence that would be useful not only
to shame perpetrators, but that would also hold up in court. This goal
of objectively denouncing state terror was extremely influential for transitional justice scholarship and practice. The search for objectivity led to
the publishing of the famous *Nunca Más* reports in the Southern Cone
and gave transitional justice one of its most distinct mechanisms: the
truth commissions.

Brazil provided the most dramatic case of unofficial truth-seeking.
Its 1979 amnesty law was meant to prevent criminal prosecutions, but
it also enabled political exiles to return to the country, provided they
offered proof of their condition.[27] To that end, their attorneys were
legally granted access to the Military Supreme Court and the right to

take any documents home for a period of twenty-four hours.[28] A group of twelve individuals soon realised the significance of what had just happened. They had been granted access by the authoritarian regime to hard evidence of atrocities committed under the dictatorship; evidence that could not be dismissed as subjective or unsupported. With the secret backing of religious leaders, they began to put a dangerous but ingenious plan into motion: within a twenty-four-hour window, lawyers would request access to documents containing evidence of atrocities, take them to a clandestine facility where they would be photocopied and, finally, return the evidence to court without raising suspicion. The photocopying machines worked non-stop, ten-hour shifts, seven days a week, over five years. By the end of that period, activists had photocopied the entire archive of the military courts: one million pages (a total of 707 lawsuits) regarding accusations of crimes against national security involving some 7,000 defendants.[29] The plan was a stroke of genius; human rights activists were now able to build a case against the regime based on 'verbatim transcripts of military trials which were never intended to be read by the public at large'.[30]

Argentina, the country that became the poster child of transitional justice, provided the most influential case. In Argentina, the anti-impunity agenda dominated the political transition to a different degree. In the context of a weakened military, demoralised by the Falklands/Malvinas War (1982) and a strong human rights movement, truth-seeking became part of the state's policy. In 1983, after enduring 7 years of a brutal regime, Argentines headed to the polls to elect the radical candidate Raúl Alfonsín as their new president. Co-founder of the APDHs, the new president was a name from the human rights movement and therefore sympathetic to demands for truth-seeking and criminal accountability. Alfonsín's name was immortalised in the transitional justice literature as the statesman behind the world's first truth commission: the Comisión Nacional sobre la Desaparición de Personas (CONADEP), a temporary official body created in 1983 with a mandate to investigate the fate of the disappeared.

Staffed by a group of 'notables', CONADEP gathered information, identified detention centres and collected the testimonies of 1,200 survivors.[31] In September 1984, the commission released a final report, entitled *Nunca Más* (*Never Again*). Endorsed with official authority, the report recognised 8,961 forced disappearances and 380 clandestine prisons.[32] Setting an important precedent for truth commissions throughout the world, CONADEP rejected the explanation of atrocities as the misdeeds of a few rogue officers. Against this common trope, the report vehemently affirmed that it was 'the whole of the system, the whole of its methodology, since its very idealisation, which constituted the great overreaction; the aberration was a common widespread practice'.[33]

The Argentine commission was extremely influential. *Nunca Más* sold more than half a million copies and was translated into five languages.[34] The report inspired similar publications such as *Uruguay: Nunca Más*, organised by the Uruguayan branch of SERPAJ, and *Brasil: Nunca Mais*, published by the Archdiocese of São Paulo.[35] The latter summarised the results of the secret plan of Brazilian activists, giving a clear idea of the extent and the systematic nature of state terror: 17,420 individuals summoned to military court; 1,843 charges of torture out of an estimate of 20,000; 283 different types of torture employed by 444 perpetrators; entire lists of collaborators and informers; 144 deaths and 125 disappearances.[36] Like its Argentine counterpart, *Brasil: Nunca Mais* was another bestseller.[37] The success of the *Nunca Más* reports helped the dissemination of truth commissions around the globe.[38] As of 2015, more than forty extrajudicial commissions had been established, making the search for knowledge and acknowledgement a standard response to mass atrocities and systematic violence.

Truth commissions are usually associated with policies of forgiveness and reconciliation as alternatives to punishment, but this was far from the case in Argentina. Apart from a truth commission, Alfonsín's transitional policies also involved the trials of the military juntas and the heads of the guerrillas.[39] In fact, the *Nunca Más* report was presented to the courts and was instrumental in the condemnation of Jorge Rafael Videla and Emilio Massera to life imprisonment during the 1985 Trial of the Juntas.[40] If the anti-impunity movement was disjointed and heterogeneous, it was at least united in a tripartite demand immortalised in the slogan *memoria, verdad y justicia* (memory, truth and justice). The *Nunca Más* reports were the product of struggles for the preservation of the archives of repression (memory); the gathering of forensic proof of atrocities (truth); and, most of all, the prosecution of perpetrators (justice). Those were not separate demands to be picked apart: they were inalienable goals of justice, the metal rings of the same chain. It was in the process of mainstreaming truth commissions that the chain was eventually 'broken'.

The Politics of Reconciliation

Ernesto Verdeja identifies two major paradigms of political reconciliation: a minimalist and a maximalist approach. For a minimalist account, reconciliation stands for the 'simple coexistence between former enemies,

premised on a rejection of violence'.[41] Minimalists abide by a thin pro-
ceduralism concerning the formal regulation of animosities in the post-
conflict scenario. They tend to frame the role of transitional interventions
as providing proper means of mediation, the re-restructuring of political representation and the reorganisation of the judiciary. This calculat-
ing perspective weighs anti-impunity drives in the aftermath of violence
against contextual political constraints.[42] Minimalist scholars see the
prospects of achieving peace and restoring decency as depending on the
'prospects for controlling the behaviour of those [. . .] who are antagonistic to democracy'.[43] Therefore, in their account, realistic transitional
responses must be attentive to the 'natural fit between the desire for reconciliation that often [. . .] animates incoming leaders and the desire for
immunity in the outgoing ones'.[44]

In abstract, minimalism sounds convincing. But in historical terms, it
cannot be disentangled from a conservative undertone present in the struggles for amnesty in the Southern Cone. In Argentina, the anti-impunity
movement revolved primarily around the phenomenon of forced disappearances. But in the other countries (Brazil, Uruguay and Paraguay), the
number of disappeared was dwarfed by the number of exiles and political prisoners. In these places, the fight for truth against impunity was also,
counterintuitively, a fight for political amnesty.[45] Amnesties were not seen
as a synonym of benevolent forgiveness but as a cry for 'freedom'[46] that
demanded the liberation of political prisoners and the return of exiles. As a
matter of fact, this type of amnesty was diametrically opposed to the theme
of reconciliation. In some contexts, the struggle for amnesty demonstrated
an immense capacity to build up social mobilisation around a political
objective. The call for amnesty was associated with two goals: a short-term
goal of finding pathways for justice for those affected by the violence of
state terror, and a long-term goal of promoting political change by striking
at the basis of legitimacy of dictatorships.

But the political allure of amnesties was a double-edged sword. If the
concept could be claimed by those advocating retribution, it could be
equally appropriated by conservative sectors fighting against retribution.
Beyond the notions of truth-seeking and justice, the concept of amnesty
was also associated with ideas of pardoning, forgetting and forgiving, all
of which possessed a strong religious undertone. They had been widely
discussed by the Christian tradition[47] and were therefore palatable and
immediately available to a wider Catholic audience. This association
between amnesty and forgiveness was frequently turned against the
activists themselves. For the ideologues of forgiveness, the fight for memory, truth and justice was a wanton form of *revanchismo* (revenge), an

enduring resentment that threatened the process of pacification. In order to 'protect' the future of peace and stability, opposing groups claimed a need to turn the page of the past,[48] a need to forget, to forgive and to let bygones be bygones. In the infamous words of Uruguayan president Julio María Sanguinetti: 'no hay que tener ojos en la nuca'[49] – there is no need for eyes on the back of the neck.

The minimalist approach to reconciliation in the Southern Cone is indissociable from this dual friction; the clash between a project of *amnesty anamnesis*, fruit of the struggle for truth against impunity, and a project of *amnesty amnesia*, fruit of the counter-struggle for forgiveness towards national reconciliation.[50] It was in the interplay between these two divergent tensions that the idea of truth-seeking as a 'second-best'[51] form of justice gained prominence.[52] And it was in Chile that truth-seeking was blatantly disconnected from the promotion of criminal prosecutions. There, the pursuit of knowledge and acknowledgement (previously at the service of punishment) appeared, for the first time in the Southern Cone, as a policy of national reconciliation against the alleged temptations of revenge: it was justice 'en la medida de lo posible',[53] as far as possible.

Chile was the second transitional country in the Southern Cone to establish a successful truth commission, following the Argentine model. In May 1990, the democratically elected president Patricio Aylwin Azócar created the Chilean Comisión Nacional de Verdad y Reconciliación (National Truth and Reconciliation Commission, CNVR) in order to investigate the crimes of Pinochet's regime. However, there were marked differences between CONADEP and the CNVR. Both symbolically and practically, the most important difference was the change in the attention granted to the theme of reconciliation. In Argentina, CONADEP rejected the possibility of 'reconciliation unless the guilty repent and unless we find justice founded upon truth';[54] reconciliation was but a by-product of the fight for justice. In Chile, it had come to the forefront of the transitional agenda. Before anything else, the CNVR was meant 'to collaborate for the reconciliation of every Chilean'.[55]

When we analyse the Chilean case, the trope of reconciliation shows uncomfortable similarities with the rhetoric of the previous regime. Conscious of the legal consequences of wrongdoing, Pinochet's regime passed an amnesty law in 1978 lifting the state of exception instituted in the wake of the 1973 coup.[56] In hindsight, the text of this amnesty law seems like a perfect summary of the arguments of those opposing truth-seeking efforts in the Southern Cone. It connected the regime's achievement of 'general tranquillity, peace and order' with the need to 'leave behind meaningless hatred' and 'to consolidate the reunification of all Chileans'.[57] In the 1980s, the regime adopted strategic measures to ensure that, even when leaving power, the military would remain powerful. By the 1990s, the dictatorship had passed a sequence of *leyes de amarre* (tie-up laws) that restricted the possibilities of criminal accountability for the foreseeable future.[58] This directly affected the political transition. In practice, Aylwin's policies faced a series of constraints. When the CNVR was created, Pinochet 'remained as head of the army, a number of Senate seats remained subject to Pinochet's appointment [. . .] and military and judicial structures remained intact'.[59] With the backing of half of the Chilean electorate,[60] Pinochet was able to dictate the order of events to a larger extent,[61] including unashamed threats that '[t]he day they touch one of my men, the rule of law ends.'[62]

The minimalist approach offered a way out of the transitional cul-de-sac, and it was enthusiastically taken forward by a president committed to 'reconciling the virtue of justice with the virtue of prudence'.[63] Aylwin appointed eight individuals of different political affiliations to assess the atrocities perpetrated by *both sides* of the so-called dirty war.[64] Like its Argentine predecessor, the Chilean commission also affirmed the systematic character of violations of human rights. But unlike the Argentine context, no trials ensued.[65] Justifying this reconciliatory prudence was no easy job. It fell upon José Zalaquett, former member of Amnesty International and member of the truth commission, to articulate a moral defence of the Chilean compromise. In his words, the reconciliatory stance of the CNVR showed a deeply courageous move; a 'less striking form of courage [. . .] to learn how to live with real-life restrictions'.[66] Reconciliation required the courage 'to advance one's most cherished values day by day to the extent of the possible'.[67]

Besides the minimalist account, Verdeja also acknowledges a second, broader take on political reconciliation. Merging religious, moral and even medicalised arguments, this maximalist account 'stipulates more extensive requirements for morally acceptable coexistence'.[68] In at least one central point, the maximalist approach holds a fundamental difference against the minimalist perspective: while the latter characterises reconciliation as a realistic political compromise (justice as far as possible), the former sees forgiveness and social restoration as superior forms of justice. Maximalists envision post-conflict justice as a restorative exercise in which punishment is secondary to 'the call *to heal*, to redress imbalances, and to reduce differences'.[69] This vision of reconciliation, as opposed to 'vengeful' punishment, had the advantage of offering a 'reparative humanism in a society trying to heal itself from a destructive past'.[70] According to maximalism, truth-seeking and forgiveness in the wake of systematic violence constitute parts of an essential post-conflict or post-authoritarian therapy.[71]

The transitional measures put in place in Argentina and Chile already showed a mix of religious and medical metaphors. In his inaugural speech as elected president, Alfonsín referred to post-authoritarian Argentina as a society that was made 'sick'[72] by the wounds of the past. Hence, 'the *Alfonsinista* experience, promised a future that would *suture these wounds*'[73] without turning to '*sterile* fixations on the past'.[74] In Chile, this pattern continued. In a speech at the mythical Estadio Nacional, Aylwin affirmed that the state of 'Chile's *spiritual health*'[75] demanded '*sanitation* measures'.[76] In both cases, by mobilising the idea of (spiritual and moral) healing, the South American leaders linked their policies with themes familiar to religious sectors of society.[77] They also suggested the endorsement of 'amnesties' as acts of sacrificial compassion. In Argentina, this connection helped to justify the passing of amnesties in 1986 and 1987 (the Full Stop Law and the Law of Due Obedience) following a series of military riots against prosecutions.[78] In Chile, it induced the theory that only exposing the 'truth also brings a measure of healthy social catharsis and helps to prevent the past from reoccurring'.[79]

In the mid-1990s, Zalaquett's ideas found many enthusiastic supporters in South Africa, a country recovering from decades of white-supremacist rule during the apartheid state (1948–94). In a somewhat similar fashion to the Southern Cone, the concept of reconciliation was originally advocated by pro-apartheid supporters, members of the National Party (NP) and president F. W. de Klerk. Like their fellow South American activists, Nelson Mandela, members of the African National Congress (ANC) and other anti-apartheid activists opposed the theme of reconciliation without accountability in the late 1980s.[80] For them, reconciliation was also supposed to be a by-product of acknowledgement and atonement, subjected upon the releasing of political prisoners and the punishment of state criminals. Attitudes towards the idea of reconciliation changed after the 1992 and 1993 Convention for a Democratic South Africa (CODESA) talks, when the concept was mobilised time and again, by both sides of the negotiation, to justify the necessity for compromise.[81] Once it became clear that reconciliation would set the tone of the bargained transition, more elaborate justifications of the policy of collective forgiveness began to appear.

Leebaw explains how the idea of reconciliation came to be treasured by circles within the ANC as a deeply transformational approach to the end of civil conflict. More than a focus on pacification and political stability, the idea of social restoration promised 'a wider vision of justice that would encompass the ongoing pursuit of political and social change'[82] to a society riddled with structural racism, violence and inequality. In 1995, the elected government of Nelson Mandela enacted the Promotion of National Unity and Reconciliation Act (1995). Following the South American example, the act established a commission of inquiry mandated to create 'as complete a picture as possible of the causes, nature and extent of the gross violations of human rights' (1995: Art. 3). The Truth and Reconciliation Commission of South Africa (TRC) became the archetypal case of maximalist reconciliation, relying on 'therapeutic assumptions and methods'[83] to reject retribution in a more substantial way.[84]

Chaired by the Archbishop of Cape Town, Desmond Tutu, a passionate advocate of the maximalist approach, the TRC acquired a deeply religious undertone, emphasising the restoration of order and political stability. But, in South Africa, order stood for more than the limits of what was politically possible. The concept of order was seen through an organic lens as that which provides the life and health of a community. This organic order was translated in the notion of Ubuntu: a traditional Bantu concept in which 'humanness' is expressed by the virtue of coexistence.[85] The concept of Ubuntu is at the heart of the TRC's creative rejection of retribution and legitimation of restoration as a better form of justice. Stressing a vision of humanness as interconnectedness, by drawing on a belief that 'people are people through other people',[86] Ubuntu leads to an interpretation of punishment as a harm done to the 'essence of shared humanity'.[87] Roughly, in this account, the anti-impunity movement risks much more than enhancing social divisions. Punishment can alienate perpetrators from the community they violated, damaging even further the social ties. Instead, 'in the spirit of Ubuntu'[88] reconciliation should work for 'the healing of breaches, the redressing of imbalances, the restoration of broken relationships'.[89]

Ubuntu preaches a sacrificial need for collective forgiveness, respecting the need for knowledge and acknowledgement, but also the need for repentance. Anti-apartheid activist Mamphela Ramphele added a medicalised tone to the logic of Ubuntu by depicting the violent past as '"an abscess," which "cannot heal properly unless it is thoroughly incised and cleaned out"'.[90] The concept of Ubuntu even came to be infused with a decolonial sense: it allegedly represented an authentic form of African justice against the foreign concept of retribution.[91] Ironically, this authentic African justice shared some of the practical consequences of the Christian politics of forgiveness, which included support for state amnesties. But the South African case provided an innovation.

The 1995 act determined amnesties to be granted to perpetrators of political violence on an individual basis, in exchange for full disclosure of past atrocities.

This provision became one of the most controversial issues involving the TRC. In accordance with the principles of Ubuntu, perpetrators were given a chance to repent, provided they offered knowledge and acknowledgement of their own misdeeds. This innovative move connected a vision of '*truth as acknowledgment* and *justice as recognition*'[92] to the confession of 'potentially penitent souls'.[93] But to make it work, the TRC had to break down the primacy of forensic truth (a constitutive aspect of the anti-impunity movement) into a plurality of truths that could accommodate the diverging accounts of victims and perpetrators. The TRC defined four different kinds of coexistent truths: (1) *factual (forensic) truth*, the gathering of legal proof of past atrocities; (2) *personal truth*, individual accounts on violent events; (3) *social truth*, a dialogic truth created out of interaction between different accounts; and (4) *restorative truth*, a truth that, by opposing the truth of the apartheid state, would heal both traumatised individuals and the wounded nation.[94]

The sheer scale of the TRC was unparalleled. Divided into three subcommittees, with a staff of 300 and several headquarters, the TRC collected the testimonies of around 22,000 survivors, broadcasting deeply emotional hearings on national television.[95] In 1998, the TRC released a five-volume report comprehensively exposing the atrocities of the apartheid state and recommending the payment of reparations to thousands of victims (between 17,000 and 23,000 rand per year, for six years).[96] By the end of its mandate, the commission had assessed over 7,000 applications for amnesty, granting immunity from prosecution to around 1,300 perpetrators who cooperated with truth-seeking.[97] As late as 2011, the TRC was still the largest, most complex and most influential of all truth commissions.[98] Like many other commissions, it was regarded as a tremendous success internationally, but it could never dispel a sense that it had been the product of a political compromise that thwarted justice.[99]

Transitional Justice in the New Millennium

The experiences of the Southern Cone and in South Africa were fundamental for the institutionalisation of transitional justice as a field of knowledge and practice. Many individuals involved with human rights activism across the South Atlantic would gain global notoriety, gathering the attention of intellectuals and policymakers around the world. Adolfo Pérez Esquivel, a survivor of torture and co-founder of SERPAJ in Argentina, was awarded the Nobel peace prize in 1980.[100] Nelson Mandela, the symbol of the new, democratic South Africa and the living personification of a reconciliatory discourse (the basis of the Rainbow Nation) attained pop-star status in the late 1990s. The apparent success of the TRC gave birth to 'a burgeoning industry, both in theory and praxis, as the politics of reconciliation',[101] exporting the South African product to the four corners of the world.

The famous Aspen, Charter 77 and IDASA conferences, held between 1988 and 1995, are illustrative of this process. Funded by organisations such as the Ford Foundation and the Rockefeller Foundation, the conferences were meant to address the dilemmas of societies facing a fragile balance between (re-)democratisation and reckoning with the legacy of past atrocities. Big names from the Southern Cone, such as Raúl Alfonsín, Jaime Malamud-Goti, José Zalaquett and Luis Pérez Aguirre, as well as from the anti-apartheid struggle, such as Alex Boraine and Nomonde Calata, were present. They were joined by recognisable scholars and practitioners such as Aryeh Neier, Diane Orentlicher, Lawrence Weschler, Tina Rosenberg, Samuel Huntington and Ruti Teitel, who would later produce the classics of the transitional justice literature. These conferences laid the academic foundations for debates on whether, and how, to punish perpetrators of heinous crimes, providing the basis for the discipline's canonical book:[102] the three-volume *Transitional Justice: How Emerging Democracies Reckon with Former Regimes*, published in 1995 by the United States Institute of Peace. They also provided the platform for a new, burgeoning group of professionals claiming expertise on the methods for implementing a just and everlasting peace in the wake of atrocities.[103]

In a sense, the synthesis of retribution and restoration was enabled by the mainstreaming of the struggles of activists into a wider project of global governance and peacekeeping.[104] As mechanisms designed to fit specific contexts were reclaimed as part of transitional justice's toolbox (e.g. truth commissions), their political commitments were lost, or at least diluted. Supporters of criminal accountability based their arguments on the concept of universal jurisdiction (reclaiming the legacy of the Nuremberg trials) to defend the irrevocable duty to punish perpetrators.[105] Likewise, the defence of reconciliation could be voiced in the abstract, as an idea dissociated from the collusion with state terror in the Southern Cone or white power in South Africa. Slowly but steadily, the punishment vs impunity debates would only superficially allude to the dilemmas faced, and the solutions found, by activists across the South Atlantic. The search for a common ground between previously intractable positions was made much easier in the context of high levels of abstraction and generalisation that characterised transitional justice debates. But it was also helped by a series of developments beyond transitional justice scholarship, in the fields of peacebuilding and legal theory. The twenty-first-century common language of justice was built based on *hybridism*, the development of *holistic* forms of peacebuilding, and the framing of *truth as a human right*.

Merging the Local and the Global

Throughout the 1990s, the United Nations (UN) became more involved with the implementation of transitional justice mechanisms. Responses to the end of conflict and the legacy of mass atrocities had always been troubled by what became a true obsession of international politics and transitional justice debates: the so-called rift between the 'global' and the 'local'. The central problem was to what extent, if at all, national sovereignty and jurisdiction should be respected when handling the end of conflict. At stake was the international community's responsibility to act when faced with crimes against humanity and unacceptable atrocities. While transitional justice was being institutionalised, the fields of peacekeeping and conflict resolution witnessed the development of a new approach: hybrid operations that employed a mix between global and local elements in the implementation of post-conflict policies. Three specific cases became paradigmatic of the development of hybridism: the establishment of a truth commission in El Salvador (1992) and the creation of ad hoc international criminal tribunals in the Balkans (1993) and Rwanda (1994).

The history of El Salvador during the 1980s was similar to that of the Southern Cone countries. Engulfed in an anti-communist atmosphere, the country was taken by a 'right-wing civilian-military alliance engaged in a counterinsurgency civil war'.[106] For twelve years, El Salvador was trapped in a conflict between leftist guerrillas and the country's military juntas. Peace talks started in the late 1980s, eventually leading to a UN-brokered peace accord in the early 1990s.[107] Following the zeitgeist, the Salvadoran peace accord established the creation of a truth commission, with a small difference: the search for truth was to be conducted by 'global' actors.[108] The exclusion of Salvadorians from truth-seeking was justified as a necessary measure, fruit of the perceived intractability of the civil war divide. In 1992, the Comisión de la Verdad para El Salvador (Commission on the Truth for El Salvador, CVES) was created under the administration of the UN.[109] El Salvador represented the first pocket of internationalisation, seen along the lines of 'neutrality', and an importance source of practical experience for 'global' actors. From the peace talks to the establishment of the CVES, 'the level and length of UN involvement was unprecedented for the organization'.[110] In later years, the Salvadoran experience would be remembered as one of the first peace operations specifically 'mandated to address transitional justice and rule of law activities'.[111]

Around the time of the Salvadoran peace accords, the world witnessed the resurgence of the term 'genocide' in the headlines.[112] The Yugoslav ethnic wars (1991–9) left 300,000 dead, thousands raped and over four million refugees, imprinting 'the term ethnic cleansing on global consciousness'.[113] During the Rwandan genocide (1994) more than 500,000 people were murdered 'at a rate of 300 murders every hour'.[114] With the apparent resurgence of an old problem, the Nuremberg model was promptly reactivated. At the same time that the concepts of reconciliation and forgiveness were gaining traction as alternatives to criminal prosecution, punishment regained momentum. Plans to establish a permanent international criminal court during the United Nations Genocide Convention[115] were later frustrated by the Cold War atmosphere of non-interference.[116] But the violence in the Balkans and Rwanda changed everything. The talk of revamping an old plan proliferated until, in 1993, Security Council Resolution 827 created the International Criminal Tribunal for the Former Yugoslavia (ICTY) to operate in the Netherlands.[117] In the following year, Resolution 955 created an International Criminal Tribunal for Rwanda (ICTR).[118]

Despite their many merits, as 'completely international'[119] mechanisms, the Salvadoran commission and the ad hoc tribunals had undesirable shortcomings. As top-down responses to atrocity, they could never overcome a certain level of 'local' suspicion. Many activists still nurtured the view that they were handled by outsiders, *gringos* who impaired rather than instigated 'genuine reform on the local level'.[120] This, at times, 'generated outright resistance and hostility'.[121] The CVES was strongly criticised for displacing the concerns of grassroots activists, who were excluded from the search for knowledge and acknowledgement as a *sine qua non* condition for truth-seeking.[122] In Serbia, the prosecution of war criminals 'from above' contrasted with the silence of the local population, who showed little interest in reassessing the past.[123] In addition to concerns over scepticism and detachment, there were logistical and financial problems. In Serbia and Rwanda, the anti-impunity drive proved particularly straining. By 2004, the ad hoc tribunals had shared 'more than 2,000 posts between them and a combined annual budget exceeding a quarter of a billion dollars'.[124] A more efficient alternative was needed.

Hybrid responses came as a logical answer to these problems. Hybrid courts function 'with international backing that combine, to differing degrees, domestic and international jurisprudence and include both international and national judges'.[125] Hybrid truth commissions were first implemented in Haiti (1995) and Guatemala (1997), where truth-seeking mixed global and local elements.[126] But hybridism also had an element of awareness to local traditions. In Rwanda, where the sheer number of those implicated in the genocide made the prospect of prosecutions daunting, the work of the ad hoc tribunal was complemented by the Gacaca courts, a reconstructed version of old communal systems of adjudication.[127] According to Roht-Arriaza, these were measures to improve the efficiency of transitional interventions. Hybridism offered a way to 'combine the independence, impartiality and resources of an international institution with the grounding in national law, realities and culture, the reduced costs, and the continuity and sustainability of a national effort'.[128] This arguably neutral, culturally sensitive and cost-effective model became the United Nations template for post-conflict justice.[129]

A Holistic Peacebuilding Project

Having found fertile ground in the punishment vs impunity debates, the reconciliation industry would reach other fields such as peace and conflict research.[130] Traditional accounts of conflict resolution were more concerned with the end of hostilities and the priorities of disarmament and demobilisation.[131] Much of the research that is known as conflict management and conflict transformation shares strong ties with minimalist accounts of reconciliation. But the atmosphere would change in the early 1990s, when a series of 'peacekeeping operations in Namibia, Cambodia, Angola, Mozambique and El Salvador seemed to offer the hope that the peace engendered by UN intervention could go beyond patrolling cease-fires'.[132] The UN document *An Agenda for Peace*, published in 1992, was instrumental, introducing the concept of post-conflict peacebuilding as a global, multilevel approach 'in order to promote a durable foundation for peace'.[133] In this new scenario, the idea of reconciliation and, in particular, the maximalist trope, offered a promising alternative towards 'more ambitious forms of peacekeeping'[134] that would seek to 'contribute to the democratisation of failing and failed states'.[135]

Understood as a policy of forgiveness, reconciliation was meant to 'humanize the perpetrators',[136] which was seen as an important way to 'engage the sides of a conflict with each other as humans-in-relationship'.[137] The politics of reconciliation promised 'bringing together people from opposing sides and encouraging them to articulate their past pain'.[138] Conceived as 'a process through which a society moves from a divided past to a shared future',[139] reconciliation became an increasingly attractive buzzword for researchers and practitioners concerned with measures 'for the prevention of further conflict'.[140] It came to be seen also as a potential contribution of transitional justice to a thicker understanding of pacification and for wider strategies of conflict transformation.[141]

The cross-field popularisation of reconciliation was more than an unreflective adoption of the South African model. In fact, it helped to reshape the maximalist approach breaching the remaining gaps between retributive and restorative justice. A growing consensus emerged that neither punishment nor forgiveness could bring about peace on their own. The same handbooks preaching the value of reconciliation were also arguing that 'compromise regarding justice, and the legal desire for retribution [. . .] innately carries the risk of silencing the past'.[142] They insisted that '[r]econciliation processes are ineffective as long as the vicious circle of impunity is not broken'.[143] Over time, this rapprochement backed by a wider peacebuilding agenda acquired its own mantra: the need for a 'holistic prism'[144] that encompasses 'all existing methods of transitional justice'[145] as means 'necessary to support sustainable peacebuilding'.[146]

The UN report *The Rule of Law and Transitional Justice in Conflict and Post-conflict Societies*[147] marks the 'official' recognition of transitional interventions as 'an apparatus within the wider peacebuilding "package"'.[148] The report shows a strong tendency to recuperate the connection between processes of reconciliation and the fight against impunity, in an attempt at 'articulating a *common language of justice* for the United Nations'.[149] Transitional justice is defined as the 'full range of processes and mechanisms [. . .] in order to ensure accountability, serve justice and achieve reconciliation'.[150] Interestingly, the common language of justice mixed the different vocabularies of retributivist and restorative approaches. It considered the faculty of punishment as part of a 'mix of complementary therapies'[151] seeking to 'heal rather than exacerbate wounds'[152] endured by 'populations traumatized by war'.[153] The merging of the two vocabularies recuperated old claims that 'truth and justice are complementary'[154] against perspectives that had framed them as 'alternative forms of accountability'.[155] Once again, scholars and practitioners were voicing the belief that 'there can be no just and lasting reconciliation unless the need for justice is effectively satisfied'.[156]

Many have criticised this progressive indistinction between retributive and restorative justice. Bronwyn Leebaw argues that the rhetoric of synthesis works to conceal a set of contradictory claims (a topic I will explore further in Chapter 4).[157] For Eric Doxtader, the synthesis risked creating a straitjacket approach, undermining the rhetorical, deconstructive and transformative potentiality present in the concept of reconciliation.[158] Eagle does not speak of a synthesis but of a true criminal turn in the human rights movement, with the entrenchment of retribution as the only possible response to the post-conflict.[159] Notwithstanding, the common language influenced several paradigmatic cases of transitional justice from the early 2000s to the present days. Both the ad hoc tribunals shared '[t]he implicit assumption [. . .] that criminal trials are an important component of reconciliation'.[160] Returning to the Argentine model, transitional responses implemented in East Timor (2001) and Sierra Leone (2002) saw truth commissions sharing space with courts, as complementary interventions.[161] More recently, the 2015 peace agreement in Colombia proposed not one or two, but a plethora of different transitional mechanisms including a truth commission, reparations, criminal trials and partial amnesties for political crimes.[162]

Truth as a Human Right

If, in 'political' terms, the synthesis between retributive and restorative justice required a wider, emancipatory peace agenda, in 'legal' terms it was brought about by an ingenious operation: the establishment of the truth about the past as an inalienable human right. In a typically legalistic fashion, scholars have traced the right to truth back to the post-1948 era (finding antecedents in the UN Declaration of Human Rights and the Geneva Conventions).[163] But this misses the fact that the right to the truth was deeply grounded in the politics of the punishment vs impunity debates. The framing of 'truth' (the knowledge and acknowledgement of past violations of human rights) as a human right cannot be disentangled from the effervescence of the anti-impunity movement in the 1990s.

In tandem with the explosive rise of the reconciliation industry, the world witnessed what Karen Eagle termed the criminal turn in human rights.[164] Those were the years of the convention against torture, drafted in 1984,[165] and the declaration defining forced disappearances as crimes against humanity,[166] drafted in 1992 and adopted by the General Assembly fourteen years later.[167] In the late 1980s, for the first time, the Inter-American Commission on Human Rights (IACHR) referred cases of violations of human rights to the Inter-American Court (IACtHR), breaking with a long period of inaction.[168] In the emblematic *Velasquez Rodríguez vs Honduras* case, the court ruled in favour of the families of individuals forcefully disappeared by state forces, emphasising the state's duty to continue to investigate the unsolved case.[169] The decision, arguably suggestive of the victim's right to know what happened, became a cornerstone of the anti-impunity movement.[170]

In 1998, the year the TRC published its final report, Spanish justice Baltazar Garzón requested the extradition of a Chilean criminal (Pinochet) from Britain to be prosecuted in Spain, sparking frenetic debates about the concept of universal jurisdiction.[171] While the South African politics of forgiveness and social healing were praised in the four corners of the world, in the Southern Cone, activists and scholars were fighting to circumvent impediments to prosecutions. In Chile, Judge Juan Guzmán came up with the ingenious doctrine of 'permanent sequestration' for which disappearances constituted an ongoing crime, thereby falling outside the temporal jurisdiction of amnesty laws.[172] In Argentina, survivors and family members were resorting to the innovative 'truth-seeking trials', special court proceedings that resembled truth commission hearings where perpetrators were subpoenaed and forced to testify.[173]

The jurisprudential efforts of the anti-impunity movement were mainstreamed in a series of bespoke UN reports from independent experts.[174] The 1997 report *Question of the Impunity of Perpetrators of Human Rights Violations (Civil and Political)*, written by Louis Joinet, was perhaps the most influential of such reports. The report clearly states the victim's and society's right 'to know what happened';[175] a fundamental right whose 'corollary is a "duty to remember", which the State must assume'.[176] In a clear defiance of the then-in-vogue notion of multiple coexistent truths, Joinet recuperated CONADEP's understanding that truth-seeking should work 'to preserve evidence for the courts'.[177] He further emphasised that '[t]he fact that [. . .] a perpetrator discloses the violations that he or others have committed in order to benefit from the favourable provisions of legislation on repentance cannot exempt him from criminal or other responsibility.'[178]

The right to the truth is a legal principle, but it was also a political necessity. Turning truth into a 'right' foreclosed the grounds for alternatives to retribution, binding the prospects of reconciliation back to the enforcement of criminal accountability. In historical terms, the theory behind this new right rode on the wave of the 1993 Vienna Convention, where human rights were reiterated as 'indivisible and interdependent and interrelated'.[179] The popularisation of the concept of 'indivisibility' in the 1990s was used to dispute claims that human rights could be split into groups following a hierarchy of importance.[180] Therefore, by rendering the knowledge of past violations a human right in itself, legal theorists could perform a similar move: reject claims that truth and justice could be separated. They were reclaiming the motto long held by memory struggles: the *equal, inalienable* and *inseparable* nature of truth (knowledge), memory (acknowledgement) and justice (criminal accountability).

As a testament to this successful operation, the right to the truth has become a constitutive part of the common language of justice. Since the 1980s, it has been continuously evoked in cases where the IACtHR found amnesty settlements to be inconsistent with human rights law.[181] In 2010, the UN National Assembly proclaimed the 24th of March as the International Day for the Right to the Truth.[182] Three years later, the organisation reinforced 'the importance of respecting and ensuring the right to the truth so as to contribute to ending impunity and to promote and protect human rights'.[183] The right has also been incorporated into the European and African systems of human rights, and provided much-needed support for the implementation of a truth commission in Brazil.[184]

Conclusion

This chapter has recounted the development of a common language of justice as part of a process of institutionalisation of transitional justice supported by changes in the fields of peacebuilding and legal theory. Its goal was to situate the central arguments of the punishment vs impunity debates both historically and politically, linking the often abstract debates between scholars over the meaning of justice in times of transition back to the political struggles in the South Atlantic from which they originated. First, the chapter looked at the origins of the anti-impunity movement and of transitional justice's most distinct mechanisms, truth commissions, in the late twentieth century (1980–90). It described how the international alliance formed between survivors of state terror, family members of the disappeared, legal practitioners and NGOs helped to mainstream the challenges faced, as well as the solutions produced by local activists as the toolbox of transitional justice. Second, the chapter looked at how the demands of activists in the Southern Cone, inalienable demands of truth, memory and justice, were split apart during the Chilean and South African transitions, when truth-seeking appeared first as a second-best (as in Chile) and later as the best alternative to criminal prosecutions (as in South Africa). Here, it emphasised the often forgotten resonance between the concept of reconciliation and the political agenda of conservative sectors in transitional societies. Lastly, the chapter explained the development of a common language of justice as the consequence of new approaches to peacebuilding and the development of a jurisprudence regarding the right to the truth.

This historical awareness of transitional justice's common language of justice is an important step, but it is by no means the only one needed. If we are willing to move towards a critical reading of transitional justice, more needs to be done. For example, we need to investigate the punishment vs impunity debates not only in terms of the historical development of the language and rationale of a given field (transitional justice), but from the perspective of the emergence of a certain *discipline*, in a Foucauldian sense. With the effort to historicise the present completed, I now turn to step two: analysing this historical development from the perspective of the rise of a new discipline of justice, imbued with the capacity to discipline the conduct of individuals and groups at a time of political and economic transformation. To enter the realm of disciplinarity, we need to perform a methodological twist unfamiliar in works on transitional justice: to move away from the *conditions of implementation* of justice in the wake of violence, towards its *conditions of possibility*. That is, from the question of 'how can we best implement peace and justice in the aftermath of violence?' to 'how we can even begin to think that violence ever ends?'. This is what the next chapter will do.

Notes

1. Kritz, 'The Dilemmas of Transitional Justice'; Hayner, *The Peacemaker's Paradox*; Henkin, 'State Crimes: Punishment or Pardon (Conference Report)'.
2. Minow, 'Between Vengeance and Forgiveness'; Teitel, 'Transitional Justice Genealogy'; Elster, *Closing the Books*.
3. Roht-Arriaza and Mariezcurrena, *Transitional Justice in the Twenty-First Century*; Sharp, *Rethinking Transitional Justice for the Twenty-First Century*.
4. Hayner, *The Peacemaker's Paradox*.
5. Arthur, 'How "Transitions" Reshaped Human Rights'; Collins, Balardini and Burt, 'Mapping Perpetrator Prosecutions in Latin America'; Lessa et al., 'Overcoming Impunity'; Waldorf, 'Anticipating the Past'.
6. Arthur, 'How "Transitions" Reshaped Human Rights'.
7. Keck and Sikkink, *Activists beyond Borders*, p. 23.
8. Gready, *The Era of Transitional Justice*.
9. Navarro, 'The Personal Is Political'.
10. Blakeley, 'Bringing the State Back Into Terrorism Studies'; Jackson, 'The Ghosts of State Terror'; Jackson, Murphy and Poynting, *Contemporary State Terrorism*.
11. Ministério da Justiça, *Relatório Anual da Comissão de Anistia 2010*.
12. D'Orsi, 'Trauma and the Politics of Memory of the Uruguayan Dictatorship'.
13. Camacho, 'Memorias enfrentadas'.
14. Crenzel, 'Argentina's National Commission on the Disappearance of Persons'.
15. Catela, *Situação-Limite e Memória*.

16. Teles, 'Entre o Luto e a Melancolia', p. 154.
17. Navarro, 'The Personal Is Political'.
18. Edkins, *Missing: Persons and Politics*; Jelin, *State Repression and the Labors of Memory*.
19. Bickford, 'The Archival Imperative'; Jelin, 'Public Memorialization in Perspective'; Weschler, *A Miracle, A Universe*.
20. Santos, 'Transitional Justice from the Margins'.
21. Keck and Sikkink, *Activists beyond Borders*.
22. The Russell Tribunals on Latin America were held in Rome (1974 and 1976) and Brussels (1975). See Greco, 'Anistia Anamnese vs. Anistia Amnésia'.
23. In Uruguay, in two referendums held in 1989 and 2009, a majority voted for the maintenance of the amnesty. See Lessa and Druliolle, *The Memory of State Terrorism in The Southern Cone*; Brito, Gonzaléz-Enríquez and Aguilar, *The Politics of Memory*.
24. Greco, 'Anistia Anamnese vs. Anistia Amnésia'; Cabrera, 'Do Luto à Luta'; Teles, 'Entre o Luto e a Melancolia'.
25. Schneider, 'The Forgotten Voices of the Militares Cassados'.
26. Santos, 'Transitional Justice from the Margins'.
27. Mezarobba, *Um Acerto de Contas com o Futuro*.
28. Ibid.
29. Catela, 'Do Segredo à Verdade . . .'.
30. Weschler, *A Miracle, A Universe*, p. 10.
31. Crenzel, 'Argentina's National Commission on the Disappearance of Persons'.
32. CONADEP, *Nunca Más*.
33. Ibid. p. 15.
34. Crenzel, 'Argentina's National Commission on the Disappearance of Persons'.
35. Vannuchi, personal interview, 17 January 2018.
36. Weschler, *A Miracle, A Universe*, pp. 44–5; Arquidiocese de São Paulo, *Brasil: Nunca Mais*.
37. Mezarobba, *Um Acerto de Contas com o Futuro*.
38. Crenzel, 'Argentina's National Commission on the Disappearance of Persons'.
39. Humphrey and Valverde, 'Human Rights Politics and Injustice'.
40. Crenzel, 'Argentina's National Commission on the Disappearance of Persons'.
41. Verdeja, 'The Elements of Political Reconciliation', p. 168.
42. Zalaquett, 'Balancing Ethical Imperatives and Political Constraints'.
43. O'Donnell and Schmitter, 'Transitions from Authoritarian Rule', p. 64.
44. Elster, *Closing the Books*, p. 27.
45. The most important groups in this regard were the 'Amnesty Committees in Brazil, the International Secretariat of Jurists for Amnesty in Uruguay (SIJAU) and the Secretariat for Amnesty and Democracy in Paraguay (SIJADEP)' (UN Sub-Commission on the Promotion and Protection of Human Rights 1997, p. 3).
46. United Nations, *The Administration of Justice and the Human Rights of Detainees: Question of the Impunity of Perpetrators of Human Rights Violations (Civil and Political)*, p. 3.
47. In Hannah Arendt's words, Christianity could be summarised as a political philosophy of forgiveness. See Arendt, *The Human Condition*.

48. Silva Filho, 'O Anjo da História e a Memória das Vítimas', p. 174.
49. Lessa and Druliolle, *The Memory of State Terrorism in the Southern Cone*, p. 179.
50. Greco, 'Anistia Anamnese vs. Anistia Amnésia'; Greco, '50 Anos do Golpe Militar/35 Anos da Lei de Anistia'.
51. Roht-Arriaza and Mariezcurrena, *Transitional Justice in the Twenty-First Century*, p. xx.
52. In Germany, as in Argentina, punishment was already seen in a form of symbolism. As 'post-conflict' trials they had a symbolic power (Shklar 1964) as 'exemplary' (Nino 1991: 2623) instances of retribution concerning 'those mainly responsible for the worst deeds' (ibid.). Nevertheless, during the Chilean transitional response, this symbolic power was turned against the possibility of punishment itself.
53. Aylwin, *La transicion chilena*, p. 33.
54. CONADEP, *Nunca Más*, p. 10.
55. CNVR, 'Informe de la comision nacional de verdad y reconciliacion', p. 10.
56. Collins, *Post-Transitional Justice*.
57. *Decreto-Ley 2119, de 1978*.
58. Brito, Gonzaléz-Enríquez and Aguilar, *The Politics of Memory*.
59. Popkin and Roht-arriaza, 'Truth as Justice', p. 84.
60. Aravena, 'Civil–Military Relations in Post-Authoritarian Chile', p. 151.
61. Collins, *Post-Transitional Justice*.
62. Pinochet cited in Rosenberg, 'Overcoming the Legacies of Dictatorship', p. 134.
63. Aylwin, *La transicion chilena*, p. 33.
64. CNVR, 'Informe de la comision nacional de verdad y reconciliacion'.
65. Ibid.
66. Zalaquett, 'Balancing Ethical Imperatives and Political Constraints', p. 1438.
67. Ibid. p. 1438.
68. Verdeja, 'The Elements of Political Reconciliation', p. 169.
69. Tutu, *No Future Without Forgiveness*, p. 81 (my emphasis).
70. Gobodo-Madikizela, 'Transitional Justice and Truth Commissions', p. 294.
71. Humphrey, *The Politics of Atrocity and Reconciliation*.
72. Alfonsín, *Mensajes presidenciales del Dr. Raúl Alfonsín*, p. 70.
73. Vezzetti, 'Los sesenta y los setenta', p. 59 (my emphasis).
74. Alfonsín, *Mensajes presidenciales del Dr. Raúl Alfonsín*, p. 15.
75. Aylwin, *La transicion chilena*, p. 21.
76. Ibid. p. 21.
77. Bonnin, 'Religious and Political Discourse in Argentina'.
78. Nino, 'The Duty to Punish Past Abuses of Human Rights Put into Context'; Di Paolantonio, 'Argentina After the "Dirty War"'.
79. Zalaquett, 'Balancing Ethical Imperatives and Political Constraints', p. 1433.
80. Renner, 'The Local Roots of the Global Politics of Reconciliation'.
81. Ibid.
82. Leebaw, *Judging State-Sponsored Violence*, p. 67.
83. Moon, 'Healing Past Violence', p. 78.

84. Leebaw, *Judging State-Sponsored Violence*.
85. Gibson, 'Overcoming Apartheid'; Gibson, 'The Contributions of Truth to Reconciliation'; Leebaw, *Judging State-Sponsored Violence*; Wilson, *The Politics of Truth and Reconciliation in South Africa*.
86. TRC, 'Truth and Reconciliation Commission of South Africa Report', vol. 1, p. 85.
87. Gobodo-Madikizela, 'Transitional Justice and Truth Commissions', p. 277.
88. Tutu, *No Future Without Forgiveness*, p. 54.
89. Ibid. p. 54.
90. Ramphele cited in Leebaw, *Judging State-Sponsored Violence*, p. 74.
91. The suggestion that retribution is somehow un-African has been proven deeply problematic. Many South Africans rejected Tutu's defence of reconciliation and forgiveness, calling into question the constitutionality of amnesty provisions. See Wilson, *The Politics of Truth and Reconciliation in South Africa*, p. 11; Moon, *Narrating Political Reconciliation*; Renner, 'The Local Roots of the Global Politics of Reconciliation'
92. Du Toit, 'The Moral Foundations of the South African TRC', p. 123.
93. Moon, *Narrating Political Reconciliation*, p. 93.
94. Moon, *Narrating Political Reconciliation*; TRC, 'Truth and Reconciliation Commission of South Africa Report'.
95. Hayner, *Unspeakable Truths*.
96. Wilson, *The Politics of Truth and Reconciliation in South Africa*, p. 22.
97. Hayner, *Unspeakable Truths*, p. 30.
98. Hayner, *Unspeakable Truths*.
99. Moon, *Narrating Political Reconciliation*.
100. Torre and De Riz, *Argentina since 1946*.
101. Moon, 'Narrating Political Reconciliation', p. 258.
102. Siegel, 'Transitional Justice'.
103. For a classic and thorough description of the Aspen, Charter 77 and IDASA conferences see Arthur, 'How "Transitions" Reshaped Human Rights'.
104. Nagy, 'Transitional Justice as Global Project'; D. N. Sharp (ed.), *Justice and Economic Violence in Transition*; Sharp, *Rethinking Transitional Justice for the Twenty-First Century*.
105. Orentlicher, 'Settling Accounts'.
106. Collins, *Post-Transitional Justice*, p. 149.
107. Ibid. p. 149.
108. Hayner, *Unspeakable Truths*.
109. Ibid.
110. Collins, *Post-Transitional Justice*, p. 159.
111. United Nations, 'The Rule of Law and Transitional Justice' (UN Security Council: S/2004/616, 2004), p. 5.
112. Lederach, *Building Peace*.
113. Mann, *The Dark Side of Democracy*, p. 356.
114. Ibid. p. 430.

115. United Nations, 'Convention on the Prevention and Punishment of the Crime of Genocide' (General Assembly: A/RES/3/260, 1948).

116. Lederach, *Building Peace*, p. 5.

117. United Nations, *Resolution 827* (UN Security Council: S/RES/827, 1993).

118. United Nations, *Resolution 955* (UN Security Council: S/RES/995, 1994).

119. Roht-Arriaza and Mariezcurrena, *Transitional Justice in the Twenty-First Century*, p. 10.

120. Arthur, '"Fear of the Future, Lived through the Past"', p. 289.

121. Ibid. p. 289.

122. Collins, *Post-Transitional Justice*.

123. Obradovic-Wochnik, 'The "Silent Dilemma" of Transitional Justice'.

124. United Nations, 'The Rule of Law and Transitional Justice in Conflict and Post-Conflict Societies', p. 14.

125. Verdeja, *Unchopping a Tree*, p. 95.

126. Wilson, 'Violent Truths'; Hayner, *Unspeakable Truths*.

127. Brounéus, 'The Trauma of Truth Telling'; Brouneus, 'Truth-Telling as Talking Cure?'.

128. Roht-Arriaza and Mariezcurrena, *Transitional Justice in the Twenty-First Century*, p. 10.

129. United Nations, 'The Rule of Law and Transitional Justice in Conflict and Post-Conflict Societies'.

130. Mani, 'Rebuilding an Inclusive Political Community after War'; Lambourne, 'Transitional Justice and Peacebuilding after Mass Violence'; Mendeloff, 'Truth-Seeking, Truth-Telling, and Postconflict Peacebuilding'; Sharp, *Rethinking Transitional Justice for the Twenty-First Century*.

131. Andrieu, 'Civilizing Peacebuilding'; Mani, 'Rebuilding an Inclusive Political Community after War'; Richmond, *Peacebuilding*; Richmond, 'The Problem of Peace'.

132. Richmond, *Peacebuilding*, p. 22.

133. United Nations, 'An Agenda for Peace: Preventive Diplomacy and Related Matters' (UN General Assembly: A/RES/47/1, 1992), p. v.

134. Richmond, *Peace in International Relations*, p. 105.

135. Ibid. p. 105.

136. Minow, 'Between Vengeance and Forgiveness', p. 338.

137. Lederach, *Building Peace*, p. 26.

138. Ibid. p. 150.

139. IDEA, *Reconciliation after Violent Conflict*, p. 12.

140. SIDA, *Reconciliation*, p. 9.

141. Andrieu, 'Civilizing Peacebuilding'; Little, 'Disjunctured Narratives'.

142. SIDA, *Reconciliation*, p. 30.

143. IDEA, *Reconciliation after Violent Conflict*, p. 108.

144. Gready and Robins, 'From Transitional to Transformative Justice', p. 6.

145. Mani, 'Rebuilding an Inclusive Political Community after War', p. 524.

146. Lambourne, 'Transitional Justice and Peacebuilding', p. 47.

147. United Nations, 'The Rule of Law and Transitional Justice in Conflict and Post-Conflict Societies'.

148. Andrieu, 'Civilizing Peacebuilding', p. 538.

149. United Nations, 'The Rule of Law and Transitional Justice in Conflict and Post-Conflict Societies', p. 4 (my emphasis).

150. Ibid. p. 4 (my emphasis).

151. Schabas, 'The Sierra Leone Truth and Reconciliation Commission', p. 21.

152. Mani, 'Rebuilding an Inclusive Political Community after War', p. 525.

153. United Nations, 'The Rule of Law and Transitional Justice in Conflict and Post-Conflict Societies', p. 11.

154. Roht-Arriaza, 'Truth Commissions and Amnesties in Latin America', p. 314.

155. Leebaw, 'The Irreconcilable Goals of Transitional Justice', p. 99.

156. United Nations, 'Impunity: Report of the Independent Expert to Update the Set of Principles to Combat Impunity, Diane Orentlicher' (UN Economic and Social Council: E/CN.4/200, 2005), preamble.

157. Leebaw, 'The Irreconcilable Goals of Transitional Justice'.

158. Doxtader, 'A Critique of Law's Violence yet (Never) to Come'; Doxtader, 'Reconciliation – a Rhetorical Concept/ion'.

159. Eagle, 'A Genealogy of the Criminal Turn in Human Rights'.

160. Halpern and Weinstein, 'Rehumanizing the Other', n. 11.

161. Schabas, 'The Sierra Leone Truth and Reconciliation Commission', p. 21; Reiger, 'Hybrid Attempts at Accountability for Serious Crimes in Timor Leste'; CAVR, 'Chega!'; TRC Sierra Leone, 'Witness to Truth'.

162. Alcalá and Uribe, 'Constructing Memory amidst War'; Hayner, *The Peacemaker's Paradox*.

163. Groome, 'The Right to Truth in the Fight against Impunity'; Naqvi, 'The Right to the Truth in International Law'.

164. Eagle, 'A Genealogy of the Criminal Turn in Human Rights'.

165. United Nations, 'Convention against Torture and Other Cruel, Inhuman or Degrading Treatment or Punishment'.

166. United Nations, 'Declaration on the Protection of All Persons from Enforced Disappearance' (UN General Assembly: A/RES/47/133, 1992).

167. United Nations, *Agenda Item 68: Report of the Human Rights Council* (UN General Assembly: A/61/PV.82, 2006).

168. Goldman, 'History and Action', p. 874.

169. Groome, 'The Right to Truth in the Fight against Impunity'.

170. The 1998 ruling on the *Blake vs Guatemala* case is another benchmark in the jurisprudence of the right to truth. The IACtHR ruled in favour of the family of American journalist Nicholas Blake, disappeared in Guatemala by state forces, recognising that the state had infringed on the victims' right to know the truth. See Groome, 'The Right to Truth in the Fight against Impunity'.

171. Collins, *Post-Transitional Justice*.

172. Lessa et al., 'Overcoming Impunity'.

173. Garibian, 'Ghosts Also Die'; Romanin, 'Decir la verdad, hacer justicia'.

174. Bassiouni, *The Right to Restitution, Compensation and Rehabilitation for Victims of Gross Violations of Human Rights and Fundamental Freedoms* (UN Commission on Human Rights: E/CN.4/2000/62, 1999); Van Boven, *Study Concerning the Right to Restitution, Compensation and Rehabilitation for Victims of Gross Violations of Human Rights and Fundamental Freedoms* (UN Commission on Human Rights: E/CN.4/Sub.2/1993/8, 1993).

175. United Nations, 'Question of the Impunity of Perpetrators of Human Rights Violations (Civil and Political)' (UN Economic and Social Council: E/CN.4/Sub, 1997), A17.

176. Ibid. A17.

177. Joinet's principles were later revised and supported by Diane Orentlicher in the 2000s. See United Nations, 'Impunity: Report of the Independent Expert to Update the Set of Principles to Combat Impunity, Diane Orentlicher'.

178. United Nations, 'Question of the Impunity of Perpetrators of Human Rights Violations (Civil and Political)', p. 24.

179. United Nations, 'Vienna Declaration and Programme of Action' (UN General Assembly: A/CN.15/23, 1993), pp. 1–5.

180. During the Cold War, legal theorists and politicians popularised the division of human rights into two main groups: civil and political rights (aka first-generation rights) and socio-economic and cultural rights (aka second-generation rights). See Brems, 'Human Rights'; Cohen, 'Minimalism about Human Rights'; Kennedy, 'The International Human Rights Movement'; Vincent, *The Politics of Human Rights*; United Nations, 'Universal Declaration of Human Rights' (UN General Assembly: 217 A (III), 1948).

181. Eagle, 'A Genealogy of the Criminal Turn in Human Rights'.

182. United Nations, 'Resolution Adopted by the General Assembly on 21 December 2010 65/196. Proclamation of 24 March as the International Day for the Right to Truth Concerning Gross Human Rights Violations and for the Dignity of Victims' (UN General Assembly: A/RES/65/1, 2011).

183. United Nations, 'Resolution Adopted by the General Assembly on 18 December 2013 68/165. Right to the Truth' (UN General Assembly: A/RES/68/165, 2014), p. 3.

184. Eagle, 'A Genealogy of the Criminal Turn in Human Rights'.

CHAPTER 2

The Making of the Post-Conflict

One of the most widespread and least disputed ideas in the literature of transitional justice is the belief that transitional interventions (such as trials, truth commissions and reparations) are *problem-solving* interventions, concerned with the *implementation* of peace and justice in the wake of violence. The vast majority of works depart from an uncritical account of the production of knowledge that assumes a relation of exteriority between the field and practice of transitional justice and the problems faced by transitional societies. This logic identifies in a given (post-conflict) situation the need to *implement* one particular solution (justice, in all its different forms). Everything began when the trauma of the Holocaust required the creation of a new, unprecedented crime and the enforcement of an international duty to punish the enemies of humankind (solving the impossibility of philosophical and legal judgement); in the Southern Cone and in South Africa, the 'trauma' of state terror (the military dictatorships and apartheid) and the regime of silence that ensued required a different approach involving the creation of truth commissions (solving the problem of disappearances and the need for reconciliation); and, from the establishment of the ICC onwards, a common language of justice connected both responses (solving the dynamics of a new era defined by the pervasive existence of cultures of impunity). What is clear from this historical reading is that knowledge and practice are always seen as responses to something exterior to them. They represent a reaction to a reality that, in the first place, they do not create.

The first step towards developing a critical method is to realise the limits of this historical account. Adopting a historical method is not enough to produce an innovative reading of transitional justice. So long as the analysis remains at the level of conditions of implementation, the resulting depiction will likely reproduce a traditional image of the field. To move forward and beyond such image, we need to go back to the works of Michel Foucault, seriously incorporating what he defined as a critical historical method or a genealogy.[1] Foucault was adamant about the need to question the *conditions of possibility* of both knowledge and practice. Through his genealogical insights, we can move away from the conditions of implementation of post-conflict or post-authoritarian justice towards an investigation of their conditions of possibility. This means leaving behind the assumption of exteriority between knowledge and experience and the vision of transitional interventions as problem-solving tools. It also means we need to reorganise the intellectual priorities of researchers and practitioners; to finally stop asking 'how can we best produce justice in a given post-conflict scenario?' and start asking 'how can we even speak of a post-conflict scenario to begin with?'.

A critical *genealogy* of the punishment vs impunity debate – an inquiry into its conditions of possibility – must proceed in three steps. First, instead of focusing on the problems that come with the end of violence, a critical genealogy must reveal how, at a particular point in history, it became possible to speak of a time when *violence had ended or could possibly end*. Second, instead of simply mentioning the disputes between retribution and restoration, a critical genealogy must situate these debates in the internal cohesion of a body of knowledge. It must show how seemingly disparate perspectives share a common ground. Finally, and most importantly, a critical genealogy must disclose how a field of knowledge and practice (such as transitional justice) emerged through a process of objectification: the production of its very object of study and intervention. In sum, this critical enterprise must dig deeper than the apparent diversity of conceptions of justice in the punishment vs impunity debates and reveal a central kernel providing such debates with a point of internal coherence. As this chapter will show, this kernel is exactly the field's narrow representation of *violence* that fundamentally produces a convincing 'myth' of the *post-conflict* era.

In the first section I present a dense but necessary explanation of Foucault's historical methodology. My exposé surrounds his idea of truth as a historical 'set of rules', suggesting that 'new' objects of analysis are, in a sense, produced by 'new' academic disciplines. This takes me away from the conditions of implementation of transitional justice to its conditions of possibility. In the second and third sections I move on to identify, in the history of transitional justice, the 'discipline's' own process of objectification; that is, how the emergence of a 'new' discipline of justice produced and was produced by a 'new' reality of the post-conflict. The second section contextualises the rise of transitional debates in the late twentieth century (1980–90) at a time of political and economic transformation when the *post-conflict* appeared in the global landscape as an attainable and sometimes irresistible reality. The third and last section analyses the function of transitional justice's narrow understanding of violence as the central assumption binding together the whole discipline. It also explains why, and in what sense, this central assumption is part of a larger ideological field.

The Two Meanings of the Word 'Discipline' in Foucault

As an extremely prolific writer, Foucault left a universe of concepts and ideas as an inheritance. In the field of critical global studies and the areas of human rights and transitional justice, researchers tend to begin by explaining the concepts of discourse or discursive practice[2] or the idea of governmentality.[3] Without discrediting these approaches, I take my own different shortcut into Foucault's power-knowledge nexus. There is, in the vast and erudite intellectual labyrinth of Foucauldian scholarship, one concept that stands out, one concept that simultaneously embodies the immediate connection between the two fundamental poles of Foucault's thoughts: the production of knowledge and the effects of power. This concept is *discipline*, a term that in Foucault departs from its common-sense meaning and gains a powerful political sense.

Foucault understands and uses 'discipline' in a volatile manner. The notion of discipline is not a static, coherently used concept; on the contrary, discipline is a notion that evolves over the years, assuming different connotations and unveiling the development of his profound theoretical acumen. Nonetheless, if one reads Foucault's works in retrospect, as he himself occasionally did,[4] the concept of discipline attains a prominent place. The concept presents the juncture connecting Foucault's incessant questioning of authoritative knowledge claims that govern our modes of life. It allows us to investigate how what we normally take for harmless disciplines (bodies of knowledge) can discipline (exercise power over) our everyday conduct. In this chapter I draw on the term 'discipline' in Foucault to contextualise the punishment vs impunity debates of the twentieth and twenty-first centuries. Finding inspiration in Foucault's early works, we can understand a discipline as a domain of knowledge characterised by rules of internal coherence.[5] This meaning of discipline is important because it offers a different perspective on the relation between bodies of knowledge and objects of knowledge. This perspective is the basis of the idea of objectification.

To understand what objectification is, we must consider Foucault's sophisticated account of truth. Foucault works with a concept of 'truth' that refers to a relation of correspondence defined by a set of rules.[6] This is to say the production of knowledge, as a general inquiry about the truth of things, is always a process constrained by specific procedures. If one desires to know the truth about a given phenomenon, one must follow specific directions provided by certain guidelines. This sounds all too technical, like a question that only concerns professional scientists, but it is a rather banal reality faced by thousands of people every single day. Any of us, despite our credentials, would resort to a set of rules in order to judge the veracity of the pettiest, most practical of questions. A hypothetical example might help to clarify this. Imagine being questioned about the whereabouts of your house keys. Now, when asked the question 'where are your keys?', any of us would promptly resort to an observational method (a rule or a set of procedures used to discover the truth about this particular situation). Simply put, if I cannot see the keys on my desk or find them in my pockets, the truth is I could have lost them. If, on the other hand, I can see the keys right in front of me, then I know where they are and there is no need to worry.

The idea of truth as a set of rules defining a relation of correspondence – be it with the visible world (my desk) or its invisible depths (my pockets) – is by no means an original contribution of Foucauldian thought. Philosophers of science have long discussed it.[7] Foucault's inventive twist was, in fact, seeing such rules as fundamentally historical. In one of his most famous works, *The Order of Things* (1966), Foucault describes, in overwhelming intellectual breadth, how the relation of correspondence between claims of knowledge and the 'objective reality' dramatically changed over the course of time.

At first sight, *The Order of Things* is an incomprehensible book. This is not due to a convoluted writing style; reading Foucault is usually much easier than reading his contemporaries. The book is simply weird. The information it conveys is irreparably strange. *The Order of Things* is full of odd historical 'anecdotes'. The first chapter takes us to the late Middle Ages, recounting a time of strong beliefs in the biblical myth of Babel (the common, primal language of humankind), the healing powers of walnuts (capable of curing headaches because of their resemblance to human brains) and the wickedness of cemetery flowers (carrying the omen of death because of their proximity to it).[8] From the beginning, we come across beliefs that seem incredible in the most archaic sense of the word, even ludicrous, to our modern minds. We are all too quick to see them as mere 'misbeliefs' of a past tainted by religious fanaticism or blinded by superstition. However, it is against this 'liberal arrogance'[9] – the presumptuous conjecture that we are right, that we hold the truth – that Foucault's writing is so powerful. *The Order of Things* describes such remarks in their opacity, without prejudice. In the 'misbeliefs' of the past it simply sees a different form of truth. This is perhaps the strongest of Foucault's political arguments. He takes us to this different reality, the *heterotopos* of an incomprehensible mode of knowledge, in order to question the 'beliefs' of the present, the 'truths' that govern our lives.

Foucault's genealogical approach creates this *heterotopia* by introducing the concept of objectification. Objectification fundamentally challenges the traditional way of looking at bodies of knowledge as if solving external problems. It refers to the process by which the objects we deem most natural (that is, the things whose existence we see as independent from our perspective) have, in fact, not always existed. Objectification supports a theory for which 'objective facts' and an 'objective reality' must first emerge as *knowable objects*. Here is where truth, as a set of historical relations of correspondence, comes in.

Perhaps the best way to explain objectification is to give Foucault's most radical account of it. In an unfathomable remark, Foucault affirms the discipline of biology was unknown prior to the late eighteenth century. His explanation is astonishing: biology did not exist because 'life itself did not exist'.[10] How can Foucault claim 'life', the most natural and self-evident reality, is, to put it crudely, a historical invention? What he means is that neither the concept of life, as we understand it today, nor the contemporary practice of studying life, the discipline of biology, could be accommodated within the dominant set of rules concerning truth-claims (an *episteme*) during premodern times. Human beings (read Europeans) had to significantly transform the way they conceived of themselves and their surroundings for both biology and life to become 'thinkable' realities.

The reason is simple. From the seventeenth to the late eighteenth century, the production of knowledge works within 'the apparent simplicity of a description of the visible'.[11] The rule of correspondence between representations (knowledge claims) and the reality they refer to locates certainty about truth in what is superficially and immediately observable. Knowing the truth about the world consists, according to this premodern rule, of knowing the visible characters of worldly things. This rule of correspondence (the visible) orbits a central idea: the visible surface of things transparently represents their true nature. In this historical context, the primacy of the visible in the order of knowledge dictates the predominance of 'sight with an almost exclusive privilege, being the sense by which we perceive extent and establish proof'.[12] Here, the metaphor of the 'Dark Ages' is quite revealing. From a historical perspective, the privilege attributed to the visible, observable superficiality of things was a way of detaching seventeenth- and eighteenth-century scholars from what they saw as the madness of medieval 'misbeliefs'. The observation of what is visible is the first step towards achieving a form of knowledge based on the 'universal form': a pristine deduction from the visible façade of the world. As part of a complex and rigorous method, the function of sight was exactly to ensure this immaculate *double representation*. Through sight one could deduct a representation (the ideal form) from the observance of what represents, in things themselves, their truthful nature (their visible surface). In observing things and extracting from them all the misleading features unrelated to sight (taste, smell, touch and, most importantly, the hearsay medieval scholars were so fond of), one can delineate a form that is universally applicable: an ideal structure.

We only have to follow the 'rule of the visible' to see through the logic of objectification, and Foucault's objection to a talk of life prior to modernity. According to the respective *episteme* of the seventeenth and the eighteenth centuries, 'life' cannot be more than an observable feature. The space of objectification – the space of what can be known – is restricted to the visible surface of things. Hence, 'life' can only become an object of knowledge in terms of what visibly denotes life. What, then, can be the distinctive features of 'life' under the rule of the visible? They can only refer to the observable character that distinguishes one group of things (things that are alive) from all the other things in nature. And the way of singling out 'things that are alive' is by seeing their movement (animation) and decay (degradation). Under the rule of the visible, life can only mean visible transformations such as moving around, ageing and eventually dying. The modern notion of life (as an invisible force and a deep organic function) cannot possibly make sense.

According to Foucault, the objectification of life – its appearance in the realm of 'knowable things' – is indissociable from the breakdown of this order of the visible. From the late eighteenth century onwards, visibility is supplanted as rule of correspondence between knowledge and truth by a 'rediscovery' of the invisible depths of the world. Notwithstanding how, why and when exactly it happened, at the advent of modernity knowledge was infused by a certain historicity – a mode of being, above all, limited by its existence in time. From a genealogical perspective, what historicity does is to create a three-dimensional picture of things, a feature Foucault calls 'verticality'.[13] Once affected by this verticality, the world discloses a depth that was not previously accounted for during the age of superficial observation. This change in the rules of correspondence regarding truth is the necessary condition for the process of objectification that gave birth to both life (as a knowable objective reality) and biology (the discipline devoted to life as its object of knowledge).

The concept of organic structure provides an interesting point of clarification. Citing Lamarck (1744–1829), Foucault explains how the notion of organic structure radically transformed the premodern classification of living beings according to visibility; how it infused the abstract, mechanical concept of life with an existence in time (historicity) and a depth in space (verticality). Lamarck criticised earlier naturalists for placing crustaceans into the same category as insects. If we consider sight alone, 'the articulations of the bodies and limbs'[14] of crustaceans and insects look reasonably similar. To put it differently, if lobsters *look like* oversized ants it makes sense, under the *rule of the visible*, 'to regard them as true insects'.[15] However, for Lamarck this was a capital mistake. He begins to think of life in terms of organic structures and their internal functions. Since crustaceans 'breathe solely by means of gills, in the same way as molluscs, and like them have a muscular heart',[16] they are fundamentally different from 'the arachnids and the insects, which do not have a like organic structure'.[17]

In the analysis of organic structures, the historicity of life comes into play and shatters the transcendentalism of premodern, ideal forms. First, the notion of organic structure suggests a hierarchy of visible features. Of all the visible characters of living beings, some are of much more importance than others. Second, this hierarchy is decided based solely on functional terms. The more important a visible feature is, the more connected it is to the deepest and most important of organic functions: the maintenance of life. Lamarck's argument is illustrative once again. The 'gills' (the respiratory visible organ) express a vital function (respiration) and the articulation of limbs (the locomotive visible organ) are expressions of a secondary one (locomotion).

For Foucault, modernity appears once the knowledge based on the visible surface of the world (sight) stops being a sign of enlightenment and starts designating superficiality. This significantly changes the procedures of knowing. Modern, 'in-depth' knowledge is the knowledge that seeks the hidden meaning of things (interpretation) and tries to describe them in an objective, neutral language (formalisation).[18] It is only in this order of knowledge that life, meaning more than simple animation, can become an objective reality. The appearance of such life is conditioned, as seen with Lamarck, by the appearance of new, methodological directives. Both life and biology are inseparable from anatomy, the modern technique that 'consists in establishing indicative relations between superficial, and therefore visible, elements and others that are concealed in the depths of the body'.[19]

If we accept Foucault's daring logic, our understanding of truth, knowledge and its relation to an external reality is significantly transformed. A genealogical account sees the production of knowledge as more than a mere representation of the objective nature of the world. By taking us back to a time when life 'did not exist', Foucault reveals how 'disciplines' and their methodologies help to produce the world they analyse. Disciplines divide, classify and order the very reality they are supposed to merely interpret in a formalised manner. They do so in a way conducive to a specific logic, following a historical set of rules (the primacy of the visible, or the privilege of the organic). This is not to say knowledge claims simply create their object of study, implying that biologists invented life, from scratch, at some point in history. It is, rather, to insist that both disciplines and their objects of study emerge in a contemporaneous relation to each other. The concept of objectification suggests a contemporaneous emergence that binds together bodies of knowledge, institutional practices and objects of knowledge. For example, the objectification of life discloses how, at a given historical moment, an object enters the space of knowable things (life), as a field enters the space of knowledge practices (biology), as procedures enter the space of rigorous methods (anatomy). To investigate the conditions of possibility of a discipline means precisely to investigate this tripartite historical process.

Foucault affirms that 'what permits us to individualize a discourse [. . .] is not the unity of an object'[20] – such as life for biology – but the series of rules of formation that define discourses 'as practices that systematically form the objects of which they speak'.[21] Departing from this sophisticated insight, I ask a simple question in this chapter. What happens to debates on truth, justice and reconciliation if we look at them as systematically forming the object they speak of? What can we see if we contextualise the punishment vs impunity debates as the enunciations of a 'discipline' (transitional justice) that can only exist through its own process of objectification? The Foucauldian method, like any good method, already suggests an answer. If we are to flip the question of post-conflict or post-authoritarian justice from its *conditions of implementation* – as the literature tends to reinforce – towards its *conditions of possibility*, we must first contextualise such debates in a manner that does not simply trace them back to a traumatic origin. A critical genealogy begins with the emergence of a new 'discipline' at a new age when the *post-conflict* became an irresistible possibility.

A New 'Discipline' of Justice at the End of History

Transitional justice is often treated with a certain level of timelessness. The challenges faced by courts, truth commissions and processes of post-conflict reconciliation are often assumed to be ahistorical. Claims that 'conflicts are a natural part of human interaction',[22] that 'transitional justice is almost as old as democracy itself'[23] or that the field arose as a response to the Nazi Holocaust[24] are far from uncommon. However, there is now a growing body of evidence suggesting otherwise. The phrase 'to end impunity' was not used in English prior to 1986.[25] There were virtually no mentions of the term 'transitional justice' before the 1990s.[26] The expression 'cultures of impunity', a central part of the transitional justice vocabulary, was only truly popularised after 1993.[27] A search in the Hansard Corpus of the British Parliament reveals that no MP ever used the term 'post-conflict' in the House of Commons before 21 April 1991.[28] Neither as old as time nor a natural part of life; the punishment vs impunity debates are well grounded in the history of the late twentieth century (1980s–1990s).

In a 2009 article entitled 'How "Transitions" Reshaped Human Rights: A Conceptual History of Transitional Justice', Paige Arthur criticises the literature for falling 'into the trap of imputing ideas about "transitional justice" to actors who, presumably, were unlikely to have held them'.[29] Her criticism is, perhaps, the earliest sign of a deeper historical awareness concerning the punishment vs impunity debates. To avoid the same mistake, Arthur contextualises the origins of transitional justice, 'examining the invention of a phrase itself [transitional justice], as representative of the emergence of a new position'.[30] Against the field's transcendentalism, her historical approach locates the rise of transitional justice – as a distinct practice of human rights – in the late twentieth century.

Strictly speaking, Arthur is not calling for a Foucauldian turn. Nevertheless, her sense of historicity offers a good starting point. The late twentieth century was marked by the intersection between a series of global events. From the mid-1980s until the mid-1990s the world witnessed the progressive demise of the Cold War between East and West, and the troubled reckoning with state terror in the Global South. The fall of the Berlin Wall, the military juntas in the Southern Cone and the apartheid regime in South Africa, to name a few cases, had a significant impact on the landscape of global political imagination. In economic terms, the dim prospects of political transitions were made even more uncertain by the perverse effects of the debt crisis in these economies[31] and restrictions to policymaking that the neoliberal structural adjustments imposed in the countries of the Global

South.[32] These transformations were fundamental for the rise of new claims of knowledge about the legal, moral and political implications of coming to terms with a heritage of systematic violence.

It is against this background of paramount political transformations (while overlooking the economic ones) that Arthur analyses the rise of transitional justice as a new 'discipline'. More specifically, she argues that the fabrics of the discipline were interwoven during a series of conferences held between 1988 and 1995. These encounters were important in creating the basis of a knowledge about justice in post-authoritarian times and of new mechanisms for the implementation of a sustainable post-conflict. Gathering recognisable experts from the field of human rights, moral philosophy and political science and addressing the dilemmas of societies facing a fragile balance between (re-)democratisation and reckoning, such conferences laid the foundations for debates on whether, and how, to punish perpetrators of heinous crimes.

In 1988, in the city of Wye, Maryland, USA, a conference entitled 'State Crimes: Punishment or Pardon?' took place at the Aspen Institute, funded by the Ford Foundation. Henkin's report of the conference proceedings is illustrative of what was at stake in the discussions. Participants from a legal background suggested that 'punishment would serve to deter the violators from future violations',[33] preventing 'human rights violations by others in the future'[34] and functioning 'to express the moral condemnation of society'.[35] While some participants did stress 'the need for national reconciliation and healing in order to establish a stable democratic society',[36] a considerable amount agreed on the successful example of 'both the German and the Argentine experiences'[37] in achieving social pacification without increasing 'social divisiveness'.[38] In 1992, in Salzburg, Austria, the project 'Justice in Times of Transition', sponsored by the Charter 77 Foundation, held its inaugural conference. This project was funded by a series of Western organisations alongside the Rockefeller Foundation, and, of course, the Charter 77 Foundation itself. This time, the considerations surrounding the problem of 'how Eastern European leaders might learn from the experience of the Latin American transitions'[39] served as the basis for the discipline's canonical book:[40] the three-volume *Transitional Justice: How Emerging Democracies Reckon with Former Regimes*, published in 1995 by the United States Institute of Peace.

The final two conferences took place in South Africa, in the years prior to the establishment of the TRC. In 1994, in Somerset West, the Institute for a Democratic Alternative for South Africa (IDASA) organised the event 'Dealing with the Past', funded by Open Society. In the following year another conference promoted by the same institution, 'Truth and Reconciliation', featured a powerful talk from José Zalaquett on the cathartic function of truth-telling. The IDASA conferences fundamentally contributed to the further development and dissemination of therapeutic accounts of reconciliation. Leebaw[41] recounts how mesmerising Zalaquett's ideas were to South Africans, especially to the poet and journalist Antjie Krog. In her memoir, Krog confesses that it only took 'precisely seven and a half minutes'[42] to be convinced by Zalaquett's powerful message that '*courage* has again evolved a new definition: [. . .] To *live within the confinements of reality*, but to search day after day for the progressing of one's most cherished values.'[43]

The Aspen, Charter 77 and IDASA conferences provide a good starting point for a reading of transitional justice based on the concept of objectification. First, because they comprised a forum, a space for the encounter of experts whose ideas modelled the 'common ground' – or the point of internal coherence – of a new discipline of justice. Some of the most prominent works discussed in the previous chapter were the fruit of these conferences. Aryeh Neier, Jaime Malamud-Goti, Diane Orentlicher, José Zalaquett and Lawrence Weschler were all present during the 1988 discussions. At the Charter 77 Foundation Conference (1992), Raul Alfonsín, Ruti Teitel and Samuel Huntington joined the network. Finally, in South Africa, Alex Boraine, André du Toit and Tina Rosenberg were added to the new, burgeoning group of experts on the problems of implementing a just and everlasting peace.[44] Second, the three conferences are interesting because, from a political point of view, they framed 'punishment or pardon' as the sole, or at least the most important, choice transitional societies could face in the aftermath of violence. Finally, they are important expressions of a time when achieving a post-conflictual state became a thinkable possibility; when, quoting Zalaquett, 'courage' became synonymous with the capacity to live 'within the confinements of reality'.

The encounters did not happen in a historical vacuum. On the contrary, the debates spurred by the Aspen, Charter 77 and IDASA conferences were heavily influenced by ideas that were rapidly gaining steam in the imaginary of the global intellectual elites during the late twentieth century. For instance, Huntington's theories of modernisation[45] were highly influential among the participants of the three conferences. They helped to frame the debates on punishment, forgiveness and forgetfulness as part of a third fundamental moment of the history of humankind. Through them, the conferences were imagined as the latest step in the fight against barbarism for the sake of peace, following the implementation of civil liberties by the American and the French revolutions and the post-war de-Nazification of Germany. They became part of a joint civilisational march whereby progress could be facilitated, and spread throughout the Third World, via the correct implementation of a set of techniques of justice (trials, truth-seeking and reconciliation programmes) being discussed during these encounters.

Likewise, the conference procedures are permeated by belief in the final breakdown of authoritarian modes of government and the predominance of liberal democracy as 'the end point of mankind's (sic) ideological evolution'.[46] And this dated expectation, known thereafter as the trope of the 'end of history', was of paramount importance. In a sense, the trope of the 'end of history' is part of what drives and enables the appearance of a body of knowledge specialised in the transition to a *post-conflictual scenario* (transitional justice). As a new discipline emerging at the endpoint of humanity's ideological evolution, transitional justice articulated a set of knowledge claims and practices that confined 'the desire to realise social transformation beyond violent conflict'[47] to the idea that 'democracies are often unruly, but they are not often politically violent'.[48] A knowledge that betrayed, in its association between courage and the capacity to remain within the confinements of reality, an uncomfortable resonance with the neoliberal banner that the world faced 'no alternative'[49] to the transformations witnessed. If we accept this logic, we start seeing the Aspen, 77 Chart Foundation and IDASA conferences as instances when this equation, known as the liberal democratic peace,[50] was affirmed, performed or, to use Foucault's terminology, objectified.

This awareness of objectification – lost within the preoccupation with the conditions of implementation of peace – is fundamental. Because the body of knowledge specialised in the transition to the post-conflict is also the knowledge drawing the limits of what such post-conflict could possibly look like. This is the most important idea behind the reformulation of responses to systematic violence in the late twentieth century; the double, historical connection between a discipline (the knowledge about justice in the aftermath of violence) and a knowable and achievable object (the *post-violent* or *post-conflictual* liberal-democratic reality). This connection was not yet at stake in the immediate aftermath of World War II.

Furthermore, this connection is important because it suggests a reading of the punishment vs impunity debates and of the techniques of *retribution* (criminal accountability) or *restoration* (national reconciliation) as *productive* of such post-violent reality not only in practical but also logical terms. The poles of punishment and pardon, the limits of trials and amnesties stand at the borders of a whole universe of possibilities, delineating the conceivable limits of both peace and justice. They alone, and their potential permutations, provide the measure of what is possible in the implementation of a future for which systematic violence is but a memory. In this sense, the theoretical profusion and practical creativity of the first transitional debates should not conceal one fact. Their fractious disagreements on whether to punish perpetrators or forgive former political radicalisms could not work without the common dissociation between democracy and violence that presents the telos of both 'history' and of political transitions.

Unpacking the Epistemological Coup

The trope of the end of history and the dissociation between liberal democracies and violence was never unanimously accepted. Some would strongly question the hypocrisy of affirming 'the ideal of a liberal democracy [. . .] as the ideal of human history',[51] reminding apologists of the end times that 'never have violence, inequality, exclusion, famine, and thus economic oppression affected as many human beings in the history of the earth'.[52] Others, in a similar vein, consider the thesis of non-convertibility of violence into democratic, institutional arrangements as an 'epistemological coup of no small import'.[53] As such, the belief in liberal, Western democracy 'as the very antithesis to state violence'[54] can only work 'despite the realities of its historical record'.[55]

There are two pathways for criticism here. We could reject the liberal idea of a democratic post-conflict either as a hypocritical claim based on an intentional blindness to the violent reality of certain liberal democracies, such as Brazil. Or we could investigate in this so-called 'epistemological coup' an element of what Žižek defined as a symptom: loosely translated, a point at the centre of any ideological field that holds both the conditions of possibility for such field while, at the same time, defining the impossible realisation of its central promise. In Žižek's own words, the symptom is 'a particular element which subverts its own universal foundation'.[56]

This formulation of the social symptom might sound complex at first, but it is actually very simple. To clarify it, Žižek goes back to the Marxist critique of bourgeois or liberal freedoms, offering his own psychoanalytically inspired reading of it.[57] According to him, the liberal political order is predicated on the preservation of fundamental individual freedoms inscribed in the foundational texts of our time (e.g., the Declaration of the Rights of Man and of the Citizen; the Bill of Rights; the Universal Declaration of Human Rights). The safeguarding of these fundamental freedoms is based on an overarching promise to protect individuals from oppression[58] and to grant them equality of treatment before the law. By safeguarding their freedoms, the liberal order provides each and every one of the citizens of a polity with equal opportunity to fulfil their potential. These freedoms are to be read in the plural; they comprise a generality of freedoms such as 'freedom of speech and press, freedom of conscious-ness, freedom of commerce, political freedom, and so on'.[59] But this apparently coherent and wholesome edifice rests on a hollow base. There is one specific form of freedom within liberal societies that simultane-ously conditions and impedes the realisation of the liberal promise: this specific freedom, related to the capitalist freedom to possess the means of production, is the freedom a worker enjoys 'to sell [. . .] his own labour on the market'.[60] It is exactly from studying the ensuing societal effects of this specific 'freedom' that Marxism gets to its theory of value, the notion of exploitation and the oppressive character of class societies.[61]

This is where the effects of the symptom become apparent. The liberal promise of liberation from oppression that is conditioned by the protec-tion of individual freedoms can never be universalised so long as one of these freedoms (the freedom to be 'economically oppressed') is pre-served. The symptom here is a point of internal exception, a ruse in the otherwise smooth façade of ideology, without which, as paradoxical as it might sound, there would be no ideology. It is a point that both sustains a promise and presents its own point of negation.[62] Most importantly, the symptom provides the central point of misrecognition[63] (the framing of exploitation as freedom) that sustains individual and collective forms of life based on what we may consider 'epistemological coups'.

In the following pages I will argue that behind the idea of a non-violent post-conflict – as the end goal of history and transitional jus-tice – there is a very narrow understanding of what counts as 'violence': a narrow understanding that can be derived from the punishment vs impunity debates. I will also explain that this concept of violence is simultaneously the point of internal coherence of the punishment vs impunity debates (in a Foucauldian sense) and the ideological symp-tom (in a Žižekian sense) of the discipline of transitional justice. It is a specific idea of violence as an *intentional, cyclical* and *exceptional* phe-nomenon that conditions the possibility of thinking of a *post-conflictual* reality with its particular ethos,[64] but also poses the biggest impediment to the transitional promise of 'never again'.

Violence and Intentionality

The Aspen, Charter 77 and IDASA conferences gathered experts with a significant background in human rights activism. It is important to acknowledge such humanitarian backgrounds for several reasons, but mainly because the discipline's underlying humanitarianism helped to settle its main representation of violence *as gross violations of human rights* (GVHRs). Brown argues that 'virtually everything encompassed by the notion of "human rights" is the subject of controversies'.[65] The doctrine of human rights has indeed a longstanding conflictual history in terms of its universal applicability, its philosophical foundations and its maximalist pretensions.[66] All these problems are, of course, important for the implementation of justice and the enforcement of humanitarian standards in transitional societies. Different researchers have, time and again, criticised the top-down, one-size-fits-all formula assumed by transitional interventions. Nevertheless, these much-discussed controversies remain at the level of conditions of implementation. It is the liberal and humanitarian representation of violence – above all, the concept of violations of rights – that directs us to the conditions of possibility of this reality named post-conflict.

Whether human rights are universal or not, whether transitional governments have a duty to punish perpetrators or not, the account of violence behind transitional interventions – in both their retributivist and restorative methods – remains delimited by the idea of violations. First, the notion of violations of rights was central for the very development of the fight against impunity post-1945, for the preservation of historical memory and the protection of human dignity. It offered a possible 'framework for human rights movements to challenge the arbitrary power of dictatorships'[67] and provided 'the legal discourse to frame investigations for truth commissions and the legal basis for the documentation of evidence of [. . .] abuse'.[68] The role of documentation was extremely invaluable. Without this humanitarian basis, truth commissions, criminal tribunals and reconciliation programmes would lack a much-required direction. It is from this understanding of violations that transitional interventions draw their clear focus on which forms of suffering to address on the road to implement justice.

The clear focus provided by this humanitarian frame, however, is also inevitably restrictive of the aims and scope of transitional interventions. In defining which forms of behaviour and which phenomena count as abusive, the humanitarian concept of violation also defines the scope of what requires reckoning. Their empowering of HRAs cannot outshine the fact that the 'coming to terms' promoted by transitional interventions orbited a rather specific account of 'wrongdoings'. Violence, in the punishment vs impunity debates, has long meant violations of specific (human) rights listed under international treaties.[69]

GVHRs are extremely important from the perspective of international law. Cases of genocide, torture, enforced disappearance and other inhuman mistreatment may seem like a disparate array of gruesome acts, but they share a common legal denominator. In order to constitute international crimes, they all require a level of intentionality (or acknowledgement thereof). Every convention typifying GVHRs shows this pattern. Genocide is characterised as a set of actions 'committed with the *intent to destroy*, in whole or in part, a national, ethnical, racial or religious group'.[70] Torture is described as 'any act by which severe pain or suffering, whether physical or mental, is *intentionally inflicted on a person* for such purpose as obtaining from him or a third person information or a confession'.[71] Finally, enforced disappearances are violations of the right to liberty and 'presumably' the right to life, which 'render their perpetrators and the state or state authorities *which organize, acquiesce in or tolerate* such disappearances liable'.[72]

The feature of intentionality (and its derivatives) is what turns a violation of a right (life, freedom of movement, liberty) into a crime that renders perpetrators accountable. As part of *mens rea* (the set of elements composing a 'guilty mind'), the concept of 'intention [. . .] is the main concept in criminal law'.[73] The assignment of responsibility for a criminal act demands a level of culpability, and culpability involves a certain understanding of intentionality.[74] The proof that an act of wrongdoing was intended is a significant way of assigning a degree of blame, and therefore of attributing adequate levels of punishment. In national legal systems, given the specificities of different traditions, intentionality (*mens rea*) is often used to suggest a worse degree of culpability in the presence of the criminal act itself (*actus reus*).[75] This does not mean that intention to commit a crime is a sufficient or *sine qua non* condition of punishment – certain crimes, in certain places, do not need an element of *mens rea*.[76] Individuals can still feel guilt for their unintended actions, and it is not always possible to evade responsibility by pleading the absence of a 'guilty mind'. It solely means that an intended wrongdoing is somehow accepted as a worse form of wrongdoing. And when it comes to international criminal law, this difference plays a fundamental part.[77] Precisely because the fight against the enemies of humankind deals with crimes that outrage humanness itself, they are among the *most heinous possible offenses*. With a few exceptions, their levels of culpability usually require that a perpetrator 'shall be criminally responsible and liable for punishment for a crime [. . .] only if the material elements are committed with intent and knowledge'.[78]

Hence, intentionality plays a fundamental role for retributivist perspectives of justice in the post-conflict. Without the assignment of responsibility to a specific group of perpetrators, neither the international duty to combat impunity nor the idea of universal jurisdiction makes much sense. The heinousness of a crime is what makes it a problem for humanity, as opposed to a local concern. Following a time when violations are often denied or excused as mere mishaps, transitional interventions use the concept of intentionality as proof of their systematic nature, that is, that the referred violations were *intentionally devised* or *knowledgably allowed* by the former regimes. But, as 'an artificial construction referring to fault',[79] the feature of intentionality also works to delimit the scope of which forms of violence are considered unacceptable.

Here we find the first clue about the social symptom supporting the objectification of the liberal post-conflict. Just like 'freedom', 'violence' is a term that could be 'applied to countless phenomena'.[80] But according to the liberal humanitarian frame, violence, or at least the worse of it, is restricted to *intentionally perpetrated violations*. It is by logically delimiting violence to a series of intentional violations that the liberal democratic state (the *post-conflictual* telos of history) can appear as the antithesis of indiscriminate violence. Hence there is no need to ignore the world's historical record; the liberal thesis does not require any blindness towards social inequality, famine and multiple forms of exclusion. On the contrary, this is simply a question of what forms of violence the liberal order is willing to accommodate. By privileging a modern humanitarian view of a highly complex and multidimensional phenomenon, scholars and HRAs can promise an *aftermath of violence* amidst enduring, and even rising, levels of suffering.

This humanitarian background, in itself, is not a sufficient condition for the objectification of the post-conflict. The idea of the end of violence requires, as the prefix *post* suggests, a particular conception of time. Most of all, it requires a conception of how violence (as intentional GVHRs) happens over time. The post-conflict can only enter the realm of thinkable objects and achievable political goals once the intentionality of perpetrators is connected with the cyclical nature of violations. It requires the danger of uncontrollable revenge and the methods devised to prevent it.

Violence and Revenge

Meister criticises modern humanitarianism for viewing the '*cyclicity* of violence – violence that begets violence – as itself the paradigm of evil'.[81] This representation of violence as a self-sustaining cycle attributes a particular temporality to intentional GVHRs. According to this logic, violations are not only problematic as individual acts, but also because of their cascading effects. For instance, liberal humanitarianism sees extrajudicial killings as abhorrent in themselves (they are, after all, offenses against the whole of humanity). But for the 'theory' of cyclicity, the real danger of a violation lies in its capacity to invite counter-violations. In a quasi-mechanical understanding, cyclicity affirms that 'a self-propelling cycle or spiral of vengeance [. . .] is the natural or predictable outcome of serious or violent wrongdoing'.[82] And if violence truly breeds violence, then a single wrongdoing has the power to trigger unstoppable carnage.

Due to their modern humanitarian legacy, measures towards post-conflict or post-authoritarian justice are endowed with the goal of breaking with 'a time of cyclical violence that is past – or can be put in the past by defining the present as another time in which the evil is remembered rather than repeated'.[83] The discipline concerned with the implementation of post-conflict justice (the justice of a time when violence never happens again) must fundamentally transcend the cycle of revenge caused by past violations. The humanitarian framework to record abuses – in which violence is represented as intentional – cannot be dissociated from the political goal of halting revenge. Violations must be named and shamed and perpetrators must be held accountable because their actions can spur an indefinite cycle, transforming social life into an endless time of conflict. Hence the concern of HRAs with the so-called 'cultures of impunity', a term whose usage skyrocketed in the early 1990s.[84]

The threat of revenge – the logical outcome of an intentional and cyclical understanding of violence – is what connects the internal debates of the 'new' discipline of justice, and its techniques of retribution, restoration and mixed approaches. It is also what explains the field's fascination with the philosophy of Hannah Arendt.[85] Hardly a single work of transitional justice goes without explaining the acts of forgiveness, promising and punishing via Arendt's thoughts on the menace of uncontrollable revenge in the public sphere. However, references to her work in the punishment vs impunity debates usually do not question her complex views on the phenomenon of violence. Presenting a rather boiled-down version that fits the liberal humanitarian narrative, they do not acknowledge how Arendt's thoughts 'avoid the liberal solution of marginalizing and effectively denying violence'.[86] They miss the point that violence, in Arendt, is an inherent aspect of the human condition inhabiting the mundane acts of consumption, fabrication and, only then, revenge.

In Arendt,[87] consumption is a necessary function connected to survival of the human species. Consumption is violent because it destroys the object it consumes. A hungry individual must eat a fruit (crushing its form) to quench her hunger. In this sense violence is, *tout court*, a constitutive part of life, a form of defence against the inevitability of death (which is nothing but life being consumed). As time passes, life constantly, violently consumes itself, taking human beings closer to their time of demise, when they themselves are extinguished. Therefore, since they are mortal beings, humans are bound to an endless and futile cycle in which their consumption of other forms of life cannot but postpone the consumption of their own. In this sense, human beings are both the agents of, and continuously subjected to, life's violent and unrestricted consumption.

A second sense of violence is found in the idea of fabrication. To prolong their lives and reduce their never-ending toil, human beings can resort to another form of violence. This violence, the act of fabrication, channels the process of consumption (and its inherent force of destruction) in order to produce a result that is everlasting and not merely evanescent (such as eating or drinking). Human beings are also working beings, who build things that will endure, and therefore never be fully consumed by time. In their daily efforts to postpone death, they are compelled to create frameworks, shelters and city walls for the sake of their own protection; for the purpose of making survival easier. And when they work, humans also make use of a form of violence that is inherent in the act of consumption (fabrication, as it were, demands the consumption of the environment). But this is not the pointless violence that gives one immediate satisfaction (natural consumption). It is a productive violence that allows humans to even fabricate an artificial sense of immortality (think of the Roman or Inca ruins).[88]

Both human consumption (a 'natural' violence) and fabrication (an 'artificial' violence) are forms of violence that are 'by nature instrumental'.[89] They are instrumental because they exist in a relationship with the final goal of survival, as a means to an end. They stand 'like all means [. . .] in need of guidance and justification through the end'[90] pursued. Now this instrumentality brings interesting consequences in Arendt's philosophy. If limited to the satisfaction of basic needs (consumption) or the fatalistic destruction required for building everlasting things (fabrication), violence is potentially justifiable. It respects the just end of survival. An end that is just insofar as it sets *predictable* and *controllable* boundaries for the violence employed. Both forms of violence involved in the act of consuming a fruit and of weaving a jumper are foreseeable (one knowns how much violence will be needed), are controllable (one can easily stop) and come to a definite halt (violence ends). This is to say that, far from completely eschewing violence, Arendt accepts as justifiable those forms of violence that are predictable, controllable and 'will bring about a particular outcome'.[91] The violence Arendt vehemently rejects is a third form of violence: 'political violence', or violence employed in the realm of politics.

Arendt rejects the idea behind 'political violence' – the idea that violence is a justified means to a given political goal[92] – as a mistake based on a misconception of the nature of human interaction. According to her, humanness is defined as the capacity to create things anew.[93] This condition marks the realm of politics, the sphere where human beings interact as equals, as, by definition, an unpredictable and irreversible realm. We never know what will come of the dealings between two equal individuals, and we can never simply undo the things that have been done between them. And this is why, in Arendt's conception, 'political violence' rests on a dangerous liaison. It endows the destructive and instrumental nature of violence (consumption/fabrication) with the unpredictability and irreversibility of human interaction. In the capricious realm of politics, every action induces an unpredictable reaction. 'Political violence' is unjustifiable because its revolutionary project involving the instrumental 'consumption of lives' for the 'fabrication of a new order' overlooks the danger of an endless cycle of revenge. Advocates of political violence mistake the realm of work for the realm of politics. For Arendt, this is the reason all modern revolutions have turned into a state of terror, when violence knows no justifiable limits.[94]

Here is the interesting part. Faced with an unpredictable and irreversible act of violence, human beings always have a choice. In Arendt's philosophy, wrongdoing can be met either with retaliation (revenge) or with actions that break the cycle of violence: most importantly, *punishment* and *forgiveness*. What differentiates punishment and forgiveness from simple revenge is their relationship with the essential political faculty of *promising*. Making and keeping promises binds human beings to an 'agreed purpose'.[95] It allows them to create 'islands of security without which not even continuity, let alone durability of any kind, would be possible in the relationships between men (sic)'.[96] Promising constitutes the very basis for political life. When human beings interact as equals, 'the force that keeps them together [. . .] is the force of mutual promise'.[97]

Punishment is radically different from revenge. It is a predictable and controlled response to violence that 'attempts to put an end to something that without interference could go on endlessly'.[98] It also differs from mere retaliation because it is infused with a political promise. Controlled instances of retribution account for the 'need of society to be protected against a crime'[99] while promising 'the improvement of the

criminal'.[100] Likewise, when retribution is undesirable, humans can forgive each other's misdeeds. Once again, this action revolves around the
faculty of promising. Wrongdoing can be forgiven so long as perpetrators promise never to wrong again. This is what prevents us from being
'confined to one single deed from which we could never recover'.[101]

Arendt's philosophy works very well for the discipline of transitional
justice. It provides a sophisticated and yet parsimonious justification for
the different methods at stake in the punishment vs impunity debates.
Drawing on the faculties of punishment and forgiveness, retribution and
reconciliation are supposed to intercede in the cycle of revenge, freeing
human beings from the shackles of the past and preventing the development of cultures of impunity. And just like the Arendtian framework,
they have nothing or very little to say about the 'natural' and 'acceptable' violence present in consumption and fabrication, which are simply
taken for granted. It is perhaps unsurprising that these two concepts (and
their respective forms of violence) can be easily translated into the problematic of economic oppression.

Violence and the Exception

We finally come to the last aspect of transitional justice's understanding
of violence: a certain idea of *exceptionality* that encompasses both the discipline and its object of study. As I have already mentioned, scholars and
practitioners have long assumed that transitional mechanisms are simply
responses to heinous crimes or, resorting to a term abundantly used in
the literature, *traumatic* events.[102] Facing the worst forms of wrongdoing
committed on an unfathomable scale, transitional justice mechanisms
must deal with *exceptional* situations demanding *exceptional* responses.
Once again, a turn to Arendt's philosophy might help to clarify matters.

When trying to make sense of the Holocaust/*Shoah*, Arendt reached
a cul-de-sac. The industrial annihilation of undesirable individuals and
the programme of elimination of European Jewry were of such magni-
tude, so incredible, that, according to Primo Levi,[103] people were likely
not to believe it had actually happened. This posed an immense challenge to post-war justice. Prosecutors would not judge common trans-
gressions of warfare, they were supposed to pass judgement over events
that have since become imprinted on the global 'Western' imaginary'[104]
as 'the epoch's inaugural historical trauma'.[105] These crimes were so horrendous, one could hardly imagine an adequate punishment, and yet
they could never be forgiven or forgotten. They pointed directly to a
paradox in the Arendtian containment of political violence; the fact that
'men (sic) are unable to forgive what they cannot punish and [. . .] they

are unable to punish what has turned out to be unforgivable'.[106] This can be called the paradox of the 'traumatic crime', to coin a term.

Judging traumatic crimes is not easy. The concept of trauma originates from medical science, as a rupture produced on the body (a wound) by an external factor (a shock).[107] When applied in the social context, as a metaphorical description, trauma usually refers to a rather different rupture: the breakdown of the faculty of understanding. The talk of Nazi crimes as an inaugural trauma suggests they induced 'the confrontation with an event that, in its unexpectedness or horror, cannot be placed within the schemes of prior knowledge'.[108] Coming to terms with such crimes forces the 'direct imposition on the mind of the unavoidable reality of horrific events [. . .] that it cannot control'.[109] What all these classic definitions of collective or historical trauma denote is the sense of disturbance caused by a traumatic event;[110] in other words, the exceptional nature of trauma. The metaphors are very enlightening. Wounds and shocks are traumatic because they are *unforeseen, uncommon* and *external to the normality of the body*. They disrupt its expected functioning. They present moments when the defences of the body are torn open and the fragility of human life is exposed.[111] When it comes to historical traumas, this disruption is supposed to affect the realms of political life and legal judgement. It is because certain crimes are traumatic from a collective point of view that they create the paradoxical, and equally exceptional, point where neither punishment nor forgiveness works satisfactorily.

Here, Teitel's concept of transitional jurisprudence is particularly enlightening. As responses to collective traumas, in the unspeakable hiatus between an unforgiving and unpunishable violation, transitional interventions play a very specific societal function as 'the engine of revolutionary change'.[112] Retributive and restorative measures in post-conflict or post-authoritarian scenarios must account for factors exogenous to the legal order but fundamental for its re-establishment. They must transcend the cycle of violence by bringing the unspeakable back into a pedagogic language, that is, by exposing 'the core illegitimacy of past rule'[113] and by promoting the 'stigmatization of past wrongdoing'.[114] This is why the extravagances and the limitations of the search for justice in times of political change, otherwise unacceptable, 'are justified [. . .] for the purpose of *construction of a new political order*'.[115]

This idea is widespread in the punishment vs impunity debates.[116] The literature usually describes transitional justice responses as inherently *exceptional measures* envisioned to overcome particularly *exceptional times*. This is part of the reason for the constant references to Nuremberg as the transitional justices' imaginary origin.[117] When the 'new' discipline of justice was being objectified, claiming the heritage of Nuremberg worked to symbolically connect the specific 'traumas' of repression in the Global South with the epoch's inaugural 'trauma' of the Holocaust. At the same time, this strategy enabled arguments from both ends of the punishment vs impunity debates. By recuperating the mythical origins of the international fight against impunity, retributivists could gain a sort of moral high ground. They could set from the beginning the problems of extremely disparate transitions as a simple decision to abide by or reject the essential, and morally imperative, Nuremberg model of criminal trials. On an abstract, argumentative level, anyone against criminal prosecutions (for whatever reason) could be described as defending the enemies of humankind. On the other hand, advocates of reconciliation could use the language of trauma to invoke a diametrically opposed solution. By resorting to medicalised language to describe the state of transitional societies as wounded societies, restorativists could oppose criminal prosecutions and propose an agenda of reconciliation based on collective forgiveness. Taken to its furthest extent, this argument could be used to frame any policies towards criminal accountability as unhealthy policies that could prevent the so-called wounds of the past from scarring.

On a deeper level, the references to trauma also reinforced the exceptionalism of the object of study and the methods of transitional justice. They helped scholars and practitioners to represent trials, truth commissions and reparations as producing a temporal break between an *exceptionally* violent past and a non-violent future; in order words, a *normal* future. This disseminated the notion of transitional justice bringing about a 'liberalizing transition'[118] that promotes a 'radical shift from repression to democracy'.[119] It is easy to see this duality of normality and exceptionality in the new discipline's burgeoning concept of cultures of impunity. At the end of history, a 'culture of impunity'[120] is nothing more than one 'in which violence becomes the norm, rather than the exception'.[121]

If we read transitional justice as an ideologically supported discipline, as I propose we do, this double claim to exceptionalism is imbued with a performative force. It becomes the last step in the making of the post-conflict. Once we accept Foucault's ideas of objectification and the productive power of knowledge claims, it makes little sense to speak of transitional mechanisms merely as responsive practices. We ought, instead, to analyse how they account for moments when an *object* enters the space of thinkable things (the post-conflict), as a field enters the space of knowledge practices (transitional justice), as procedures enter the space of rigorous methods (punishment or forgiveness). The central point here is exactly the objectification of a *post-conflictual* reality, a process enabled by a specific representation of violence. This representation acted as the point of internal coherence of the punishment vs impunity debates as they were framed in the late twentieth century (the end of history). The vision of the post-conflict promised by narratives of 'never again', in whichever form they took, could only become intelligible once the phenomenon of violence was restricted to *intentional* GVHRs and their *cyclical* consequences. This was, logically speaking, the condition of possibility of a *post-conflictual* time, which both informed and enabled the methodologies and techniques of transitional justice.

As part of a discipline of justice in the aftermath of violence, retributive and restorative measures are instances of liberal humanitarianism that produce an association between violence and the exception. This association is created by making visible intentional GVHRs and their cyclical consequences. It is this representation that is behind the idea of politics within liberal democracies as the non-violence realm *par excellence*. And it is only through this representation that scholars and practitioners within this discipline can promise a future where violence (in its intentional, cyclical and exceptional facet) never happens again. Once we accept Žižek's theorisation of the social symptom, it becomes clear that the foundational promise of this discipline is bound to be disturbed by its excesses: the specific forms of violence that remain unaccounted for and create the illusion of an 'epistemological coup' behind the slogan of 'never again'. And if this slogan persists, despite the promise to deliver an everlasting peace purged of violence being frustrated time and again, it is because its appeal lies elsewhere. As I show in the following chapter, the promise of 'never again', as part of a larger ideological field, creates an easy explanation for a much more complex reality. At an age pervaded by violence in many identifiable sources, its power and appeal come from promising to sort out the issue by focusing on a specific violence that as intentional can be held accountable, as cyclical can be stopped, and as exceptional can be normalised.

Conclusion

In this chapter I have presented the first sketch of a critical reading of the punishment vs impunity debates. This analysis flips traditional explanations of transitional justice measures as responses to the problems posed by post-authoritarian or post-conflict scenarios. By bringing in the Foucauldian concept of objectification I suggested that the question of whether or not to punish perpetrators of mass atrocities is, in a certain sense, partially performative or productive of the *post-conflictual* reality is it supposed to implement. This is not to say that post-conflict scenarios do not exist, nor that a certain type of violence never recedes during political transitions. Civil wars certainly end, authoritarian governments certainly fall, and political oppression at least changes its form (from centralised and overt during dictatorships to decentralised and covert under certain democracies). Reading transitional justice through the lens of disciplinarity and accepting the performative or productive character of this discipline means something else entirely. It means to acknowledge that the theories, debates and practices that emerged with this new discipline were part of a historical process that shaped the *post-conflict as a thinkable and achievable political reality* by narrowing down the meaning of violence to an *intentional, cyclical and exceptional phenomenon*.

But to fully grasp the significance of this historical making of the post-conflict, we need to look at more than mere logical conditions of possibility. Liberal humanitarianism is much older than the Aspen, Charter 77 and IDASA conventions, and so is its specific representation of violence. We need to look at what was specific to the late twentieth century in terms of concrete historical events; that is, what enabled actors in that period to effectively mobilise a pre-existing humanitarian logic to create a new political reality. In the next chapter, I will turn to the history of the Years of Lead (1964–88) in Brazil to answer this question. More specifically, I will focus on the different movements of popular resistance that antagonised the regime, from the emergence of the guerrilla movement in the 1960s to the groups of family members of victims in the mid-1970s. My goal will be to show how the appearance of a new democratic resistance against the dictatorship, based on the language of human rights and the slogan of 'never again', was conditioned by a concrete historical fact: the double disappearances that characterised the making of a *post-conflictual* Brazil.

Notes

1. Foucault, 'History, Discourse and Discontinuity'; Foucault, *The History of Sexuality*; Foucault, *Language, Counter Memory, Practice*.
2. Ditrych, 'From Discourse to Dispositif'; Dunne and Wheeler, '"We the Peoples"'; Evans, 'International Human Rights Law as Power/Knowledge'; Frazer and Hutchings, 'Avowing Violence'; French, 'Technologies of Telling'; Humphrey, *The Politics of Atrocity and Reconciliation*; Moon, 'Narrating Political Reconciliation'.
3. Campbell, *Writing Security*; Fourlas, 'No Future without Transition'; Katz, 'A New "Normal"'; Odysseos and Selmeczi, 'The Power of Human Rights/the Human Rights of Power'; Dillon and Reid, 'Global Liberal Governance'; Jabri, 'Michel Foucault's Analytics of War'.

4. Foucault and Rabinow, *The Foucault Reader*.
5. Foucault avoids the term 'discipline'. He more commonly refers to savoir, discourse or discursive formations. One of the main reasons for this difference in terminology is Foucault's inclination to look at claims of knowledge that were not validated as modern, academic fields of inquiry: knowledges that were left behind as the debris of immature, mad, or improper forms of investigation and are not considered 'disciplines' in a serious sense. Nonetheless, I recuperate the term 'discipline' here because of its semantic value, emphasising the link between claims of knowledge and the power to discipline the conduct of individuals. See Foucault, *Archaeology of Knowledge*; Foucault, *The Order of Things*.
6. Foucault and Rabinow, *The Foucault Reader*; Harrison, 'Madness and Historicity'.
7. Popper, *The Logic of Scientific Discovery*; Kuhn, *The Structure of Scientific Revolutions*; Feyerabend, *Against Method*.
8. Foucault, *The Order of Things*.
9. Bartelson, *A Genealogy of Sovereignty*, p. 66.
10. Foucault, *The Order of Things*, p. 139.
11. Ibid. p. 149.
12. Ibid. p. 144.
13. Foucault, *Archaeology of Knowledge*, chapter 8.
14. Foucault, *The Order of Things*, p. 248.
15. Ibid. p. 248.
16. Ibid. p. 248.
17. Ibid. p. 248.
18. Foucault, *The Order of Things*.
19. Ibid. p. 294.
20. Foucault, 'History, Discourse and Discontinuity', p. 227.
21. Foucault, *Archaeology of Knowledge*, p. 54.
22. Bar-tal, 'From Intractable Conflict through Conflict Resolution to Reconciliation', p. 351.
23. Elster, *Closing the Books*, p. 3.
24. Teitel, 'Transitional Justice Genealogy'.
25. Moyn, 'Anti-Impunity as Deflection of Argument'.
26. Arthur, 'How "Transitions" Reshaped Human Rights'.
27. Arthur, 'How "Transitions" Reshaped Human Rights'; Eagle, 'A Genealogy of the Criminal Turn in Human Rights'.
28. Alexander and Davies, 'Hansard Corpus 1803–2005'.
29. Arthur, 'How "Transitions' Reshaped Human Rights", p. 328.
30. Ibid. p. 328.
31. Ocampo, 'The Latin American Debt Crisis in Historical Perspective'.
32. Babb, 'The Washington Consensus as Transnational Policy Paradigm'.
33. Henkin, 'State Crimes', p. 185.
34. Ibid. p. 185.
35. Ibid. p. 185.
36. Ibid. p. 185.

37. Ibid. p. 185.
38. Ibid. p. 185.
39. Leebaw, 'The Irreconcilable Goals of Transitional Justice', p. 100.
40. Siegel, 'Transitional Justice'.
41. Leebaw, *Judging State-Sponsored Violence*, p. 71.
42. Krog, *Country of My Skull*, p. 35.
43. Ibid. p. 35 (my emphasis).
44. Arthur, 'How "Transitions" Reshaped Human Rights'.
45. Huntington, *The Third Wave*.
46. Fukuyama, *The End of History and the Last Man*, p. xi.
47. Jabri, 'War, Government, Politics', p. 41.
48. Huntington, *The Third Wave*.
49. Harvey, 'A Brief History of Neoliberalism', p. 40.
50. Andrieu, 'Civilizing Peacebuilding'; Fourlas, 'No Future without Transition'.
51. Derrida, *Specters of Marx*, p. 106.
52. Ibid. p. 106.
53. Williams, *The Divided World*.
54. Ibid.
55. Ibid.
56. Žižek, *The Sublime Object of Ideology*, p. 16.
57. Ibid. p. 16.
58. Balibar, *Masses, Classes, Ideas*.
59. Žižek, *The Sublime Object of Ideology*, p. 16.
60. Ibid. p. 16.
61. Marx, *Capital*.
62. Žižek, *The Sublime Object of Ideology*, p. 18.
63. Althusser, *For Marx*.
64. Williams, *The Divided World*.
65. Brown, 'Universal Human Rights', p. 41.
66. Beitz, 'Human Rights as Common Concern'; Brems, 'Human Rights'; Freeman, 'The Philosophical Foundations of Human Rights'; Griffin, 'First Steps in an Account of Human Rights'; Nickel, 'Rethinking Indivisibility'.
67. Humphrey, *The Politics of Atrocity and Reconciliation*, p. 117.
68. Ibid. p. 117.
69. United Nations, 'Convention on the Prevention and Punishment of the Crime of Genocide'; United Nations, 'Declaration on the Protection of All Persons from Enforced Disappearance'; United Nations, 'Convention Against Torture and Other Cruel, Inhuman or Degrading Treatment or Punishment'; United Nations, 'An Agenda for Peace: Preventive Diplomacy and Related Matters'; United Nations, 'Vienna Eclaration and Programme of Action'.
70. United Nations, 'Convention on the Prevention and Punishment of the Crime of Genocide', Art. 2 (my emphasis).
71. United Nations, 'Convention Against Torture and Other Cruel, Inhuman or Degrading Treatment or Punishment', Art. 1 (my emphasis).

72. United Nations, 'Declaration on the Protection of All Persons from Enforced Disappearance', Art. 5 (my emphasis).
73. Douzinas, *The End of Human Rights*, p. 239.
74. Moore, *Placing Blame*.
75. Ibid. Part II.
76. Lacey, 'A Clear Concept of Intention'.
77. Schabas, 'Mens Rea and The International Criminal Tribunal for the Former Yugoslavia'.
78. United Nations, 'Rome Statute of the International Criminal Court', Art. 30.
79. Douzinas, *The End of Human Rights*, p. 239.
80. Wieviorka, *Violence: A New Approach*, p. 3.
81. Meister, *After Evil*, p. 41.
82. Walker, 'The Cycle of Violence', p. 81.
83. Meister, *After Evil*, p. 25.
84. Eagle, 'A Genealogy of the Criminal Turn in Human Rights', p. 20.
85. Arendt, *The Origins of Totalitarianism*; Arendt, *The Human Condition*; Arendt, *Responsibility and Judgment*.
86. Frazer and Hutchings, 'On Politics and Violence', p. 93.
87. Arendt, *The Human Condition*.
88. Ibid.
89. Arendt, *On Violence*, p. 51.
90. Ibid. p. 51.
91. Frazer and Hutchings, 'On Politics and Violence', p. 100.
92. Laqueur, *The Age of Terrorism*.
93. Arendt, *The Human Condition*.
94. Arendt, *On Revolution*; Arendt, *On Violence*.
95. Arendt, *The Human Condition*, p. 245.
96. Ibid. p. 237.
97. Ibid. p. 244–5.
98. Ibid. p. 241.
99. Arendt, *Responsibility and Judgment*, p. 25.
100. Ibid. p. 25.
101. Arendt, *The Human Condition*, p. 237.
102. Moon, 'Healing Past Violence'; Nytagodien and Neal, 'Collective Trauma, Apologies, and the Politics of Memory'; Mendeloff, 'Trauma and Vengeance', *Human Rights Quarterly*; Brounéus, 'The Trauma of Truth Telling'; Humphrey, 'From Terror to Trauma'.
103. Levi, *The Drowned and the Saved*.
104. Edkins, *Trauma and the Memory of Politics*; Zehfuss, *Wounds of Memory*.
105. Luckhurst, 'The Trauma Question', p. 13.
106. Arendt, *The Human Condition*, p. 241.
107. Edkins, 'Ground Zero'; Leys, *Trauma: A Genealogy*; Luckhurst, 'The Trauma Question'; Alexander, *Trauma: A Social Theory*.
108. Caruth, 'Recapturing the Past', p. 153.

109. Caruth, *Unclaimed Experience*, p. 57.
110. Furtado, 'When Does Repression Become Political?'
111. Edkins, 'Ground Zero'.
112. Teitel, *Transitional Justice*, p. 149.
113. Ibid. p. 26.
114. Ibid. p. 50.
115. Ibid. p. 169.
116. Sharp, 'Emancipating Transitional Justice from the Bonds of the Paradigmatic Transition'.
117. Orentlicher, 'Settling Accounts'; Teitel, 'Transitional Justice Genealogy'.
118. Teitel, 'Transitional Justice as Liberal Narrative', p. 101.
119. Kritz, 'The Dilemmas of Transitional Justice', p. xxi.
120. Sadat, 'The Effect of Amnesties Before Domestic and International Tribunals', p. 227.
121. Ibid. p. 227.

CHAPTER 3

The Brazilian Case

The previous chapter introduced the core of my theoretical framework. Inspired by Foucault's concept of objectification, I proposed to read the scholarship and practice of transitional justice as a form of discipline: a body of knowledge, a set of technologies (practices) and a group of institutions that both produce, and are produced by, the historical emergence of their own object of study. From a critical historical perspective, I suggested that the emergence of a body of knowledge specialised in post-conflict or post-authoritarian justice was the by-product and the co-producer of a post-conflictual economy of signification characteristic of the late twentieth century. The discipline of transitional justice has been continuously criticised for the 'mistake' of seeing violence merely in terms of violations of civil and political rights. I argued that this narrow understanding of violence was not a mistake, but the logical hardcore of such post-conflictual economy of signification. The central argument was that the end of violence (e.g., civil war, terrorism, authoritarianism) was not a sufficient condition for the emergence of the post-conflict, as an object of study and political intervention. This new political reality called the post-conflict also required the emergence of a new discipline that defined violence as an intentional, cyclical and exceptional phenomenon.

In this chapter I turn to the history of political violence in Brazil from the early 1960s to the late 1970s. The events narrated here serve two main purposes. First, they are meant to introduce the uninitiated reader, providing the background knowledge required by my analysis of the CNV. Aside from this introductory function, the chapter serves another important function: it completes the theoretical argument of the previous chapter with an empirical example. The contemporary history of political violence in Brazil illustrates what I call the constitutive absence of the post-conflictual economy of signification: the practices and ideas that cannot be incorporated by its narrow representation of violence. The question this chapter seeks to answer is very simple. Which practices and ideas needed to 'disappear' in order to pave the way for a post-conflictual reality?

The choice of the word 'disappear' is not arbitrary. As Chapter 1 argued, the discipline of transitional justice owes much to the struggle of family members of the disappeared in the Southern Cone. Both the scholarship and practice of transitional justice have, to a sensible degree, been shaped and evolved as responses to the forced disappearance of political dissidents. But while rightfully condemning forced disappearances as crimes against humanity, the literature has lost sight of a more subtle, but nevertheless important meaning of the word 'disappearance'. The historical emergence of the post-conflictual reality cannot be dissociated from the so-called disappearance of its constitutive absence: the competing visions of justice for which there can be no end to conflict. The new discipline of transitional justice could only emerge and become naturally accepted as a form of justice 'as far as possible' once previous conceptions of justice had been declared impossible. This chapter is essentially about the rise and fall of these competing visions of justice (the constitutive absence of the post-conflictual economy of signification) as it happened in Brazil, from the early 1960s to the late 1970s.

In the first section, I begin by describing the political crises of the 1961–3 triennium that ended in the 1964 military coup. This provides the historical context in which support for political violence was normalised within the new left, far-right anti-communist groups and the armed forces. The next section describes the events that preceded the 1964 coup until the institutionalisation of state terrorism after 1968. This section pays particular attention to the rise of the urban guerrilla movement, analysing the perspectives of left-wing clandestine organisations regarding their understanding of violence, their vision of social justice and their radical political project. The last section describes how the fall of the urban guerrilla movement in Brazil affected the rise of an anti-impunity movement, uniting exiles, family members and human rights activists in a struggle for truth, memory and justice. The chapter ends by discussing how the metamorphosis experienced by leftist militants during exile and the dilemmas faced by the anti-impunity movement left a deep mark in the Brazilian transition.

Political Violence in Context

Every story has to start somewhere. A tale that has no point of origin is unintelligible. This truism works from unpretentious conversations about the weather to the most sophisticated historiographical works. But, as necessary as they may be, points of origin 'divide more than just time'.[1] Depending on when and where we decide our story begins, we might already define how the story will end and what lessons we can actually learn from it. This is why there is always 'a critical political dimension to the way we [. . .] begin a particular historical narrative'.[2]

It is hard to say exactly when political violence first appeared in Brazil during the Cold War. We find diverging accounts in both the historiography and remembrance of the period concerning both extremes of the political spectrum. Did state terror and the persecution of left-wing 'subversion' begin after the military coup d'état in 1964, or did state-led violence precede the coup? Was the leftist armed struggle a response to the military coup, or was it the expression of an international movement inspired by the success of liberation struggles in Algeria, Cuba and Vietnam? At stake here is a question that emerges time and again when it comes to the memory of political violence: the question of blame or, as Marchesi and Yaffe put it, of 'who threw the first stone?'.[3] In the past decade, this historical version of a blame game heated up with the increased scholarly interest in the topic of revolutionary violence; acts of political violence committed by leftist clandestine organisations in the 1960s.[4] It is not in the interest of the present work to join this game. From a Foucauld-inspired perspective, it makes little sense to pose the question of who threw the first stone. It is much more useful to ask *how* violence was made into a possible and, for some, even desirable political act.

Political violence in Latin America is almost always remembered in light of the ideological antagonisms that characterised the Cold War. The left is accused of nurturing a dangerous Leninist disregard for democratic institutions[5] while the right is unanimously blamed for its hysterical anti-communism.[6] Instead of beginning from the perspective of ideology (in the common-sense use of the term), I propose a different starting point: the perspective of development. I do not mean to say that ideological differences played no role in the violent past; they obviously did. It is merely a question of perspective. To search for the causes of state terrorism in the ideas behind the torturers and their supporters (their visceral anti-communism) only tells half of the story. After all, according to Anibal Quijano, if any spectre was haunting Latin America after World War II, it was first and foremost the spectre of socio-economic development.[7]

Without getting into too much detail about the vast, interdisciplinary literature on development studies, it suffices to say that the 1960s presented a turning point in Latin America. Since the 1940s, nationalist-populist movements such as *Peronismo* in Argentina and *Varguismo* in Brazil were based on a central promise: to overcome the region's dependency on commodity markets (seen as a sign of 'underdevelopment' and a cause of inequality) through state support for industrialisation.[8] The inward-looking model of development, as it became known, was based on three pillars: fomenting the development of local manufacture with the aim of substituting imported goods; raising protective barriers (e.g. multiple exchange rates, capital controls and import restrictions) to enable nascent industry to flourish; and financing the process of industrialisation via the traditional export-looking sector (appropriating part of the surplus from the sales of raw materials). For decades, the industrialisation strategy was the golden hen of nationalist-populist governments, generating rates of GDP growth of 4.8 per cent to 5 per cent a year.[9] But by the 1960s, the dream of achieving national 'independence' through economic self-sufficiency was showing clear signs of fatigue.

Brazil was a paradigmatic case. Inward-looking policies started during *Varguismo* (1930–45, 1951–4) and intensified during the presidency of Juscelino Kubitschek (1956–61) had transformed the country's social fabric and its productive structure. The urban population had grown from 16 per cent in 1940 to 50 per cent in the wake of the military coup.[10] Brazilian industry enjoyed rates of growth of around 10 per cent a year and became vertically integrated, with the capacity of producing capital goods.[11] Nonetheless, the project of industrialisation did not resolve the central issue of inequality. Despite the economic boom, in the 1950s only 12 per cent of families owned refrigerators.[12] Circa 1960, the richest 20 per cent owned 58.6 per cent of national income, whereas the poorest 20 per cent were left with 3.8 per cent.[13] According to critics on the left, the inward-looking model was structurally flawed. The highly protected, dynamic economy created by decades of industrialisation relied on the sales of durable consumer goods (like refrigerators) to a minuscule market of well-educated and well-paid groups. This industrialisation for the few was anchored on the vast, informal economy that supplied basic necessities at negligible costs for the working masses (therefore keeping wages at low levels).[14] This structural contradiction exploded in the 1960s, when the combination of protectionism, unequal growth and receding demand for raw materials generated levels of inflation reaching 75 per cent per year in 1963.[15]

Institutional design also helped to create a political crisis out of an economic one. The Brazilian electoral system had an interesting feature in the 1960s: separate national elections were held for the positions of president and vice president. In this system the major parties still composed a single list and, ideally, because they shared a common political agenda, candidates from the same party should technically receive a similar amount of votes. Nevertheless, in practice the people could still elect a president and a vice president who came from the extreme opposites of the political spectrum. And this is exactly what happened in 1961. Originally, the elected president was Jânio Quadros, an independent candidate who personified the expectations of a more conservative electorate. Quadros's campaign slogan promised a 'crusading attitude toward corruption, a suspicion of grandiose reforms, a preference for free enterprise, and an emphasis on the values of home and family'.[16] The elected vice-president was João Goulart (aka 'Jango'), a politician from the Partido Trabalhista Brasileiro (Brazilian Labour Party, PTB), who served as minister of labour during the last Vargas government in 1954. Often described as a *peronista* and the major architect of the communisation of Brazil, Jango was *persona non grata* among the liberal elite, conservative urban segments and, of course, the extreme right.[17]

How such an uncommon political arrangement could work and which problems it would face remains a question for imagination, because Quadros resigned after little more than six months.[18] Before resigning, the conservative president made a series of odd decisions, such as awarding state honours to Che Guevara and re-establishing diplomatic relations with the Soviet Union. The resignation came when the vice president, Jango, was in the middle of a diplomatic mission to the People's Republic of China.[19] The mix of ideological and practical confusion set a 'red alert' in many sectors who supported Quadros, but most of all, in the high echelons of the armed forces. The clear possibility of a 'Peronist-syndicalist' as a president prompted the first orchestrated attempt at a coup. General Denys (minister of war), Admiral Heck (minister of the navy) and Brigadier Grün Moss (minister of the air force) released a joint manifesto to veto the succession.[20] But the incipient military putsch faced strong resistance from pro-legality sectors. Governor Leonel Brizola, a southern politician from the PTB and Jango's brother-in-law, organised a network in defence of Jango's right to return as the legitimate president. Brizola's network gathered support from communists, students, intellectuals and the clergy,[21] eventually joined by the military command of the 3rd Army, the southernmost section of Brazilian terrestrial forces.[22] With the risk of a further escalation of conflict, including the possibility of a civil war, Jango's return to Brazil was assured.

At the time, the return of the legitimate, although unexpected, president was considered a major victory of popular forces.[23] But in the long run, it would begin to look more like a Pyrrhic victory. Jango's presidency came with a caveat: he was forced to share space with newly instituted prime ministers, in a newly created semi-parliamentarian system.[24] Moreover, the presidency also struggled with labour demands for structural reform (there were 435 workers' strikes from 1961 to 1963)[25] and a climate of increasing political polarisation.[26] As a bureaucrat from the PTB, Jango was no 'man of the revolutionary Left',[27] despite the claims from his opponents.[28] It is true that his government enjoyed the support of the Partido Comunista Brasileiro (Brazilian Communist Party, PCB), recently legalised for the second time in its history.[29] But the alliance was more suggestive of the particular agenda of Brazilian communists at the time than of Jango's 'radical' inclinations.[30] In fact, the Labour politician was criticised by radical leftist sectors that were increasingly discontented with the pacifist agenda of the *Partidão* (big party). Rather than an agent of international communism, he became entangled in a historical process of fragmentation of the Brazilian leftist camp,[31] a process that would break with the historical monopoly of the PCB and the PTB.[32]

This fragmentation started earlier in 1961, even before Jango became president, and after Cuba assumed a socialist perspective.[33] In that year, a group of Trotskyists and Luxemburgists organised the first congress of a new clandestine organisation in the countryside of São Paulo, the Organização Revolucionária Marxista (Revolutionary Marxist Organisation, POLOP).[34] The POLOP was the first group of dissidents from the PCB to question the pacifist route to socialism and, in particular, the belief in institutional reforms. Its clandestine organisation was followed by the Maoist Partido Comunista do Brasil (Communist Party of Brazil, PCdoB, founded in 1962), the peasant's Movimento Revolucionário Tiradentes (Tiradentes Revolutionary Movement, MRT, founded in 1962) and the Christian-Maoist Ação Popular (Popular Action, AP, founded in 1963).[35] Jango, the peaceful southerner with limited political skills,[36] witnessed the rise of an influential new left, outside the control of the PCB, that disturbed both his and the PTB's historical strategy of conciliation. The new left was joined by a rising movement of peasants denouncing the dire conditions of the countryside and demanding an extensive programme of land reforms 'under the law or under force'.[37]

Far-right groups were also mobilising, fuelled by dissatisfaction with the eccentricity of Quadros's decisions. Two organisations stood out in the universe of far-right extremism: the Movimento Anti Comunista (Anti-Communist Movement, MAC), founded in 1961, and the Comando de Caça aos Comunistas (Command of Communist Manhunting, CCC), founded by students at the prestigious Law School of the University of

São Paulo shortly before the 1964 coup. Although largely neglected by the literature, these groups played a fundamental role in the dynamics of polarisation and radicalisation in the 1960s. As early as 1961, graffiti calling for the death of communists appeared in Rio de Janeiro. By 1962, the headquarters of the national student's union was machine-gunned, bombs were thrown at left-wing newspapers, and a ticking bomb was found and disarmed by the police at a Soviet industry exposition.[38]

The radicalisation of anti-communism also found fertile ground in the armed forces. From 1957, official publications of the armed forces such as the periodical *O Mensário de Cultura Militar* translated and disseminated a series of texts from the *Revue Militaire d'Information* regarding the concept of *guerre révolutionnaire* (revolutionary warfare).[39] The doctrine emerged as the theorisation of French military defeats during the first Indochina War (1946–55) and the Algerian War (1954–62).[40] Popularised by the writings of Colonel Jacques Hogard, widely read within Brazilian military circles, the French doctrine described international communism as a new, highly coordinated enemy that would stop at nothing to achieve its ultimate goal: the total submission of the Western world.[41] For the French doctrine, the new enemy had no face; it operated in disguise amidst the civilian population and was virtually omnipresent, always attempting to win over hearts and minds via a campaign of indoctrination.[42] Differing from conventional warfare, revolutionary warfare was a total war that would be fought between 'individuals and parties'[43] over the control of 'opinions and ideas'.[44] Its battlefields were limitless, including the political arena, industrial relations and even popular culture.[45] The defeat of French forces was explained by a failure to recognise this reality: that the new war merged military and non-military elements, effacing the boundaries between peace and war in a new state of *paix-guerre* (peace-war).[46] The effectiveness of counterinsurgency practices required the 'decisive control of information'[47] and, if need be, 'unification between the political and the military commands'.[48]

For those inspired by the paramilitaries or versed in the French doctrine, Jango's return was akin to a state of emergency. As new cadets were being instructed in the methods of anti-subversive warfare, the Brazilian political landscape was changing. The proportion of seats in the national congress held by centre/left and leftist parties significantly increased from 4 per cent in 1954 to 12 per cent in 1962, when the PTB became the second largest party in the chamber of deputies.[49] It mattered little that Jango was no communist. Read through the lenses of the new doctrine, Brazil could be experiencing a dangerous 'psychological transference of a population from a given political universe to a different political universe [. . .] favourable to the USSR'.[50] The fact that no one had yet 'thrown any stones at anyone' also mattered little for a doctrine that failed to see the difference between strikes, soap operas and acts of terrorism, all bundled together under the vague concept of 'subversion'.[51]

In 1963, Jango won the right to restore presidentialism with an outstanding majority in a national referendum.[52] At the same time, the social mobilisation around basic reforms hit the lower ranks of the armed forces, also suffering from the high rates of inflation.[53] In May 1963 around a thousand non-commissioned officers joined the struggle for reform and, in September of the same year, 600 sergeants started a mutiny in the federal capital, Brasília, for the right of non-commissioned officers to run for legislative elections, a possibility forbidden at the time.[54] Empowered by the recent show of popular support, Jango made one of the most consequential decisions in Brazilian contemporary politics. He chose to 'radicalise' his own agenda while 'breaking' with military hierarchy by supporting 'the unionization of enlisted men'.[55]

On 13 March 1964, the president held the first of a sequence of national rallies in Rio de Janeiro, at the Square of the Central Railway Station. In a spontaneous, impassioned speech broadcast nationwide, the president filled the radical wing with hope by publicly announcing a new plan for basic reforms[56] and 'the nationalization of land lying within six miles of federal highways, railways, or national borders'.[57] Two days later Jango addressed the national congress, emphasising the urgency of the land question and the need to widen suffrage legislation, as well as calling for an extraordinary council in order to change the federal constitution.[58] The response from the conservative side came in two ways. While civilians organised an open demonstration against the president, the high ranks of the military organised a secret plot to overthrow him. In São Paulo, 500,000 people took to the streets in a large 'March with God, for the Family and Liberty', calling for the end of Jango's government. Placards showed slogans conflating anti-communist and misogynist tropes such as *'verde e amarelo, sem foice nem martelo'* (green and yellow, no sickle or hammer) and *'vermelho bom, só batom'* (red only looks nice on lipsticks).[59] From his position as chief of the army, General Castello Branco issued a top secret communication to every Brazilian general accusing the Labour government of working against the interests of the fatherland.[60] Castello Branco, a longstanding defender of legality, denounced Jango's agenda of constitutional change and called for a counter-coup.[61]

Castello Branco's communication was followed by a tense stand-off. Jango still had the support of powerful segments of the military such as the 2nd Army in São Paulo, the 3rd Army in Porto Alegre and the 4th Army in Recife.[62] On the morning of 31 March, the commander of the 4th military region, General Mourão Filho, moved 4,000 troops from Juiz the Fora to Rio de Janeiro, intending to topple the 'communist' president.[63] According to Elio Gaspari, even the inner circles of the conspiracy were taken by surprise by Mourão's bold move, including Castello Branco and the entire Ministry of War.[64] On 1 April, Jango was finally betrayed. On the verge of an open engagement with the insurrection forces, General Kruel, the commander of the 2nd Army and, until the very end, a Jango supporter, made an ultimatum to the President: he was to leave the radical leftist support behind and dismantle his plans of basic reforms if he wanted to remain in power.[65] The president refused to accept, flying from Rio to Brasília and then to his southern stronghold, where Brizola was making plans for resisting the military putsch from the South. After a tense period of deliberation, Jango chose exile in Uruguay over the possibility of sparking a national bloodbath.[66] With his response, Brazil entered a period of twenty-one years of military dictatorship.

The Years of Lead

April Fool's Day seemed like an appropriate date for what had happened. The legitimate government had been overthrown by a disorganised, small-scale military operation that faced no real confrontation,[67] no popular resistance,[68] and lasted less than a couple of days.[69] Suddenly, the armed forces took power 'virtually without firing a single gun at anyone'.[70] For the left, this unbelievable coup d'état felt like an earthquake, releasing decades of anti-communist hatred. In the Institutional Act No. 1 (AI-1), the first of many authoritarian decrees, the putschists were self-proclaimed as the new constituent power, representative of the 'victorious revolution' against the 'bolshevisation' of the country.[71] AI-1 emphasised the military 'mission to restore in Brazil the economic and financial order and to take the urgent measures needed in order to drain the purulent communist boil that had long infiltrated the government and the state bureaucracy'.[72] The text also mentioned the need for a political and moral reconstruction of the country.[73] Through AI-1, the high command of the armed forces institutionalised a witch-hunt atmosphere that fuelled the extreme right's desire 'to clean everything'.[74] In the immediate aftermath of the coup, around 50,000 'undesirables' were victimised by purges, arrests, torture and bans, losing their political rights for a decade.[75]

The symbolism of April Fool's Day is important. More than just truculence, 1964 represented a demoralising defeat from which the PCB would never recover.[76] Ever since the Cuban Revolution, the new left had treated the project of a pacifist transition to communism with scorn. But after being made 'fools' of, this disdain became a radical rejection. After a demoralising coup that sounded more like a joke than a serious military operation, reacting became a question of honour.[77] Moreover, the resort to force by conservative sectors eager to reconstruct the economic and financial order was read as a clear diagnosis: in the writings of clandestine organisations and militants, pacifism appears an illusory fantasy[78] and reformism is but a sign of co-optation.[79]

In this new context, the Cuban revolution became an even greater yardstick for the new left. Cuba was not simply the 'the first liberated territory of Latin America',[80] it was also 'a small island'[81] only '120 kilometres away from the Yankee (sic) Empire'.[82] The victory of the guerrilla movement in such conditions only magnified the failure of reformism in the largest and most industrialised Latin American country. In the imaginary of the new left, the 1964 coup highlighted the importance of the theory of the guerrilla focus known as *foquismo*.[83] Based on the military reflections of Ernesto Guevara considering the success of the Sierra Maestra guerrillas, *foquismo* proposed a new theory of revolutionary action that purportedly broke free from party politics.[84] Instead of waiting for the perfect time when the perfect material conditions were met, the revolutionary could seize history by the horns and create subjective conditions themselves, meaning popular support for the revolution. Via the establishment of guerrilla camps (the foci) in the mountainous regions, surrounded by deprived areas, the revolutionary would engage with the masses of peasants, learn from their experience and incorporate Marxism through practice.[85] He was to quit the safety of reformism and become a true 'social reformer who takes up arms [. . .] against special institutionalised conditions of a given moment and dedicates himself to rupture these frames, with all the vigour allowed by the circumstances.'[86] With military actions targeting individuals and institutions 'symbolising oppression', the revolutionary would gain the 'the entire support of the local population'.[87]

From a military reflection in the early 1960s, *foquismo* became the foundational mythology of the Cuban revolution and, in particular, of sectors in support for Castro.[88] Its account of the revolution accorded a special place to the Sierra Maestra guerrillas, painting Castro as the natural commander of the newly liberated Cuba. But by ignoring and downplaying the fundamental role of urban political mobilisation during the struggle,[89] it created an alluring legend that the country had been liberated from imperialism by no more than a group of twelve revolutionaries.[90] From 1960 until Che's death in 1967, *foquismo* was actively disseminated by the Cuban state, other guerrilla groups and Latin American and European intellectuals. It found its most cherished spokesperson in the French philosopher Regis Debray, a former student of Althusser who proclaimed the revolutionary nature of the new method.[91]

No other individual embodied the promises of *foquismo* in Brazil as Carlos Marighella, longtime member of the PCB and anti-fascist militant, did.[92] In a moment when resistance was a question of honour, Marighella was one of the few members of the PCB to outspokenly confront the military putsch. Figuring in the regime's top list of undesirables, on the day of the coup Marighella was cornered by the police in a local cinema in a middle-class neighbourhood in Rio de Janeiro. He resisted the order of arrest, shouting 'Down with the fascist military dictatorship! Long live democracy! Long live the communist party!'[93] The police opened fire. Marighella was injured in the chest by a bullet, but survived and was taken prisoner.[94] It was a short and vain act of resistance, but it was enough to secure a privileged place in the imaginary of the new left. In 1965, Marighella published the book *Por que resisti à prisão* (*Why I Resisted Arrest*), providing a lengthy critique of the 'American-backed, fascist military dictatorship' and characterising 'conformism' as worse than death.[95]

In the years following the coup, Marighella continued trying to persuade other members of the PCB of the virtues of operating through 'a small nucleus of combatants [. . .] immune to the conventionalism of traditional leftist political parties'.[96] His definite break with the *Partidão* only came after the party's decision to boycott the first congress of the Organisation of Latin American Solidarity (OLAS), an international socialist encounter held in Havana, in August 1967.[97] Unauthorised by the central committee, Marighella travelled to Cuba and joined the conference, which cost him his membership.[98] Convinced of the necessity of the armed struggle, he formed a new clandestine organisation: the Ação Libertadora Nacional (National Liberation Action, ALN). Alongside the Uruguayan Tupamaros, the leader of the ALN became one of the central theorists of urban guerrilla action.[99] Whereas for Guevara the cities were to be avoided at all costs, since they represented the impenetrable stronghold of state forces, for Marighella urban military actions were a vital step in the armed struggle, first in preparation for, and later in support of, the rural guerrillas.[100] The guerrilla foci would be supplied by urban actions, which would theoretically expropriate funds and at the same time cut the enemy's lines of supply. Terrorism was supposed to disorient the forces of the regime, creating a second internal front.[101]

Marxism, and in particular Marxist-Leninism, has always had a complicated relationship with the question of violence.[102] The new left was indeed part of a broader tradition that justified the resort to political violence as a progressive force. Jacob Gorender famously classified Marighella, the son of a descendant of slaves and an Italian migrant, as a cross between Franz Fanon's decolonial politics and Georges Sorel's anarcho-syndicalism.[103] Regardless of the question of morality and means, what is interesting about this tradition is that its conception of violence is irreducible to a narrow view of violence as an intentional, cyclical and exceptional violation. Violence, for the Marxist tradition, and specially for the new left, is 'not an extraordinary phenomenon in bourgeois societies' but a fundamental 'part of the everyday'.[104] This is why the analysis of Marighella and the armed struggle matters to a critical genealogical reading of the late twentieth century in Brazil and the world: in this irreducibility we find a sense of violence that allows no possibility of a *post-conflictual*.

In the foundational writings of the new left, violence appears as the fruit of the 'original sin'[105] of Latin American societies: the exploitation of the gargantuan masses across the region by a minuscule elite. The understanding of exploitation comes from Marx, where exploitation appears as the necessary by-product of a system of production and distribution of wealth based on the generalised production of commodities (saleable goods) by privately owned firms.[106] Differing from oppression (caused by exclusionary and unjust legal-political arrangements, e.g. dictatorships), the concept of exploitation merges the political and economic spheres of life. It addresses a fundamental relationship between those who work in a society and those who enjoy the benefits of that work. In an orthodox reading of Marx, exploitation can be measured between the time spent working to feed oneself (necessary labour) and the extra time required by profit-making (surplus labour).[107] In a more humanist reading, exploitation denotes the major form that alienation takes under the system described above. The vast majority of people, possessing no land or capital, see themselves estranged (alienated) from their means to survive and compelled into working in exploitative conditions. They are not only materially alienated from the benefits of their work but also, in a more existential sense, alienated from a full and meaningful life and, at times, from the very recognition of their humanity.[108] This is the first point of contention between the thoughts of the new left and the new post-conflictual ethos. The reality of exploitation in capitalist conditions leaves very little room, and credibility, for Arendt's precious principle of *men qua men* (human beings as equals) as the promise sustaining life in community.

The second point of contention refers to the vision of violence as primarily or fundamentally destructive. A society that requires the reproduction of exploitation at an ever-expanding rate is not a society that has overcome the barbarism of violence, as preached by the enlightenment tradition.[109] It is a society that has simply incorporated destructive violence (war, political repression, terror) into a latent state, always ready to resurface once the system is threatened.[110] With this particular reading, the new left recuperated the tradition in Marxist thought that emphasised the intimate relation between capital and conquest.[111] In Latin America, this tradition naturally focuses on the history of European colonialism or, more specifically, colonial land-grabbing, to explain the region's insurmountable levels of inequality as the historical by-product of development.[112] It is the accumulation of land in the hands of a few, a phenomenon that Marx defined as primitive accumulation, that produced the masses of landless workers required by the process of accumulation.[113]

In Brazil, after 1964, this reading of political events seemed unquestionable. First, the era of industrialisation was carried out at the cost of workers. Between 1955 and 1959, 'during the developmental euphoria [. . .] while the productivity of work increased by 37%, the gross profit of entrepreneurs increased 76%, and the minimum wage was raised by around 16%'.[114] Second, the country's colonial heritage had created a situation in the 1960s in which '2.2% of agricultural lots amassed 59% of occupied land in the country'.[115] This inequality of land ownership was held responsible for 'pressurising the great rural masses to offer both their muscles in exchange for the lowest pay, sometimes a simple plate of food'.[116] Faced with democratic demands for land reform, the violence of the system leaves its state of 'latency' and rises to the surface in an authoritarian coup with the goal of achieving '"order", whatever the costs, and "progress" integrated to neocolonialism'.[117]

The theoretical debates of the radical left seemed to be confirmed by the regime's economic policy. From the very dawn of the 1964 coup, the military sought to strengthen what the Brazilian-born, American-educated economist Roberto Campos (Mr Bob Fields for the critics) defined as a vital 'interdependency'[118] with the global economy. As the dictatorship's first planning minister, under the rule of General Castello Branco, Campos represented a liberal wing of technocrats that sought to contain inflationary pressures by reducing the general levels of liquidity and controlling public expenditure.[119] The regime also aimed at solving some of the contradictions of the inward-looking model by creating an attractive atmosphere for foreign investors. The new model of growth through debt[120] involved three central pillars: the issuing of treasury bonds indexed to inflation (protecting their value in the long run); the relaxing of federal legislation on remittances of profit abroad;[121] and the depression of real wages (systematically raised below levels of inflation).[122] For the new left, this was a clear sign that the military dictatorship was a 'neo-colonial troop of occupation'[123] interested in the exploitation of the masses and the preservation of large plantations[124] and subjugated to the interests of the North American empire.[125]

The third and final point of contention regards the 'techniques' or methods of justice. In an exploitative order – where the original and natural equality among humans is continuously broken – the 'techniques' of forgiveness, promising and punishing are incapable of controlling the violence required by the system's reproduction. If oblivious to the productive-destructive link, they risk making the very concept of democracy seem like an illusion.[126] The new left was certain that there could be no peaceful coexistence in a context of subjugation. The creation of a new world order can only emerge from the complete dialectical denial of the old one.[127] It was in this context and for this purpose that violence was legitimised and, in a very few instances, glorified as a heroic act. Much has been said of Marighella's thoughts on terrorism in the literature on political violence, which all too often reduces the complexity of his conjectural analysis to a single quote: that terrorism is 'a quality that ennobles any honorable man'.[128] This widely mischaracterised statement is neither representative of the view of members of clandestine organisations, nor a carte blanch for murder.[129] First, it is important to clarify what is meant by 'terrorism', which Marighella clearly distinguishes from assassinations. According to his *Mini-Manual of the Urban Guerrilla* (1969), terrorism primarily means blowing things up:[130] the tactical use of explosives for the sake of sabotage. There was nothing particularly honourable in blowing things up. What he truly considered as an honourable quality was the political label of terrorism, that is, the sign that the guerrillas were fighting 'against the shameful military dictatorship and its monstrosities'.[131] This second part of the sentence is all too often ignored.

The tactics of *foquismo* were extremely successful until 1969. In the convulsive atmosphere of 1968, the urban guerrilla movement was but one element of the opposition. Like their peers in Mexico City and Paris, Brazilian students took to the streets.[132] The loss of purchasing power among industry workers also sparked a series of strikes across the country.[133] Unidentified and employing sophisticated methods, radical militants faced little opposition from the state apparatus. They benefited from the weakness of a divided regime, stuck in internal disputes, and the precarious state of Brazil's regular police force.[134] In preparation for the guerrilla movement, the number of bank robberies in São Paulo jumped from two in 1967 to eleven in 1968, and to thirty-one in 1969.[135] In May 1969, militants of the Vanguarda Armada Revolucionária Palmares (Armed Revolutionary Vanguard, VAR-Palmares) expropriated 2,500,000 dollars (equivalent to approximately 17,000,000 in 2019) from the personal safe of the late Adhemar de Barros, an ex-governor of São Paulo accused of corruption.[136] These acts of 'revolutionary expropriation' were the perfect expression of the urban struggle: their practical function was to raise funds for the guerrillas, and their symbolic function was to generate popular support by 'taking back from bankers what they take from the people'.[137]

This period also witnessed the first campaign of targeted assassinations and kidnappings.[138] In 1966, a bomb targeting General Costa e Silva, the first in the regime's line of succession, exploded at the international airport of Recife. The attempt failed, sparing the general's life, but left fourteen people injured and two dead.[139] In 1968, Charles Chandler, an American Vietnam War veteran suspected of disseminating torture methods in Brazil, was killed by the Vanguarda Popular Revolucionária (Popular Revolutionary Vanguard, VPR).[140] On 4 September 1969 (three days before Independence Day), militants of the ALN and the Movimento Revolucionário 8 de Outubro (Revolutionary Movement 8 of October, MR-8) kidnapped US ambassador Charles Burke Elbrick.[141] The targeted assassinations of 'executioners and torturers'[142] were seen as *justiçamentos*, forms of justice carried out by revolutionary tribunals that were meant to disseminate 'terror and fear in the exploiters'.[143] The kidnappings also mixed pragmatic and symbolic motivations. For example, in exchange for the life of the American ambassador, the ALN and the MR-8 demanded the liberation of political prisoners and the reading of a manifesto on national television. This tactic, used many times in the course of the armed struggle, was particularly uncomfortable for the regime. The manifestos often made public facts that government officials vehemently denied, such as the existence of political prisoners and the practice of torture.[144]

At first, the response to the success of the armed struggle came through a wave of paramilitary terrorism. Far-right, anti-communist organisations such as the MAC and the CCC were joined in their crusade by the Grupo Secreto (Secret Group) a death squad formed by members of the intelligence services operating off-duty.[145] Frustrated with the softness of the state's response, the anti-communist far right triggered terror campaigns in the hope of promoting political radicalisation.[146] Largely ignored by the police, they too resorted to kidnappings and targeted assassinations, including a series of twenty bomb attacks[147] and a failed plan to explode a gas plant in Rio de Janeiro that could have cost the lives of approximately 100,000 people.[148] On 13 December 1968, pressed by the rising tide of extremism within its ranks, the regime finally decreed its draconian legislation, the Fifth Institutional Act (AI-5). Curbing civil liberties, AI-5 shut down the national congress for an indeterminate time, ruled out the right to *habeas corpus* and established an indefinite state of exception.[149] AI-5 inaugurates the phase of 'undisguised dictatorship'[150] in Brazil, when the presidency was controlled by the extreme right, the channels of political opposition were dissolved, and dissidents (whether armed or unarmed) were subjected to a violent programme of extermination.

The Two Meanings of the Word 'Disappearance'

Richard Jackson et al. define state terrorism as 'the intentional use or threat of violence by state agents or their proxies against individuals or groups who are victimized for the purpose of intimidating or frightening a broader audience'.[151] As a specific form of terrorism, state terror involves the production and management of fear in order to achieve a political goal.[152] The direct consequence of the mainstreaming of the anti-communist far right after 1968 was that the production and management of fear became official state policy. The incorporation of the language and tactics of right-wing terrorists by the state meant a more radicalised and brutal response from state officials, no longer seeking to pacify but also to terrorise any source of dissent. As paramilitary terror waned, terror was institutionalised and intensified under the rule (1969–74) of General Emílio Garrastazu Médici, a defender of the idea that 'those who sow violence will fatally reap violence'[153] and a detractor of the policy of keeping prisoners.[154]

The institution of the political police usually engraves the horror of authoritarian and totalitarian violence in a simple acronym, such as the Nazi Gestapo, the Stasi in the GDR, and the Dina during Pinochet's rule. The Brazilian regime had not one, but many 'political police' organisations during the most intense phase of state terror. In order to suppress subversion, the dictatorship built a vast and heterogeneous counterinsurgency network formed by military intelligence agencies, a civilian central intelligence service, a gendarmerie and police departments. This complex and confusing network had continental proportions, spanning a territory twice the size of western Europe. In the literature and in common parlance, the entire network is simply referred to as the *Repressão*, the Portuguese word for repression. In the 1970s, with Médici, the *Repressão* was centralised in the DOI-CODI system, a joint operation between Destacamentos de Operações de Informacões – Centros de Operações de Defesa Interna (Deployment Groups for Intelligence Operations – Centres for Operations of Internal Defence). Each DOI-CODI was composed of civilian and military officers (from the three forces) stationed in one of the six zones of internal defence established by the army's military command. DOI-CODI officers reported to the Serviço Nacional de Informação (National Information Service, SNI), instituted by General Castello Branco after the 1964 coup.[155] DOI-CODI agents were given carte blanche to kidnap, torture and assassinate by the high command of the armed forces. To cover their tracks, they resorted to hundreds of forced disappearances, dismembering the bodies of their victims and dumping their remains into the sea or into unidentified mass graves.

No one has ever conveyed the inequality of forces between the *Repressão* and insurgent groups better than General Fiúza de Castro, co-founder of the army's intelligence agency and chief of Rio de Janeiro's CODI between 1972 and 1974. According to the veteran, working for the DOI-CODI system felt like using a 'helve hammer in order to kill a bunch of flies'.[156] Overall, 4,935 individuals were accused by the dictatorship of participating in clandestine organisations from 1964 to 1979.[157] Of this total, only 1,464 were charged with taking part in violent or armed actions.[158] In the end, the *foquista* assumptions regarding the immediate link between violence and popular support turned out to be a gross misreading of reality. Militarised, direct action was never 'clean' and hardly ever went according to plan. Bomb attacks, such as the 1966 attempt, could result in the deaths of innocent people who had virtually nothing to do with the intended targets.[159] 'Revolutionary justice' was often seen by the larger public, and widely reported by the mass media, as nothing but cold-blooded murder. Even 'revolutionary expropriations' eventually led to the deaths of innocent guards, usually working-class people who were not the perpetrators of neo-colonial exploitation but the very victims of a system that forced them to risk their lives in order to make a living.[160] All this had a profoundly negative impact on the image of the radical left, especially among its natural audience. 'Stood up' by the revolution, the dozens of isolated groups that took part in the armed struggle did not stand a chance against the helve hammer of the *Repressão*.[161]

The assassination of Carlos Marighella on 4 November 1969 by Operação Bandeirantes (Operation Bandeirantes, OBAN), the embryo of the DOI-CODI system, was the prelude to this tragic fall.[162] In a period of approximately four years (from 1970 to 1974) most clandestine organisations had been 'dismantled' and 'neutralised', to use the

regime's euphemisms. In the most astonishing display of dispropor-
tional force, the Brazilian army deployed around 5,000 personnel and
extensively employed napalm to hunt down and murder around sixty
members of a guerrilla focus established in the south-eastern borders
of the Amazon.[163] Unsurprisingly, the end of the armed struggle did
not mean an end to violence. Kidnappings, assassinations and forced
disappearances continued well into the 1980s.[164]

The concept of state terror should not be confused with Arendt's idea
of totalitarian violence, indiscriminate and arbitrary in its essence.[165]
Political violence can seem arbitrary to a wider audience, but it is hardly
ever completely indiscriminate.[166] Even the regime's vague and omnipresent concept of subversion respected certain ideological/practical contours. This is not an excuse for torturers, and it is far from the myth of the
so-called dirty war. It is merely a reminder of the uncomfortable fact that,
just like everything else, suffering was also unequally distributed during
the civic-military dictatorship. At the apex of terror, the regime's model of
growth through debt was starting to pay off. The early stabilisation measures taken at the costs of workers in 1964 would bear fruit from the late
1960s to the 1970s, in the period known as the 'economic miracle'. With
global interest rates at negligible, sometimes negative levels,[167] foreign
capital flooded the Brazilian economy in unforeseen levels, financing
growth rates of 11 per cent per year and the expansion of manufactured
exports.[168] Far from a terrorising scenario, it seemed as though the world
was witnessing the 'birth' of a future world power; a suspicion almost
confirmed by the magic of the national football team. While political dissidents were being murdered in torture cells, Pelé and Brazil's unbeatable
'Golden Squadron' became the World Cup title-holders for the third time
in history with a mesmerising performance in Mexico in 1970.[169] Médici,
himself an inveterate football fan, enjoyed 82 per cent popular support.[170]
State terror had an indistinguishable double face in Brazil: '*years of lead,
but also years of gold*'.[171]

It took a long and tortuous time before 'the years of gold' were finally
acknowledged as 'years of lead'. As discussed in Chapter 1, the disappearances of the bodies of clandestine militants, and the process of
politicisation of grief that this generated, played an important part. They
paved the way for the emergence of a new movement of resistance, led
by the family members of the disappeared and based on an agenda of
denouncing state terrorism and holding perpetrators accountable. However, aside from the absence of bodies, grief and graves, it is possible to
see yet another dimension to the word 'disappearance'. This dimension,
rarely explored in the literature, relates to the disappearance of a whole

political project. In the 1970s, this second meaning of the word is closely linked with a particular metamorphosis experienced by exiles and the choices faced by the human rights movement.

The Diaspora (1973) and the Amnesty Movement (1975–1979)

The experience of forced migration is a heterogeneous experience, depending on individual choices and trajectories.[172] But, in a certain sense, the Brazilian diaspora in the 1970s showed a more general meaning regarding the fate of militancy. Rollemberg describes the concept of the exile as the embodiment of the defeat of a 'socio-political project'.[173] It is 'the defeat of this project or the unsurmountable difficulties for its implementations'[174] that creates the exile. The first leftist militants to leave Brazil after the 1964 coup did not immediately experience the defeat of a political project. Remaining in Latin America, at that time, the geopolitical forefront of the revolution, they were still fighting, resisting, regrouping. *Foquistas* could seek guidance in Havana or Montevideo, and more traditional grassroots activists could experience the effervescence of Salvador Allende's socialism in Chile.[175] This situation would, nonetheless, dramatically change following the internationalisation of the fight against communism, terrorism and subversion in the Southern Cone. Between 13 December 1968 (the Brazilian state of exception) and 11 September 1973 (the Chilean state of exception) leftist militants outside of Brazil were forced into the strange experience of 'exile within the exile'.[176] Even more so than Guevara's death in 1967, Pinochet's victory carries the weight of a serious 'political defeat'.[177] In 1976, Uruguay, the second leftist safe haven in the Southern Cone, also fell to a right-wing coup. Everything seemed to signal the endgame for the Latin American revolution and 'the defeat of a continent'.[178]

The year 1973 also saw a rapprochement between liberal professionals and Christian humanists and the families of the disappeared. The president of the CJP, Don Evaristo Arns from the Archdiocese of São Paulo, was one of the central figures in this process.[179] The cardinal used his political influence to unite relatives around demands for accountability and, at the same time, protect them through the prestige enjoyed by religious leaders within conservative circles.[180] In a bold move in 1974, the CJP requested clarification on the whereabouts of twenty-two disappeared and was granted a meeting with the regime's authorities.[181] Arns also coined what would become the historical motto of the new emerging movement of democratic resistance: *para que não se esqueça* (so it's not forgotten), *para que nunca mais aconteça* (so it never happens again). This incipient new form of resistance intersected with the devastating precariousness experienced by exiles. Defeated, wounded and unprotected, certain groups of survivors saw in the works of human rights organisations the possibility of continuing their struggle by other means. Paradoxically, the 'disappearance' of their political project also offered a 'liberation'[182] from the military discipline, the almost ascetic denial of the self into the collective, and the violence that were required by the armed struggle.

Here lies the transformation: if they reconsidered the rejection of legality as co-optation and democracy as an inherently flawed regime,[183] exiles could overcome their powerlessness and defeat and come back to a different, albeit equally important struggle.[184] This metamorphosis was especially intense in those leaving for western European countries such as France, Sweden, Portugal and the United Kingdom.[185] Now transformed into exiles proper, they were outside the horizons of the socialist world, living on a continent where belief in the promises of the Enlightenment and a certain civilisational narrative were still very strong. They were embraced by human rights NGOs such as Amnesty International, who remained receptive to the Brazilian cause. At this point, some exiles slowly reconsidered the belief that violence could possibly have any progressive function. Immersed in this new reality, they were more and more drawn to the ideas of the emerging green movement or the defence of universal human rights.[186]

As attorneys continued to provide support for political prisoners and relatives in Brazil, in cases more likely to draw public attention,[187] exiles participated in the Bertrand Russell tribunal on Latin America held in Rome (1974 and 1976) and Brussels (1975).[188] In 1975, members of the democratic opposition gathered 138 signatures requesting the institution of a commission of inquiry concerning violations of human rights.[189] In the same year, the demand for a state pardon for exiles and political prisoners first appeared in the *Manifesto da Mulher Brasileira pelo Movimento Feminino pela Anistia* (*The Brazilian Woman's Manifesto by the Feminists for Amnesty Movement*).[190] The appearance of the Feminists for Amnesty was a turning point. From 1977 to 1978, different groups of feminists congregated as oppositional forces towards the creation of the first Comitê Brasileiro pela Anistia (Brazilian Amnesty Committee, CBA).[191]

In the eyes of the military, the mobilisation around humanitarian issues was a clear 'defamatory campaign against Brazil, as an integral part of the psychological warfare planned by the communist movement overseas'.[192] Even for liberal officers sympathetic to the 'anxiety of relatives and friends',[193] the activists asked for too much. There would be no freedom for terrorists or sympathisers with terrorism.

Between Innocence and Utopia

The framework of human rights and the requirements of the struggle for amnesty seemed to complement each other, as a perfect fit. Most of all, the language of rights offered an impeccable mix of neutrality and non-partisanship to Brazilian activists. It allowed some feminists to claim association with 'no ideologies nor political jargons',[194] representing the struggle for amnesty as a defence of the principles of 'love, liberty and justice'[195] that 'exist in the hearts of every men (sic)'.[196] But the framework of human rights had yet another contribution, of a more practical nature. Its idea of justice was simple: due process. This vision of justice involved no revolution in the basics of society and no knowledge of the dialectic. All that it required was the political will to free those arbitrarily incarcerated and punish those responsible for committing, ordering or condoning gross violations of human rights. This justice, based on a clear and feasible idea, offered an endpoint to the endless mourning of relatives.

There was, however, one central problem, and it concerned the question of political violence. International human rights organisations had been raised under the defence of the principle of non-violence,[197] which sometimes presented a problem to political prisoners and family members. This was the case with Amnesty International's concept of prisoners of conscience. When British activists Peter Benenson and Eric Baker co-founded the movement for amnesty in 1961, the forerunner to Amnesty International, they were far from advocating for the universal and indiscriminate defence of political prisoners. The early campaigns to name and shame had very specific contours and objectives: 'to bear witness to the private suffering of nonviolent innocents'[198] and 'to demand their release on the sole ground that such suffering was *unjust*'.[199] Restricted to prisoners of conscience (those incarcerated for voicing a belief or opinion), the movement was, to put it mildly, less keen on supporting those who, at some point in time, had advocated violence in one way or another.

The non-violence caveat naturally drove a wedge between the new left and a movement that was 'unable to find a suitable prisoner in Northern Ireland'[200] and considered Nelson Mandela unworthy of support.[201] But the insistence on the question of innocence presented yet another problem, of a more serious nature. The concern to determine the worth of political prisoners with reference to the question of personal guilt represented an uncomfortable common ground between human rights activists and members of the authoritarian regime. Within military ranks and in the conservative media, the lack of innocence of those fighting against the dictatorship was constantly mobilised as some sort of distorted justification for the crimes of state terror. The guilt of the radical left was the central pillar supporting the regime's narrative of pacification, the mythology that the *Repressão* was fighting a dirty but just war against subversion.[202]And by drawing on the idea of non-violence as irreproachable, human rights activists were playing straight into the regime's mythology. Irrespective of their intentions, they ended up reinforcing, or at least they failed to repudiate, the conservative blame game that justified state terror on the basis that the other side had thrown the first stone, or in this case, that it had thrown stones at all.

Amnesty International's defence of non-violence was highly problematic for the Brazilian amnesty movement. By 1976, Amnesty International supported the 'humane treatment of all prisoners',[203] which did not go against the CBA's agenda, but also continued to endorse only the 'release of [. . .] non-violent prisoners'.[204] This policy was inconsistent with the demands of Brazilian activists for an *anistia ampla, geral e irrestrita* (ample, generalised and unrestricted amnesty): a state pardon encompassing every oppositional group (ample), releasing every victim of the *Repressão* (generalised) and punishing every state agent who committed violations of human rights (unrestricted).[205] The resonance between the ideas of innocence and moral worth and the myth of the 'dirty war' also divided activists. In the end, this unlikely common ground enabled the rearticulation of the demands for amnesty in more conservative terms. In 1979, the ruling General Figueiredo promised to send the draft of an amnesty bill to the National Congress, breaking with the previous policies of the military.[206] The dictatorship now accepted the possibility of pardoning political dissidents and exiles, under the condition that violent terrorists remained between bars.

The regime's U-turn was a response to a rather larger and more significant turn of events. By the time of the amnesty movement, the 'years of gold' were beginning to fade away as the Brazilian economy struggled to assimilate the oil shock of 1973. Foreign indebtedness was once again the response of policymakers, now more intensely seeking the dollars needed to cover balance of payment deficits (due to oil imports) in the private financial market.[207] With receding levels of growth (relative to the years of the miracle) and mounting inflationary pressures, the spectre of labour unrest was once again haunting the minds of technocrats. The struggle for amnesty had never been restricted to the defence of civil liberties. The CBAs envisioned their activism as a plural and open struggle and were keen on supporting the demands of workers.[208] What the military feared the most was the appearance of a new, united front against the regime. Conservative circles were horrified when, in 1979, a general strike of metallurgists demanding better wages was met by a nationwide hunger strike of political prisoners demanding their freedom.[209] In this context, the military's amnesty proposal was swiftly marketed as a more reasonable and pragmatic means to reconcile a wounded society.[210]

At the International Conference in Rome (1979), when survivors, exiles and relatives engaged in direct collaboration for the first time, Brazilian feminists rose up against the non-violence caveat. They advocated unreserved and unconditional solidarity with the victims of state terror. Helena Greco, one of the most prominent Feminists for Amnesty, reaffirmed the overarching and non-discriminatory terms of the CBAs: 'we cannot agree with the attempt to classify [. . .] as "terrorists" or "non-terrorists", as "guilty" or "non-guilty"'.[211] Going against the grain of the international human rights movement, she emphasised that 'all who opposed the dictatorship [. . .] deserve the same respect'.[212] At the end of the conference, this became the central tenet of the fight for amnesty in Brazil.

Discussions on the themes of innocence, worth and violence went far beyond the CBAs. They also became the central theme of an emerging memoir literature. Simultaneously to the feminist mobilisation, survivors and journalists were recounting their experiences of torture as a form of unofficial truth-seeking.[213] Of all the memoirs released during the struggles for amnesty and criminal accountability, *O que é isso, Companheiro?* (*What's going on, Comrade?*, 1979) by Fernando Gabeira is the one that most clearly articulates the emerging consensus regarding the relationship between innocence and political violence. In a very clear sense, Gabeira's life story was the story of the new left. He had first-hand experience of all the processes and metamorphoses experienced by those who took part in the armed struggle. As a former member of the MR-8, he had actively participated in the spectacular kidnapping of Charles Elbrick and escaped unharmed. After living clandestinely for a while, he was found and shot by the *Repressão*. He became a political prisoner, suffered at the hands of torturers and felt the weight of political defeat during the Brazilian diaspora (first in Algeria, then Chile and later in Sweden).

The most remarkable feature of *O que é isso, Companheiro?* is the level of humour. Gabeira's story of armed struggle is a tragicomic tale, populated by hilarious anecdotes on the verge of absurdity. Prime among these is the case of an old couple who, in the middle of an act of revolutionary expropriation, begin to argue about whether or not the militants are robbing the place. The old lady approaches a militant, who is armed with a rifle and stands guard, and kindly asks, 'Young man, you are robbing this place, aren't you?'[214] Once her suspicion is confirmed, she turns back to her husband: 'I told you, I told you, Decio, you never listen to me.'[215] Gabeira's humour masterfully plays the big stereotypes of the age, such as the monstrous torturer and the heroic freedom fighters, against a reality that more often than not turns out to be pathetic. There is the case of the torturer who cannot handle the sight of blood;[216] the case of militants who seek to overthrow a military dictatorship, but fail to assemble their weapons and showcase terrible marksmanship;[217] and, of course, the anecdotes involving the kidnapping of the American ambassador. Moments before the ambassador is bound to be released, the militants have a crisis meeting: they cannot let him go without at least buying him a souvenir. All of a sudden, the revolutionaries committed to the overthrow of the capitalist system rush through a local market in search for something suitable. They finally settle on the only book they can find in English: a pocket version of Ho Chi Minh's poems. Then, the writing of the dedication becomes a problem. Should it begin with 'Dear hostage'?[218] Gabeira's sharp, sophisticated and irreverent writing style provokes outbursts of laughter. But there is a very serious point behind all the fun. His depiction of the tragicomic struggle further problematises the humanitarian caveat regarding political violence. In *O que é isso, Companheiro?* the equation between innocence and non-violence is far from uncomplicated.

This question is clearly stated when it comes to the kidnapping of the ambassador. In one scene, Gabeira recounts a conversation between himself and Elbrick on the topic of political violence:

> Once, I talked about the Black Panthers movement. I said that I saw them with sympathetic eyes and that I believe they could represent a lot for American democracy, for the humanisation of Babylon. He disagreed. The Black Panthers were too radical and did not stand the slightest chance. Because there was a window to his left, I had my gun pointed at him. I immediately put the gun down to continue with the discussion. He realised my discomfort with the circumstances. After all, my arguments were good enough and there was no need to expose them at gunpoint. He understood that we had an uncomfortable relationship with guns. We were intellectuals, wanting to say something, while the tanks were pointed at us in Brazil. Under no circumstances would we have wished to swap places.[219]

The idea of innocence as non-violence does not disappear from the text. At times, Gabeira does describe those who did not take part in the armed struggle but were nonetheless targeted by the *Repressão* as 'the innocent'.

However, innocence also acquires a more ambiguous meaning, shifting from an association with the sphere of action (e.g. non-violent means) to the sphere of ideas (as a sign of naiveté). Gabeira could be easily placed as one of the founding fathers of a now almost unavoidable trope in the literature on political violence in Latin America: the naive revolutionary. In a sense, revolutionary naiveté is one of the central themes of his memoir, understood as the inability to act according to reality. This critical appraisal of the past is first and foremost directed at the militarisation of the political struggle. Gabeira was one of the first members of the urban guerrilla movement to publicly articulate a *mea culpa* for the resort to political violence. *O que é isso, Companheiro?* is a harsh critique of *foquismo*, described as the 'great illusion of the period'.[220] It positions the belief in the possibility of victory for the guerrilla movement without the popular support of the masses as one of the 'particular mythologies'[221] of the new left, inciting the wildest 'fantasies' of militants.[222] Time and again, the memoir describes the degrees of self-deceit that militants went through when faced with clear and unambiguous defeat. It also mourns those who were unnecessarily 'crushed by their utopian dreams'.[223] In the context of the dilemmas faced by the amnesty movement and the metamorphosis experienced during the diaspora, Gabeira provides an argument for which the very resort to violence was, in fact, the sign of a certain innocence.

O que é isso, Companheiro? was published in 1979, the year the National Congress voted in favour of the military's blanket amnesty, which triggered the dissolution of the CBAs and the reorganisation of the anti-impunity movement. According to Daniel Reis, former member of the ALN and historian of the period, the amnesty law was responsible for three fundamental silences that endured in post-transitional times: (1) the silence about human rights violations perpetrated by state agents; (2) the silence about society's connivance with state terror; and (3) the silence about the radical political project of the armed struggle.[224] It is in relation to that last silence that the diaspora and the discussions regarding violence and innocence become illustrative of a deeper, less explored meaning of the word 'disappearance'. Gabeira's mixture of humour and an overt *mea culpa* was not unanimously treasured. He faced and still faces considerable criticism from those on the left who rejected his hindsight/fatalism and also those who did not think their grief was a laughing matter. But his critique of *foquismo* as an unrealistic strategy was one step from the extrapolation that everything the left had fought for constituted an unrealistic illusion. The memoir was a huge bestseller, with more than more than 250,000 copies sold by 2009.[225] Its tone was a perfect fit for the masses of bystanders seeking to consume recent political history in a palatable way. Regardless of Gabeira's intentions, his work became the *magnum opus* of a society wishing to leave the past behind, willing to treat torture with a pinch of laughter, and eager to declare the disappearance of past 'utopias'.

Conclusion

The objective of this chapter was to ground the emergence of a post-conflictual reality and its narrow representation of violence in the contemporary history of Brazil. My intention was to offer a clear empirical and theoretical account of two historical processes that became constitutive of a post-conflictual economy of signification. The first is the widely studied phenomenon of the forced disappearance of the bodies of radical militants. The second is an often overlooked, but nonetheless related phenomenon: the disappearance, or rather, the eager proclamation of the disappearance, of the ideas these militants were fighting for. These two different but connected processes of disappearance are not restricted to the Brazilian case. Happening at different places and paces throughout the world, they helped to pave the way for the emergence of a post-conflictual reality that came to support and legitimise the mainstreaming of transitional justice.

The central theme connecting the emergence of the armed struggle, the Brazilian diaspora and the fate of the amnesty movement is a certain sense of loss. More specifically, it describes the absence of certain practices and ideas without which a 'common language of justice', based on the power of consensus, cannot stand. It draws attention to a sort of constitutive absence of the post-conflictual economy of signification, represented by two elements that cannot be incorporated by its logic: the first is the militarised reading of political struggles as armed struggles (a reading shared by the far left, the military and the far right in the 1960s); the second is the Marxist reading of the capitalist system as the constant reproduction of conflict. None of these elements can find space in a post-conflictual reality and, therefore, they needed to have their 'disappearance' proclaimed loud and clear. While the rejection of militarisation, at least by the radical left, is a cause to be celebrated, the exclusion of Marxism and, in particular, a Marxist understanding of violence, is a cause for concern. Nevertheless, as the following chapters will show, these elements that cannot be incorporated by the post-conflictual economy never really go away. Their presence remains a constant obstacle, threatening to expose the failures of the common language of justice.

Notes

1. Zerubavel, 'In the Beginning', p. 457.
2. Ibid. p. 485.
3. Marchesi and Yaffe, 'La violencia bajo la lupa', p. 95.
4. There is usually a fine line between sophisticated accounts of the language and aesthetics of revolutionary violence and an uncomfortable similarity with far-right myths such as the dirty war or the communist threat. For an example of the former see Vezzetti, *Sobre la violencia revolucionaria*; for the latter see Brands, *Latin America's Cold War*.
5. Marchesi and Yaffe, 'La violencia bajo la lupa'.
6. Osiel, 'Constructing Subversion in Argentina's Dirty War'.
7. Quijano, 'El fantasma del desarrollo en América Latina'.
8. Cardoso and Faletto, *Dependency and Development in Latin America*; Baer, 'Import Substitution and Industrialization in Latin America'; Bulmer-Thomas, *The Economic History of Latin America Since Independence*; Coatsworth, 'Structures, Endowments, and Institutions in the Economic History of Latin America'.
9. Bulmer-Thomas, *The Economic History of Latin America Since Independence*.
10. Silva, 'Brazilian Society: Continuity and Change, 1930–2000'; The World Bank World Development Indicators, 'Urban Population (% of Total)'.
11. Bulmer-Thomas, *The Economic History of Latin America Since Independence*.
12. Silva, 'Brazilian Society: Continuity and Change, 1930–2000', p. 460.
13. Bulmer-Thomas, *The Economic History of Latin America Since Independence*, p. 340.
14. Oliveira, *Crítica à Razão Dualista/O Ornitorrinco*.
15. Gaspari, *As Ilusões Armadas*.
16. Skidmore, *The Politics of Military Rule in Brazil 1964–85*, p. 7.
17. Chirio, *A Política nos Quartéis*.
18. Gaspari, *As Ilusões Armadas*; Bethell, 'Politics in Brazil under the Liberal Republic, 1945–1964'; Skidmore, *The Politics of Military Rule in Brazil 1964–85*.
19. Gaspari, *As Ilusões Armadas*.
20. Ibid.
21. Reis, 'Ditadura e Sociedade'.
22. Gaspari, *As Ilusões Armadas*.
23. Ibid.
24. Reis, 'Ditadura e Sociedade', p. 33.
25. Bethell, 'Politics in Brazil under the Liberal Republic, 1945–1964'.
26. Ibid.
27. Ibid. p. 144.
28. Chirio, *A Política nos Quartéis*.
29. Carvalho, 'Breve História do "Comunismo Democrático" no Brasil'.
30. Carvalho, 'Breve História do "Comunismo Democrático" no Brasil'; Gorender, 'Combate nas Trevas'.
31. Rollemberg, 'Esquerdas Revolucionárias e Luta Armada'.
32. Reis and Sá, *Imagens da Revolução*.
33. Rollemberg, 'Esquerdas Revolucionárias e Luta Armada'.

34. Reis and Sá, *Imagens da Revolucão*.
35. Arquidiocese de São Paulo, *Brasil: Nunca Mais*; Gorender, 'Combate nas Trevas'.
36. Bethell, 'Politics in Brazil under the Liberal Republic, 1945–1964', p. 148.
37. Rezende, *Suicídio Revolucionário*, p. 54.
38. Motta, *Em Guarda contra o 'Perigo Vermelho'*; Argolo, Ribeiro and Fortunato, *A Direita Explosiva no Brasil*.
39. Chirio, *A Política nos Quartéis*.
40. Martins Filho, 'Tortura e Ideologia'.
41. Finch, 'A Total War of the Mind'.
42. Ibid.
43. Estado Maior das Forcas Armadas, 'C-85-59', p. 2.
44. Ibid. p. 2.
45. Martins Filho, 'Tortura e Ideologia'.
46. Finch, 'A Total War of the Mind'.
47. Martins Filho, 'Tortura e Ideologia', p. 182.
48. Ibid. p. 182.
49. Bethell, 'Politics in Brazil under the Liberal Republic, 1945–1964', p. 143.
50. Estado Maior das Forcas Armadas, 'FA-E-01/61', p. 7.
51. Chirio, *A Política nos Quartéis*.
52. Bethell, 'Politics in Brazil under the Liberal Republic, 1945–1964'.
53. Chirio, *A Política nos Quartéis*.
54. Ibid.
55. Skidmore, *The Politics of Military Rule in Brazil 1964–85*, p. 17.
56. Gaspari, *As Ilusões Armadas*.
57. Skidmore, *The Politics of Military Rule in Brazil 1964–85*, p. 15.
58. Bethell, 'Politics in Brazil under the Liberal Republic, 1945–1964'.
59. Starling, *Os Senhores das Gerais*, pp. 33–4.
60. Gaspari, *As Ilusões Armadas*.
61. Chirio, *A Política nos Quartéis*.
62. Ibid.
63. Bethell, 'Politics in Brazil under the Liberal Republic, 1945–1964'.
64. Gaspari, *As Ilusões Armadas*.
65. Ibid.
66. Congresso Nacional, 'Diário do Congresso Nacional. Ano XIX: N. 154. Seção I. 25 de Agosto de 1964', 6899.
67. Chirio, *A Política nos Quartéis*.
68. Reis, 'Ditadura, Anistia e Reconciliação'.
69. Bethell, 'Politics in Brazil under the Liberal Republic, 1945–1964'.
70. Reis, 'Ditadura, Anistia e Reconciliação', p. 178. As a measure of comparison, while in Chile Pinochet's 1973 putsch caused approximately 1,000 deaths, the Brazilian coup 'only' produced seven fatal casualties. For more information see Instituto de Estudos da Violência, *Dossiê dos Mortos e Desaparecidos Poléticos a partir de 1964*; Collins, *Post-Transitional Justice*.
71. 'Ato Institucional Nº 1, de 9 de Abril de 1964', preamble.

72. In the original: 'missão de restaurar no Brasil a ordem econômica e financeira e tomar as urgentes medidas destinadas a drenar o bolsão comunista, cuja purulência já se havia infiltrado não só na cúpula do governo como nas suas dependências administrativas'. Ato Institucional N° 1, de 9 de Abril de 1964, preamble.
73. In the original: 'reconstrução econômica, financeira, política e moral do Brasil'. Ato Institucional N° 1, de 9 de Abril de 1964, preamble.
74. Colonel Martinelli cited in Chirio, *A Política nos Quartéis*, p. 90.
75. Chirio, *A Política nos Quartéis*.
76. Ridenti, *O Fantasma da Revolução Brasileira*.
77. Reis and Sá, *Imagens da Revolucão*.
78. Marighella, *Escritos de Carlos Marighella*.
79. COLINA, 'Concepção Da Luta Revolucionária (Abril 1968)'.
80. Rollemberg, *O Apoio de Cuba à Luta Armada no Brasil*, p. 15.
81. Ibid. p. 15.
82. Debray, *Révolution dans la révolution?*, p. 116.
83. Rollemberg, 'Esquerdas Revolucionárias e Luta Armada'; Gorender, 'Combate nas Trevas'.
84. Childs, 'An Historical Critique of the Emergence and Evolution of Ernesto Che Guevara's Foco Theory'.
85. Guevara, *Escritos revolucionarios*.
86. Ibid. p. 26.
87. Ibid. p. 23.
88. Childs, 'An Historical Critique of the Emergence and Evolution of Ernesto Che Guevara's Foco Theory'.
89. Ibid.
90. Gorender, 'Combate nas Trevas'.
91. Debray, *Révolution dans la révolution?*
92. Sales, 'A Ação Libertadora Nacional, a Revolução Cubana e a Luta Armada no Brasil'.
93. Betto, *Batismo de Sangue*, p. 36.
94. Skidmore, *The Politics of Military Rule in Brazil 1964–85*, p. 86.
95. Marighella, *Escritos de Carlos Marighella*, p. 9.
96. Marighella, *Escritos de Carlos Marighella*, p. 122; Ridenti, *O Fantasma da Revolução Brasileira*.
97. Rollemberg, *O Apoio de Cuba à Luta Armada no Brasil*.
98. Ibid.
99. Marchesi, 'Revolution Beyond the Sierra Maestra'; Sales, 'A Ação Libertadora Nacional, a Revolução Cubana e a Luta Armada no Brasil'.
100. Marighella, 'Minimanual of the Urban Guerrilla'.
101. Ibid.
102. For good introductions to a very long discussion see Cohen-Almagor, 'Foundations of Violence, Terror and War in the Writings of Marx, Engels, and Lenin'; Gilbert, 'Salvaging Marx from Avineri'; Avineri, 'How to Save Marx

from the Alchemists of Revolution'; Balibar, 'Reflections on "Gewalt,"'; Basso, 'The Ambivalence of Gewalt in Marx and Engels'.

103. Gorender, 'Combate nas Trevas'.
104. Ibid. p. 226.
105. Marighella, *Escritos de Carlos Marighella*, p. 9.
106. Marx, *Capital*, vol. 1.
107. Ibid. chapters 9 and 11.
108. Fanon, *The Wretched of the Earth*.
109. Sorel, *Reflections on Violence*.
110. Gorender, 'Combate nas Trevas'.
111. Marx and Engels, *Collected Works*, vol. 25.
112. Fanon, *The Wretched of the Earth*.
113. Marx, *Capital*, vol. 1.
114. POLOP, 'Programa Socialista para o Brasil (Setembro 1967)', p. 97.
115. Ibid. p. 99.
116. Ibid. p. 99.
117. PCdoB-AV, 'Os Dezesseis Pontos (Novembro 1969)', p. 279.
118. Skidmore, *The Politics of Military Rule in Brazil 1964–85*.
119. Ibid.
120. Bulmer-Thomas, *The Economic History of Latin America Since Independence*.
121. 'Lei N° 4.390, de 29 de Agosto de 1964'.
122. Oliveira, *Crítica à Razão Dualista/O Ornitorrinco*.
123. AV, 'Crítica ao Oportunismo e ao Subjetivismo da "União dos Brasileiros para Livrar o País da Crise, da Ditadura e da Ameaça Neocolonialista" (Dezembro 1967)', p. 123.
124. Marighella, *Escritos de Carlos Marighella*.
125. PCdoB, 'Manifesto-Programa (Fevereiro 1962)'.
126. Marighella, *Escritos de Carlos Marighella*.
127. Martuccelli, 'Reflexões sobre a Violência na Condição Moderna'; AP, 'Documento Base (Fevereiro 1963)'.
128. Marighella, 'Minimanual of the Urban Guerrilla', p. 71.
129. Rollemberg, *O Apoio de Cuba à Luta Armada no Brasil*.
130. Marighella, 'Minimanual of the Urban Guerrilla'.
131. Ibid. p. 71.
132. Ventura, *1968: O Ano que não Terminou*.
133. Between 1964 and 1967 the mean salary dropped approximately 17.2 per cent in Rio de Janeiro and 19.7 per cent in São Paulo. For the metalworkers of the city of João Monlevade, in the state of Minas Gerais, the loss was close to 40 per cent. See Costa, 'A Política Salarial no Brasil, 1964–1985', pp. 164–5.
134. Chirio, *A Política nos Quartéis*.
135. Gorender, 'Combate nas Trevas'.
136. Ibid.
137. ALN and MR-8, 'Manifesto da ALN e do MR-8 (1969)', p. 227.
138. Gaspari, *As Ilusões Armadas*.

139. Ridenti, *O Fantasma da Revolução Brasileira*, p. 58.
140. Gorender, 'Combate nas Trevas'.
141. Ibid.
142. ALN and MR-8, 'Manifesto da ALN e do MR-8 (1969)', p. 227.
143. Ibid. p. 228.
144. Rollemberg, 'Esquerdas Revolucionárias e Luta Armada'.
145. Chirio, *A Política nos Quartéis*; Coimbra, 'Doutrinas de Segurança Nacional'.
146. Gorender, 'Combate nas Trevas'.
147. Chirio, *A Política nos Quartéis*.
148. Ventura, *1968: O Ano que não Terminou*.
149. 'Ato Institucional N° 5, de 13 de Dezembro de 1968'.
150. Coimbra, 'Doutrinas de Segurança Nacional', p. 7.
151. Jackson, Murphy and Poynting, *Contemporary State Terrorism*, p. 5.
152. Laqueur, *The Age of Terrorism*.
153. Médici cited in Figueiredo, *Ministério do Silêncio*, p. 186.
154. Gaspari, *As Ilusões Armadas*.
155. Fico, *Como Eles Agiam*.
156. General Fiúza de Castro cited in D'Araujo, Soares and Castro, *Os Anos de Chumbo*, p. 75.
157. Arquidiocese de São Paulo, *Brasil: Nunca Mais*.
158. Ibid.
159. Ridenti, *O Fantasma da Revolução Brasileira*.
160. Gorender, 'Combate nas Trevas'.
161. Reis, *A Revolução Faltou ao Encontro*.
162. Betto, *Batismo de Sangue*.
163. A journalistic account originally speaks of the figure of 10,000; Portela, *Guerra de Guerrillas no Brasil*.
164. Instituto de Estudos da Violência, *Dossiê dos Mortos e Desaparecidos Políticos a partir de 1964*.
165. Arendt, *On Violence*.
166. Drake, 'The Role of Ideology in Terrorists' Target Selection'.
167. Ocampo, 'The Latin American Debt Crisis in Historical Perspective'.
168. Veloso, Villela and Giambiagi, 'Determinantes do "Milagre" Econômico Brasileiro (1968–1973)'; Bulmer-Thomas, *The Economic History of Latin America Since Independence*; O'Donnell, 'Reflections on the Patterns of Change in the Bureaucratic-Authoritarian State'.
169. Ridenti, *O Fantasma da Revolução Brasileira*.
170. Figueiredo, *Ministério do Silêncio*, p. 194.
171. Reis, 'Ditadura, Anistia e Reconciliação', p. 178.
172. Rollemberg, 'Nômades, Sedentários e Metamorfoses'; Paiva, 'Memórias de Uma Herança'; Cavalcanti and Ramos, *Memórias do Exílio, Brasil 1964–19??*.
173. Rollemberg, 'Exílio: Refazendo Identidades', p. 25.
174. Ibid. p. 25.
175. Ibid. p. 25; Marchesi, 'Revolution Beyond the Sierra Maestra'.

176. Rollemberg, 'Cultura Política Brasileira', p. 168.
177. Rollemberg, 'Nômades, Sedentários e Metamorfoses', p. 282.
178. Glória Ferreira cited in Rollemberg, 'Exílio: Refazendo Identidades', p. 38.
179. Panizza and Brito, 'The Politics of Human Rights in Democratic Brazil'.
180. Pereira, 'An Ugly Democracy?'
181. Teles, 'Entre o Luto e a Melancolia'; Teles, 'Políticas do Silêncio e Interditos da Memória na Transição do Consenso'.
182. Rollemberg, 'Cultura Política Brasileira', p. 164.
183. Rollemberg, 'Nômades, Sedentários e Metamorfoses'.
184. Greco, 'Anistia Anamnese vs. Anistia Amnésia'.
185. Rollemberg, 'Cultura Política Brasileira'.
186. Rollemberg speaks of the metamorphosis of Brazilian exiles as as a process in which 'provincialism gave way to cosmopolitanism [o provincialismo cedeu lugar ao cosmopolitanismo]'; Rollemberg, 'Nômades, Sedentários e Metamorfoses', p. 293. Interestingly, explanations of this metamorphosis in the literature on Latin American exiles in the late twentieth century are pervaded by culturalist undertones. The rethinking of radical left-wing positions is often read as part and parcel of a natural process of modernisation alongside the dichotomy global-liberal-advanced/local-radical-backward. According to this trope, exiles were faced with, and realised the benefits of, more civilised forms of political culture in European countries. For works on Latin American exiles, see Roniger et al., *Exile, Diaspora, and Return*; Sznajder and Roniger, *La política del destierro y el exilio en América Latina*; Markarian, *Left in Transformation*; Franco, 'Les exilés Argentins en France'.
187. Santos, 'Transitional Justice from the Margins'.
188. Greco, 'Anistia Anamnese vs. Anistia Amnésia'.
189. Gaspari, *O Sacerdote e o Feiticeiro*, p. 32.
190. Greco, 'Dimensões Fundacionais da Luta pela Anistia'.
191. Ibid.
192. Golbery do Couto e Silva cited in Gaspari, *O Sacerdote e o Feiticeiro*, p. 33.
193. Golbery do Couto e Silva cited in Gaspari, *O Sacerdote e o Feiticeiro*, p. 33.
194. Zerbine, 'Anistia Semente da Liberdade', p. 8.
195. Ibid. p. 8.
196. Ibid. p. 8.
197. Williams, *The Divided World*.
198. Hopgood, *Keepers of the Flame*, p. 62.
199. Ibid. p. 62.
200. Buchanan, '"The Truth Will Set You Free"', p. 586.
201. Williams, *The Divided World*.
202. Huggins, 'Legacies of Authoritarianism'.
203. Cited in Meirelles, 'A Anistia Internacional e o Brasil', p. 335.
204. Cited in ibid. p. 335.
205. Greco, 'Dimensões Fundacionais da Luta pela Anistia'.
206. Skidmore, *The Politics of Military Rule in Brazil 1964–85*; Gaspari, *O Sacerdote e o Feiticeiro*.

207. Bulmer-Thomas, *The Economic History of Latin America Since Independence*.
208. Greco, 'Dimensões Fundacionais da Luta pela Anistia'.
209. Ibid.
210. Ibid.
211. Greco, 2010.
212. Greco, 2010.
213. Martins Filho, 'The War of Memory'.
214. Gabeira, *O Que é Isso, Companheiro?*, p. 88.
215. Ibid. p. 88.
216. Ibid. p. 88.
217. Ibid. p. 88.
218. Ibid. p. 126.
219. In the original: 'Certa vez, falei sobre o movimento Panteras Negras. Disse que os via com muita simpatia e achava que poderiam representar muito para a democracia americana, para a humanização de Babilónia. Ele discordou. Os Panteras Negras eram muito radicais e não teriam a mínima chance. Eu estava com o revólver apontado para ele, por causa da janela à sua esquerda. Imediatamente baixei o revólver para prosseguir a discussão. Ele percebeu que fiquei perturbado em discutir nessas circunstâncias. Afinal meus argumentos eram bastante bons para que eu apontasse uma arma para o interlocutor. Ele captou muito bem a relação incómoda que tínhamos com a arma. Éramos intelectuais, querendo dizer alguma coisa, e os tanques estavam apontados contra nós, no Brasil. Não queríamos de forma alguma trocar de papel'. Gabeira, *O Que é Isso, Companheiro?*, p. 119.
220. Ibid. p. 18.
221. Ibid. p. 36.
222. Ibid. p. 36.
223. Ibid. p. 147.
224. Reis, 'Ditadura, Anistia e Reconciliação'.
225. Martins Filho, 'The War of Memory', p. 92.

CHAPTER 4

The Value of Resistance*

This chapter presents an analysis of the Resistance Memorial of São Paulo (RM-SP), a memorial whose mandate is to preserve the history of contemporary political struggles in Brazil. The RM-SP is an example of a site of memory,[1] a space 'where memories converge, condense, conflict, and define relationships between past, present, and future'.[2] Built in a former iconic site of torture, the RM-SP was one of Brazil's first public institutions to openly address the topic of political violence during the civic-military dictatorship (1964–85). In a country marked by the legacy of a blanket amnesty and the relative absence of measures of accountability, the site has become a reference centre, reaching an annual viewership of 78,000 persons on average.[3]

The RM-SP is one of the most important, but unfortunately least studied, transitional justice initiatives in Brazil. But my decision to focus on the memorial at this point in the book is also strategic. The history of the RM-SP as an institution is, in many ways, representative of the history of the Brazilian transition. Inaugurated in 2003 as an ode to liberalisation and re-inaugurated in 2009 with its current focus, the memorial's trajectory was shaped by the contextual changes of the post-transitional scene. The institutional mission statement, the architecture and the very designation of the RM-SP are witnesses to the different policies of accountability that characterised the democratic transition, from the fall of the military regime to the leftist turn in the 2000s. Put simply, the RM-SP provides the perfect shortcut to explain the history of transitional justice in Brazil, from the publication of *Brasil Nunca Mais* to the creation of the CNV.

But this is not only a historical chapter. The analysis presented here is also an investigation of the wider aspects of the particular languages

* This chapter is adapted from Furtado, Henrique Tavares, 'The Memory of Militarism and the Value of Resistance: an Analysis of the Resistance Memorial of São Paulo', *Critical Military Studies* 6, no. 3–4 (2020), 376–96, and is reproduced with permission.

that characterise the discipline of transitional justice. As a site of memory situated in the present, the RM-SP is also *a site of struggle* expressing the dilemmas of a (neo)liberal society, torn in between the *liberal* defence of democratic principles and the reorganisation of social relations according to the *neoliberal* market. In the spirit of a political economy of memory,[4] this chapter analyses how the RM-SP's duty to remember the past is contrasted with, and sometimes shaped by, the (neo)liberal urge to sanitise the present and to celebrate the future. Drawing on poststructuralist/post-Marxian critiques of representation,[5] this chapter argues that the narrative of the RM-SP is constantly held back by what I call the 'language of (neo)liberalism': the set of equivalences and differences between concepts, practices and experiences that constitutes the frame through which the past is represented and communicated to present audiences. This language affects the RM-SP in two ways: first, by introducing a temporal break between past and present that explains *present-day political violence as an abnormality*; and second, by providing a *commodified memory of resistance* whereby the values that make different struggles 'exchangeable', or equivalent, in the eyes of the present are concealed as the natural values of resistance. Together, these two effects work to render the overall narrative much less disturbing for the (neo)liberal order.

This chapter is the fruit of two short-term visits to the RM-SP in 2014 and 2018 and a series of informal meetings with the curatorial team and former political prisoners. The first section introduces the historical trajectory of the RM-SP, contextualising it in the Brazilian post-authoritarian scene. The second section investigates the RM-SP's permanent exhibition, most specifically modules A, B and C, where the exhibition deals with themes of militarism and resistance. The third section reveals the ways in which the representations and memorialisation practices at work in the RM-SP are affected by the language of (neo)liberalism. The chapter ends by proposing an interpretation of the RM-SP as a complex site of struggle; a space of remembrance in which the meanings and values attributed to the (neo)liberal order are endlessly disrupted, reinstated and reproduced.

Settling the Debt with Survivors

In 2002, the Secretariat of Culture of the State of São Paulo became the main administrator of a five-storey edifice right at the historical centre of the Latin American metropolis. This was no ordinary building. Originally raised in 1914 to house the offices of a defunct railway company,[6] from 1940 to 1983 the site had served as the headquarters of the Departamento de Ordem Política e Social (State Department of Social and Political Order, DOPS). Created in the 1920s to contain the spread of

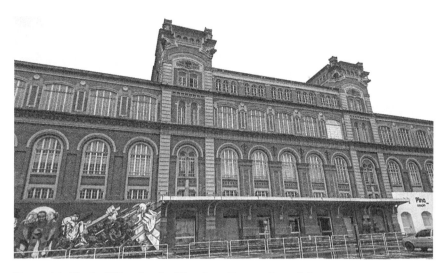

Figure 4.1 The building façade (Henrique Tavares Furtado).

anarchist strikes and the appearance of communism,[7] the DOPS functioned as a political police organisation prior to the dictatorship and was later incorporated within the structure of the *Repressão*.[8]

The DOPS has a special place in the history of political violence in Brazil. Violence was a common currency of the organisation from its early days. Officers arbitrarily incarcerated and often tortured political dissidents such as anarchists and communists, but also other individuals and groups seen as undeserving or undesirable, such as prostitutes, transvestites, the homeless and unemployed vagrants. The question of political regime mattered little in this case. Torture coexisted as easily with periods of authoritarianism (1937–45; 1964–83) as with periods of democratic rule (1945–64).[9] Nevertheless, it was during the Cold War that the DOPS became known as one of the most iconic torture chambers of São Paulo. In the early 1970s, the DOPS became the centre of a plan to reorganise the regime's counteroffensive against the urban guerrilla movement. Under the command of police deputy Sérgio Paranhos Fleury, a notorious torturer and leader of a paramilitary death squad, the state's response soon derailed into terror.[10] Underneath the beautiful high ceilings and modern façade of the early 1914 edifice, hundreds were incarcerated, mistreated, raped and eventually deemed to have 'committed suicide' or 'disappeared'.[11]

As the years passed and the threat of communism 'passed away', the military successfully bargained the terms of a long period of re-democratisation. No longer possessing an immediate *raison d'être*, the

DOPS was dismantled in 1983. The headquarters of the former political police were to host a different agency, the police department for the protection of consumer's rights, illustrating the links between political violence and economic development like no academic critique ever could. Before vacating the site, DOPS officers were careful to destroy the physical evidence of torture, scraping off the walls the inscriptions left by political prisoners.[12]

This would not be the last attempt at whitewashing the building's history in the reconciliatory atmosphere of the democratic transition. In fact, the years following the 1979 amnesty can be defined by a double sense of indebtedness. The legitimacy of the dictatorship relied on an economic policy of strong and sustained growth financed by foreign private banks. During the apex of political violence, the regime enjoyed rates of growth of 10 per cent a year, but this came with a cost. The sovereign debt, which stood at around 3 billion dollars in 1964, reached more than 95 billion dollars by 1985.[13] The return to democracy came amidst a deep economic crisis, mounting inflation and international pressures for debt repayment/rescheduling. The debt crisis not only imposed severe constraints on public policies, but it also influenced the language and symbology in which policies of accountability were framed. Unlike in Argentina and Chile, the process of re-democratisation in Brazil included no trials or truth commissions. The blanket amnesty for torturers included a tacit, unofficial policy of silence regarding the crimes of state terror. This policy of institutionalised impunity came to represent another sense of debt owed by the authorities, who remained in silence, to the victims of terror, who were denied justice.[14]

These two senses of 'debt' met in the 1990s, when policies of austerity, liberalisation and privatisation formed the background to the first official measures of accountability. Slowly but surely, the archives of the political police were made partially public[15] as state officials responded to global enthusiasm for the thematic of human rights. In 1995, President Fernando Henrique Cardoso (1995–2002) acknowledged 136 disappearances as political assassinations. This was the first time a state representative had officially recognised the crimes of the military regime. While Cardoso would not risk reviewing the amnesty law, his administration offered reparations to the families of victims and created a commission of inquiry to investigate the practice of forced disappearances.[16] The Comissão Especial sobre Mortos e Desaparecidos Políticos (Special Commission on the Dead and Political Disappeared, CEMDP) provided reparations to the families of victims ranging from R$100,000 to approximately R$150,000, based on a calculation of the victim's life expectancy.[17] Following on the footsteps of the 1993 Vienna Conference, the Cardoso administration also devised two national plans for the dissemination and protection of human rights and created a secretariat to handle the process of implementation.[18] In 2001, in the later stages of Cardoso's administration, a second commission, the Comissão de Anistia (Amnesty Commission), was created to expand the policy of reparations beyond the families of the disappeared to other groups affected by political repression.

The policy of 'settling the debt' with relatives and survivors was informed by a context of excitement about the prospects of the future and an urge to let bygones be bygones. Both the opening of archives and the reparation commissions showed a clear conciliatory streak. Although the records of political polices were slowly transferred to public archives and became accessible to individuals, Law 8.159/91 specified that documents pertaining to national security issues could remain secret for up to 200 years from the date of issue.[19] In the same vein, at the establishment of the CEMDP, Cardoso defended the amnesty law as a *sine qua non* condition for democratic coexistence.[20] Mixing a certain level of *doisladismo* (a local version of horseshoe theory preaching the false equivalence between the guerrilla movement and the armed forces) and the South African narrative of reconciliation, the president stated: 'The forgetfulness of acts practised by any sides of the political spectrum enabled the full reconstruction of democracy. Thus, the values of liberty and respect for human rights could triumph in Brazil [. . .] in this context, of a reconciled nation willing to repair injustices.'[21] His national human rights initiatives were important, but remained focused on so-called 'first generation' rights (civil and political rights), sidelining the urgent issue of inequality precisely at the time it had become the Achilles heel of neoliberal policies.[22] Importantly, the plans made no mention of transitional justice whatsoever.[23]

This reconciliatory context also affected the fate of the former DOPS. In the late 1990s the building was included in an exciting wave of urban renewal in São Paulo, reimagined as a lively cultural space.[24] It was granted cultural heritage status, but the renovation destroyed most of the DOPS, leaving the ruins of four cells as its main legacy. In the early 2000s, the State Secretariat of São Paulo decided to open a museum celebrating the successes of the Brazilian transition.[25] This new museum was named the Memorial da Liberdade (Freedom Memorial), and it was inaugurated with an exposition celebrating the legacy of human rights.[26]

Figure 4.2 The ruins of the former DOPS (Fernando Braga. Acervo Público do Estado de São Paulo).

Attempts to 'settle the debt' with survivors were not without controversy. Many activist groups regarded the policy of reparations without justice as a way of buying their silence.[27] Likewise, the association between the former DOPS and the word 'freedom' profoundly displeased survivors and the relatives of the disappeared. Maurice Politi, the president of an association of former political prisoners, explained that 'freedom was precisely the only thing you couldn't find in the DOPS'.[28] Politi's association demanded a change in focus from the celebration of freedom to the commemoration of the resistance movement against the dictatorship and the struggles of the prisoners themselves.

The demands of former prisoners benefited from an atmosphere of political change in the Southern Cone, defined by growing dissatisfaction with the consequences of the neoliberal reforms of the 1990s. Between 2003 and 2011, the Southern Cone witnessed the coming to power of left-of-centre leaders promising to roll back austerity measures, stop privatisation and address rising levels of inequality.[29] In Brazil, the rampant levels of informality and unemployment that constituted the atmosphere of neoliberal insecurity produced strong anti-neoliberal sentiments. The centre-left Workers' Party fiercely capitalised on this atmosphere, winning presidential elections against the right-leaning Social

Democracy Party in 2002, 2006, 2010 and 2014. The rise of the Workers' Party was part of a leftist turn that also promised a different politics of memory in the region. Many of the new leaders, such as Lula da Silva and Dilma Rousseff (Workers' Party), Pepe Mujica in Uruguay and Michelle Bachelet in Chile, were themselves former political prisoners. Others, like Néstor Kirchner and Cristina Fernández in Argentina, promised to overrule the country's impunity laws.

The swing to the left intensified processes of transitional justice. By the end of the decade, thousands of former agents of state had been prosecuted or were under investigation in Argentina and Chile.[30] In Brazil, the year 2007 marked a shift to a more active policy of accountability, beginning with the publication of the report of the CEMDP, *Direito à Memória e Verdade* (*The Right to Memory and Truth*). The report was facilitated by Paulo Vannuchi, a former political prisoner nominated minister of the Secretariat for Human Rights in 2005, during the Lula years (2003–10). Vannuchi's idea was to synthesise the content of previous unofficial reports into an official publication carrying the stamp of the state.[31] Moreover, the minister of human rights played an important role in incorporating the demands of activists and civil society groups towards the writing up of a new, more expansive national plan of human rights.

Another significative twist was the appointment of Paulo Abrão, an expert in transitional justice, as the new head of the Amnesty Commission.[32] Under Abrão's leadership, the members of the commission begun to make more explicit references to the goals of transitional justice.[33] In particular, they emphasised the need to re-signify the concept of amnesty, dissociating it from the regime of silence and forgetfulness that defined the Brazilian transition. For the new commissioners, the granting of amnesties was reconceptualised as an apology, a symbolic act whereby state representatives ask for forgiveness on behalf of perpetrators, recognising and accepting the existence of a preceding crime.[34] Through the project Caravanas da Anistia (Amnesty Caravans), members of staff travelled to the deep countryside, providing guidance on how to fill the commission forms, giving lectures, organising debates, holding art exhibitions and public hearings.[35] By the end of the decade the Amnesty Commission had received 70,000 requests of political amnesty, accepting 35,000, and expanding the right to reparation to 15,000 individuals.[36]

In this context, the administration of the former DOPS, then in the hands of the Pinacotheca de São Paulo (a public art gallery), started a project to remodel the Freedom Memorial in line with the demands, and with the participation of former political prisoners.[37] The memorial was renamed Memorial da Resistência (Resistance Memorial) on 1 May 2008, the same year the Brazilian bar council officially disputed the legitimacy of the amnesty law *vis-à-vis* the federal constitution.[38] The RM-SP was inaugurated on 22 September 2009 by Paulo Vannuchi. Three months later, the Secretariat for Human Rights published the 3° Programa Nacional de Direitos Humanos (3rd National Plan for Human Rights, PNDH-3). More extensive than its predecessors, this new plan contained the demands of thousands of organisations over 200 pages. PNDH-3 also broke the silence on transitional justice initiatives for the first time, announcing plans for the establishment of a truth commission.[39]

Remembering and Resisting Militarism

The RM-SP is situated within a longstanding tradition of memorialisation in Latin America: that of regarding *remembrance* as a quintessential *act of resistance*. Anchored on global narratives of transitional justice, this idea promotes the fight against state terror as a struggle to grant victims a platform to express themselves. In the context of widespread silence on past violations that often define post-authoritarian/post-conflict polities, the mere act of remembering the past becomes a form of resistance and an imperative to make sure political violence never happens again.

The inscription *lembrar é resistir* (to remember is to resist) is one of the first things visitors see when entering the RM-SP via module A (focused on the building's history). Situated on a corner wall, above the memorial's logo (a lockup grid resembling a hashtag), the inscription pays homage to a homonymous play written by Analy Álvarez and Izaías Almada and enacted in the ruins of the DOPS in 1999, in commemoration of the 20th anniversary of the amnesty of political prisoners.[40] Against the conciliatory urge to 'settle the debt' in the 1990s, the play *Lembrar é resistir* invited members of the public to witness the violence perpetrated by DOPS officers as well as the courageous acts of resistance staged by political prisoners.[41] The play emphasised the systematicity of violations of human rights during the military regime; that is, the fact that torture, extrajudicial executions and forced disappearances were not exceptional misdeeds, but a central part of the state's response to dissent.[42] Module A has other installations detailing the history of the building, but it is this inscription that produces a powerful and immediate effect, dictating the tone of the visit. By reminding visitors of the play, the inscription strengthens the links between the memorial's pathos, its political commitment to non-recurrence ('never again'), and a narrative that explicitly connects violence to the unrestrained militarisation of the state.

Figure 4.3 Module A, entrance (Pablo Di Giulio. Acervo Memorial da Resistência de São Paulo).

Module B handles the question of militarism more explicitly by situating the history of the DOPS within the development of a wider *geopolítica do controle* (geopolitics of control).[43] The module comprises one large rectangular room with a miniature model at the centre (a reconstitution of the DOPS in the 1960s based on the accounts of survivors) and two interactive screens opposite a large wall mural showing a timeline of Brazilian history (1889–2008). The interactive screens invite visitors to learn more about the rationale and the logistics behind the DOPS, carefully avoiding traditional liberal representations of political violence as the dissolution of order. Instead, the screens explain state-led violence as an expression of the modern state's drive to institutionalise its authority via the control of a given population. Political violence is discussed alongside three axes: *controle* (control or surveillance), *repressão* (political repression) and *resistência* (resistance). Visitors learn that the institutionalisation of political authority is not violence-free but involves the identification of pockets of the population whose very existence is deemed subversive of such authority. The constant surveillance and repression of these pockets, commonly seen as illiberal excesses, are described as the requirements of the continuous processes whereby control is ascertained. As every action has an

Figure 4.4 Module B, interactive screens (Pablo Di Giulio. Acervo Memorial da Resistência de São Paulo).

opposite reaction, the screens also emphasise that resistance emerges as a natural consequence of the geopolitics of control. Because state-led violence poses a constant threat to the lives of 'marginal' groups (those living at the ideological or economic margins of society), their very existence leads to acts of resistance.

The text acknowledges the role of the geopolitics of control in structuring roughly sixty years of DOPS activity, from the 1920s to the 1980s, but it also gives particular attention to the military regime (1964–85).[44] It is with this focus that Module B invites a reflection about the concept of militarism and the recent calls to bring militarism to the forefront of critical security studies.[45] Since the heyday of the study of militarism in the 1980s, there has been no single, undisputed definition of the term (see introduction). Militarism can mean an ideology that glorifies war, a simple increase in military spending and operational capacity or, in institutionalist terms, the interference of the military in the domain of public society.[46] Regardless of this fluidity of meaning, uses of the concept often evoke an element of preparation for, and the normalisation of, war as a social phenomenon.[47] Despite efforts to enrich the study of militarism by locating new manifestations of the concept in its civil-society or neo-liberal varieties,[48] war has largely remained its guiding principle, uniting different conceptualisations of the term.

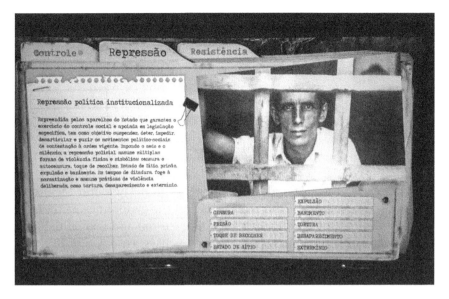

Figure 4.5 Module B, interactive screens – closer look (Henrique Tavares Furtado).

The problem is that state-led violence in the Southern Cone does not abide by this characterisation. The RM-SP's explanation for the focus on the military regime is illustrative here. Far from mentioning warfare, it simply states that 'under dictatorial rule [repression] *escapes from the norm*, assuming the form of practices of *deliberate violence* like torture, disappearances and extermination' (translated from Figure 4.5; my emphasis). This view of state-led violence is situated in between traditional liberal approaches that assume an essential separation between the state and the military, and Agamben-inspired works that argue that 'the separation [. . .] is always contingent and indeterminate'.[49] Divided between the geopolitics of control, for which political violence is always already at work, and a liberal approach, for which it is a sign of illiberalism, Module B is nonetheless unequivocal in its sidelining of war from the memory of militarism. From the perspective of the Southern Cone, militarism appears as a moment of crisis when the state's capacity to repress dissent is brought into question and a recalibration is needed. In a way that resembles critiques of pacification more than works on militarism,[50] the RM-SP treats war as part of the 'mythology' and symbolism of social control; not so much as an external phenomenon for which society needs preparation, but as a 'reality' socially fabricated to justify the radicalisation of political violence from above.

This mix of liberal and critical perspectives on political violence generates tensions and contradictions that can be seen in the large wall mural. Breathtaking in scope, the mural displays a timeline with seven rows detailing the international facts, presidents, state governors, statutes, political organisations and events of political violence during 119 years of republican history (1989–2008). The timeline shows elements of the liberal approach, marking a clear distinction between the decades of democratic rule (colour-coded in a green and yellow) and the decades of military rule (colour-coded in grey). Indeed, the order of the rows is suggestive of the centrality of the decision-making process and the question of legislation in relation to political violence. Nevertheless, the liberal frame coexists with a more critical viewpoint. The timeline is entitled 'Control, Repression and Resistance: Political Time and Memory', which reminds visitors of the central axes of the geopolitics of control. The last two rows of the timeline provide pictorial and textual descriptions of measures of control (e.g. draconian laws, emergency decrees), acts of state-led violence (e.g. the purging of public officials, extrajudicial killings, military occupations) and, at last, acts of resistance (e.g. pro-democracy demonstrations, workers' strikes).

Considered in isolation, the interplay between control, repression and resistance has the interesting effect of disturbing the centrality, maybe even the relevance, of the liberal perspective. The further away from the

Figure 4.6 Module B, the wall mural (Pablo Di Giulio. Acervo Memorial da Resistência de São Paulo).

wall we stand, as if adopting the perspective of the *longue dureé*, the more indistinguishable the green and yellow of democracy becomes from the grey of authoritarianism. This is particularly true of the years of (neo) liberalisation following the democratic opening and the retreat of the military in 1985. Instead of an abrupt end to political violence, the timeline shows a sequence of brutal events in democratic times: the assassination of environmentalist leader Chico Mendes in 1988; the slaughter of 111 inmates by the police during the Carandiru Penitentiary massacre in 1992; the killings of nineteen members of the landless workers' movement in 1996; the arrest of hundreds of Indigenous leaders boycotting the 500th anniversary of the Portuguese 'discoveries' in 2000. This chilling reminder of the violent face of Brazilian democracy is counterposed by uninterrupted acts of resistance. The Black movement in the 1880s, the anti-fascist movement in the 1930s, the urban guerrilla movement in the 1960s, the alter-globalisation movement in the 2000s – all are linked in a continuum of acts of resistance that ends with the inauguration of the RM-SP in 2009. Contrary to the standard narratives of transitional justice, this perspective enables visitors to hear the delicate echoes of a leftist reasoning for which resistance to political violence is not a thing of the past, but a struggle that goes on.

Figure 4.7 Module C, the first prison cell (Pablo Di Giulio. Acervo Memorial da Resistência de São Paulo).

Module C shifts the focus away from the historical to the personal level, recounting everyday acts of resistance by prisoners during the dictatorship. This space occupies the four remaining prison cells, restored with the help of former political prisoners. The first cell works as the institution's mission statement, recounting the events organised by staff and the links built with civil society since the inauguration of the RM-SP. This cell explains the RM-SP's main goals of promoting the historical memory of resistance and educating new generations about the authoritarian past. Here visitors are also introduced to one of the most interesting and invaluable activities of the RM-SP: the Sábados Resistentes (Defiant Saturdays), whereby members of staff organise guest talks, book launches, guided visits and other activities in order to engage the public in the thematic of political resistance.

The second cell pays homage to survivors of violations of human rights perpetrated by agents of the DOPS. In the centre of the room is a device projecting the individual stories of those 'who fought for justice and democracy' (see Figure 4.8) on a glass screen that hangs from the ceiling. The third cell is a faithful historical reconstitution based on the testimony of survivors. Everything in the cell, from the mattresses to the foul toilet,

Figure 4.8 Module C, the second prison cell (Pablo Di Giulio. Acervo Memorial da Resistência de São Paulo).

from the inscriptions carved on the walls to the hefty wooden door, is meant to provide a vivid and authentic experience of what it was like being a political prisoner. The effect works, creating a truly chilling atmosphere.

Module C also hosts one of the most beautiful and poetic parts of the RM-SP: cell number four, a space commemorating the stories of solidarity, hope and tenacity of political prisoners. At the end of the long corridor, the last cell is purposefully made darker than the other rooms, with two long wooden benches placed against the two side walls and headphone sets sitting on top of nails hammered into the walls. Here, visitors can listen to the stories of survivors, narrated by themselves, in edited testimonies collected by the curatorial team. In the middle of the room, in front of a rusty central column, is a red carnation in a transparent PET bottle, lying on top of a wooden crater. The carnation is the only thing illuminated in the room, catching the eyes of visitors once the audio begins.

Sitting on the bench in the dark cell, visitors listen to tales ranging from the abhorrent to the tragicomic, never losing sight of the red carnation, a symbol of hope turned into the room's focal point. In the recorded testimonies, different voices explain that the experience of imprisonment was not the end of their struggle –far from it. Life in a DOPS cell

Figure 4.9 Module C, the third prison cell (Henrique Tavares Furtado).

Figure 4.10 Module C, the fourth prison cell (Fotógrafo não identificado. Acervo Memorial da Resistência de São Paulo).

required the constant articulation of innovative and ingenuous everyday acts of resistance. The audio recounts how political prisoners continuously played the system against itself by using their sunbathing time to communicate with each other, preparing common stories to be told under torture. They tried to buy themselves some time at all costs, not only for the cause, but also hoping to save the lives of comrades on the regime's murder list. When the DOPS bureaucracy bluffed, setting up a no-bathing policy for weeks in order to dehumanise prisoners and break their morale, inmates raised the stakes, making the cells dirtier than even the bureaucrats themselves would accept, forcing their retreat.

The different stories of cell number four are united by a sense that humanity and hope will always prevail. In one story a survivor recounts the profound feeling of happiness and relief they felt when, years after the dictatorship, a cellmate presumed dead was found alive. In another, visitors learn about the petty, almost metaphorical, similarities between life inside and outside the DOPS. As good public servants, the DOPS agents never worked weekends, and political prisoners, just like everyone else in society, looked desperately forward to Friday nights, when their torture ended for a brief time. There are also stories of how terror was resisted with irony and the memory of loved ones, such as the story

Figure 4.11 Module C, the fourth prison cell with the red carnation (Henrique Tavares Furtado).

of a prisoner who left a message to her fiancé shortly after a torture session. Using her own blood as ink, she apologised for not having resisted the urge to confess under torture as much as she had resisted going out with him when they first met.

The experience in cell number four is not only touching because of the stories told, but also tasteful because of what it carefully omits. In an all too literal and unsubtle age, the installation touches only indirectly on the experience of torture. Mistreatment and disappearances provide the backdrop against which the stories of survivors make sense, but at no point do they become the centre of attention. There are no graphic displays of lacerated bodies or lengthy typologies of torture methods, as commonly found in the reports of commissions of inquiry. Politi explains that two concerns of former political prisoners directly influenced this choice. First, they preferred to raise public awareness without the cheap trick of naked violence (which could repel visitors or, worse, trivialise torture). Second, they felt it was important to avoid reducing the lives of survivors to their experiences of victimhood, suffering and helplessness.[51] Instead, cell number four depicts survivors in all their complexity and humanity, as individuals who faced the direst of situations without ever giving up their combination of hope and defiance.

Resistance as Currency: The Language of (Neo)liberalism

As an act performed in the present, remembering is never far detached from the socio-economic context of the present. Dwelling in the memories of the past can provide a false sense of security and stability to counter the insecurities of the ever-changing present.[52] The way individuals remember the past can itself change as a response to new conceptions of time and space, new technologies and the restructuring of economic production.[53] Memories are also mobilised in response to present concerns and political dilemmas; the past is recreated as a model, providing lessons from the present and the future.[54] Therefore, memory is often as much *about the present* as it is about the past. In the context of the Southern Cone, the memory of militarism happens in, is shaped by, and responds to a (neo)liberal context defined by an unstable relationship between two poles: the *liberal* defence of democratic principles and the *neoliberal* framing of the market as the template of all existence.

There are obvious reasons why curators make the decisions they make, impacting on the narrative of a particular exhibition. I have explained some of these decisions in the context of the RM-SP, such as the choice to include political prisoners and to leave the details of torture outside the narrative. As a public institution, the RM-SP also faces constraints that impact heavily on the story it tells. Members of staff have to find creative ways of squaring their social mission with budget constraints and even the political sensitivities of different administrations. There is also a more fundamental sense in which their memorialisation practices are shaped, or at least constrained, by the language of post-authoritarian times.

Remembrance is a representational practice. To remember something is to bypass its actual absence through an act of representation, that is, an interplay of resemblances that fabricates a sense of 'presence'.[55] As an instance of representation, memory requires a certain language with which to translate sensuous experiences into thought, speech and even complex stories.[56] The term 'language' here is not only restricted to the vernacular but refers to any system or chain of equivalences that attributes meaning to experience. The language that remembrance needs to mobilise, as it were, is also always situated in and shaped by the present. It is in this sense that memory meets the market. The relationships between words, sounds, concepts and the phenomena they describe are always inserted in wider social dynamics where the circulation of goods and people affects the circulation of signs and symbols. The constraints imposed by the market on institutions go far beyond the idea of budget constraints or the demands of those 'consuming' the memory of the past.[57] The market is also a language, operating via representational practices that determine the value of things and persons.

It makes sense to speak of a political economy of memory from the recognition that acts of remembrance and markets are instances of representation mediated by, and constitutive of, a certain language. Marxian critiques of political economy were not only preoccupied with exploitation within the sphere of production. They were also concerned with the attribution of meaning and value to things and persons in societies where production was dictated by the market.[58] For traditional Marxian critiques, the expansion of commodity production (goods produced for exchange) that characterised capitalist economies was accompanied by a general process of *commodification of life*, whereby everything and everyone was *made replaceable*.[59]

Scholars influenced by French structuralism, and to an extent Marx himself, have analysed the question of commodification through the lenses of representational practices.[60] In these works, the economic sphere appears as another language, that is, a set of equivalences between different goods (signs) that opens the possibility of trade (communication) and defines their value (meaning) according to a system of exchanges. The defining feature of commodification is the production of a certain 'fetishism': the belief that the value of goods is a representation of their own utility, according to the natural needs they fulfil, whereas, in fact, value is defined by circulation.[61] Likewise, in the sphere of representation, signs and concepts are also thought to be meaningful in themselves due to their natural relationship with the phenomena they refer to, such as 'militarism' or 'resistance'. Nonetheless, their meaning is also a function of circulation; it is not in relation to the phenomena they represent, but due to the position they occupy in a wider chain of equivalences that such concepts acquire any meaning. In other words, it is not from what they are in themselves, but from what *they are not*, in relation to other concepts, that they become intelligible.

The similarities between the two spheres do not stop there. Representational practices are also assumed to rely on a chain of production-exclusion-domination. The system of equivalences that produces meaning (value) in a given language is also a system that produces exclusion. To define a phenomenon or an event according to a system of equivalences is to repress its radical ambivalence, excluding possible meanings that could destabilise the whole language. Thus, it is via the exclusion of ambiguity and the 'repression' of indeterminacy that representational practices preserve the stability of a given language. And by preserving the stability, that is, the internal order of a given language, they also help to preserve the wider socio-political order supported by this system of equivalences.

I have already provided some ideas of how the language of (neo) liberalism shaped the memory of political violence. At the apex of neoliberal restructuring programmes, the former DOPS was envisioned as a memorial in *commemoration of freedom*. Remodelled and re-inaugurated, the RM-SP evidenced the shifts, hopes and dilemmas that characterised the Latin American turn to the left, torn between *liberal democratic* principles and *neoliberal market* imperatives. As the analysis has shown so far, the narrative of the RM-SP is pervaded by a sense of ambiguity, providing both radical and not-so-radical ways in which to remember the state-led violence and political struggles of the past. What I define here as the language of (neo)liberalism is the set of equivalences established at certain points throughout the exhibition, which work to control the radical ambiguity of the overall narrative. Paraphrasing JanMohamed,[62] this language has the effect of appropriating a certain surplus morality for the (neo)liberal present, infusing it with meaning, value and legitimacy exactly in opposition to the past.

Making use of critical perspectives, the permanent exhibition invites readings of political violence that transcend concerns with civic-military relations. In the timeline of social control, the distinction between democratic and authoritarian rule seems arbitrary at best. As I have suggested, this perception of arbitrariness could lead visitors to question the centrality of the military regime, or the centrality of militarism, in the dynamics of political violence. But the full potentiality of this reading is foreclosed by a move commonly seen in narratives of human rights and transitional justice: the need to re-establish a temporal break between a militaristic past and a democratic present, as fragile as this break may be.[63] This is where the critique of social control is suddenly transformed into a critique of militarisation; as a concept, militarisation is suggestive of a similar temporal break whereby the natural liberal order is encroached and corrupted by the principles and practices of the military.[64] It is exactly this logic that pushed the RM-SP to define the dictatorship as a moment when social control *exceeds its normal function*, adopting a systematic and deliberate use of political violence.

The equivalence between the military regime and the idea of abnormality has the effect, intended or otherwise, of normalising the present liberal order. Hence, the radical effect that cases of present-day violence could have, in terms of subverting the liberal narrative, is tamed via the suggestion that they constitute an *abnormality*: not a direct consequence of neoliberalism, exclusion and insecurity, but an authoritarian remnant of militarism; the sign of an incomplete transition. Any association between state-led violence and the fabrication of the politico-economic order,[65] such as the fact that the DOPS persecuted beggars, vagrants and prostitutes as much as anarchists, is shifted to the background of the narrative. The memory of political violence is translated into a language that assigns meaning and value to the present exactly in opposition to the illiberal and militarised past. Excluded from any disturbing links with the present context, seen almost as an anachronism, political violence loses its uncomfortable complexity and becomes palatable to (neo)liberal audiences.

There is a second way in which the radical potentiality of the RM-SP is held back. The duty to keep the memory of political struggles alive is constantly unsettled by a certain process of commodification: a tendency to delimit the scope of what resistance could possibly mean. The RM-SP shows a commendable effort to democratise resistance, linking the struggles of former political prisoners with those of peasants, Indigenous people, human rights and anti-globalisation activists. The equivalence between acts of resistance has a progressive effect, emphasising the urgency of an ethics and practice of resistance based on plural struggles in the present. But again, this radical replaceability is constantly subjected to the risk of commodification: the confusion of the plurality of values associated with resistance for that which makes them all equivalent in the eyes of the liberal present (as an opposition to militarism/ illiberalism).

The risk of commodification is particularly clear in the way the dynamics of social control are translated into the chronology of surveillance-repression-resistance. In this chronology, the moment of resistance appears mainly as a reactive act; that is, in the strict sense of an act in reaction to original breaks of the natural liberal order (the military coup, disappearances, present-day massacres). While the reading of resistance as an act in the form of dissent is very clear (and accessible to wider audiences), the complex reasons why individuals resisted are less so. The exposition refers to the ideals of *justice and democracy*, but their possible meanings are never explored. Justice and democracy could be associated with that which the *neoliberal present lacks* as much as with that which the *liberal present provides*. The risk of commodification is, therefore, expressed by a twist that superimposes the latter onto the former; a moment when resistance is tamed, becoming synonymous with the defence of the present order.

Conclusion

Through the advocacy of former political prisoners and the hard work of its curatorial team, the RM-SP became one of the most important centres for the preservation of the memory of state-led violence in Brazil. The memorial's permanent exhibition offers a privileged point from which to start a conversation between the field of critical military studies and accounts of state-led violence from the Global South. The RM-SP invites an interesting reassessment of the concept of militarism, the centrality often assigned to the phenomenon of war and the possibility of analysing political violence from the perspective of a geopolitics of control. The site also excels at preserving and disseminating an account of resistance based on everyday experiences of former political prisoners without trivialising the pain and suffering they endured or victimising them. On both accounts, the RM-SP is a commendable institution, committed to the deepening and strengthening of Brazilian democracy.

But sites of memory are always also sites of struggle. The duty to keep the memory of the past alive is never detached from the struggle to avoid the risk of commodification in the present. As institutions that rely on representational practices mediated by systems of equivalence, memorials are always at risk of reducing the radical ambiguity of what they represent. When it comes to the RM-SP, the central paradox faced by curators is that, in order to keep the memory of political prisoners alive and to communicate it in an accessible way, they must translate it into the language of the (neo)liberal present. Sometimes, this is masterfully done through the setting of equivalences between political struggles across time, or the immediate connection created between prisoners and visitors by the centrality assigned to the themes of humanity and hope. Other times, the language employed risks reproducing an unreflective legitimation of the present political order. This is what happens when the narrative re-establishes the centrality of civic-military relations in the analysis of political violence; it is also what happens when the concept of resistance is dissociated from its subversive value.

Notes

1. Nora, 'Between Memory and History'.
2. Davis and Starn, 'Introduction: Memory and Counter-Memory', p. 3.
3. Maurice Politi, personal interview, 4 July 2014.
4. Allen, 'The Poverty of Memory'.
5. Baudrillard, *For a Critique of the Political Economy of the Sign*; Žižek, *The Sublime Object of Ideology*; Rancière, *The Emancipated Spectator*; Laclau and Mouffe, *Hegemony and Socialist Strategy*.

6. Gumieri, 'Espaços de Memória'; Gumieri, 'O Memorial da Resistência de São Paulo'.
7. Gumieri, 'Espaços de Memória'; Gumieri, 'O Memorial da Resistência de São Paulo'.
8. Skidmore, *The Politics of Military Rule in Brazil 1964–85*; D'Araujo, Soares and Castro, *A Volta aos Quartéis*.
9. D'Araujo, Soares and Castro, *Os Anos de Chumbo*.
10. Ibid.
11. Atencio, 'Acts of Witnessing'.
12. Ibid.
13. Instituto de Pesquisa Economica Aplicada, 'Ipeadata: Dívida Externa Registrada'.
14. Bilbija and Payne, 'Introduction. Time Is Money'.
15. Catela, 'Do Segredo à Verdade . . .'.
16. Mezarobba, *Um Acerto de Contas com o Futuro*; Mezarobba, 'Entre Reparações, Meias Verdades e Impunidade'.
17. Comissão Especial sobre Mortos e Desaparecidos Políticos, *Direito à Memória e à Verdade*.
18. Pinheiro and Neto, 'Direitos Humanos No Brasil Perspectivas No Final Do Século'.
19. *Lei Nº 8.159, de 8 de Janeiro de 1991*, Art. 23, paragraph 3.
20. Cardoso, 'Assinatura do Projeto de Lei sobre Desaparecidos Políticos', pp. 257–8.
21. In the original: 'O esquecimento dos atos praticados por qualquer dos lados do espectro político permitiu a plena reconstrução da democracia. Com isso, os valores da liberdade e do respeito aos direitos humanos puderam triunfar no Brasil [. . .] nesse contexto, de uma Nação reconciliada e desejosa de reparar injustiças'.
22. Adorno, 'História e Desventura'; Pinheiro and Neto, 'Direitos Humanos no Brasil Perspectivas no Final do Século'; Pinheiro and Neto, 'Programa Nacional de Direitos Humanos'; Neto, 'Programa Nacional de Direitos Humanos'.
23. Adorno, 'História e Desventura'.
24. Menezes and Neves, 'Rotas para um novo Destino'.
25. Gumieri, 'O Memorial da Resistência de São Paulo'; Soares and Quinalha, 'Lugares de Memória no Cenário Brasileiro de Justiça de Transição'.
26. Menezes and Neves, 'Rotas para um Novo Destino'.
27. Francisco Calmon, personal interview, 9 July 2014; Vitoria Grabois, personal interview, 22 July 2014.
28. Politi, personal interview, 4 July 2014.
29. Grugel and Riggirozzi, 'Post-Neoliberalism in Latin America'; Arditi, 'Arguments about the Left Turns in Latin America'; Beasley-Murray, Cameron and Hershberg, 'Latin America's Left Turns: An Introduction'; Cameron, 'Latin America's Left Turns: Beyond Good and Bad'; French, 'Understanding the Politics of Latin America's Plural Lefts (Chávez/Lula)'.
30. Collins, Balardini and Burt, 'Mapping Perpetrator Prosecutions in Latin America'.
31. Vannuchi, personal interview, 17 January 2018.
32. Santos, 'Transitional Justice from the Margins'.

33. Ibid.
34. Silva Filho, 'Dever de Memória e a Construção da História Viva'; Abrão and Torelly, 'Justiça de Transição No Brasil'.
35. Coelho and Rotta, *Caravanas da Anistia*; Silva Filho, 'O Anjo da História e a Memória das Vítimas'.
36. Coelho and Rotta, *Caravanas da Anistia*.
37. Seixas and Politi, 'Os Elos que Vinculam as Vivências Encarceradas com as Perspectivas de Comunicação Museológica'.
38. Schneider, 'Impunity in Post-Authoritarian Brazil'.
39. Secretaria de Direitos Humanos da Presidência da República, *Programa Nacional de Direitos Humanos (PNDH -3)*.
40. Atencio, 'Acts of Witnessing'.
41. Ibid.
42. Ibid.
43. Carneiro, 'Caixa de Pandora'.
44. Ibid.
45. Mabee and Vucetic, 'Varieties of Militarism'; Stavrianakis and Selby, 'Militarism and International Relations in the Twenty-First Century'; Shaw, 'Twenty-First Century Militarism'; Ferguson, 'The Sublime Object of Militarism'; Basham, 'Raising an Army'; Howell, 'Forget "Militarization"'.
46. Stavrianakis and Selby, 'Militarism and International Relations in the Twenty-First Century'.
47. Mann, 'The Roots and Contradictions of Modem Militarism'; Stavrianakis and Stern, 'Militarism and Security'.
48. Mabee and Vucetic, 'Varieties of Militarism'.
49. Ibid. p. 101.
50. Neocleous, *The Fabrication of Social Order*; Neocleous, '"A Brighter and Nicer New Life"'; Neocleous, 'Security, Commodity, Fetishism'; Kienscherf, 'Beyond Militarization and Repression'; Kienscherf, 'A Programme of Global Pacification.
51. Lacerda, '"Victim": What Is Hidden behind This Word?'; Baines, '"Today, I Want to Speak Out the Truth"'; Humphrey, 'From Victim to Victimhood'; McEvoy and McConnachie, 'Victims and Transitional Justice'.
52. Edkins, *Trauma and the Memory of Politics*; Nora, 'Between Memory and History'.
53. Huyssen, *Present Past*.
54. Zehfuss, *Wounds of Memory*.
55. Ricoeur, *Memory, History, Forgetting*.
56. Halbwachs, *On Collective Memory*; Freud, *The Complete Psychological Works of Sigmund Freud*, vol. 4; Freud, *The Complete Psychological Works of Sigmund Freud*, vol. 5.
57. Bilbija and Payne, 'Introduction. Time Is Money'.
58. Marx, *Capital*, vol. 1; Debord, *The Society of the Spectacle*; Horkheimer and Adorno, *Dialectic of Enlightenment*.
59. Lijster, '"All Reification Is a Forgetting"'.
60. Baudrillard, *For a Critique of the Political Economy of the Sign*; Žižek, *The Sublime Object of Ideology*; Rancière, *The Emancipated Spectator*.

61. Baudrillard, *For a Critique of the Political Economy of the Sign*; Žižek, *The Sublime Object of Ideology*.
62. Abdul JanMohamed, 'The Economy of Manichean Allegory'.
63. Meister, *After Evil*.
64. Howell, 'Forget "Militarization"'; Kienscherf, 'Beyond Militarization and Repression'.
65. Neocleous, *The Fabrication of Social Order*.

CHAPTER 5

The Search for Truth

The previous chapters have offered a historical account of the long struggle for truth, memory and justice in Brazil. Chapter 3 begins by recounting the history of the 1964 coup, the emergence of the armed struggle and the ensuing Years of Lead (1968–74), when state agents systematically resorted to GVHRs against political dissidents. I have explained how the regime's gruesome tactics, in particular the forced disappearances, had unforeseen consequences that contributed to the fall of the dictatorship. By 'disappearing' members of clandestine organisations, the regime paved the way for the appearance of another movement of resistance: the mothers, daughters and partners who, in the absence of bodies and death certificates, were unable to mourn their loved ones. In this atmosphere, when personal grief became politicised, the Feminists for Amnesty (1975) spearheaded a nationwide movement demanding the amnesty of exiles and political prisoners and the punishment of perpetrators. This movement was frustrated by the 1979 unilateral amnesty passed by the military. The chapter also traced the long march towards the institutionalisation of the right to the truth in Brazil, from the first unofficial attempts to break with the regime of silence that followed the amnesty law (1985), to the officially sanctioned national plans for human rights (1996, 2002, 2009).

This exercise of historical contextualisation was driven by a central goal; I wanted to show that HROs operating in Brazil during the transition were not only seeking the *implementation* of justice but, in a disciplinary and ideological sense, were also creating the *conditions of possibility* for such justice. By framing their demands in the language of human rights and tactically promoting the imperatives of international law, they associated their struggle with the tenets of an emerging discipline. A discipline that, as part of a larger ideological field described in Chapter 3, was partially responsible for *disciplining* the political transition by defining what counted as unacceptable violence, delimiting the goals of justice and drawing the boundaries of the promise of 'never again'. These practices also had their own unintended consequences: if the authoritarian regime 'disappeared' the bodies of radical leftist militants, it was the unreflective acceptance of the liberal and humanitarian vocabularies that, in a sense, 'disappeared' their radical project of deep structural change. In the following chapters, I investigate how this double process of disappearances, the vanishing of bodies and of ideas, still affects present-day truth-seeking and the seemingly never-ending quest for justice in Brazil.

This chapter analyses the CNV's 'failure' to deliver the longstanding demands of HRAs concerning truth (knowledge about GVHRs), memory (acknowledgement of state terror) and justice (the prosecution of perpetrators). In the first section I provide a brief overview of the truth commission, disclosing its mandate, organisational structure, sources of funding and size of membership as well as the disparities between the international and domestic responses to the final report. The second section investigates the relationship between the CNV and HRAs, focusing on recurrent critiques that truth-seeking was mishandled in Brazil. This section also discusses the internal tensions and the methodological decisions that affected the work of commissioners and technical advisors, including the CNV's theory of truth and its representation of truth-seeking as an archaeological enterprise. The third section re-inscribes the CNV's 'failure' as a failure of transitional justice's twenty-first-century or 'common-language' approach, which merged the contradictory goals of criminal accountability and reconciliation. By analysing the efforts of the CNV, in particular the reconciliation of the armed forces with society, I explain that the 'failure' of justice in Brazil goes well beyond a mere case of mismanagement. My objective is to show how the implementation of transitional justice processes is intimately connected to the theoretical possibilities delimited by the discipline and the larger ideological field these processes mobilise.

The National Truth Commission (CNV)

After decades of political pressure from HROs – including the mobilisation of the IACHR, which lead to a condemnation by the IACtHR in 2010[1] – the Brazilian state created a truth commission on 18 November 2011 as an official policy for the implementation of the right to memory and truth. The CNV was charged with the investigation of GVHRs – 'illegal and arbitrary detentions; torture and other inhumane, cruel or degrading

penalties; summary, arbitrary and extrajudicial executions; and forced disappearances, contemplated in cases where the mortal remains were concealed'[2] – committed between the years of 1946 and 1988.[3] Envisioned as
a measure for the defence of basic human rights in the present, the truth
commission was expected to draw lessons from the past towards a future
of non-recurrence. The CNV was based in the Federal District (Brasília)
and funded by the Brazilian presidency. Although there is little information regarding this aspect of truth-seeking in the final report, federal law
shows that by the end of the CNV's mandate, the budget amounted to
R$19.3 million (approximately $5 million as of 2015).[4] As for human
capital, the *colegiado* or coordinating board of the CNV originally comprised seven members, all Brazilians and mostly individuals identified
with the cause of human rights, and fourteen technical advisors.[5] As time
progressed and the enormity of the commission's task became apparent,
the number of technical advisors jumped from fourteen to twenty-five.[6]
In the end, the final report listed 245 members, including technical advisors, researchers and independent experts.[7]

The staff were allocated into three sub-commissions: (1) research,
generation and systematisation of information; (2) civil society and
institutional relations; and (3) external communications. Each sub-commission was further divided into thirteen thematic working groups.[8] The
CNV enjoyed a strong network of international support. Commissioners
were granted access to archives in Argentina, Chile, Paraguay, Germany
and the former Czech Republic, and even to classified documents from
the US State Department. They liaised with recognised experts like José
Zalaquett[9] and received technical support from the ICTJ.[10] The CNV also
signed a cooperation agreement with the UNPD, through which fifty-
nine new technical advisors' posts were advertised by 28 February 2014.[11]

Perhaps the most innovative aspect of the Brazilian experience was
the process dubbed 'capillarisation', or the dissemination of truth-seeking.[12] Following the establishment of the CNV, around one hundred
sub-national commissions were created nationwide. Working at all levels of the federation (states and municipalities), across the three powers
(executive, legislative and judiciary) and in the public and private sectors
(universities and professional organisations), these bodies were sponta-
neously created and operated independently from the national commission. Around thirty of them ended up working in collaboration with the
CNV, so as to prevent multiple investigations from overlapping.[13]

The CNV was originally granted a two-year mandate,[14] but again things
had to change in the face of a series of structural and organisational challenges. The mandate was extended by seven months in May 2014 to allow

appropriate time for the writing up of the final report,[15] released on 10 December 2014 (International Human Rights Day). This highly anticipated report was immediately made available online, on the commission's website.[16] Its extensive historical recollection and legal analysis was presented in three volumes: 976 pages presenting the CNV's official narrative of the violent past, alongside recommendations for the enhancement of human rights (volume 1); over 400 pages of thematic essays produced under the responsibility of technical advisors (volume 2); and a 2,000-page biographical account of the killed and disappeared (volume 3). Physical copies of the three volumes were delivered to President Rousseff during an official ceremony held at the presidency's headquarters in Brasilia. Celebrating both the international date and the completion of the CNV's work, Rousseff offered the official report as a tribute to 'all the women and men of the world who have fought for liberty and democracy'.[17]

Outside the country, the response to the final report could not have been better. The text was praised within the circles of international advocacy as yet another achievement of the global fight against impunity.[18] According to well-known experts, the CNV 'scored a six on the seven-point scale'[19] regarding the general quality of truth commissions worldwide. In Brazil, however, the results were not so unanimously acclaimed. Indeed, some activists saw the mere fact that a truth commission was finally implemented as excellent.[20] But for many others, expectations were not met. For HRAs, the CNV was a parody of their struggle: a non-ideal[21] form of redress that by respecting the amnesty law was merely bound to deliver what was conveniently possible.[22] Voicing their extreme frustration[23] throughout the commission's mandate, HRAs still viewed the CNV as just another expression of a longstanding strategy of political forgetfulness.[24] Even independent experts who ended up collaborating with the CNV were at some point displeased. Their discontent ranged from comparisons between truth-seeking and the Greek myth of Sisyphus[25] (who was forced by the gods to roll a giant rock uphill only to watch it roll back again, eternally) and the feeling that transitional justice had, despite the best of efforts, failed Brazilian society.[26]

Between Criticisms and Contradictory Demands

The criticism of HRAs focuses on the primary (and primarily superficial) aspect of truth-seeking: an analysis of its practical operation connected to the conditions of implementation of post-authoritarian justice. From the beginning to the end, and all over the political spectrum, the Brazilian government was accused of mishandling the implementation of the CNV.

Criticism abounded about the absence of a vital preparatory time before the beginning of the mandate; the political composition of the CNV's *colegiado*; and the alienation of HRAs from truth-seeking. Most of the criticism was compiled by the periodic reports of the *Instituto de Estudos da Religião* (Institute of Religion Studies, ISER) an NGO based in Rio de Janeiro that closely monitored the CNV. According to ISER, the commission's working methodology seemed to follow a make-it-up-as-you-go-along rule of thumb. Almost seven months after its legal creation, the CNV still lacked an internal charter. Until July 2012, the truth commission remained unstructured and its members remained without more substantial guidelines concerning their mandate, duties and activities.[27] As late as November 2012, almost a year after the law that created the CNV was passed, members of staff were still establishing new working groups on different possible themes of research.[28] These organisational measures, at such a late stage, suggest an initial void in the space between the commission's legal creation (18 November 2011) and its effective establishment (16 May 2012). By the time members of the *colegiado* were appointed by the president, very little had been done, or at least publicly advertised, in terms of planning and preparation.

The absence of a clear, preconceived plan significantly affected the CNV's initial activities. According to the testimonies collected by ISER researchers (alongside their own impressions), the first half of the commissioner's mandate was permeated by an embarrassing sense of disorganisation.[29] According to HRAs who attended the first public events organised by the CNV, the commission's agenda sounded, first, unclear. The fact that public hearings were often scheduled shortly after newspaper reports raised criticisms that 'the media seemed to play a central role in orienting the CNV and its decision-making concerning the steps of investigation'.[30] Second, the meetings were repeatedly criticised for basic faults such as 'last-minute bookings; the partial presence of staff members; little time for civil society speakers; confusing objectives'.[31] There were even complaints about the quick invention of ad hoc coffee breaks as soon as controversial issues were raised.[32]

Besides the question of disorganisation, the CNV was also affected by what one advisor defined as a high level of internal friction.[33] The first cause of this friction concerned its political neutrality. Neutrality had been, from the beginning, a very real concern. Law 12.528/2011 defined impartiality as a *sine qua non* condition for holding a commissioner position.[34] During the CNV's inauguration, the president herself insisted she 'was not moved by personal criteria or subjective evaluations'[35] when selecting members of the *colegiado*. And this idea of political neutrality displeased some activists. In the very early stages, one of the commissioners appointed by Rousseff pushed the boundaries of non-partisanship too far. In a newspaper interview, Gilson Dipp, then coordinator of the CNV's *colegiado*, revived the controversial concept of *doisladismo* (two-sidedness). Committing a capital mistake, Dipp pondered the possibility of looking at both sides of the story.[36] The remark was the last straw, saturating activists' discomfort with the text of Law 12.528/2011. The text had originally left unaddressed whether survivors from the radical left would also be investigated by the commission.

For HROs, this was preposterous. To speak of 'both sides' is to accept the fiction created by the military dictatorships in the Southern Cone; the supposed threat of insurgency used to justify the widespread use of VHRs as the means to wage a dirty but necessary war against communist subversion. To speak of both sides is to forget the imbalance of power between the armed forces and the armed struggle and to conveniently overlook the fact that Brazil had never endured a civil war,[37] but had witnessed a massacre.[38] Furthermore, even if HRAs were to accept this fiction, the distasteful suggestion that truth-seeking should encompass the actions of radical leftists was off limits. HRAs could never accept the investigation of individuals who had already been thoroughly investigated by the political police, who had been judged without a semblance of due process and, in numerous cases, executed by agents of state still enjoying impunity.[39] Outraged, HROs urged the withdrawing of any remnants of *doisladismo* from the activities of the CNV, including Dipp's resignation.[40] This strong refusal echoed within the CNV, as other members of the *colegiado* reaffirmed the commitment to only 'investigate the conduct of these delinquents, the ruffians who compromised the institutions they served'.[41] In response, the internal charter of the CNV was reformulated in August 2012, when the qualifier violations perpetrated by state agents was added to the commission's mandate.[42] Gilson Dipp distanced himself from the CNV in September of the same year, ostensibly for health reasons. He would officially announce his resignation in April 2013.[43]

The CNV also suffered from the lack of a clear leadership role.[44] There was no clarity about how decisions were to be made, or by whom. This offered fertile ground for the entrenchment of different camps within the *colegiado*, holding opposing methodological views. During the first year of the CNV's mandate, one particular episode reached the news: the alleged dispute involving the *colegiado* members Claudio Fonteles and Paulo Sérgio Pinheiro concerning the CNV's relationship with HROs and the general public. In the capacity of coordinator, Fonteles released a series of twenty-four short essays entitled *Exercitando o diálogo* (*Practising Dialogue*) – revealing the ongoing research of the working groups. Appearing as a frank enthusiast of a pluralist form of truth-seeking where 'everyone, together, would get involved, everlastingly, in the defence of democracy',[45] he came to be celebrated by HRAs as the best of the whole lot.[46] Allegedly, this vision of truth-seeking clashed with the vision of other commissioners, like Pinheiro himself, who disliked the unfinished and rough style of Fonteles' essays. This camp believed that truth-seeking should follow a rigorous format and present robust findings in a finished report, at the end of the CNV's mandate. Despite much noise, the parties to the quarrel hardly spoke of it in public. In fact, the episode was handled in a tabloid-like way by the Brazilian press, devoted to squeezing every single drop of intrigue out of a controversial topic. The case ended with Fonteles' voluntary resignation in June 2013 due to personal reasons.[47]

Regardless of its anecdotal nature, the dispute between Fonteles and Pinheiro does point to the theory of truth-seeking adopted by the CNV. Unlike the South African TRC, and similar to other Southern Cone commissions, the CNV's report does not discuss but rather assumes what constitutes the 'truth' about the past. However, one can see in the language with which the CNV described its own work a theory of truth-seeking and truth-telling connected to the discipline of transitional justice. In the first place, the commission repeated the common liberal humanitarian vision of official remembrance and policies of redress as the *opposite of forgetting or denial*.[48] At the CNV's inauguration ceremony, the presidency endorsed this opposition by regarding truth as the opposite of forgetfulness.[49] Referring back to what she claimed as a millenary Hellenistic heritage, Rousseff defined truth as a force that could not be hidden nor prevented by tyranny.[50] This distinction between truth (the object of knowledge) and tyranny (a metaphor for power) also replicates a common trope in liberal circles, and consequentially in the transitional justice literature, concerning neutrality and non-partisanship: the idea that truth-seeking involves telling truth to power,[51] in other words, that it is an act of resistance *par excellence*.

In 2013, the Special Secretariat for Social Communications of the Brazilian presidency (Secom) released a public campaign featuring the CNV and in celebration of the international day for the right to the truth. On 24 March, Secom published an advert in the largest-circulation newspapers explaining the role of the CNV and calling for contributions from individuals in possession of any evidence about HRVs in the past. Interestingly, but unsurprisingly, those responsible for designing the advert chose to depict the past as a jigsaw puzzle.[52] Once again, this is a common trope in the literature. For transitional justice scholars and practitioners, the apolitical practice of truth-seeking resembles a puzzle-solving exercise; it involves gathering 'pre-shaped jigsaw pieces of memory that refer to a completed picture, a completed narrative'.[53] Secom's piece reproduced this idea word by word: it explained that 'The truth commission exists so as to complete the [missing] pieces [of the past] and clarify what happened between 1946 and 1988,' ending with a witty slogan: 'Truth Commission. Here to complete our history. Truthfully.'

It is almost a settled tradition in the Southern Cone that efforts for truth-seeking and truth-telling should focus on the search for, the opening or the preservation of archives.[54] In this context, the jigsaw puzzle metaphor went beyond the sphere of public relations. Commissioners themselves adopted the metaphor on plenty of occasions, adding their own twist. They framed the missing pieces of truth as the archaeological remnants of Brazil's political past.[55] Seeing truth-seeking as an archaeology is very illustrative of an understanding of its ensuing practice. As an archaeology, the search for truth must be meticulous, intricate and at times exhaustive. It requires extreme attention to what is said 'in between lines, in the headers, in the subtleness and scattered details of documentary sources'.[56] In line with the standards set by *Brasil: Nunca Mais*, this practice demands a level of objectivity that dismisses, above all, charges of partisanship and revenge. Archaeologists are concerned with material vestiges from the past, disregarding other subjective sources. But the archaeological metaphor has yet another benefit: it implies a technocratic understanding of truth-seeking. Archaeology demands a set of skills and know-how beyond the grasp of the uninitiated. This technocratic element helps to accommodate the theme of 'speaking truth to power' by dissociating the former from the latter. It is a liberal commonplace that experts never do politics, they merely do their jobs.

It is not hard to see how this vision of truth-seeking can lead to a series of contradictions. Truth-seeking should be, at the same time, an act of resistance and apolitical; a means to provide victims a voice[57] but also technocratic; and an investigation that rejects the idea of two sides, but is non-partisan. In the end, these contradictions negatively affected the CNV's work and its relationship with HROs. From the beginning, HRAs questioned the CNV's focus on material evident to the detriment of personal testimonies.[58] The commission was criticised for remaining distant to civil society,[59] for its excessive academic formality[60] and lack of transparency.[61]

On 21 May 2013, the CNV released a partial report in response to the demands of HRAs and intellectuals, which was received by the public as an expected but nonetheless unfortunate disappointment. Critics pointed out that the twenty-page report resembled a 'cover letter'[62] stating 'more of a future project of information-management [. . .] than of current data processing'.[63] Perhaps more importantly, the report spelled out the CNV's hierarchy of methods. While its archival research seemed solid (the report provided a thorough map of the archives of political repression), the CNV disclosed it had only held fifteen public hearings[64] and collected 268 testimonies[65] in the span of a whole year: half of its original mandate. This hierarchy, as it were, would continue to define the CNV's working methodology. In the end, the commission organised seventy-five public hearings,[66] collecting a meagre 1,116 testimonies.[67] As a measure of comparison, CONADEP took around 7,000 testimonies in six months;[68] the CAVR received 7,669 statements;[69] and the South African TRC listened to over 21,000 individuals.[70] Those who were supposed to be given a voice also figured very little in the final report, where testimonies were used mostly for the sake of supporting hard evidence, in quotations or in chapter epigraphs. It is hard to say for certain what caused this detachment between the CNV and HRAs. But it is equally hard to dismiss the clear links between the commission's image of truth-seeking, involving a technocratic, objective and neutral practice, and the secondary role assigned to individual testimonies (which struggled to fit in any of these demands).

The 'Failure' of the Common Language

The final report places the CNV in the 'strict list of truth commissions whose work was justified based on the exercise of the right to the truth'.[71] As seen in previous chapters, the right to the truth assumes a holistic 'common language' of justice whereby the fight against *impunity* (justice as criminal accountability) is inextricably connected with the fight against *obliviousness* (justice as historical acknowledgement). This idea progressively emerged as a means to protect the imperative for retribution from the challenges of projects of reconciliation. Once knowledge became a right indissociable from the right to justice, two things followed: 'truth' could never again stand for a second-best form of justice (minimalist reconciliation) nor be bargained with for the sake of national healing (maximalist reconciliation).

The long trajectory of the right to the truth overlapped with a time when peacebuilding was envisioned in more all-encompassing terms.

Part of the reason this new right emerged as jurisprudence in the IACtHR was to fight back against attempts to dissociate between retribution and restoration. Since the 1990s, several transitional interventions designed to promote criminal accountability in the aftermath have kept the trope of reconciliation intact. The Rwandan and the Yugoslavian tribunals, the ICC, the CARV and the Sierra Leone TRC (among others) have maintained that the pursuance of justice (as the joint enforcement of criminal and historical accountability) leads to an endpoint of national reconciliation. This new 'common language' of justice devised to assist a new global agenda for peace posed a holistic methodology that moved beyond previously intractable positions.[72] Holding 'the conviction that historical truth has not only the affirmation of justice, but also the preparation of national reconciliation as its main objective'[73] and in line with 'the imperatives of international human rights law',[74] the CNV was inserted at the heart of this new transitional jurisprudence. And, in many senses, this is what makes Brazil such an interesting case. We must situate the contradictory demands of the CNV's theory of truth-seeking with the limits of a 'common' language of justice that has 'moved beyond problematic dichotomies that characterized'[75] transitional justice but has 'not entirely resolved major dilemmas'.[76]

The Burden of Time

The best way to reveal these contradictions is to judge the CNV's work on its own terms, or rather, on the terms of HRAs: the demands of truth (knowledge), memory (acknowledgement) and justice (criminal accountability). In relation to truth (knowledge), the CNV faced a logical, or rather chronological, abyss. As a 'delayed' transitional intervention, the Brazilian truth commission was separated in time from the actual political transition by almost three decades of rich unofficial and official forms of truth-seeking. In this context, knowledge meant *unavailable, new information*. A more-of-the-same approach simply does not work. HRAs often emphasise that their story is always told, one way or another,[77] pointing towards the need to know what the other side did.[78] In their eyes, the temporal lag works against truth-seeking in a very simple way. Whatever findings the final report could disclose would be contrasted with an overwhelming background of old information (a story that had been told, one way or another). To compensate, the CNV would have to stand out, over and above more than twenty years of research in a two-year mandate. From the beginning, the prospects were very low.

Against the odds, staff carried out ninety-eight visits to public and institutional archives[79] and, in the end, made 100,000 digitalised documents available online.[80] On many occasions, their efforts were fruitful. The CNV discovered small public archives that had previously been thought destroyed,[81] and recovered 'new' lawsuits and microfilm documentation that could potentially help future investigations.[82] It also retrieved the private archive of a deceased veteran, willingly offered to the CNV by his family.[83] The CNV's international channels of cooperation also proved vital; in German archives the commissioners collected 3,500 documents concerning the surveillance of 'undesirable' Brazilians during the Cold War.[84] And, in a remarkable move, the Obama administration accepted the CNV's request to declassify more than 600 documents that were shipped to Brazil in a series of three instalments.[85]

Other times, however, what seemed like bombastic revelations led to disappointing results. Pressed by HRAs, the CNV investigated the deaths of two former presidents who opposed the dictatorship: Juscelino Kubitschek (who died on 22 August 1976) and Jango (who died on 6 December 1976). Both deaths occurred in a short period of time alongside the death of a third political leader of the oppositional moment, Carlos Lacerda (who died on 21 May 1977). Hence, they raised suspicions over a coordinated plot to eliminate the leaders (or potential symbols) of political dissidence in the Southern Cone.[86] Stirring up the controversy, another truth commission in São Paulo publicly declared Kubitschek the victim of a political assassination.[87] However, further investigations commissioned by the CNV contradicted the São Paulo commission, stressing the absence of 'any material element capable of even suggesting that former president Juscelino Kubitschek de Oliveira and Geraldo Ribeiro [his driver] were assassinated, victims of intentional homicide'.[88] Jango's case was more complex. A former Uruguayan veteran suggested Jango's medicines were adulterated during his time in exile, causing a poison-induced heart attack. In this case, verification involved an exhumation, anthropological analysis and further laboratorial tests looking for any traces of poisoning. Notwithstanding all of this, the results were inconclusive.[89] But the biggest disappointment concerned the fate of the disappeared. Since the 1970s, only thirty-three mortal remains had been recovered, leaving 210 victims still missing.[90] Politically sold as a form of remembrance that concedes no space for oblivion, the CNV was only capable of identifying and recovering the mortal remains of a single victim, Epaminondas Gomes de Oliveira, a community leader disappeared in 1971.[91]

It is easy to confuse the question of truth (knowledge) with another important demand of HRAs, the question of official memory (acknowledgement). With little prospect of obtaining any substantial new information, the CNV still relied on 'the symbolic recognition of what is already known but was officially denied'.[92] Here, the truth commission achieved better results. While its hierarchy of truth-seeking largely failed to give victims a voice, it offered a strong official endorsement of the historical memory of the defeated. As the third official institution to validate the memory of state terrorism, the CNV ensured a commitment to humanitarianism by the Brazilian state, at least to a certain extent. The CNV raised the number of recognised victims of the dictatorship to 434.[93] It produced twenty-one forensic reports countering previous versions of the authoritarian regime about the assassination of dissidents,[94] for which it was widely praised. Staff also requested new obituaries for major, public cases of death under incarceration, putting an end to falsified official accounts of suicides and runaways. The most emblematic case concerned Vladmir (Vlado) Herzog's new obituary. Herzog was a journalist accused of having connections with the PCB by conservative MPs in 1975. He was subpoenaed by the political police to clarify his ties with the clandestine organisation. Herzog voluntarily walked into a police station in São Paulo (the DOI-CODI of the II Army) but he never walked out. State agents claimed Herzog had hanged himself after the session of so-called interrogations, a version later refuted by the CNV's forensics. Proving Vlado's suicide had been forged by the authorities, the CNV requested a change in the official cause of his death to 'deceased due to mistreatment'. The new document was promptly delivered to Vlado's family.[95]

The decision to reopen Jango's grave, a necessary step for investigating his supposed assassination, was also a big symbolic moment. In a complex joint operation involving the Federal Public Prosecutor's Office, the presidency and an international forensics team, Jango's mortal remains were carefully exhumed and transported over a distance of 2,000 kilometres to the capital.[96] Once in Brasília, the mortal remains of the president deposed by the 1964 coup were received with military honours in a ceremony broadcast nationwide. Towards the end of the ceremony, President Rousseff laid a wreath of white flowers upon Jango's coffin and presented the former first lady with the Brazilian flag. The commemoration performed a symbolic refusal of the conservative historical version of 1964 as a legitimate 'revolution'. In a sense, the event carried the implicit tone of an official apology (perhaps not from the military, some of whom looked visibly uncomfortable, but from Rousseff, their commander in chief). When the president returned the flag covering Jango's coffin to his widow, she was also returning their legitimacy; the idea that they were and would always be remembered as the country's rightful president and first lady.

The CNV also sought an overt apology, this time directly from the armed forces. In 2014, prior to the writing up of the final report, the

CNV launched a series of reconnaissance visits to military facilities identified as previous sites of GVHRs. In total, the commission investigated seven military facilities belonging to the *Repressão*'s apparatus: three DOI-CODI, the army's military village, the 12th Infantry battalion, Galeão Airbase, and the Ilha das Flores naval base. Besides identifying the loci of past mistreatments, the reconnaissance expeditions also functioned as another means to objectively override the memory of 1964 as a 'revolution' and of the so-called dirty war as a just war against terrorism. The conclusions were released in a partial report where the pattern of violations was found to be *inconsistent with the original purpose of the military facilities*. According to the CNV, these facilities – belonging to the Brazilian state – possessed an original determination to defend the public good and ensure the 'satisfaction of society's general necessities'.[97] Instead, they were *misused* for the systematic GVHRs of political dissidents, *which significantly deviated* from these determinations.

The Response of the Military

Seen as the first step to promote the reconciliation with the armed forces,[98] the partial report was used to support an official solicitation issued directly to the Ministry of Defence. Via *Ofício n° 124/2014*, the CNV specifically requested the opening of internal administrative investigations by the high commands of the army, navy and the air force on the aforementioned charges. The need for clarification was based on a simple question: 'How was it possible to employ [the facilities] for purposes other than their original ones?'[99] This exchange between the CNV and the armed forces is very interesting. It reveals the limits of the synthesis between retribution and the idea of political reconciliation, and also suggests a different meaning of 'reconciliation' associated with the archaeological metaphor.

On the eve of the 50th anniversary of the military coup, the Ministry of Defence communicated its acceptance of the request. Investigations were to be established and should proceed according to the determinations of the truth commission.[100] Such a positive response was cherished by the staff. On 1 April, the CNV released a public note praising the military for 'an extremely important gesture [. . .] that could represent a great step forward in the investigation of gross violations of human rights'.[101] The response of the armed forces crushed this hope. In June, the command of the three forces denied any grounds for supporting the accusation of misuse of public facilities in the past. Lieutenant-Brigadier Saito blamed the difficulties posed by the passage of time,[102] nonetheless stating that Galeão's airbase had never diverged from its public duty: the provision of support to stationed units. Vice Admiral Luz Filho also dismissed accusations that Ilha das Flores naval base had deviated from the defence of the public good. He emphasised that the base – turned into a prison during the dictatorship – functioned in strict conformity with the National Security Law.[103] Finally, General Peri affirmed the DOI-CODI system had been created in the 1970s for the purpose of 'combating subversion and terrorism [. . .] there being no records of the employment [of such facilities] for ends other than those originally assigned'.[104]

Albeit somehow expected, the response outraged members of the CNV, putting the minister of defence (a civilian extremely cooperative with truth-seeking) in a difficult situation. Seemingly astonished, members of staff required further clarification; how could the armed forces ignore *objective facts*, denying the occurrence of GVHRs in their own facilities?[105] The minister of defence, himself a former diplomat, responded that, looking carefully, no force had either denied or confirmed these objective facts.[106] This response sheds light on the idea of national reconciliation behind the CNV's investigation; behind the expectation that acknowledgement would create a future of reconciliation with the armed forces. This form of reconciliation is very different from the minimalist idea of 'justice' within the realms of the possible, and also from the maximalist belief in mutually coexistent truths. Anchored in and working for the excavation of past state terror (the archaeological metaphor) and towards the purpose of criminalisation (a regime of forensic truth), 'national reconciliation' has less to do with the production of *consensus* than with the *assimilation* and *acceptance* of a factual occurrence. This form of 'reconciliation' requires compromises not only of a political nature, but also at the order of interpretation.

From a theoretical perspective, this is but a consequence of the discipline's 'common language' and its conflation between historical and forensic 'justice'. The CNV asserted the *objective* fact that those incarcerated by the military regime were murdered by agents of the state; it commemorated the *objective* fact that the rightful ruler of the Brazilian people was the one democratically elected (Jango); and it requested an explanation from the armed forces for their *objective* deviation from the determination of protecting the Brazilian people. Those were not frivolous claims; on the contrary, commissioners openly disavowed theories they believed were lacking in empirical support. These conclusions that qualified national reconciliation were based on a rigorous method of *neutral* and impartial truth-seeking. They were ensured by a centralised and technocratic truth commission. And it is here that the theoretical architecture of the common language of justice reveals a fissure: The CNV's project of reconciliation failed. However, it did not fail only because the military was extremely uncooperative (although that was certainly the case), but also because of a weary, liberal belief that *neutrality* would inevitably bring about *a common ground of reconciliatory policies.*

The liberal ideological field indiscriminately amalgamates different (and opposing) aspects of *neutrality*. We can conceive of neutrality as a methodological imperative, or, in Rousseff's own words, the absence of any personal criteria or subjective considerations spoiling the investigations. In this case, neutrality is coterminous with *objectivity*. Otherwise, we can also think of neutrality as a political stance, an *impartial* attitude privileging no side of a dispute. In this case, referring again to Rousseff's words, neutrality opposes the drive towards revenge. As I have explained, the 'common language' of transitional justice works by merging forensic and historical 'truths', thereby equating these two different forms of neutrality. Without going into intricate debates in the philosophy of science and historiography, from the aspect of forensic truth, *there is one and only one objective truth.* Everything that cannot be proven via an objective assessment of a given situation (via a neutral methodology independent from each part's interpretation of the event) cannot be true. The problem is, from the aspect of historical truth (the representation of historical events) the question of interpretation plays a massive role. Events (such as the Brazilian dictatorship) generate a move towards 'identification, description, determination, interpretation on the basis of a horizon of anticipation, knowledge, naming, and so on [. . .] that remains evasive, open, indeterminate'.[107] They depend on historical representations that inevitably leave behind an unrepresented residue, an outside, *another possible representation.* And even though anti-impunity struggles drew on the concept of *objective neutrality* (from *Brasil Nunca Mais* to the CNV), its advocates could never relinquish a representation of the past as a period of state terror – a representation that was not only based on objective, forensic evidence but on the necessarily partisan description of the Brazilian 'years of gold' in the 1970s as 'years of lead', torture and assassination.

The idea of a common language of justice, based on the interchangeability between retribution and reconciliation, is misleading because it overlooks this fundamental distinction. Because the fight towards 'historical justice' (the acknowledgement of *violence as violations*) and the fight towards 'forensic justice' (the prosecution of *perpetrators of misdeeds*), once merged, offer no space for 'reconciliation' in the terms of the South African TRC, as the coexistence of multiple truths. Because neither of these goals, even when supported by an objective methodology, supposed a non-partisan account of the past. On the contrary, there can be no middle ground founded on forensic evidence alone; the effort to 'plainly reconcile them [the military] with Brazilian society'[108] is indissociable from the 'imperative acknowledgment, by the armed forces, of their institutional responsibility'.[109] In this misleading 'common language of justice', not only were the armed forces required to acknowledge their role in the violent past (which they in fact did) but to acknowledge their role as an instance of state terror (which they refused to do, exploring loopholes with a touch of cynicism). Determined to support their historical, institutional account of the so-called just war, the armed forces reinforced the version of the 1964 'revolution' as an internal war *against terrorism and subversion*. An internal war that did not deviate from the purpose of protecting the public wellbeing (as the CNV suggested), but was, in their understanding, waged precisely to protect the nation against the communist infection. The armed forces, and in particular the army, never denied that violence took place. What they refused to do was to acknowledge *violence as violations*; that is, as a distortion of their original determination and as a misuse of their authority. A chilling reminder that a certain authoritarian imaginary had outlived authoritarianism. After the end of the CNV's mandate, prominent members of the armed forces came to publicly denouncing the final report as ideologically biased.[110]

With the response of the armed forces, the commission lost its trump card. Bound by the amnesty law and without prosecutorial powers, the CNV could only recommend future action. There were, however, a few gains in terms of justice (criminal accountability). First, and for the first time in Brazilian history, the state recognised the names of 377 state agents who had been held responsible for gross violations of human rights in the past. The CNV situated these names alongside three different degrees of responsibility: (1) a politico-institutional responsibility for the doctrine behind repression; (2) responsibility over the control of the procedures in which violations of human rights were perpetrated; and (3) responsibility for the direct authorship of violations.[111] In reprisal, a group of veterans' associations released the names of 126 state agents who allegedly lost their lives due to leftist violence (the list included officers killed by friendly fire and, tragicomically, an officer who turned out to be alive).[112]

Conclusion

In terms of practical implementation, the CNV fell short of satisfactory. The lack of preparation time, internal divisions and a technocratic take on truth-seeking alienated the commission's historical bases of support, affecting its results and reception. However, an analysis at the level of conditions of implementation leads to a simple question: would things have *turned out differently* had the conditions *also been different*? Suppose the CNV was implemented in an immaculate manner, precisely as international handbooks on transitional justice recommend. Suppose it was given a six-month period to organise an internal charter and a clear methodology, and, in this period, it had built up consensus within its ranks. Would the results have been different? Would the CNV have been able to ensure an end to impunity were it not for the wide political bargain that curtailed its powers? This is the peculiarity of analyses of implementation. Because they assume a relation of exteriority between the intervention (a truth commission) and its goal (truth, justice and reconciliation) they inevitably lead to a certain level of speculation. Rigorously speaking, there is no evidence pointing to an affirmative answer in any of the questions above. And, to say that yes, truth, justice, and reconciliation would have been delivered 'were the CNV not the CNV' is nothing but an article of faith.

Moving away from criticisms of the CNV as a 'failure' or as a 'mishandled' intervention towards the conditions of possibility of post-conflict or post-authoritarian justice is a paramount move. This move is important because it questions a simple analysis of specific transitional cases as individual, isolated processes. It also comes with a political decision to stop outsourcing responsibility for the failure of justice to those handling concrete cases. It is a move that focuses on the relationship between specific practices and the general discipline they abide by. In the Brazilian case, this means that the 'failure' to promote retribution or restoration is to be blamed on international standards as much as it is to be blamed on the implementation of the CNV. It was a failure that speaks of the irreducible limits of a 'common language' of justice that presents mutually exclusive choices and of a liberal ideological field oblivious to the differences between neutrality and non-partisanship.

We can ask the same question again. Could things have been different? Maybe. I affirmed earlier that, from the beginning, the CNV was unlikely to produce any new information about the past. This is not completely true. There was at least one way to potentially produce ground-breaking revelations: by opening the archives of the armed forces. Had the commission decided to investigate 'both sides' or had it implemented a more dialogical or social theory of truth-seeking (as in South Africa), maybe the military would have cooperated. But then again, all we are left with is speculation – a form of speculation that sounds offensive and obscene to those whose loved ones were treated as 'terrorists', and presupposes a false equivalence between militarism to the left and the right. What we can know, given the way things developed, is that the archaeological merging between 'forensic' and 'historical' truth dismissed this possibility. Incapable of seeing the differences between different ideas of neutrality, unresolved between retribution and restoration, the CNV was either seen as 'ideologically contaminated' – by those it was supposed to reconcile – or a vain 'labour of Sisyphus' – by those it was supposed to empower.

Notes

1. *Case of Gomes Lund et al. ('Guerrilha Do Araguaia') v. Brazil.*
2. In the original: 'detenções ilegais e arbitrárias; tortura e outros tratamentos ou penas cruéis, desumanos ou degradantes; execuções sumárias, arbitrárias e extrajudiciais; e desaparecimentos forçados, contemplados, aqui, os casos de ocultação de cadáveres.' Comissão Nacional da Verdade, *Relatório da Comissão Nacional da Verdade*, vol. 1, p. 38.
3. *Lei No 12.528, de 18 de Novembro de 2011*, Art. 1º.
4. *Lei Nº 12.952, de 20 de Janeiro de 2014; Lei Nº 12.798, de 04 de Abril de 2013; Lei Nº 13.115, de 20 de Abril de 2015.*
5. *Lei No 12.528, de 18 de Novembro de 2011*, Art. 9.
6. 'Resolução Nº 8, de 4 de Março de 2013'.
7. Comissão Nacional da Verdade, *Relatório da Comissão Nacional da Verdade*, vol. 1, p. 43.
8. 'Comissão da Verdade Define Estratégias de Funcionamento e Estrutura'.
9. 'CNV Vai ao Chile Apurar Cooperação entre Ditaduras'.
10. Comissão Nacional da Verdade, *Relatório da Comissão Nacional da Verdade*, vol. 1, p. 70.
11. 'Acordo de Cooperação Técnica Internacional com o PNUD'.
12. Institutos de Estudos da Religião, *Um Ano de Comissão da Verdade.*
13. *Resolução Nº 4, de 17 de Setembro de 2012*, edição ext.
14. *Lei No 12.528, de 18 de Novembro de 2011.*
15. 'Nota sobre a Prorrogação do Mandato da CNV'.
16. 'Relatório da Comissão Nacional da Verdade'.
17. In the original: 'a todas as mulheres e homens do mundo que lutaram pela liberdade e pela democracia'. Rousseff, 'Discurso da Presidenta da República, Dilma Rousseff, durante Entrega do Relatório Final da Comissão Nacional da Verdade'.
18. 'Secretary-General's Message on the Occasion of the Presentation of the Final Report of the Brazilian National Commission of Truth'; 'OHCHR Statement on Brazilian Truth Commission's Final Report'; 'Brazil: Truth Commission Opens Route to Justice for Victims of Military Rule'.
19. Sikkink and Marchesi, 'Nothing but the Truth'.

20. Rubinho Gomes, personal interview, 17 July 2014.
21. Calmon, personal interview, 9 July 2014.
22. Monteiro, 'Comissão da Verdade ou Comissão do Possível?'.
23. Grabois, personal interview, 22 July 2014.
24. Greco, '50 Anos do Golpe Militar/35 Anos da Lei de Anistia'.
25. Teles and Quinalha, 'O Trabalho de Sísifo Da Comissão Nacional Da Verdade'.
26. José Luiz del Roio, personal interview, 17 January 2018.
27. *Resolução Nº 1, de 2 de Julho de 2012.*
28. *Resolução Nº 5, de 5 de Novembro de 2012.*
29. Institutos de Estudos da Religião, *Comissão Nacional da Verdade: Balanços e Perspectivas da Finalização de Seu Processo Político-Institucional*; Institutos de Estudos da Religião, 'I Relatório Semestral de Acompanhamento da Comissão Nacional da Verdade (Maio a Novembro de 2012): Documento-Base para Discussão'; Institutos de Estudos da Religião, 'III Relatório de Monitoramento da Comissão Nacional da Verdade'; Institutos de Estudos da Religião, *Um Ano de Comissão da Verdade*.
30. In the original: 'a mídia parece desempenhar um papel central na orientação dos trabalhos da CNV e em suas tomadas de decisão sobre seus passos investigativos'. Institutos de Estudos da Religião, 'I Relatório Semestral de Acompanhamento da Comissão Nacional da Verdade (Maio a Novembro de 2012): Documento-Base para Discussão', p. 34.
31. In the original: 'pouca antecedência de agendamentos; presença parcial dos comissionados; pouco tempo de fala para participantes; objetivos confusos'. Institutos de Estudos da Religião, *Um Ano de Comissão da Verdade: Contribuições Críticas para o Debate Público (II Relatório de Monitoramento da Comissão Nacional da Verdade)*, p. 22.
32. Calmon, personal interview, 9 July 2014.
33. Antonio Mesplé, phone interview, 6 January 2018.
34. *Lei No 12.528, de 18 de Novembro de 2011*, Art. 2, paragraph 1, ii.
35. In the original: 'Ao convidar os sete brasileiros que aqui estão e que integrarão a Comissão da Verdade, não fui movida por critérios pessoais nem por avaliações subjetivas'. Rousseff, 'Discurso da Presidenta da República, Dilma Rousseff, na Cerimônia de Instalação da Comissão da Verdade – Brasília/DF'.
36. 'Comissão da Verdade Deve Analisar Os Dois Lados, Diz Integrante'.
37. Calmon, personal interview, 9 July 2014.
38. Politi, personal interview, 4 July 2014.
39. Grabois, personal interview, 22 July 2014.
40. 'Comitês Protocolam Demandas a Comissão Nacional da Verdade'.
41. In the original: 'Nossa função é apurar as condutas desses delinquentes, fascínoras que comprometeram as instituições a que serviam'. 'Havendo Precedentes, Comissão da Verdade Pedirá Novas Retificações de Óbitos, Como a de Herzog, Afirma Fonteles no RJ'.
42. *Resolução Nº 2, de 20 de Agosto de 2012.*
43. 'Por Motivo de Saúde, Gilson Dipp Deixa Comissão da Verdade'.

44. Mesplé, phone interview, 6 January 2018.
45. 'Textos de Claudio Fonteles: Exercitando o Diálogo'.
46. Calmon, personal interview, 9 July 2014.
47. In the original: 'o objetivo desse diálogo é que todos, juntos, nos envolvamos, perenemente, na defesa da Democracia'. 'Claudio Fonteles Anucia Saída da Comissão da Verdade'.
48. Eastmond and Selimovic, 'Silence as Possibility in Postwar Everyday Life'; Malksoo, '"Memory Must Be Defended"'; Misztal, *Theories of Social Remembering*; Obradovic-Wochnik, 'The "Silent Dilemma" of Transitional Justice'; Zehfuss, *Wounds of Memory*.
49. Rousseff, 'Discurso da Presidenta da República, Dilma Rousseff, na Cerimônia de Instalação da Comissão da Verdade – Brasília/DF'.
50. Ibid.
51. Douzinas, *Human Rights and Empire*; Gready, *The Era of Transitional Justice*; Richmond, 'The Problem of Peace'.
52. The image can be found at: 'Secom: Comissão da Verdade'.
53. Humphrey, 'From Terror to Trauma', p. 11.
54. Bickford, 'The Archival Imperative'; Collins, *Post-Transitional Justice*.
55. Pinheiro and Pereira, 'Comissão Nacional da Verdade, CNV, e os Arquivos'.
56. In the original: 'deve-se estar-se atento às entrelinhas, aos cabeçalhos, às sutilezas e aos detalhes dessas fontes documentais'. Pinheiro and Pereira, 'Comissão Nacional da Verdade, CNV, e os Arquivos'.
57. Pinheiro, 'Apresentação de Paulo Sérgio Pinheiro no Seminário sobre o Primeiro Ano de Trabalho da Comissão Nacional da Verdade'.
58. Institutos de Estudos da Religião, 'III Relatório de Monitoramento da Comissão Nacional da Verdade', p. 71.
59. Institutos de Estudos da Religião, *Comissão Nacional da Verdade: Balanços e Perspectivas da Finalização de Seu Processo Político-Institucional*, p. 138.
60. Ibid. p. 83.
61. Ibid. p. 138.
62. In the original: 'O relatório acaba assumindo caráter de carta de intenções'. Teles and Quinalha, 'O Trabalho de Sísifo da Comissão Nacional da Verdade'.
63. In the original: 'o que parece apontar mais para um projeto futuro de gestão da informação e do conhecimento produzido pela CNV do que para um atual processamento de dados'. Institutos de Estudos da Religião, *Um Ano de Comissão da Verdade: Contribuições Críticas para o Debate Público (II Relatório de Monitoramento da Comissão Nacional da Verdade)*, p. 103.
64. Comissão Nacional da Verdade, *Balanço Atividades: 1 Ano de Comissão Nacional da Verdade*.
65. Ibid. p. 11.
66. Comissão Nacional da Verdade, *Relatório da Comissão Nacional da Verdade*, vol. 1, p. 43.
67. Ibid. p. 55.
68. Hayner, *Unspeakable Truths*, p. 46.

69. Ibid. p. 40.
70. Ibid. p. 28.
71. In the original: 'coloca a CNV no restrito rol das comissões da verdade cujo funcionamento foi justificado com base no exercício do direito à verdade'. Comissão Nacional da Verdade, *Relatório da Comissão Nacional da Verdade*, vol. 1, p. 34.
72. Roht-Arriaza and Mariezcurrena, *Transitional Justice in the Twenty-First Century*.
73. In the original: 'Baseia-se na convicção de que a verdade histórica tem como objetivo não somente a afirmação da justiça, mas também preparar a reconciliação nacional'. 'Nota Oficial da CNV 50 Anos do Golpe de 64'.
74. In the original: 'adequar os trabalhos da CNV aos imperativos do direito internacional dos direitos humanos e seus corolários'. Comissão Nacional da Verdade, *Relatório da Comissão Nacional da Verdade*, vol. 1, p. 36.
75. Leebaw, 'The Irreconcilable Goals of Transitional Justice', p. 106.
76. Ibid. p. 106.
77. Grabois, personal interview, 22 July 2014.
78. Grabois, personal interview, 22 July 2014.
79. Comissão Nacional da Verdade, *Relatório da Comissão Nacional da Verdade*, vol. 1, p. 53.
80. 'Comissão Nacional da Verdade Entrega Relatório Final ao Arquivo Nacional'.
81. 'Comissão da Verdade Pede que Governo de MG Tome Medidas para Conservar Documentos da Ditadura'.
82. 'Trabalho Conjunto da CNV e da Petrobras Localiza Acervo na Estatal'.
83. 'Comissão Nacional da Verdade Recebe Complemento de Documentação Recolhida no Rio Grande do Sul'.
84. 'Alemanha Vai Cooperar com a Comissão da Verdade'.
85. 'Documentos Recebidos dos EUA'.
86. 'CNV, MPF-RS e SDH Conduzem Exumação dos Restos Mortais de João Goulart'.
87. 'Juscelino Kubitschek Foi Assassinado, Conclui a Comissão da Verdade de SP'.
88. In the original: 'Não há nos documentos, laudos e fotografias trazidos para a presente análise qualquer elemento material que, sequer, sugira que o ex-Presidente JUSCELINO KUBITSCHEK DE OLIVEIRA e GERALDO RIBEIRO tenham sido assassinados, vítimas de homicídio doloso'. Comissão Nacional da Verdade, *Relatório Preliminar de Pesquisa: O Caso Juscelino Kubitschek*, pp. 8–9.
89. Comissão Nacional da Verdade, *Relatório da Comissão Nacional da Verdade*, vol. 1, p. 79.
90. Ibid. p. 500.
91. Ibid. p. 55.
92. Cohen, *States of Denial*, p. 13.
93. Comissão Nacional da Verdade, *Relatório da Comissão Nacional da Verdade*, vol. 1, p. 68.
94. Ibid. p. 53.
95. Santos, 'Transitional Justice from the Margins'.
96. 'Brasília Sedia Reunião Técnica sobre a Exumação de Jango'; 'CNV, MPF-RS e SDH Conduzem Exumação dos Restos Mortais de João Goulart'.

97. In the original: 'satisfação das necessidades gerais da sociedade'. Comissão Nacional da Verdade, 'Ofício Nº 124 de, 18 de Fevereiro de 2014'.

98. 'Ex-Presos Políticos Reconhecem Local de Tortura na Antiga 1ª. Cia de PE da Vila Militar'.

99. In the original: 'De que forma se tomou possível o uso para fins diversos dos da destínação?' Comissão Nacional da Verdade, 'Ofício Nº 124 de, 18 de Fevereiro de 2014'.

100. Ministério da Defesa, 'Ofício Nº 3329/MD'.

101. In the original: 'é um gesto muito importante das Forças Armadas, que pode representar um grande avanço para a apuração das graves violações de direitos humanos ocorridas durante o regime militar'. 'Forças Armadas Aceitam Investigar Centros de Tortura'.

102. Comando da Aeronáutica, 'Ofício Nº 386/GCL/7618'.

103. Força Naval, 'Fis Nº 260 M.Defesa/SG/SEORI/DEADI/DIPOD/PGA'.

104. In the original: 'combater a subversão e o terrorismo [. . .] não havendo qualquer registro de utilização para fins diferente do que lhes tenha sido atribuído'. Exército Brasileiro, 'Ofício Nº 027-A2.2.1/A2/GaCcmtEx. EB: 64536.013874/2014-75', p. 36.

105. Comissão Nacional da Verdade, 'Ofício Nº 585/2014-Cnv'.

106. Ministério da Defesa, 'Ofício Nº 10944/Gabinete'.

107. Borradori, Derrida and Habermas, *Philosophy in a Time of Terror*, pp. 90–1.

108. In the original: 'consolidando em base permanente o compromisso dos militares com o Estado democrático de Direito, e reconciliando-os plenamente com a sociedade brasileira'. Dallari, 'Verdade, Memória e Reconciliação'.

109. In the original: 'é imperativo que haja, por parte das Forças Armadas, o reconhecimento de sua responsabilidade institucional'. Dallari, 'Verdade, Memória e Reconciliação'.

110. 'Comissão da Verdade Deixa Uma Grande Mágoa, Diz General'.

111. Comissão Nacional da Verdade, *Relatório da Comissão Nacional da Verdade*, vol. 1, p. 844.

112. 'Lista de Vítimas da Esquesda Tem Ex-PM ainda Vivo'.

CHAPTER 6

The Enclosure of Blame

In Chapter 5 I analysed the implementation of the CNV (2012–14), focusing on the challenges and problems faced during the commission's mandate as well as its alleged failure to deliver truth, justice and reconciliation. In this chapter I move away from the conditions of implementation of justice to its conditions of possibility: the historical and logical assumptions grounding the works of transitional justice mechanisms. This chapter investigates the shape and substance given to the promise of 'never again' in the Brazilian case; in other words, it seeks to clarify what exactly the Brazilian truth commission meant by justice. Therefore, the chapter focuses on the set of recommendations provided in the end of the first volume of the CNV's final report.

The final report of the CNV is an impressive historical document. The text narrates with rigour and overwhelming breadth the socio-political foundations, the ideological origins and the most perverse consequences of political repression in Brazil. As a historical document, it expresses the longstanding demands of survivors and family members for accountability. Any critique of the truth commission must acknowledge these facts to avoid falling into vulgar historical revisionism, right-wing sophistry or pure nonsense. But even a sympathetic critique, such as the present one, must be critical at some level. It must point out the blind spots, the internal contradictions and the political consequences that can always be drawn from even the most important of historical documents. In the present case, the point is to identify how the recommendations of the CNV ended up incurring two fundamental problems: (1) the unreflective acceptance of logical assumptions dear to the discipline of transitional justice and (2) the reproduction of a limited, parsimonious promise of justice that overlooks the complexity of violence in Brazil. The thesis presented here is that these two problems are indicative of what I call the *economy of anti-impunity*: a set of assumptions about wrongdoing and blame that, together with transitional justice's narrow understanding of violence, result in an equally narrow form of accountability.

In the first section, I analyse the main conclusions of the final report, including a list of twenty-nine policy recommendations. I argue that the measures and policies proposed by the truth commission follow the five interrelated themes of punishment, demilitarisation, re-education, restitution and protection. The purpose of the next section is to connect these themes to my explanation of the economy of anti-impunity. First, I describe how the recommendations of the CNV reveal strong links with what I call a *market model of accountability*: the assumption that power is a commodity individuals may or may not possess, that the violent use of this commodity constitutes a misuse of authority, and that such misuses can be prevented by a process of redistribution of rights. Second, I explain the problems that come from unreflectively adopting the market model, by tracing its central assumptions to the production of a certain *fetishism of responsibility*: the hypervisibility enjoyed by perpetrators of GVHRs in the reports of truth commissions/commissions of inquiry. In this section, I also explain that this hypervisibility (or the focus on those who misuse their authority) comes at the cost of neglecting a series of violent social relations that help to constitute perpetrators as such (introducing a fundamental blind spot in the work of transitional justice mechanisms). In the final section, I look at how this fetishism of responsibility affected the promise of justice woven by the recommendations of the CNV. More specifically, I argue that the attribution of responsibility for wrongdoing in the final report is akin to a process of *enclosure of blame* that produces a singular and exclusive source of blame for the violent past; an individual or group of individuals who can be held accountable, either in court or in history books. Finally, I briefly discuss the implications for the scope and quality of the promise of justice provided by transitional justice mechanisms.

The Recommendations of the Final Report

Transitional justice is always legitimised by the promise of non-recurrence (bringing violence and impunity to an end) central to the discipline's vision of a *post-conflictual* future. When it comes to truth commissions, this promise must be translated into a set of policy recommendations usually placed at the end of a long historical scrutiny of the violent past. Unsurprisingly, the final recommendations enjoy an unmatched level of importance in the work of truth commissions. It is in the recommendations that we find the results of the investigatory work, including the most important lessons to be drawn from the past, and it is through the recommendations that society must find justice. As the culmination of a long-drawn-out process of historical and legal analysis, the recommendations represent the near impossible task of distilling the complexity of thousands of pages into a few policies. Thus they represent prime research material, illustrating the tensions, limitations and contradictions of a given truth commission as well as the deeper politics of the discipline of transitional justice.

The recommendations of the CNV respect the overarching tone of investigations, rejecting the conservative notion of *doisladismo* and focusing instead on the crimes of state terror in which 'the armed forces were the protagonists'.[1] From the perspective of anti-impunity struggles in Brazil, this focus might seem like an obvious choice or, in fact, the only morally acceptable choice. But this was far from obvious when the commission was created. The legal mandate of the CNV stretched the timeframe of investigations beyond the limits of the military dictatorship (1964–85) into democratic periods (1946–64 and 1985–8),[2] which could in theory dilute the importance of the armed forces. Members of staff themselves recognised that GVHRs were not invented in the wake of the 1964 coup,[3] but had been a constant presence in Brazil's '"parallel regime of exception" [. . .] that always validated illegality and overt physical violence'.[4] But those following the early days of the CNV feared that, with a broad mandate, the investigations would be at risk of misappropriation. Instead of providing a narrative denouncing the military regime, the report could be misused by far-right revisionists portraying the dictatorship as a tough but mild 'dicta-light'.

In a wise twist, the CNV used its enlarged temporal horizons to reinforce the responsibility of the armed forces. The investigation goes further back into the past, but instead of diluting the importance of the military regime it exposes the historical rise of 'ideologies', techniques and prejudices employed by the military to legitimise crimes against humanity. The first volume of the report traces the spread of anti-communism from at least since the mid-1920s into the Cold War, when the idea of subversion became an umbrella term, conjuring up the different fears of the military intelligentsia (order), the conservative elites (property) and the traditional middle classes (morality). The text identifies the theoretical basis for the banalisation of GVHRs in the French theories of counterinsurgency of the 1950s (extensively read at Rio de Janeiro's War College) and in the pan-American doctrine of national security.[5] Page after page, the first volume deconstructs accounts of torture as rampant acts of rage or unprofessionalism, revealing a serious methodology behind physical and psychological torments[6] as well as their official endorsement.[7]

Acts of political repression and GVHRs are not depicted as reactions to insurgent violence. As the reading proceeds, it becomes crystal clear that they were part of a carefully planned, meticulously waged strategy to eliminate dissent. The first volume provides plenty of evidence that violations committed during the military regime 'resulted from the generalised and systematic actions of the Brazilian state'.[8] This idea of *systematicity* is central, working as the link between the report's historical narrative and the ensuing recommendations. By proving the *systematic nature* of violations during the civic military regime – that is, the fact that they had been part of an *intentional plan of extermination* carried out by the state at a large scale – the CNV could denounce them as heinous crimes against humanity.[9] As previously explained, crimes against humanity are treated in international law as *jus cogens* norms that impose on states the non-derogable obligation to punish perpetrators. In other words, these crimes cannot be pardoned by any circumstances or relaxed by extenuating factors.[10] The proof of systematicity and the ensuing state duty to prosecute perpetrators of GVHRs was the necessary condition for fulfilling the demand of anti-impunity struggles: the end of the blanket amnesty. Therefore, the report demands the withdrawal of the protections granted by the 1979 amnesty law to the 377 perpetrators named in the final report.[11]

But the lifting of the blanket amnesty does not exhaust the anti-impunity agenda. In fact, the first volume provides a list containing twenty-nine recommendations, divided into institutional measures, constitutional and legal reforms, and follow-up recommendations. The list contains a vast range of policy measures, but it is still possible to identify a few unifying themes without misrepresenting their content too much: punishment, demilitarisation, re-education, restitution and protection.

The lifting of the blanket amnesty has a straightforward connection with the theme of *punishment*. But the list of recommendations regarding the punishment of perpetrators goes beyond the confines of past harm. The first volume recognises that 'the practices of unlawful and arbitrary detentions, torture, executions, forced disappearances [. . .] are no strangers to Brazil's contemporary reality'.[12] Hence, the text emphasises the need to bring present-day perpetrators of GVHRs to justice by implementing measures to prevent the occurrence of violations and, when prevention fails, to ensure criminal accountability (see Table 4.1, recommendations 9 and 24). These measures also include the development of legislation to provide further legal support for prosecutions (see Table 4.1, recommendation 19).

Table 4.1 The 29 Recommendations of the Final Report

Demilitarisation	[10] The establishment of independent forensic departments separated from the security forces (pp. 968–9) [18] The annulment of the 1984 National Security Law (p. 971) [20] The demilitarisation of state police forces (p. 971) [21] The extinction of military state courts (p. 972) [22] The exclusion of civilians from the jurisdiction of the military federal court (p. 972)
Re-education	[1] The official acknowledgement of the armed forces (p. 964) [4] The prohibition of official events celebrating the 1964 coup (p. 967) [5] The reformulation of processes of admission and evaluation for the armed forces and public security forces (p. 967) [6] The introduction of pro-democracy and human rights values in the curriculum of military and police academies (pp. 967–8) [16] The promotion of pro-democracy and human rights values in the national curriculum (p. 970) [23] The suppression of homophobic references in legislation (p. 972) [28] The preservation of the memory of GVHRs (e.g. withdrawing honours granted to perpetrators in the past) (p. 974) [29] The continuation of efforts in search of the remaining archives of the dictatorship (p. 975)
Restitution	[3] The repayment of public funds used to support GVHRs (p. 967) [7] The issuing of new death certificates to family members of victims with the correctly stated cause of death (p. 968) [8] The withdrawal of the names of those politically persecuted in the past from intelligence databases (p. 968) [15] The provision of medical and psychological treatment to victims of GVHRs (p. 970) [17] The provision of support to institutions and public sector organisations committed to the promotion and protection of human rights (p. 970) [27] The continuation of efforts in search for the mortal remains of the disappeared (p. 974)
Protection	[11] The strengthening of public defenders' offices (p. 969) [12] The end of inhuman conditions of incarceration; the end of humiliating procedures inmates' families must go through; more re-integrative policies (p. 969) [13] The establishment of independent ombudsman services for the prison system (p. 969) [14] The strengthening of community councils (p. 970) [25] The implementation of procedures in conformity with article 7.5 of the American Convention on Human Rights (ACHR) (p. 972)

Members of staff occasionally voiced the belief that transitional justice should help to 'excise the enduring metastasis of the dictatorship'.[13]
Among the twenty-nine recommendations, the policies that most clearly
illustrate this belief are those focusing on the *demilitarisation* of Brazilian institutions. These measures aim at identifying and neutralising areas
in which military principles and codes of practice have spilled over into
civilian life. The merging of the two spheres is seen as an 'anomaly'[14] in
itself: the outdated remnants of an authoritarian past that have no place
in a democratic society. The theme of demilitarisation draws special attention to one of the most problematic legacies of the military regime: the
militarisation of law enforcement. Thus, the final report recommends the
end of institutions (e.g., pieces of legislation, official bodies, public sector organisations) that in any way or form represent the invasion of the
civilian sphere by military hierarchical principles, doctrines and practices
(see Table 4.1, recommendations 10, 18, 21 and 22). In a brave move, the
first volume recommends the complete demilitarisation of police forces,
affirming that the methods of the gendarmerie are 'incompatible with the
exercise of public security in the democratic rule of law'.[15]

The remaining themes move away from the perpetrators of GVHRs to
their victims, including a strong emphasis on policies seeking to redress
past harms, to promote democratic values and to extend current mechanisms of protection to vulnerable populations. This victim-oriented set of
recommendations also incorporates traditional ideas of historical or symbolic justice tied to the need to *re-educate society*. This is where the distinctive meaning attributed by the CNV to the practice of reconciliation stands
out. In fact, the first recommendation to appear in the final report calls for
the acknowledgement by the armed forces of their own protagonist role
during the violent past.[16] Recalling the official exchanges between the CNV
and the army, the navy and the air force concerning misuses of authority
in the past, the report criticises the cynical policy of neither denying the
existence of documented abuses nor acknowledging their criminal status.
One of the central conclusions of the final report is that the continuation of
GVHRs by state agents in Brazil 'comes, to a large extent, from the fact that
gross violations of human rights witnessed in the past were not adequately
denounced'.[17] Thus, the report states, once again, that national reconciliation can only happen once the armed forces are finally reconciled with
their criminal past. It also explains the importance of opening the remaining archives of repression and the need to reject allegations that they were
destroyed.[18] Other measures of re-education include preventing historical
revisionism (see Table 4.1, recommendations 4 and 28), the re-training of
the security forces (see Table 4.1, recommendations 5, 6 and 23) and the

promotion of societal support for human rights (see Table 4.1, recommendation 16).

The theme of restitution is present in efforts to address 'the marks of traumatic suffering'[19] left by the dictatorship in the lives of survivors and family members. The final report recommends continuing the search for the disappeared[20] and the lifelong provision of medical and psychological support to survivors,[21] in order to offer some level of closure and proper care to those directly or indirectly victimised by the regime. Measures with the goal of restitution also include amending the lies commonly used by state agents in order to conceal extrajudicial killings (see Table 4.1, recommendations 7 and 8) and even the call for a very specific form of 'reparation': payments made by perpetrators to the state, their former employer, on account of their misappropriation of public funds for criminal goals (see Table 4.1, recommendation 3). On the other side of the temporal spectrum are recommendations that share a similar concern with the wellbeing of victims but focus on present-day GVHRs committed by agents of the criminal justice system. These measures denounce the lack of appropriate protections enjoyed by individuals accused of wrongdoing, urging the state to strengthen mechanisms of due process, transparency and accountability (see Table 4.1, recommendations 11, 13, 14 and 25). Here, special attention is drawn to Brazilian prisons, seen as 'places where multiple violations of rights happen systematically'.[22] The report admirably calls for an end to the inhumane conditions currently witnessed in overpopulated, unsanitary prison cells, demanding a more dignified system and 'policies focused on the social re-integration of prisoners'.[23] Interestingly, this theme illustrates the CNV's sophisticated treatment of the problematic of punishment, which situates the commission apart from some facile claims usually implied by the idea of a 'culture of impunity'. Members of staff do not condemn Brazil as the land of indiscriminate impunity; in fact, they regard such claims as deceptive clichés.[24] What is condemned in their work is something else: the essential imbalance between the impunity enjoyed by agents of state throughout history and the excessive punishment hanging over the heads of non-white, working-class individuals who committed petty crimes.[25]

The Economy of Anti-Impunity

The five themes running through the recommendations proposed by the final report are essential for the purposes of the present work. Essential not only because the future of Brazilian democracy would be jeopardised without their implementation (which is certainly true), but also because they provide us with a fundamental clue about the promise of transitional justice. To be more specific, the themes of punishment, de-militarisation, education, restitution and protection are not simply straightforward directives devised by a group of experts. They are policies that rely on certain assumptions about redress, mobilise imaginaries of blame and reinforce specific forms of responsibility over others. It is by investigating these assumptions that we can further contextualise the reasons for transitional justice's narrow understanding of violence as part of what I choose to call the *economy of anti-impunity*: the acceptance of a *market model of accountability* and a certain *fetishism of responsibility* that create a parsimonious promise of justice.

The Market Model of Accountability

Foucault was deeply critical of what he identified as the '"economism" in the theory of power'[26] more or less shared by juridical, liberal and even Marxist approaches. In the context of legal and political thought, this economism refers to the framing of power (meaning a potential or a capacity) as 'something that can be possessed and acquired, that can be surrendered through a contract or by force, that can be alienated or recuperated, that circulates and fertilizes one region but avoids others'.[27] Conveniently, the English language expresses this sense of 'ownership' in a clear way. In English, one speaks of those who enjoy their economic, social and personal potential to its full extent as the *powerful* – that is, those who are filled with power. At the other end of the spectrum are the *powerless* – those who are destitute of power and, hence, lack the capacity to achieve their full potential. In this economic model, what dictates the relationship between the powerful and the powerless is the possession of a scarce commodity. If an individual – let us say *A*, to paraphrase Robert Dahl's classic scheme[28] – seizes the sources of power, it decreases the power available to other individuals, for example *B*. For the sake of simplicity, I will call this approach the market model.

According to the market model, politics is dictated by a fundamental equation: power can either be taken away from the market or it can be put back there, as it were, redistributed. It is a mere question of institutional adjustment. What is important here is to understand that, from a market model perspective, it is the number of empowered individuals that defines the number of individuals who will enjoy the benefits of such possession (who will be able to exercise their potential).

With his characteristic historical awareness, Foucault traces this model to late medieval times during 'the reactivation of Roman law around the problem of the monarch and the monarchy'.[29] More specifically, he identifies it with the political philosophy of Thomas Hobbes. And it is not by mere chance that the *Leviathan* – known for founding Western political theory around the themes of violence, power and authority – is also seen as 'the founder of the modern tradition of individual rights'.[30] Theories about rights often follow this economic logic. Rights are powers, entitlements, capacities attributed to individuals[31] that have been, to different degrees, 'embedded in domestic legal systems'.[32] The promotion, protection and enforcement of human rights, in this perspective, has a very specific function. They offer at least a 'minimal level of protection'[33] that 'decreases the probability of harm'[34] when society is faced with the 'misuse of state power'.[35] In other words, they function as a strategy of *redistribution of power* in a system suffering from an imbalance between the powerful (the state) and the powerless (the individuals). *Misuse* is the central term here. It connects the perspective of power as a scarce commodity to the representation of violence as an *intentional, cyclical and exceptional phenomenon*.

The term *misuse* points to the way in which the market model conceives of the *dynamics of wrongdoing*, in particular the relationship between the resource *power* and the act of *violence*. Scholars within this tradition see the relationship as a relation of reciprocity. They see the instrumental resort to violence (often defined as the potential for destruction) as an empowering force in at least two different senses. First, there is an understanding that violence is somehow necessary to sustain the conditions for the establishment and maintenance of a political community. As one should conclude from the truisms about life in communion with others, covenants required the support of force.[36] So 'force', here, is a prerequisite to ensure promises between individuals are kept. It is in this sense that we need the faculty of punishment (a controlled and perfectly legitimate resort to violence) to protect the 'promises' binding together a political community.

But the assumptions of the market model are incredibly flexible, allowing those who employ it to conceptualise the relationship between power and violence in a plethora of different ways. Some commentators understand the use of violence (or the threat to use violence) as a strategy to enhance what they believe is the quintessential feature of power: the potential to command. In the context of transitional justice debates, we can see this idea beneath a minimalist approach to reconciliation. Minimalists see the resort to violence (destruction) as empowering when they emphasise the need to pay attention to the different demands of post-authoritarian, 'authoritarian enclaves'. Because these 'authoritarian enclaves' retain control over the means of violence, they can endanger the implementation of transitional measures by threatening to reinstitute a cycle of revenge. And because they can impose their interests via this resort to violent means, they are seen as 'powerful', or still holding too much power.[37] In this equation, to be capable of acting through violent means is to be in possession of *power* (empowered) and to enjoy a sharp increase in the capacity to exercise *authority* (command).

In yet a third way, scholars can think of the instrumental resort to violence as the opposite of empowerment. They believe, as Arendt herself does, that the intersection between violence and politics could become extremely dangerous. According to this rationale, once violence is waged upon the political arena it risks assuming the uncontrolled nature of revenge. At first, the resort to violent means might offer a short-term sense of empowerment (based on the capacity to command others through fear), but what it actually does is to dissolve the fabric that holds a political community together.[38] In Arendt's perspective, the simple equation between violence and power is misleading, since the most powerful of all human things is the potential to create things anew (a potential embodied in a political community) and not the potential to destroy. Thus, instead of translating power into authority, political violence simply corrupts political authority into plain authoritarianism.

The market model takes the question of accountability, rather literally, as an act of counting: counting the parties that were wronged, the amount of damage endured and the amount of resources (power) that each party holds.[39] The practice of redressing past or present-day wrongs is envisioned as a process of institutional adjustment shaped by two central operations: an arithmetic of victims and perpetrators that aims to stop 'individuals who live together from doing each other reciprocal wrongs [. . .] re-establishing the balance of profits and losses whenever they do so';[40] and a geometric redistribution of resources (power) across society, making sure that 'each party takes only what is its due'.[41] At the core of these operations is the problematic of *Gewalt* or the legitimacy of the use of force defining the boundaries between authority and authoritarianism.[42] This is a question that, overtly or tacitly, recurs in works on transitional justice, since it is related to the foundation or re-foundation of a political community. To be very succinct, the problematic refers to the difficulties involved in quantifying the optimal amount of power amassed by the party that rules the whole, separating legitimate from illegitimate uses of violence. It involves the drawing of a delicate line, defining what constitutes *misuses of power* in a given legal, moral and political arrangement. This is why the problematic of *Gewalt* occupies such a central place in the discipline.

Here, we can make a clear parallel with the twenty-nine recommendations of the CNV. First, one of the central conclusions of the commission was that the anti-communist crusade of the 1970s constituted a misuse or distortion of state authority. Now, for the armed forces to re-establish their legitimacy as *power holders*, they need to acknowledge their past wrongdoing. As an institution they need to understand why, and publicly accept that their actions represented *misuses of power*, so as to make sure they do not reproduce them in the future. This also requires changes in the legal system. In order to promote a liberalising transition away from the remnants of authoritarianism, Brazilian legislators must make sure everyone else realises the nature of *violations as misuses*, thereby pedagogically combating impunity. Finally, the promotion of human rights in terms of education follows a logic of redistribution of 'powers'; they are meant to re-establish the balance of the Brazilian system between the powerholders and the powerless, to expand legal protections until the point where no party is left unprotected from the abuses of state authorities.

This approach uses a simple logic to define which wrongs will fit into the category of misuse. Because it sees power as an identifiable commodity, it searches for those empowered; and because it reads the relationship between power and violence as a question of legitimacy, it measures the rightfulness or rightlessness of their actions. This procedure is *juridical* because it is concerned with the question of *jurisdiction*, in other words, the right (*ius*) to dictate (*dictio*) the boundaries between the uses and the misuses of power. This procedure is also *philosophical* because the question that follows, that of legitimacy, necessarily spurs an abstract metaphysical dilemma about the search for the origins of political authority.[43]

That such abstract discussions often end in the question of 'exceptionalism' is hardly surprising. Because the market model understands power as a possession (a right or an entitlement) and sees violence as instrumental (a means to an end), what concerns this tradition the most is the figure of the *dictator* – the identifiable individual (and indivisible) powerholder who misuses authority – and the period of the *dictatorship* – the identifiable timeframe when the systematic wrongdoing leads to authoritarianism. The question of the exception or the exceptionalism of violence naturally leads to a question about the rightfulness or the rightlessness of *dictator*s. This is a question that has enjoyed disproportionate attention in debates within political theory and international relations,[44] fields that have long nurtured, even among critical scholars, a simplistic view of power as the capacity to 'dictate who may live and who must die'.[45] It is this question that, taken to an extreme degree, drives scholars to the absurd point of enquiring whether or not there is or should be a 'right' to torture 'dangerous' individuals based on the threat they pose to a political community.[46]

To fully appreciate the consequences of this perspective, we need to go back to Foucault's and Rancière's critiques of the central assumptions of the market model. Although the topic of power was one of his chief concerns, Foucault rejected the economism of theories of power. He saw both the view of power as a commodity and the central focus on the figure of the dictator (the apex of a power structure) as rather misleading. For Foucault, the question of what constitutes misuse of authority is oblivious to different forms of power that do not fit in the economic schemata. While focusing excessively on the 'legitimate forms of power which have a single centre',[47] this approach neglects the 'smallest details of everyday life'[48] where power is not possessed by anyone in particular but experienced by all through relations of 'subjection':[49] a form of power that 'categorizes the individual, [. . .] imposes a law of truth on him which he must recognise, and which others have to recognise in him'.[50]

It is here that Foucault provides his most fundamental contribution to a critique of the market model of accountability. The response of 'redistribution' – the endowment of rights to the dispossessed in order to protect them from the misuses of power – is not only inefficient against the exercise of power in term of subjection. It is also part of it. Relations of subjection are produced and reproduced through claims of knowledge that assign 'to each individual [. . .] his "true" name, his "true" place, his "true" body'.[51] Therefore, the moment of redress that requires the identification and measurement of wrongs as well as the 'counting' of victims and perpetrators is also a moment of reorganisation of power relations; a moment where the truth about those who suffered and committed wrongdoing is expected to come to light. Acts of accountability are assumed to be responding to an external reality; a situation where wrongdoing has already been committed by some to others. All that accountability is assumed to do in this scenario is identify which parties were wronged (victims) and which ones committed the wrongdoing (perpetrators), and take appropriate action. But, just like the discipline of transitional justice, the moment of accountability also has a productive facet. As Rancière elegantly puts it, 'parties do not exist prior to the conflict they name and in which they are counted as parties'.[52] The counting of victims and perpetrators, the assignation of their 'true' names and places in the causality chain of wrongdoing, is also productive of these identities. No victims or perpetrators exist prior to the articulation of their identities as such.

Both critiques are relevant to understanding the limitations and even the so-called failures of transitional justice, since the discipline is based around the central assumptions of the market model. Transitional justice values the promotion and protection of rights (human rights included) precisely to end with the domination that comes from the misuse of authority in an unbalanced system. Following the market model of accountability, transitional justice mechanisms aim to redistribute powers (rights) and impose duties (limits) on the functioning of sovereign authority exactly to normalise the situation, to put violence and authoritarianism under control. But the domination Foucault speaks of is situated at the blind spots of the discipline. It relates less to the illegitimate misuses of authority (which the market model certainly tackles) than to the dynamics of subjection and control at work even in well-intended truth commission reports. Fundamentally, the counting of wronged parties that seeks to rebalance the sheet of society is also a miscounting of the number of 'victims' and 'perpetrators'.

The Fetishism of Responsibility

That truth-seeking and truth-telling are mechanisms of control is no news to transitional justice scholars. As we have seen throughout this book, truth commissions are often justified as victim-centred approaches to conflict transformation.[53] They are supposed to be non-partisan institutions that provide victims with a voice, breaking with decades of regimes of silence and obliviousness; but the reality is far more complex. As instances of memorialisation (when different interpretations of the past collide), truth commissions are pervaded by silence.[54] They are sold as forums where survivors speak freely but often adopt confessionary practices saturated by rituals, predefined expectations and hierarchical relations. Indeed, truth commissions decry instances of past abuse, which in itself is irreproachable, but because they adopt a limited understanding of violence, what they consider to be 'abuse' is often also very limited.[55] Furthermore, the famous imperatives of 'Never again!' or 'Enough!' have frequently operated as overstated declarations that violence has already ended or will end, provided the rule of law is re-established and maintained.[56]

The more we delve into the prehistory of truth commissions, the clearer this function of control or subjection becomes. In effect, when truth commissions appeared in the late twentieth century in Argentina,[57] they were deliberately meant to replicate the much older body of commissions of inquiry,[58] extrajudicial mechanisms that sought to investigate and produce the truth about specific events based on the testimony of witnesses.[59] Truth commissions were 'invented' in Latin America, but the form of the inquiry they adopted is an integral part of European history. Prior to the modern age, the *inquisitio* (inquiry or inquest) referred to an administrative-religious mechanism employed for solving disputes, collecting taxes, clarifying questions of property rights, recording faults and correcting sins.[60] Between the ninth and the eleventh centuries ecclesiastical and secular authorities made extensive use of *inquisitiones* in order to gather information about, and subsequently exert control over, their respective constituencies.[61] In its earlier form, as it was employed by agents of the Carolingian empire, *inquitisiones* worked by gathering a group of notable and knowledgeable individuals who would independently discuss an object of controversy, reach an agreement and propose a solution.[62]

By the twelfth and thirteenth centuries, through a complex process involving the expansion of the Church's jurisdiction and the rediscovery/reactivation of Roman law (in particular the Justinian codes), the *inquisitio* became a central part of medieval due process.[63] The expansion of the inquisitorial form not only replaced previous, traditional forms of adjudication, but also revolutionised European modes of veridiction (Foucault's neologism for historical processes of producing/telling the truth).[64] As time passed, the inquiry would become the quintessential method shared by the natural sciences and, later, the humanities.[65] With colonialism the inquisition was exported to the four corners of the world, making a mark in the Americas and late colonial possessions.[66] Before reappearing as mechanisms of transitional justice, commissions of inquiry abounded in Victorian times, when dozens of reports (known as blue books) were written condemning the insalubrious and inhumane conditions faced by workers in mines, workshops and factories.[67]

Foucault discusses the inquiry as a clear example of where the production of knowledge meets the reproduction of power. Throughout history, the evolving form of the inquiry has been employed and adapted to gather information about the forms of conduct that were good practice, that needed correction or that were subversive and required repression. More than an instrument of political repression, this was all part of a *productive affair*. By knowing those they ruled, rulers could make use of their capacity, explore their unexplored potential, pitch them against each other, pre-empt uprisings, and even create a feeling (misplaced or not) among their subjects that their voices were being heard while at the same time legitimising the status quo.[68] And amidst the multiple uses of truth-telling as a mechanism of power and an exercise of control, the act of placing blame, or the assignment of responsibility for past misdeeds, is the most interesting one for the purposes of the present work. This is where modernity made a quintessential contribution to the form of the inquiry.

In modern liberal societies, the form of the inquiry takes on a different substance defined by a new mode of subjectivity; exit the criminal act, enter the criminal individual.[69] Under this new condition, culpability is somehow modified. As a secularised version of the penitent soul, the guilty mind is defined by the central assumptions of rationality, free will and intentionality reinforced in the classic works of Hobbes, Locke, Rousseau and Beccaria.[70] What defines this new logic is the fundamental idea or worldview that Stuart Hall et al. defined as 'possessive individuality'.[71] Those who transgress the social code (defined by a contract between individuals) are to be held responsible on account of their possession of themselves and their surroundings; their mastery over their inner desires, control over their actions, and transparent, rational understanding of the harms that such actions can bring to others. Put simply, wrongdoing becomes a matter of rational choice, which affords an irrevocable tautological sense to the question of accountability. If rational individuals choose to break the contract (what should be, at least in principle, irrational), they must face the appropriate consequences (criminal or administrative procedures) precisely because they are rational individuals. It is alongside this idea of possessive individuality that impunity appears as the thing to be avoided: the absence of punishment affects the cost/benefit calculus of misbehaving and hence risks jeopardising the whole of the social edifice.[72]

This logic is less problematic for the assumptions it holds than for the practical and symbolic effects it produces. In effect, the model of 'possessive individuality' with which inquiries begin to operate in the transition from medieval to modern times defines the question of responsibility as an *individual*, and above all, *indivisible* possession. In this rationalised framework, concerns over the so-called conditions of possibility of a given misdeed – the role of the historical context, the socio-economic background, the contingent nature of the category of misdeed, etc.[73] – are sidelined for a simplistic, individualising gaze that reduces human interaction to the abstract template of the marketplace: as exchanges between individuals of equal standing. When it comes to placing blame in the aftermath, this gaze works to create a certain 'optical illusion', not in the sense of creating something false, but of establishing a game of lights that affects the visibility of a given phenomenon. In classic Marxist parlance, the form of possessive individualism produces a *fetishism of responsibility* whereby perpetrators become hyper-visible through the occultation of the social relations that have constructed them as such.

Justice and the Enclosure of Blame

The staff of the CNV were by no means unaware of the social relations that transformed agents of state into state terrorists, nor of the role of the military regime in preserving and in some cases reinforcing existing violent social relations. In effect, the second volume of the final report, a compilation of 9 *textos temáticos* (thematic essays), is almost entirely dedicated to this theme. For over 400 pages the essays expose the complexity of the civic-military regime beyond the abstract context of anti-communist struggles, situating it at the intersection of a long historical continuum of violent struggles over land and the beginnings of a process of reorganisation of global productive forces. They explain the dictatorship's project for the implementation of a new mode of capital accumulation in Brazil based on extreme levels of exploitation in the cities and the intensification of land-grabbing in the countryside. The question of inequality takes a prominent place, as the essays explore the exclusionary practices and ideals at the core of the regime's project of conservative modernisation. The volume also makes it patently clear that the regime enjoyed the strong support of business elites interested in deepening the process of industrialisation in Brazil and demobilising populist promises of inclusion through consumption.

The most interesting aspect of the second volume is the intrinsic and indistinguishable link built between the *repressive* and the *productive* facets of the dictatorship, clearly articulated by the essay 'Violações de direitos humanos dos trabalhadores' ('Violations of workers' human rights'). In this essay we find out that despite the gains from the 'economic miracle', the real minimum wage index fell approximately 38 per cent between 1961 and 1975,[74] and the Gini coefficient increased from 0.50 in the 1960s to 0.59 in 1980s.[75] To maintain this unequal pattern of accumulation, the regime relied on a practice of pacifying distributional conflicts through terror, tightening its grip on organised labour. Agents of state treated unionisation as a subversive activity, passing legislation that virtually criminalised any form of industrial action[76] and actively intervened in 536 unions. The essay estimates that 10,000 syndicalist leaders lost their political rights.[77] The strategy of pacification through terror involved multiple episodes of mass arrest, including the detention of 600 workers in the 1968 Osasco city strike and the detention of 334 workers during the 1979 steelworkers' strike in São Paulo.[78] It was also behind the intelligence services' decision to establish a network of surveillance sections inside the headquarters and industrial plants of major companies (including branches of the multinationals Volkswagen, Fiat, Ford, Toyota, Chrysler, General Motors, Scania, Rolls-Royce and Mercedes-Benz). These sections were responsible for compiling blacklists of individuals made redundant for politically motivated reasons and meant to remain redundant for as long as the regime lasted.[79] The essay devotes special attention to the Volkswagen section, devised and operated with the assistance of Franz Stangl, former commander of the Nazi extermination camps Sobibór and Treblinka.[80]

The links between repression and production are also present in two other essays: 'Violações de direitos humanos dos camponeses' ('Violations of peasants' human rights') and 'Violações de direitos humanos dos povos indígenas' ('Violations of the human rights of Indigenous peoples'). Both essays acknowledge that the historical inequality and the violence characteristic of the Brazilian countryside predated the dictatorship. They remind us that in 1961, 3.5 per cent of agricultural properties owned 62.33 per cent of the country's entire arable land,[81] and that successive governments turned a blind eye to the criminal actions of landowners who forged property titles, maintained working conditions similar to slavery and formed countryside militias. But the already precarious situation of peasants and Indigenous groups was worsened after the 1968 state of exception. With the hardlines in power, the regime abandoned prospects for redistribution of land (legislated in 1964 partially out of fear that extreme inequality would develop into revolutionary resentment) and promoted a change in the national indigenist police towards a sped-up process of acculturation.[82] The founding of the National Institute for Colonisation and Land Reform (Incra) in 1969, and the National Integration Plan (PIN) of 1970 were some of the landmarks of the new, aggressive policy. The plan was to fight pockets of underdevelopment by building a network of major highways that would stimulate the settlement of the Amazon. The plan to further colonise the Brazilian interior was 'also an attempt to reduce tension in countryside areas marked by conflict over land'.[83] The regime's target was to 'settle around 100,000 families alongside the highways, over more than 2 million square metres of expropriated land'[84] in what can be easily described as a massive, coordinated effort of land-grabbing. According to the authorities, the project required the 'pacification of thirty unruly Indigenous groups'.[85]

But the unequal nature of state terror goes beyond questions of income, assets or occupational categories in the second volume. The collection also discloses the homophobic, racist and neocolonial ideals about civilisation and progress cherished by the military intelligentsia at the time of the coup and during the Years of Lead. One essay, entitled 'Ditadura e homossexualidades' ('The dictatorship and homosexuality') explains that the military regime 'had a clear homophobic perspective, relating homosexuality to the left and to subversion [. . .] harmful, dangerous and opposite to family values and the prevailing morality'.[86] Another essay, 'A resistência da sociedade civil' ('Civil society resistance'), discusses the colour-blind racism of state officials, who denied the existence of racial oppression in the country and disseminated the 'idea of "racial democracy", spread by the nationalist propaganda of the military dictatorship'.[87] The essay on the fate of Indigenous communities is also worth mentioning here, mostly because it denounces the mobilisation of the old colonial trope of *terra nullius*[88] by the military – in which the 'Amazon is represented as a "demographic vacuum"'[89] – as another way 'to consolidate the image of Indigenous peoples as hindrances to the country's development'.[90] This ethnocentric view was not only an expression of unenlightened prejudice. It was the condition for a tacit policy of expropriating the lands inhabited by Indigenous groups and redistributing them 'between entrepreneurs interested in running agribusiness companies or extractivist projects as though they were uninhabited'.[91] It was also the condition for pitching subaltern groups against each other, promising the partition of 'no man's land for the landless men'.[92]

Overall, the second volume recounts a truly nauseating litany of horrors, often left outside the scope of transitional justice in Brazil and around the world. Hundreds of families forcefully removed from their lands as part of the counterinsurgency effort,[93] rubber tappers murdered for refusing to sell their product below the controlled prices,[94] activists burned alive,[95] and even genocidal actions including the 'deliberate introduction of smallpox, influenza, tuberculosis and measles amongst Indigenous peoples'.[96] The volume also problematises the real number of victims of violence in the past. In places, it moves away from transitional justice's template of victims as victims of GVHRs (the essay on worker's rights goes as far as to say that 'workers and the syndicalist movement were the primal targets of the 1964 coup').[97] Elsewhere, it puts the figure of 434 victims (as acknowledged in the first volume) in a wider context. For example, we learn that in the countryside 1,603 individuals were assassinated between 1964 and the 1990s,[98] and a possible estimate of at least '8,350 Indigenous people were killed during the CNV's period of investigation, as a result of direct action by government agents or the lack thereof'.[99]

Therefore, the problem with the final report is not a lack of knowledge about the violent social relations behind the emergence of the authoritarian regime. The problem is that this robust knowledge of violent relations is almost entirely absent from the final list of twenty-nine recommendations. With the exception of the theme of homophobia (see Table 4.1, recommendation 23), the recommendations make no genuine effort to push the boundaries of what is considered violence (for example, the characterisation of the dictatorship as a 'new articulation of the violence typical of the capitalist system [. . .] and state-led violence',[100] or even the notion of 'employers' terrorism').[101] Instead, the commission's strategy of punishment, demilitarisation and the promotion of human rights emphasises the narrow understanding of violence found in the scholarship and practice of transitional justice. In fact, the very authorship of the second volume is ambiguous. While the collection was released alongside the first and the third volumes, and while it is normally counted as part of the final report, its place in the official narrative is made unclear by the strange way in which the volume is introduced: 'The present volume of the report of the National Truth Commission contains an ensemble of texts produced under the individual responsibility of some of the commissions' advisors.'[102] In any case, the result is that the complexity of violent relations gives way to a weak understanding of the link between violence and responsibility whose sole purpose is to render someone or something accountable.

Members of staff knew that an estimated 9,500 human beings lost their lives during the period of investigation. But since they had to accept violence as *intentional violations* of human rights, the recommendations end up marginalising suffering caused in the absence of a clear intent expressed in explicit state policies. The second volume is filled with qualifications such as 'the disrespect of labour norms established by law and the concentration of land in the hands of a few do not constitute violations of human rights',[103] or 'there was no formalised and coherent state policy of extermination of homosexuals'.[104] Eschewing promising ideas such as 'quotidian violations'[105] or the violent nature of economic systems, the recommendations reproduce an understanding of violence as an *exceptional phenomenon*, repeating the word 'anomaly' several times when demanding the demilitarisation of the gendarmerie and the criminal justice system. The point is not that these policies are unimportant, but that they help to solidify a counterproductive notion that violence is something external to the present political and economic order, that it is a strange abnormality. In line with a market model of accountability, this abnormality is explained as the consequence of an incomplete transition to democracy, jeopardised by a blanket amnesty and a veil of silence that normalised the *misuses* of authority by the civic-military dictatorship. Essentially, a complex problem that involves the exploitation of workers, the inequality of land and the colonial heritage of euro-centrism is reduced to the simplicity of a calculator: there is a surplus of power still enjoyed by the military in post-transitional times and a deficit of power that continues to characterise the lives of Brazilian citizens.

The way in which the problematic of blame is simplified is emblematic of a certain fetishism of responsibility. Of all possible chains of responsibility that could emerge from the complexity of the dictatorship as a historical period, the focus of accountability is reduced to 377 individuals and the indivisible responsibility of the institution they served (the military). The recommendations rightfully accuse perpetrators of GVHRs of crimes against humanity due to the *systematic* nature of their offences. But the concept of *systematic* – as it is philosophically and legally used by transitional justice scholars and practitioners – is miles away from a *systemic* understanding of violence. The promise of transitional justice is thus reduced to a promise of criminal accountability that involves attributing blame to a specific group of individuals who are identified as responsible for a very specific form of violence: violations that can be seen and held accountable; that are intentionally committed or acknowledged; that pose the risk of a returning cycle of revenge; and that are contained in the well-drawn boundaries of states of exception.

I am not the first to share a certain discomfort with the absence of a productive facet of the dictatorship in the CNV's recommendations. Critics have emphasised how the report missed a golden opportunity to hold to account those who financed the repressive apparatus.[106] Even staff members who acknowledged the full support offered by the state throughout the commission's mandate also complained about the difficulties of discussing the role of enterprises and companies in supporting and collaborating with state terror.[107] These are vital criticisms, as they do point to the blind spots of the rather parsimonious justice promised by the CNV. But they are insufficient insofar as we consider what I call here the economy of anti-impunity. The problem I identify in the final recommendations is not a simple legal problem that could be easily avoided by employing better legal frameworks (such as adding more names of perpetrators to the list). The invisibility of social relations that help to shape perpetrators of GVHRs as such is problematic, first and foremost, because of its non-legal or extra-legal dimension: the material basis that connects the economy of anti-impunity to the continuation of multiple violent relations. To put it differently, the central question is not so much who is responsible for past misdeeds, but how the assignment of responsibility normalises violent social relations in the present.

Abiding by the principle of *systematicity* was a necessary move. It was the condition for framing the crimes of the military as heinous crimes against humanity and of overruling, or attempting to overrule, the amnesty law. As I have repeatedly insisted throughout this book, the CNV cannot be faulted for this choice in isolation. The problem is much wider and much more difficult to handle than the decisions made within the confines of a relatively small body. Nonetheless, we need to investigate this practical need because, in many senses, it is precisely what accounts for the 'optical illusion' seen in the recommendations: the *hypervisibility* accorded to the 377 perpetrators of GVHRs that has the effect of rendering a series of other forms of 'violations' *invisible or less-than-visible*. The other side of the focus on anti-impunity is the silencing of violations and forms of suffering that cannot be proven systematic – for they are not the fruit of intentionally devised policies drawn by powerholders, but are *systemic* and *relational* because they are deeply entrenched in the ways in which human beings live, work and produce in cooperation with each other. In this game of lights, the *productive facet* of the authoritarian regime; the fact that it reorganised industrial relations, opened the gates for an unprecedented inflow of foreign capital, modernised agriculture while maintaining unequal ownership, increased work flexibility and systematically depressed real wages; is almost entirely sidelined by its *repressive facet*. The myriad of social relations created, destroyed and re-created by the historical movement known as the dictatorship fades away, so that individuals and the individual corporation (the armed forces) can be held responsible for the GVHRs.

To keep within the imagery of political economy, the promise of justice based on the market model of accountability and a fetishism of responsibility could be characterised as a process of *enclosure of blame*. In a historical sense, the term 'enclosure' refers to the process that transformed the English countryside during the fifteenth and seventeenth centuries. Roughly speaking, enclosures consisted in the fencing off of areas of the English medieval estate traditionally used by commoners for their own subsistence (for grazing livestock, hunting, gathering berries or timber), which enforced a system of private (exclusive) ownership of resources and arguably provided the conditions for the industrial revolution.[108] The term 'enclosure' can also be used in a broader sense, meaning instances in which communal resources are expropriated during the expansion of market relations (e.g. the colonisation of the Americas, the neoliberal waves of privatisation in Latin America during the 1990s or even the depletion of pension funds during the 2007 financial crisis).[109]

I do not wish to discuss the historical process of enclosure as such, but simply to borrow the powerful imagery and the immediate connection with a certain materiality present in the idea of 'fencing off'. To speak of a process of enclosing blame is to point out the circumscription of responsibility that fabricates a singular source of blame (both in the sense of a single person or group, and in the sense of an exceptional person or group). The production of a singular and therefore exclusive source of blame is, in many ways, akin to the fabrication of exclusive ownership rights during the dawn of the modern era, or even during the dictatorship's project of national integration. In both senses, either in the realms of justice or production, the fabrication and enforcement of the notion of *individuality* as *indivisibility* leaves a trace of dispossession behind. In the context of the enclosure of blame, we are left dispossessed of other possible forms of justice that require more collective effort than is needed by the relatively parsimonious promise of criminal accountability, demilitarisation and the redistribution of civil and political rights.

Conclusion

My aim in this chapter has been to provide an analysis of the final report of the CNV that moved away from the problematic of implementation into the workings of the economy of anti-impunity. The chapter has focused on the twenty-nine policy recommendations produced by the truth commission in the first volume of its final report. The point was very simple. I intended to showcase that the recommendations were more than mere neutral, technocratic policies against impunity; that, in fact, they were supported by certain logical and philosophical assumptions that privileged some ideas about violence, authority and accountability over others. And more than the beliefs of staff members, these ideas revealed larger and wider problems: the blind spots and contradictions shared by works within the discipline of transitional justice. At this point, the centrality of the economy of anti-impunity (the tripartite connection between the market model of accountability, the fetishism of responsibility and the enclosure of blame) became apparent. I explained that despite being aware of the *productive facet* of state-led violence in the past and of all the violent social relations that constituted perpetrators as such, the CNV reproduced a narrow sense of responsibility, focusing on the *repressive facet* of dictatorship. The result was the reproduction of a certain optical illusion concerning violence in the recommendations of the final report: the hypervisibility attributed to those who committed systematic GVHRs *vis-à-vis* the relative invisibility of violent relations that are not simply systematic, but systemic; violent social relations such as exploitation, inequality, racism and neo-colonial imaginaries of development that had no place in the CNV's promise of justice. They were left behind by the process of *enclosure of blame*, which consists in the fencing off of 'areas' of individual and indivisible responsibility and, consequentially, the reduction of the complexity of responses to violence.

In a sense, the promise of justice (seen in the recommendations) based on the economy of anti-impunity is a parsimonious promise. The twenty-nine recommendations are indeed vast and cover a series of important points, translated in five different themes. However, parsimonious does not mean simple. Some measures, such as the demilitarisation of the police or the end of the blanket amnesty, are definitely not simple; their implementation would require a concerted effort on the part of state officials as well as the willingness and capacity to overcome the strong resistance posed by certain segments. What I mean by a parsimonious promise of justice has nothing to do with the degree of difficulty of each recommendation. Parsimony, here, refers to the scope and depth of what is meant by justice. In this case, the recommendations of the CNV are parsimonious insofar as they propose to overcome longstanding, complex socio-political problems via legal and institutional reform. Their parsimonious nature comes from the intersection between a narrow understanding of violence (as an *intentional, cyclical and exceptional* phenomenon) and a limited economism (the market model of accountability and the fetishism of responsibility) that end up reducing the complexity of blame beyond any helpful measure.

The problem with such parsimonious justice is not the fact that it operates through state institutions. Legal and institutional reforms are fundamental for tackling systematic cases of violence in society. The problem is that a parsimonious promise of justice is a promise that conforms to the limits imposed by a given political and economic system. It is a promise that enables the *post-conflictual* future as a credible reality precisely because the idea of justice emanating from its recommendations does not seem impossible; that is, it is justice that can be achieved *en la medida de lo posible* (as far as possible). It is obviously important to have a credible promise of justice in post-authoritarian or post-conflict scenarios. Those are often moments when inaction and silence cost society dearly, and something must be done. But a form of justice that only goes 'as far as possible' is blind to the violent social relations at the core of the present political and economic order. It is our duty as scholars to point out the moment when practicality becomes dangerously close to omission.

Notes

1. In the original: 'o protagonismo foi das Forças Armadas'. Dallari, 'Verdade, Memória e Reconciliação'.
2. *Lei No 12.528, de 18 de Novembro de 2011.*
3. D'Araujo, Soares and Castro, *Os Anos de Chumbo.*
4. In the original: '"regime de exceção paralelo", protegido pela dissimulação, que validou sempre a ilegalidade, a violência física aberta'. Pinheiro, 'Notas sobre o Futuro da Violência na Cidade Democrática', p. 43.
5. Comissão Nacional da Verdade, *Relatório da Comissão Nacional da Verdade,* vol. 1, pp. 333–6.
6. Ibid. chapter 9.
7. Ibid. p. 321.
8. In the original: 'foram o resultado de uma ação generalizada e sistemática do Estado brasileiro'. Ibid. p. 963.
9. Ibid. p. 964.
10. Bassiouni, 'International Crimes'.
11. Comissão Nacional da Verdade, *Relatório da Comissão Nacional da Verdade,* vol. 1, p. 966.
12. In the original: 'prática de detenções ilegais e arbitrárias, tortura, execuções, desaparecimentos forçados e mesmo ocultação de cadáveres não é estranha à realidade brasileira contemporânea'. Ibid.
13. Dias, 'Precisamos Extirpar as Metástases Da Ditadura'.
14. Comissão Nacional da Verdade, *Relatório da Comissão Nacional da Verdade,* vol. 1, p. 972.
15. In the original: 'incompatíveis com o exercício da segurança pública no Estado democrático de direito'. Ibid. p. 971.
16. Ibid. p. 964.
17. 'resulta em grande parte do fato de que o cometimento de graves violações de direitos humanos verificado no passado não foi adequadamente denunciado' In the original. Ibid. p. 965.
18. Ibid. p. 975.
19. In the original: 'as marcas do sofrimento traumático'. Ibid. p. 426.
20. Ibid. p. 974.
21. Ibid. p. 970.
22. In the original: 'Os presídios são locais onde a violação múltipla desses direitos ocorre sistematicamente'. Ibid. p. 969.
23. In the original: 'políticas voltadas à reintegração social dos presos'. Ibid. p. 969.
24. Paulo Sérgio Pinheiro, Skype interview, 9 January 2018.
25. Paulo Sérgio Pinheiro, Skype interview, 9 January 2018.
26. Foucault, *Society Must Be Defended,* p. 13.
27. Ibid. p. 14.
28. Dahl, 'The Concept of Power'.
29. Foucault, *Society Must Be Defended,* p. 34.
30. Douzinas, *The End of Human Rights,* p. 69.

31. Wenar, 'On the Nature of Rights'.
32. Beitz, 'Human Rights as Common Concern', p. 269.
33. Brems, 'Human Rights', p. 355.
34. Brandt, 'The Concept of a Moral Right and Its Function', p. 37.
35. Beitz, 'Human Rights as Common Concern', p. 271.
36. Thomas Hobbes, *Leviathan*.
37. Elster, *Closing the Books*; O'Donnell and Schmitter, 'Transitions from Authoritarian Rule'; Verdeja, 'The Elements of Political Reconciliation'.
38. Arendt, *On Violence*.
39. Rancière, *Disagreement: Politics and Philosophy*.
40. Ibid. p. 5.
41. Ibid. p. 5.
42. Agamben, *Homo Sacer*; Benjamin, 'Critique of Violence'; Derrida, 'Force of Law'; Schmitt, *Political Theology*; Balibar, 'Reflections on "Gewalt."'
43. Derrida, 'Force of Law'.
44. Huysmans, 'The Jargon of Exception'; Aradau and van Munster, 'Exceptionalism and the "War on Terror"'; Neal, 'Foucault in Guantánamo'; Walker, 'Lines of Insecurity'.
45. Mbembe, 'Necropolitics', p. 11.
46. Allhoff, 'A Defense of Torture'.
47. Foucault, *Society Must Be Defended*, p. 27.
48. Foucault, *Discipline and Punish*, p. 198.
49. Foucault, 'The Subject and Power', p. 781.
50. Ibid. p. 781.
51. Foucault, *Discipline and Punish*, p. 198.
52. Rancière, *Disagreement: Politics and Philosophy*, p. 27.
53. Hayner, *Unspeakable Truths*; Baines, '"Today, I Want to Speak Out the Truth"'; Nwogu, 'When and Why It Started'; McEvoy and McConnachie, 'Victims and Transitional Justice'.
54. Jelin, *State Repression and the Labors of Memory*.
55. Laplante, 'Transitional Justice and Peace Building'; Fourlas, 'No Future without Transition'; Furtado, 'On Demons and Dreamers'.
56. Bevernage, 'The Past Is Evil/Evil Is Past'; Meister, *After Evil*; Wilson, *The Politics of Truth and Reconciliation in South Africa*.
57. Hayner, *Unspeakable Truths*.
58. Crenzel, 'Genesis, Uses, and Significations of the Nunca Más Report in Argentina'; Teitel, 'Transitional Justice Genealogy'.
59. Foucault, *A Verdade e as Formas Jurídicas*; Foucault, *Society Must Be Defended*; Foucault, *Wrong-Doing, Truth-Telling*.
60. Foucault, *A Verdade e as Formas Jurídicas*; Foucault, *Wrong-Doing, Truth-Telling*; Eichbauer, 'Medieval Inquisitorial Procedure'.
61. Foucault, *A Verdade e as Formas Jurídicas*.
62. Ibid.
63. Fraher, 'The Theoretical Justification for the New Criminal Law of the High Middle Ages'; Kelly, 'Inquisition and the Prosecution of Heresy'; Stein, *Roman Law in European History*; Berman, 'The Origins of Western Legal Science'.

64. Foucault, *A Verdade e as Formas Jurídicas*; Foucault, *Society Must Be Defended*; Foucault, *Wrong-Doing, Truth-Telling*.
65. Balibar, 'Foucault's Point of Heresy'.
66. Laidlaw, 'Investigating Empire'; Balint, Evans and McMillan, 'Justice Claims in Colonial Contexts'; Tieffemberg, 'Deber de responder'.
67. Frankel, 'Scenes of Commission'.
68. Foucault, *Wrong-Doing, Truth-Telling*; Gilligan and Pratt (eds), *Crime, Truth and Justice*; Ashforth, 'Reckoning Schemes of Legitimation'.
69. Foucault, *Discipline and Punish*.
70. Stuart Hall et al., *Policing the Crisis*; Neocleous, *The Fabrication of Social Order*.
71. Hall et al., *Policing the Crisis*, p. 172.
72. Foucault, *A Verdade e as Formas Jurídicas*.
73. Hall et al., *Policing the Crisis*.
74. Comissão Nacional da Verdade, *Relatório da Comissão Nacional da Verdade, vol. 2: Textos Temáticos*, p. 70.
75. Ibid. p. 70.
76. Ibid. p. 69.
77. Ibid. p. 61.
78. Ibid. p. 76.
79. Ibid. p. 66.
80. Ibid. p. 67.
81. Ibid. p. 96.
82. Ibid. p. 213.
83. In the original: 'tentativa também de reduzir a tensão no campo em áreas marcadas pelo conflito por terras'. Ibid. p. 137.
84. In the original: 'A meta era assentar umas 100 mil famílias ao longo das estradas, em mais de 2 milhões de quilômetros quadrados de terras expropriadas'. Ibid. p. 209.
85. In the original: 'pacificação de 30 grupos indígenas arredios'. Ibid. p. 209.
86. In the original: 'Essa ideologia continha claramente uma perspectiva homofóbica, que relacionava a homossexualidade às esquerdas e à subversão. Acentuou-se, portanto, assumida agora como visão de Estado, a representação do homossexual como nocivo, perigoso e contrário à família, à moral prevalente e aos "bons costumes"'. Ibid. p. 301.
87. In the original: 'a ideia de "democracia racial" pregada pelas propagandas ufanistas da ditadura militar'. Ibid. p. 395.
88. Neocleous, 'International Law as Primitive Accumulation'; Wolfe, 'Settler Colonialism and the Elimination of the Native'.
89. In the original: 'A Amazonia é representada como um "vazio demográfico"'. Comissão Nacional da Verdade, *Relatório da Comissão Nacional da Verdade, vol. 2: Textos Temáticos*, p. 209.
90. In the original: 'que tenha se consolidado a imagem dos povos indígenas enquanto 'empecilho para o desenvolvimento do país'. Ibid. p. 251.
91. In the original: 'as terras do interior do Brasil foram distribuídas entre empresários interessados em tocar empresas agropecuárias ou projetos extrativistas como se ali não existissem moradores'. Ibid. p. 97.

92. In the original: 'o projeto de "terra sem homens para homens sem-terra"'. Ibid. p. 137.
93. Ibid. p. 123.
94. Ibid. p. 139.
95. Ibid. p. 126.
96. In the original: 'a introdução deliberada de varíola, gripe, tuberculose e sarampo entre os índios'. Ibid. p. 207.
97. In the original: 'Os trabalhadores e seu movimento sindical constituíram o alvo primordial do golpe de Estado de 1964'. Ibid. p. 58.
98. Ibid. p. 145.
99. In the original: 'foi possível estimar ao menos 8.350 indígenas mortos no período de investigação da CNV, em decorrência da ação direta de agentes governamentais ou da sua omissão'. Ibid. p. 205.
100. In the original: 'estabelecer-se-á uma nova articulação entre a violência típica do sistema capitalista contra os trabalhadores das cidades e a violência estatal'. Ibid. p. 64.
101. In the original: 'Terrorismo patronal'. Ibid. p. 142.
102. In the original: 'O presente volume do Relatório da Comissão Nacional da Verdade contém um conjunto de textos produzidos sob a responsabilidade individual de alguns dos conselheiros da Comissão'. Ibid. p. 9.
103. In the original: 'O desrespeito às normas trabalhistas já estabelecidas por lei e a concentração de terras nas mãos de poucos proprietários não constituem graves violações de direitos humanos'. Ibid. p. 96.
104. In the original: 'Não houve uma política de Estado formalizada e tão coerente no sentido de exterminar os homossexuais'. Ibid. p. 301.
105. In the original: 'Violações cotidianas'. Ibid. p. 65.
106. Torelly, 'Assessing a Late Truth Commission'; Bohoslavsky and Torelly, 'Financial Complicity'.
107. Roio, personal interview, 17 January 2018.
108. Chambers, 'Enclosure and Labour Supply in the Industrial Revolution'; Wood, The Origin of Capitalism; Vasudevan, McFarlane and Jeffrey, 'Spaces of Enclosure'.
109. Wood, The Origin of Capitalism; Harvey, 'The "New" Imperialism'; Mezzadra, 'The Topicality of Prehistory'; Bonefeld, 'Primitive Accumulation and Capitalist Accumulation'; Sassen, 'A Savage Sorting of Winners and Losers'.

Conclusion: Politics of Impunity

Transitional justice initiatives do not happen in a vacuum. They are shaped by, and also shape, a universe of events, narratives and practices. The assessment of their performance and legacy cannot be easily isolated from their formative role in the political and economic contexts that provide the milieu in which transitional justice happens; the backdrop against which the promise of 'never again' is to be realised. These may seem like obvious statements, but they are often disregarded by the transitional justice literature. To put it simply, we need to understand in which ways the 'common language of justice' and the wider language of (neo)liberalism constituted the *linguae francae* of the years of hope in Brazil. Only then can the full impact of what I call the politics of impunity become clear.

There is no better place to start this conclusion than at the end: the dramatic fall of the Workers' Party from power and grace, an event that shook the foundations of Brazilian politics. The coming to power of the Workers' Party in the early 2000s was significative in terms of expanding the human rights agenda of previous administrations and introducing a new transitional justice agenda at the state and federal levels. But the Brazilian turn to the left was no radical break with the past. The party that united syndicalist leaders, the Catholic youth, and urban intellectuals around an impassionate defence of social justice in the 1980s had changed. After losing the presidential election in 1989 by the tiniest of margins, the Workers' Party eventually fell prey to the blackmail of 'the end of history', sensibly rethinking its core socialist principles under the pretext of winning over the centre ground.[1] No one personified this slow shift more than the party's historical leader, Lula da Silva. Lula, the face of new syndicalism in São Paulo's industrial belt during Brazil's civic-military dictatorship (1964–85), dropped his fiery anti-capitalist rhetoric after three frustrated attempts to run for office. Reimagined as a reasonable politician,[2] mindful of the limitations and restrictions inherent in Brazil's complex political system, he was elected the first president with working-class origins in 2002. In his first presidential address, Lula was clear enough about his priorities: 'First, I am going to do what needs to be done, then I am going to do what can be done, and, when there is nothing left to the imagination, I shall be doing the impossible.'[3] He, too, had moulded himself *en la medida de lo possible*.

The political stability of the Workers' Party governments depended on a delicate political balance that sought the support of the two extreme poles of Brazilian society: the financial sector, and those below the extreme poverty line.[4] The party's early commitment to pursue an anti-capitalist agenda had transformed into a commitment to eradicate hunger and extreme poverty, always perceived in a somehow apolitical way as misfortunes that could be solved by the political will to take the gradual steps.[5] Despite riding on the wave of dissatisfaction with neoliberal adjustments, the strategy of governing 'in the interests of everybody' while keeping a 'keenest eye out for those at the bottom of the heap'[6] effectively meant the continuity of old neoliberal policies.[7] The Lula da Silva administration was defined by this duality. On one hand, the government expanded the famous Bolsa Familia (Family Bursary), providing monthly cash transfers of R$105 on average to families whose per capita monthly income was lower than R$70.[8] Aided by legislation, real minimum wages increased 6.8 per cent between 2003 and 2005 and 5.9 per cent between 2006 and 2010.[9] On the other hand, the economic team reassured sceptics by keeping interest rates high and inflation controlled, and setting fiscal surplus goals even higher than those required by the International Monetary Fund.[10] This delicate balance was facilitated by the boom in the prices of crude oil, soy and iron (some of Brazil's largest exports) in the 2000s.[11] The relentless international demand for Brazilian raw materials took the fiscal pressure off the Workers' Party administration, creating the true sense of a win-win situation. The once radical socialist leader was now extremely dependent on the performance of the international commodity markets.

This win-win game was disturbed by the 2008 financial crisis. The ensuing global economic slowdown forced the second Lula administration to readjust its economic strategy, intensifying its minimum wage policy and increasing real governmental investments (from –4.7 per cent a year in the first term to 27.6 per cent a year in the second term).[12] The strategy to boost the internal market in hope of offsetting the fall in exports proved successful. Amidst a global recession, the second Lula administration could boast about achieving rates of GDP growth of 4.5 per cent a year on average between 2006 and 2010 (when the transitional justice agenda was introduced).[13] But the country's trade balance deteriorated rapidly.[14] A wealthier society with an appreciated currency (due to the entrance of foreign capital) meant that imports continued to increase in a scenario where exports continued to fall. By 2009, commodity prices suffered a devaluation of 28.35 per cent in relation to the previous year. After a brief period of recovery in 2011, when prices exceeded the levels of 2008, new devaluations came in 2012 (–4.51 per cent), in 2013 (–3.04 per cent) and 2014 (–5.68 per cent),[15] going into a freefall in 2016 (–31.89 per cent) as the economy plummeted into a deep recession (GDP reduced 3.5 per cent and household consumption fell 3.8 per cent).[16]

From Hope to Madness (2014–2018)

The establishment of a truth commission was not the only fact to displease conservative segments in the beginning of Rousseff's presidency. Faced with the signs of an economic downturn in 2012, the president doubled down on the heterodox bet: she lowered interest rates, devaluated the currency and indirectly subsidised manufacturers (controlling energy prices and granting tax cuts to selected industries).[17] All of this was done in hope of creating the conditions for a return to economic growth led by an increase in private investment. But, once again, reality struggled to follow the script. Rousseff's plan to revitalise the national economy ended up paving the way for one of the deepest economic crises in Brazilian history. The devaluation of the currency corroded real wages without seriously affecting the competitiveness of national manufacture. The package of lower interest rates, price controls and tax rebates failed to promote new investments, contributing instead to a revenue crisis and the rise of inflationary pressures (on average 1.5 per cent a year higher than in the previous period).[18] By 2014, the rebates amounted to R$222,46 billion,[19] which further deteriorated government accounts (government deficit reached US$100 billion)[20] in the delicate context of expansion of vital benefits (the Bolsa Familia programme, for instance, reached 50 million beneficiaries).[21] The deepening of the crisis also meant widespread discontent with the government, translated into a series of nationwide protests.

Despite the gloomy atmosphere, the 2014 presidential elections ended as a victory for the Workers' Party, but at a great political cost. Plagued by the misfortune of her economic packages and a new corruption scandal, the elected president enjoyed a very small margin in the polls (51.64 per cent), inheriting a divided party base and, more generally, an opposition unwilling to accept its fourth consecutive defeat in twelve years of Workers' Party dominance (2002–14).[22] Less than a week after election day, the defeated party (Social Democracy Party) requested an investigation of the electoral process by a panel of independent experts,[23] emulating the strategies of right-wing parties in other Latin American countries.[24] Party officials claimed they had no doubts over the legitimacy of the process itself, but were only acting to discredit conspiracy theories circulated on social media. No irregularities were found in the electoral process, but the opposition's strategy regained momentum in the second semester of 2015, when Brazil's Federal Accounting Court found irregularities in the government's accounting.[25] Fuelled by the fiscal charges and a power-hungry opposition, Rousseff's impeachment was triggered in December 2015. The impeachment process symbolised the erosion of parliamentarian support for the Workers' Party, and the beginning of what former members of the CNV defined as a 'conservative counter-offensive'.[26] On the legislative branch, the 2014 elections strengthened the 'Bible, Beef and Bullets' caucus, MPs representing the interests of Christian fundamentalists, agribusiness and pro-armament groups in congress. In effect, the Brazilian congress came to display the most conservative composition since the fall of the military dictatorship. And out of this explicit, sometimes raw conservativism, borne out of the entrails of Brazil's *post-conflictual* present, came the frightening ghosts of a violent past that transitional justice interventions had worked so hard to dispel.

The 17th of April 2016 was a turning point: 17 months after the CNV's report exposed the names of 377 state terrorists during the dictatorship, 367 legislators in the lower chamber voted in favour of Rousseff's impeachment, sealing the president's fate.[27] The voting session itself was described as a 'horror show'.[28] During their speeches, MPs from the pro-impeachment camp made almost no mention of the 'creative accounting' of which the president was accused; revamping the banners of marches in support of the military coup in 1964, most MPs chose to justify their decision in the name of God, the sacredness of the family and the value of liberty. Standing out amidst this anachronistic show was Jair Messias Bolsonaro, a former paratrooper court-martialled for insubordination and suspected involvement in a terrorist plot in the 1980s.[29] Bolsonaro had spent twenty-seven years as an unremarkable MP but was now steadily rising in the ranks of the Brazilian far right. An unapologetic supporter of the dictatorship, stark anti-communist and, for all purposes, a neo-fascist, Bolsonaro experienced a stratospheric rise in notoriety towards the end of the Workers' Party decade. His speech in defence of Rousseff's impeachment was perhaps the most chilling expression of the failure of transitional justice's pedagogic project and the promise of reconciliation.

> Glory to the Brazilian people [. . .] they lost in '64. They lost now in 2016. For the family and for the innocence of schoolchildren, that the Workers' Party never had. Against communism, for our freedom, against the Foro de São Paulo [an association of leftist parties in Latin America], for the memory of Col. Carlos Alberto Brilhante Ustra [a former torturer], Dilma Rousseff's dread! For the Army of Caxias. For our armed forces. For Brazil above everything else and for God above everything else, I vote yes.[30]

The long series of protests that started in June 2013 already suggested a certain ideological shift. What began as demonstrations against a raise of 20 cents in public transport fares in the city of São Paulo soon expanded under conditions of general discontentment with Rousseff's government, incorporating the most varied, at times openly authoritarian agendas.[31] Under the banner of 'It isn't just for 20 cents',[32] the protests turned against the economic crisis, the poor quality of public health, widespread corruption, police brutality, and the exorbitant costs of mega-events such as the 2013 Confederations Cup, the 2014 World Cup and the 2016 Olympics. It did not take long before the theme of public transport was put aside and protesters, now dressed in green and yellow and 'armed' with old anti-communist tropes, started taking to the streets against Rousseff's re-election, denouncing the Workers' Party as part of the international communist movement.[33] When the first small groups appeared backing a new military regime, they were taken for an amusing anachronism. But by 17 April 2016, when the 'conservative counter-offensive' was clearly delineated, the laughing had stopped.

The new transitional administration, under the leadership of Michel Temer, Rousseff's vice president turned impeachment advocate, quickly worked towards the demobilisation of the historic gains accrued during the years of hope. In a highly criticised measure, the transitional government amended the constitution, instituting a new fiscal regime that effectively froze social spending for a period of twenty years. The redactor's introductory statement in the Chamber of Deputies warned that only the new regime could protect families, pensioners and entrepreneurs from the impending 'fiscal judgement day'.[34] His use of the apocalyptic metaphor in the service of extreme austerity transmitted with mastery the particular blend of Christian fundamentalism and ultra-liberalism that characterised the ascending right.

The stunning shift to the right was greatly aided by the series of corruption scandals that provided the proper ammunition to longtime critics of the Workers' Party. By the time the discontent with Rousseff's government was intensified in 2013, the Workers' Party had just survived a massive corruption scandal in which party officials had been accused of buying parliamentarian support with monthly bribes.[35] In 2014, a money-laundering investigation initiated by the Federal Police – the *Lava Jato* (Car Wash) operation – ended up revealing yet another, much larger corruption scandal: the Petrobras racketeering scheme. The scheme consisted of channelling systematic overpayments to contractors of the Brazilian multinational company (a giant in the oil sector) in order to finance electoral campaigns. The more the details of systematic corruption were exposed, the more the operation affected the country's political and economic stability, cornering a big part of the political class and stalling the operations of one of Brazil's largest state-owned enterprises. With unemployment levels reaching 13.7 per cent in March 2017,[36] the distrust of politicians sparked by the scandal soon turned into outrage. Eventually the investigations reached Lula da Silva, the historical leader of the Workers' Party. Facing charges that ranged from embezzlement and misuse of political prestige to attempts to obstruct justice, Lula was convicted to serve a nine-year sentence in June 2017 (later extended to twelve years and one month).[37] He would be released after 580 days, once the Supreme Court found the circumstances of his arrest and imprisonment unlawful.[38]

This 'perfect storm' scenario proved an extremely fertile ground for the rise of *Bolsonarismo* and the particular brand of far-right militarism and historical revisionism espoused by the former paratrooper. Taking advantage of the global rise of the far right (including Trump's election in the United States and the Brexit vote in the UK) as well as the domestic outrage with the economic crisis and the anti-political atmosphere, the longtime politician managed to sell himself as an outsider unsullied by the sins of the political class. Bolsonaro was enormously aided by the unfolding of the Car Wash operation, as Lula was leading the polls by the time of his imprisonment. His fiery rhetoric, unconstrained by any sense of humanity or even by the requirement to make sense, was particularly effective in rousing conservative segments eager to frame the Workers' Party as a criminal organisation that had to be stopped.[39] More fundamentally, the rise of *Bolsonarismo* shows the shifting meanings of the concept of impunity, and how politically volatile its mobilisation has become in the course of re-democratisation in Brazil. If 'anti-impunity' had played the role of the central banner around which the resistance against the military regime had mobilised in the late 1970s, decades of public insecurity and penal popu-lism had turned 'impunity' into one of the central signifiers of extreme militarisms. In a sober reminder of this conceptual indeterminacy, the army general Villas Boas, in a country where no veteran of the *Repressão* ever faced a day in prison, tweeted that conceding a *habeas corpus* to Lula would amount to the condonement of impunity.[40] In the end, Bolsonaro played on the myth that rendered the country of 60,000 deaths a year as the 'land of impunity' like no other candidate.

During the wave of discontent that ravaged the country, Bolsonaro relentlessly made inconsistent, often bombastic associations between the Workers' Party's humanitarian agenda, the corruption scandals and a hid-den communist plot. The ideas of Jacques Hogard and the French tradi-tion of colonial counterinsurgency lived on in the paratrooper's effort to denounce an ongoing 'covert war' waged by the left (the so called commu-nist-globalist-feminist movement) under the façade of peace. Year after year, he religiously celebrated the anniversaries of the 1964 coup,[41] taking every opportunity to remind other MPs of Rousseff's 'terrorist' past.[42] The far-right leader went as far as to propose a distasteful comparison between the president and the Tsarnaev brothers, culprits of the Boston Marathon Bombings.[43] A stark opponent of the human rights agenda as policy that only benefited 'tramps', 'rapists' and 'crooks',[44] Bolsonaro took every chance to oppose truth-seeking. After the release of the CNV's final report, he shamelessly referred to Rousseff as a 'pimp' who had appointed seven 'prostitutes' (the members of staff) to adulterate history.[45] This fiery mix of slurs, Cold War-style conspiracy theories and unashamed hate speech continued throughout the 2016 impeachment and well into the 2018 presidential campaigns. The former paratrooper was portrayed as a fearless strongman in defence of conservative values and the only one capable of cleaning up the mess left by 'politics as usual'. In the 1990s, Bolsonaro had openly praised the Argentine junta for murdering 30,000 dissidents; now he showed no qualms to suggest that 'supporters of the Workers' Party should be gunned down'.[46] With Lula imprisoned and ineligible for office, the far-right leader took the lead in the polls, later surviving an attempt on his life at a political rally. On 28 October 2018, he was elected president of Brazil with 55 per cent of valid votes,[47] sealing the fate of Brazilian society in a way that no one could have possibly predicted.

The Return of the Repressed?

Transitional justice is always faced with huge expectations. In societies beset by high levels of violence, such as Brazil, the promise of 'never again' is sometimes infused with an almost mythical aura. Remembrance is supposed to provide closure to survivors of terror and family members of the disappeared. Truth-telling is supposed to reconcile incommensurable world views. Criminal accountability is supposed to put an end to endless abuses of power. Thus, it is unsurprising when these expectations are shown to be unrealistic, considering the usual scope of transitional justice interventions in terms of staffing, timeframe and budget. Truth commissions, reparations programmes and courts are often, and mostly unfairly, criticised for having failed to deliver. The Brazilian case is no exception.

The sense that transitional justice 'failed to deliver' was more palatable and symbolic in Brazil than in perhaps any other recent case. The intensification of transitional justice initiatives from the mid-2000s to the creation of the CNV in 2012 signalled a time of hope. Even as a delayed response by the government to the condemnation by the IACtHR, the CNV still symbolised the possibility of redress for thousands of individuals whose lives were affected in an irreversible way by decades of authoritarianism. It represented the possibility of deepening Brazil's commitment to the ideals of democracy, the rejection of authoritarianism and the protection of human rights. But, contrary to the traditional script of transitional justice, hope turned into madness in the space of four years (2014–18). Brazil was hit by a deep economic and political crisis. The society supposed to be reconciled by the forensic truth about the past was experiencing mounting political divisions. The promise that the 1964 coup would never be forgotten and never happen again was sharing space with denunciations of the 2016 impeachment as a veiled coup d'état.[48] Far-right historical revisionism, although never entirely absent from Brazil's political scene, was becoming visibly normalised with the new far-right president. At times, it seemed as though the new political agenda had been carefully tailored to go against every single one of the twenty-nine recommendations of the final report.[49]

Such an unexpected and dramatic turn of events magnified, in retrospect, assessments that the truth commission itself had failed. Despite being almost unanimously praised overseas, the CNV was heavily criticised in Brazil as yet another frustrating case of 'mishandling'. In this manuscript, I have analysed this criticism in terms of the irreducible and interconnected historical demands of survivors and the anti-impunity movement: truth (knowledge), memory (acknowledgement) and justice (criminal accountability). In light of all these aspects, the truth commission falls short of satisfactory. Most of its findings were based on decades of unofficial and official research, and the commissioners could only find the mortal remains of one single disappeared. In other words, it failed to produce new, substantial information about the violent past. Activists and researchers claimed the CNV was, from the beginning, a non-ideal intervention. In other words, due to the compromises made during its phase of constitution and the absence of a period of preparation, the CNV lost precious powers (such as the power to hold trials or to make binding recommendations) and precious time (in effect, the first six months were extremely unproductive). The CNV obtained important victories, such as the declassification of documents from the US Department of State, the rediscovery of archives thought to be lost, the raising of the number of officially recognised victims to 434, and the procurement of new, individual obituaries. But none of these victories could erase what seemed like the biggest defeat of transitional justice. In the end, no criminal trials were held, and the final report failed to reconcile the armed forces with the rest of Brazilian society, in the terms of the 'common language of justice'.

The rise of *Bolsonarismo* added another layer to this sense of failure: seen in hindsight, the events from the '2016 coup' to the election of the neo-fascist leader in 2018 seemed suggestive of the old trope of the 'return of the repressed'. This trope, abundant in the transitional justice and memory studies literatures, is very similar to the concept of 'cultures of impunity', focusing on the risks of leaving past historical traumas unaddressed for too long. In its most common-sense form, the trope suggests that when past events are repressed (unacknowledged, silenced, denied) there is a risk they might somehow return to haunt the present and that history might repeat itself. Inspired by Freudian psychoanalysis, the idea assumes that societies that fail to properly 'work through' their past traumas, that is, articulate and make sense of them, addressing their causes, are doomed to 'act them out' in the future, in other words, to repeat them. Writing on the Brazilian elections for the British newspaper *The Guardian*, the writer and journalist Eliane Brum was among the first to mobilise the trope, arguing that 'Jair Bolsonaro is the monstrous product of the country's silence about the crimes committed by its former dictatorship'.[50] There was no shortage of explanations connecting the rise of the far right to the failure of transitional justice in the country. When transitional justice interventions were intensified in the mid-2000s, the intentions were good, but it was unfortunately too little, too late.

The idea of a 'culture of impunity', the criticism that the reparations and truth commissions were 'mishandled', and the trope of the 'return of the repressed' showcase the same problem. Their individual merits aside, they all tend to rely on an essentially counterfactual, 'if only' hypothesis:

if only the transition to democracy had been completed, if only a truth commission had come earlier, if only the military had acknowledged their crimes, if only perpetrators had been punished. The list is almost endless. The first problem is that there is no way of knowing. To accept these hypotheses, we need nothing short of an act of faith. The second problem regards the extent of our criticism to the very basis of the discipline of transitional justice. This act of faith is also a political act: what the 'if only' hypothesis does is to shift criticism away from the discipline of transitional justice, reinvigorating a certain hope that the 'failure' at stake is the failure of implementation and not the failure of unrealisable promises. Consequently, the appeal of transitional justice is reinstated precisely at the moment of crisis, emptying the effects of a more substantial critique.

This manuscript was written against this act of faith, so common in the transitional justice literature. I proposed a critique of transitional justice interventions that did not shy away from a critique of the very theoretical basis, the promises and the political consequences of what I described as a historically grounded discipline. This critique moves beyond the critique of ad hoc failures of implementation, redirecting blame away from practitioners working in suboptimal conditions upwards, towards the directives stipulated by the discipline they followed. As such, this critique of transitional justice focuses on the disciplinary character of interventions: the necessity to fabricate a post-conflictual reality, the affinities between a common language of justice and a certain language of (neo) liberalism, and the effects of the economy of anti-impunity in our general understandings of violence. It assesses the question of accountability in the aftermath by incorporating the problematics of the *fetishism of responsibility* and the *enclosure of blame* into the explanation of why certain traumatic pasts tend to recur in the present. In relation to the case study at stake, this critique offers a reading of contemporary Brazilian politics in which the 'optical illusion' of responsibility expressed in transitional justice interventions played an active part in the build-up to the crisis in which we currently live.

Disciplines work by disciplining the conduct of individuals and groups. It is in relation to this point, more so than any other, that transitional justice reveals a successful face as a discipline that infuses the present political order with legitimacy. In Brazil and throughout the world, transitional justice debates have succeeded in portraying the techniques of retribution and restoration as apolitical, technocratic measures to promote a liberalising transition. They have succeeded in framing the theme of impunity as the most important topic in post-conflict/post-authoritarian scenarios.

Most of all, they have succeeded in reducing the complexity of what we understand as 'violence' – breaking it away from its relational character into discrete units of blame, properly fenced off from the rest of society – the domesticating struggles of 'resistance' in the present and circumscribing the achievable limits of 'justice' in the future.

In Brazil, the effects of disciplinarity are clear in the way transitional justice interventions remember the radical left (in particular the ones analysed in this book). Despite a genuine effort to do justice to the memory of political struggles, the permanent exhibition of the RM-SP is always haunted by what I have called a commodified memory of resistance: a representation that reduces the historical complexity of struggles of resistance, representing them primarily or naturally as resistance against illiberalism/authoritarianism. A commodified memory of resistance is, therefore, a memory that equates the values of political struggles (in the past and the present alike) with the values of the present politico-economic order. It is a memory, that is, a representational practice, that defines the acceptable limits of political conduct while providing the present with a certain surplus morality. This is a practice very much present in the report of the CNV. The first volume does not discuss in depth the complexities of the political project of the radical left. The text not only shows a paltry engagement with the documents of clandestine organisations, but it also sidelines the complex ideas of a recurrent and normalised violence, intrinsic to capitalist societies, relegated to a couple of essays in the second volume. But even in the second volume, generally the space for less constrained, more 'radical' reflections, we still find the signs of a commodified memory of resistance. The only essay that addresses the theme of resistance in the past, 'A resistência da sociedade civil' (civil society's resistance), states that: 'the struggle of resistance (in any form it takes) [. . .] is a struggle about rights, legality and justice. Those who take part in the struggle do not do so exclusively or mainly in the name of an ideological banner or a partisan political project. The essence of their struggle is the defence of liberty'.[51]

The question of historical accuracy aside, a commodified memory of resistance is problematic because it delimits the space of present political conduct. In the end, this non-partisan (one could say depoliticised) concept of resistance appears as nothing other than the defence of a vague idea of liberty, which could easily split into a defence of the present politico-economic order. And this argument can be equally extended to transitional justice's promise of justice, translated in the recommendations of the CNV, deemed fundamental for the restoration of normality according to a post-conflictual economy of signification.

The twenty-nine recommendations exhibited a limited understanding of the complexities of political violence, proposing a certain market model of accountability. The themes of punishment, demilitarisation, education and the promotion of human rights were based on an idea of power as a possession. They envisioned the redistribution of liberties and rights and the rebalancing of the systemic gap between the powerful and the powerless as possible ways of redressing the historical wrongs of the Brazilian polis. But a market model of accountability, based on an economistic or fictitious arithmetic solution, can never fully deliver. The process of recounting the wronged parts of society is always a miscount that leaves the unidentified 'parts' or unacknowledged 'victims' uncovered by the promise of justice.

This miscount is very clear in the workings of CNV. The adoption of a narrow understanding of violence and a depoliticised representation of resistance led to accusations that the final report produced an uncomfortable hierarchy of victims: privileging the 434 victims of GVHRs to the plight of thousands of peasants and Amerindians. The primary identification of VHRs as the wrongs to be addressed and the focus on the dictatorship produced a parsimonious promise of justice: a policy of redress that is easily understood and feasible in time, providing hope to parts of survivors and family members without shaking the foundations of the *post-conflictual* state. Nonetheless, this parsimonious promise of justice rested on a double act of marginalisation; the focus on *systematic violations of human rights* marginalised the concern with *systemic forms of violence* decreeing the further marginalisation of those affected by the latter in present-day Brazil. Their lived reality of exclusion was doubled by their exclusion from the category of 'victims' of political violence, worthy of being remembered in their individuality, in the final report.

A critique of disciplinarity does not see this double act of marginalisation as a failure, but as part of a process of *enclosure of blame* that enables a parsimonious promise of justice. Transitional justice can only promise a future of 'never again' by fending off responsibility for past and present wrongs in an individual and indivisible source of responsibility (in Brazil, the dictatorship and the military). A promise of justice based on a narrow understanding of violence and supported by a depoliticised idea of resistance, in the sense that the justice pursued is, in the end, justice *en la medida de lo posible*. It is unsurprising that this justice, tailor-made to go only as far as politically possible, influenced by the language of (neo) liberalism, flourished under the delicate political balance (some would say conservative compromise) of the Workers' Party administrations.[52] So many comparisons could be made between the two in terms of historical silences and processes of depoliticization. The silencing of a past ethos of justice as refusal, the depoliticization of present-day strategies to redress wrongs, the effort to fabricate a non-conflictual/post-conflictual atmosphere, the unwillingness to push the boundaries of the pursuit of justice beyond what is conveniently possible. One could certainly point out here the uncomfortable coincidence that peasants and Indigenous peoples were left outside the state's policy of redress precisely during the boom of mining and agribusiness; or that critiques of the militarisation of law enforcement by transitional justice practitioners were voiced as the armed forces were authorised by the president to take control of policing duties in Rio de Janeiro; or yet the irony that Rousseff, still accused of terrorism by the far right, would be the president to give in to international pressure and pass controversial anti-terrorism legislation.

The Paratrooper and the Gravediggers

The word *paraquedista* (parachutist) has a quirky use in Portuguese. In informal settings, calling someone a parachutist evokes the idea of being improvised in their role, of lacking the proper qualifications for the task they are mandated to accomplish. Perhaps no other historical moment has infused a simple slang term with such prescience like the first two years of Bolsonaro's government. The former paratrooper's time in office can be defined by what I propose to call the Bolsonaro Paradox: one cannot claim to be surprised by the actions of a man who spent decades unashamedly showing no regard for human life. Yet, the extent of the inhumanity of his words and actions is so enormous that being surprised and shocked by them is almost inevitable.

Bolsonaro composed a government based on an unsavoury but common combination in the history of Latin America: economic policy-making was handed over to the uber-liberal economist Paulo Guedes, a University of Chicago alumnus with first-hand experience of Pinochet's rule (Guedes lectured at the University of Chile during the dictatorship). Guedes pressed for pension reforms and more waves of privatisation. The Ministry of Justice and Public Security was offered to Justice Moro, one of the central actors during Operation Car Wash and main articulator of Lula's imprisonment. His agenda was based on more 'penal populism', bringing forth, among other 'anti-impunity' measures, proposals to legalise police killings in terms of the officer's right to self-defence or due to an altered emotional state. Government positions were opened to members of the so-called ideological wing, the disciples of the former journalist turned extremist pundit Olavo de Carvalho, who kept on stirring hate and misinformation, leading the crusade against 'cultural Marxism' from his residency in the American state of Virginia. The new government was also marked by a strong military presence. Aside from Bolsonaro's vice president, General Mourão, ten other ministers and heads of secretariats were servicemen, reservists or had received military training at some point in their careers. The military presence in civilian-related government positions more than doubled from 2,957 posts in 2016 to 6,157 posts in 2020.[53]

Bolsonaro's government quickly sunk the fantasy, already nurtured during the days of Temer's transitional government, that sustained economic growth would magically resume with the ousting of the Workers' Party. After a long recession, economic recovery showed the uninspiring rate of 1.41 in 2019, only to plunge to −10.90 in the second trimester of 2020, once the Covid-19 crisis was fully delineated.[54] The government was unable to deliver on its neoliberal promises. Guedes's dream of a Chilean-style, fully capitalised pension scheme was blocked by congress and privatisations stalled, forcing Bolsonaro, the outsider, to ally himself with the traditional centre right. Unsurprisingly, Bolsonaro interfered with transitional justice programmes, restructuring the Amnesty Commission – exchanging members for servicemen antagonistic to the very project of truth-seeking – and reducing the powers of the CEMDP.[55] His government came under international scrutiny for the levels of deforestation of the Amazon forest, which once again surpassed the threshold of 10,000 km^2 in 2019, when the biome suffered from widespread fires.[56] In the domestic sphere, the candidate who promised to excise corruption from the entrails of the state witnessed the personal aid of his eldest son, Senator Flávio Bolsonaro, become the centre of a corruption scandal that also involved his ex-wife, his present wife and two of his other sons.[57] More dramatically, the paratrooper was also confronted by the unfolding of the investigations of Marielle Franco's and Anderson Gomes's murder. Two of the prime suspects were found to have met prior to the crime in the gated community Vivendas da Barra, located in an upmarket neighbourhood of Rio de Janeiro. According to the bombastic testimony of a porter, one of the suspects was granted permission to enter the estate by the resident of house number 58, Bolsonaro's property.[58] While Bolsonaro's participation was ruled out (he was in Brasília at the time), the testimony reignited concerns regarding proven ties between his family and local militiamen and death squads.

The former paratrooper dealt with the almost constant state of crisis that marked his early government in the only way he knew: by vociferating patriarchal, militaristic and conspiratorial views. The Amazon fires were misleadingly blamed on pro-Indigenous NGOs and HROs. In a statement that would have been comic were the situation not so tragic, even Leonardo DiCaprio was accused of financing the wildfires.[59] Bolsonaro threatened to physically attack reporters who raised his family's involvement in corruption rings and,[60] on one occasion, even hired a professional comedian to impersonate him in a press conference, handing over bananas to journalists.[61] Examples of Bolsonaro's contempt for his position in office and the fate of the country, like the examples above, sometimes on the verge of delusional acts, and are far too numerous to be mentioned here. But nothing could have prepared anyone for the grotesque levels of inhumanity that the former paratrooper would show during the global pandemic.

Faced with a deadly pathogen spreading quickly around the world, Bolsonaro's reaction ranged from complete indifference to near excitement at the possibility of mass death. From day one, following on the footsteps of other far-right denialists, Bolsonaro dismissed Covid-19 as no more dangerous than a minor cold and omitted data about the disease's spread.[62] Bolsonaro had been openly at war with the educational system (which he saw as dominated by partisan Marxists and 'gender ideologists'), axing public funding for scientific research and interfering with the governance of higher education institutions. At the hight of the pandemic, he boycotted efforts to approve the CoronaVac (a vaccine developed by the Chinese company Sinovac Biotech) for large-scale production in the country, on account of crude Sinophobia.[63] He continued to scorn the disease, reject the need for protective equipment and incite mass public gatherings of his supporters throughout the crisis, which he constantly attended, even when infected by the virus.

The more dead bodies were piling up – to the point that cemetery workers in some states of the federation were resorting to mass graves[64] – the more the former paratrooper showed his usual brand of cruelty and contempt, firing one health minister after another. In March, as infections and deaths were escalating rapidly, he opposed the implementation of local lockdowns by state governors using devolved powers to diverge from the path of negligence. By late April 2020, the country had reached a total of 70,000 infection cases and 5,000 virus-related deaths; Bolsonaro's response was simply 'So what?' With 162,000 accumulated deaths by November, Bolsonaro's verdict, proffered in a conference on the hospitality and tourism sectors, was that Brazil had to quit being 'a country of sissies' and face Covid-19 'like a man'.[65] At the time of writing, with the death toll surpassing 197,000,[66] Bolsonaro's stance remains unchanged. Backed by important members of the business class, the former paratrooper still insists that death must run its course so that the Brazilian economy, or whatever is left of it, may survive. His words 'Everyone will die one day', voiced in the early days of the pandemic, are beginning to sound more like a promise.

However bleak the present may look, not everything is cause for concern. Bolsonaro's election also had the unintended, but much welcomed, effect of rearticulating new foci of resistance, especially from the feminist movement, the Black movement and some segments of precarised workers. In this context of political articulation against the former paratrooper's extremist agenda, a group of twenty-two intellectuals and legal practitioners, including former CNV staff members, launched the Comissão de Defesa dos Direitos Humanos Dom Paulo Evaristo Arns (the Arns Commission for Human Rights Defence, aka Arns Commission). Its 2019 manifesto begins with the important statement that 'Brazilian history is characterized by serious violations of the most fundamental human rights.'[67] It also affirms the commission's duty as a naming and shaming body, engaged in the prevention of 'setbacks'[68] to the process of democratisation enshrined in the 1988 constitution. Importantly, the manifesto recognised how the present political context posed a particular threat to 'the most discriminated sectors of society, made vulnerable by their race, religion, gender, sexual orientation, social and economic status'.[69] The activities organised in its short period of operations seem to incorporate both the conclusions of the second volume of the CNV's final report and the general transformational zeitgeist of the discipline of transitional justice. Alongside the more traditional naming and shaming of state killings and mistreatments, the commission has issued statements against the eviction of groups of peasants and traditional communities, demanding the consultation of Indigenous peoples before the implementation of development projects. Its most important, or at least noticeable, act so far was to co-file a suit with the ICC accusing Bolsonaro of committing crimes against humanity and inciting genocidal acts against the Indigenous peoples of Brazil. The commission argues that Bolsonaro's acts, words and policies showcase *a clear intention to destroy the leaders and the livelihood of Indigenous peoples* through the contamination of rivers and through land grabbing by miners, loggers and settlers.[70]

I would like to conclude by highlighting the actions of the Arns Commission as symbolic of the impasse I attempted to translate in terms of the enclosure of blame, an impasse I believe to be representative of the current state of the discipline of transitional justice. It is far too early to make a profound assessment, but some problems are already very clear. Despite an extensive knowledge of the foundational wrongs that define contemporary societies, the commission, much like its predecessor, can only translate this knowledge into calls for parsimonious justice; making the face of the former paratrooper hyper-visible as the congealment of the violent social relations that sustain everyday life. Make no mistake: a conviction in the ICC would be welcomed, but it could be dangerously counterproductive if perceived as an end in itself.

Notes

1. Antunes, 'Fenomenologia da Crise Brasileira'; Singer, 'Raízes Sociais e Ideológicas do Lulismo'; Loureiro and Saad-Filho, 'The Limits of Pragmatism'.
2. Castaneda, 'Latin America's Left Turn'.
3. Silva, Sader and Gentili, 'The Necessary, the Possible, and the Impossible', p. 225.
4. Singer, 'Raízes Sociais e Ideológicas do Lulismo'.
5. Singer, *Os Sentidos do Lulismo*.
6. Silva, Sader and Gentili, 'The Necessary, the Possible, and the Impossible', p. 230.
7. Singer, 'Raízes Sociais e Ideológicas do Lulismo'.
8. Saad-Filho, 'Social Policy for Neoliberalism'.
9. Carvalho, *Valsa Brasileira*.
10. Flores-Macias, *After Neoliberalism?*; Singer, 'Raízes Sociais e Ideológicas do Lulismo'.
11. Beasley-Murray, Cameron and Hershberg, 'Latin America's Left Turns'; Panizza, *Contemporary Latin America*; Loureiro and Saad-Filho, 'The Limits of Pragmatism'.
12. Carvalho, *Valsa Brasileira*.
13. Ibid.
14. Loureiro and Saad-Filho, 'The Limits of Pragmatism'.
15. 'IMF DATA: Primary Commodity Price System'.
16. Carvalho, *Valsa Brasileira*.
17. Morais and Saad-Filho, 'Neo-Developmentalism and the Challenges of Economic Policy-Making under Dilma Rousseff'; Carvalho, *Valsa Brasileira*; Singer, 'Cutucando Onças com Vara Cutra'.
18. Carvalho, *Valsa Brasileira*.
19. 'Dilma Deu R$ 458 Bilhões em Desonerações'.
20. Loureiro and Saad-Filho, 'The Limits of Pragmatism', p. 9.
21. Saad-Filho, 'Social Policy for Neoliberalism'.
22. Antunes, 'Fenomenologia da Crise Brasileira'; Nunes and Melo, 'Impeachment, Political Crisis and Democracy in Brazil'.
23. 'PSDB Pede Auditoria Especial do Resultado das Eleições ao TSE'.
24. Cannon, *The Right in Latin America*.
25. 'TCU Conclui Parecer sobre Contas Prestadas pela Presidente da República Referentes a 2014'.
26. Mesplé, phone interview, 6 January 2018; Pinheiro, Skype interview, 9 January 2018.
27. 'Câmara Autoriza Instauração de Processo de Impeachment de Dilma com 367 Votos a Favor e 137 Contra'.

28. 'Show de Horrores nada Surpreendente: Cientistas Políticos Analisam a Votação do Impeachment'.
29. 'O Artigo em VEJA e a Prisão de Bolsonaro nos Anos 1980'.
30. In the original: 'Perderam em 1964. Perderam agora em 2016. Pela família e pela inocência das crianças em sala de aula, que o PT nunca teve . . . Contra o comunismo, pela nossa liberdade, contra a Folha de S. Paulo, pela memória do Cel. Carlos Alberto Brilhante Ustra, o pavor de Dilma Rousseff! [. . .] Pelo Exército de Caxias, pelas nossas Forças Armadas, por um Brasil acima de tudo, e por Deus acima de todos, o meu voto é sim!' *Diário da Câmara dos Deputados. Ano LXXI – Nº 056 Segunda-Feira, 18 de Abril de 2016*, p. 91.
31. Tatagiba and Galvão, 'Os Protestos no Brasil em Tempos de Crise (2011–2016)'; Saad-Filho and Morais, 'Mass Protests'; Telles, 'A Direita Vai às Ruas'; Singer, 'Brasil, Junho de 2013'.
32. '"Não São Só 20 Centavos", Dizem Manifestantes na Avenida Paulista'.
33. Telles, 'A Direita Vai às Ruas'.
34. 'Relator da PEC do Teto Diz que "dia do Juízo Fiscal" Virá se Projeto não for Aprovado'.
35. 'Brazil "Mensalao" Corruption Trial Concludes'.
36. Instituto de Pesquisa Economica Aplicada, 'Ipeadata: Taxa de Desocupação das Pessoas de 14 Anos ou Mais de Idade, na Semana de Referência'.
37. 'Veja as Principais Decisões da Justiça sobre a Prisão de Lula'.
38. 'Brazil's Former President Lula Walks Free from Prison after Supreme Court Ruling'.
39. Misse, 'Crime, Sujeito e Sujeição Criminal'; 'Brazil Elections: Prospect of Bolsonaro Victory Stokes Fears of Return to Dictatorship'.
40. 'Na Véspera de Julgamento sobre Lula, Comandante do Exército Diz Repudiar Impunidade'.
41. *Diário da Câmara dos Deputados. Ano LXX – Nº 049 Quarta-Feira, 1 de Abril de 2015*, p. 17.
42. *Diário da Câmara dos Deputados. Ano LXVIII – Nº 088 Sexta-Feira, 24 de Maio de 2013*, 19970.
43. *Diário da Câmara dos Deputados. Ano LXVIII – Nº 067 Quarta-Feira, 24 de Abril de 2013*, 11968.
44. *Diário da Câmara dos Deputados. Ano LXIX – Nº 190 Quarta-Feira, 10 de Dezembro de 2014*, p. 41.
45. *Diário da Câmara dos Deputados. Ano LXIX – Nº 152 Quinta-Feira, 16 de Outubro de 2014*, p. 25.
46. 'Campanha Confirma Vídeo em que Bolsonaro Fala em "Fuzilar Petralhada do Acre": "Foi Brincadeira"'.
47. 'Jair Bolsonaro é Eleito Presidente e Interrompe Série de Vitórias do PT'.
48. Jinkings, Doria and Cleto (eds), *Por Que Gritamos Golpe?*; Franco, 'After the Take-Over'; Loureiro and Saad-Filho, 'The Limits of Pragmatism'; Encarnación, 'The Patriarchy's Revenge'.
49. Westhrop et al., *As Recomendações da Comissão Nacional da Verdade*.

50. 'How a Homophobic, Misogynist, Racist "Thing" Could Be Brazil's next President'.
51. 'a luta de resistência (sob qualquer forma) que ocorre quando se quebra o Estado de Direito e se rompem os princípios e valores que o organizam. Essa é uma luta que se forma em torno dos direitos, da legalidade, da justiça. Quem participa dela não o faz exclusiva ou prioritariamente em nome de uma bandeira ideológica ou de um projeto político partidário. Sua essência é a defesa da liberdade'. Comissão Nacional da Verdade, *Relatório da Comissão Nacional da Verdade, vol. 2: Textos Temáticos*, p. 342.
52. Singer, *Os Sentidos do Lulismo*.
53. 'Governo Bolsonaro mais que dobra Número de Militares em Cargos Civis, Aponta TCU'.
54. Instituto de Pesquisa Economica Aplicada, 'Ipeadata: Simópse Macroeconômica'.
55. *Comissão Arns: Annual Report Feb 2019 – Feb 2020*.
56. Instituto Nacional de Pesquisas Espaciais. Coordenação Geral de Observação da Terra, 'Programa de Monitoramento da Amazônia e Demais Biomas – Desmatamento – Amazônia Legal'.
57. 'Queiroz Preso: Entenda a Investigação Envolvendo o Ex-Assessor de Flávio Bolsonaro'.
58. 'Bolsonaro Attacks "putrid" Media over Marielle Franco Murder Claims'.
59. 'Brazil's Leader Falsely Blames Leonardo DiCaprio for Amazon Fires'.
60. 'Brazilians Back Reporter Whom Bolsonaro "Felt like Punching"'.
61. 'Bolsonaro Faz Piada com PIB Usando Humorista Carioca em Entrevista'.
62. 'News Organizations Team up to Provide Transparency to Covid-19 Data'.
63. 'Brazil's Bolsonaro Claims Victory as Sinovac COVID-19 Trial Halted'.
64. 'Cemitério de Manaus Faz Hora Extra para Dar Conta de Enterros em Massa'.
65. A succession of his grotesque statements can be found here: 'Coronavírus: "país de Maricas" e Outras 8 Frases de Bolsonaro sobre Pandemia que Matou 162 Mil Pessoas no Brasil'.
66. World Health Organization, 'WHO Coronavirus Disease (COVID-19) Dashboard'.
67. *Comissão Arns: Annual Report Feb 2019 – Feb 2020*, p. 4.
68. Ibid. p. 4.
69. Ibid. p. 4.
70. 'TPI Informa Avaliação Preliminar da Jurisdição do Caso contra Bolsonaro'.

BIBLIOGRAPHY

Abrão, Paulo, Flavia Carlet, Daniela Frantz, Kelen Meregeli Model Ferreira and Vanda Oliveira, 'Educação e Anistia Política: Idéias e Práticas Emancipatórias Para a Construção Da Memória, Da Reparação e Da Verdade No Brasil', in Boaventura de Sousa Santos, Paulo Abrão, Cecília MacDowell dos Santos and Marcelo D. Torelly (eds), *Repressão e Memória Política no Contexto Ibero-Brasileiro: Estudos sobre Brasil, Guatemala, Moçambique, Peru e Portugal* (Brasília; Coimbra: Ministério da Justiça; Comissão de Anistia; Centro de Estudos Sociais Universidade de Coimbra, 2010), pp. 60–87.

Abrão, Paulo and Marcelo Torelly, 'Justiça de Transição no Brasil: A Dimensão da Reparação', in Boaventura de Sousa Santos, Paulo Abrão, Cecília MacDowell dos Santos and Marcelo D. Torelly (eds), *Repressão e Memória Política no Contexto Ibero-Brasileiro: Estudos sobre Brasil, Guatemala, Moçambique, Peru e Portugal* (Brasília; Coimbra: Ministério da Justiça; Comissão de Anistia; Centro de Estudos Sociais Universidade de Coimbra, 2010), pp. 26–59.

'Acordo de Cooperação Técnica Internacional com o PNUD', <http://www.cnv.gov. br/component/content/article/20-parcerias/444-acordo-de-cooperacao-tecnica-internacional-com-o-pnud.html> (accessed 20 July 2015).

Adorno, Sérgio, 'Exclusão Socioeconômica e Violência Urbana', *Sociologias* 4, no. 8 (2002): 84–135.

Adorno, Sérgio, 'História e Desventura: O 3º Programa Nacional de Direitos Humanos', *Novos Estudos* 86 (Marco 2010): 4–21.

Adorno, Sérgio, 'Insegurança versus Direitos Humanos: Entre a Lei e a Ordem', *Tempo Social: Revista de Sociologia Da USP* 11, no. 2 (1999): 129–54.

Adorno, Sérgio, 'Monopólio Estatal da Violência na Sociedade Brasileira Contemporânea', in Miceli Sérgio (ed.), *O Que Ler na Ciência Social Brasileira (1970–2002)*, vol. 4 (São Paulo: Sumaré, 2002), pp. 1–32.

Agamben, Giorgio, *Homo Sacer: Sovereign Power and Bare Life* (Stanford, CA: Stanford University Press, 1998).

Agamben, Giorgio, Lorenzo Fabbri and Elisabeth Fay, 'On the Limits of Violence', *Diacritics* 4 (Winter 2009): 103–11.

Åhäll, Linda, 'The Dance of Militarisation: A Feminist Security Studies Take on "the Political"', *Critical Studies on Security* 4, no. 2 (2016): 154–68, <https://doi.org/10.1080/21624887.2016.1153933>.

Alcalá, Pilar Riaño and María Victoria Uribe, 'Constructing Memory amidst War: The Historical Memory Group of Colombia', *International Journal of Transitional Justice* 10, no. 1 (2016): 6–24.

'Alemanha Vai Cooperar com a Comissão da Verdade', <http://www.cnv.gov.br/outros-destaques/269-alemanha-vai-cooperar-com-a-comissao-da-verdade.html> (accessed 10 December 2015).

Alexander, Jeffrey C., *Trauma: A Social Theory* (Cambridge: Polity, 2012).

Alexander, Marc and Mark Davies, 'Hansard Corpus 1803–2005' (2015), <https://www.hansard-corpus.org/x.asp> (accessed 20 September 2021).

Alfonsín, Raul, *Mensajes presidenciales del Dr. Raúl Alfonsín a la honorable asamblea legislativa: Período 1983–1987* (Buenos Aires: Imprensa del Congreso de la Nación, 1987).

Allen, Matthew J., 'The Poverty of Memory: For Political Economy in Memory Studies', *Memory Studies* 9, no. 4 (2016): 371–5.

Allhoff, Fritz, 'A Defense of Torture: Separation of Cases, Ticking Time-Bombs, and Moral Justification', *International Journal of Applied Philosophy* 19, no. 2 (2005): 243–64.

ALN and MR-8, 'Manifesto da ALN e do MR-8 (1969)', in Flamarion Maués (ed.), *Versões e Ficções: O Sequestro da História* (São Paulo: Fundação Perseu Abramo, 1997), pp. 227–30.

Althusser, Louis, *For Marx* (London; New York: Verso, 2005).

Amnesty International, 'Brazil: "They Treat Us Like Animals": Torture and Ill-Treatment in Brazil: Dehumanization and Impunity within the Criminal Justice System' (2001).

Andrieu, K., 'Civilizing Peacebuilding: Transitional Justice, Civil Society and the Liberal Paradigm', *Security Dialogue* 41, no. 5 (14 October 2010): 537–58.

Antunes, Ricardo, 'Fenomenologia da Crise Brasileira', *Lutas Sociais* 19, no. 35 (2015): 9–26.

AP, 'Documento Base (Fevereiro 1963)', in Daniel Aarão Reis and Jair Ferreira de Sá (eds), *Imagens da Revolução: Documentos Políticos das Organizações Clandestinas de Esquerda dos Anos 1961–1971* (Rio de Janeiro: Marco Zero, 1985), pp. 7–47.

Aradau, C. and R. van Munster, 'Exceptionalism and the "War on Terror": Criminology Meets International Relations', *British Journal of Criminology* 49, no. 5 (12 June 2009): 686–701.

Aravena, Francisco Rojas, 'Civil–Military Relations in Post-Authoritarian Chile', in Patricio Silva (ed.), *The Soldier and the State in South America: Essays in Civil–Military Relations*, 151–74. Basingstoke: Palgrave Macmillan, 2001.

Arditi, Benjamin, 'Arguments about the Left Turns in Latin America: A Post-Liberal Politics?' *Latin American Research Review* 43, no. 3 (2008): 59–81.

Arendt, Hannah, *On Revolution* (London: Penguin Books, 1990).

Arendt, Hannah, *On Violence* (New York; London: Harcourt Brace Jovanovich, 1970).

Arendt, Hannah, *Responsibility and Judgment* (New York: Schocken Books, 2003).

Arendt, Hannah, *The Human Condition* (Chicago: The University of Chicago Press, 1998).

Arendt, Hannah, *The Origins of Totalitarianism* (New York: Harcourt Brace & Company, 1973).

Argolo, José, Kátia Ribeiro and Luiz Fortunato, *A Direita Explosiva no Brasil* (Rio de Janeiro: Mauad, 1996).

'Armed Forces', <https://academic.oup.com/ijtj/search-results?page=1&q=armed forces&fl_SiteID=5176&SearchSourceType=1&allJournals=1> (accessed 5 June 2021).

Arquidiocese de São Paulo, *Brasil: Nunca Mais* (Petrópolis: Vozes, 1985).

Arthur, Paige, '"Fear of the Future, Lived through the Past": Pursuing Transitional Justice in the Wake of Ethnic Conflic', in Paige Arthur, *Identities in Transition: Challenges for Transitional Justice in Divided Societies*, 271–302 (Cambridge: Cambridge University Press, 2011).

Arthur, Paige, 'How "Transitions" Reshaped Human Rights: A Conceptual History of Transitional Justice', *Human Rights Quarterly* 31, no. 2 (2009): 321–67.

Ashe, Fidelma, 'Sexuality and Gender Identity in Transitional Societies: Peacebuilding and Counterhegemonic Politics', *International Journal of Transitional Justice* 13, no. 3 (2019): 435–57, <https://doi.org/10.1093/ijtj/ijz022>.

Ashforth, Adam, 'Reckoning Schemes of Legitimation: On Commissions of Inquiry as Power/Knowledge Forms', *Journal of Historical Sociology* 3, no. 1 (1990): 1–22.

Atencio, Rebecca J., 'Acts of Witnessing: Site-Specific Performance and Transitional Justice in Postdictatorship Brazil', *Latin American Theatre Review* 46, no. 2 (2013): 7–24.

Ato Institucional N° 1, de 9 de Abril de 1964 (1964).

Ato Institucional N° 5, de 13 de Dezembro de 1968 (1968).

AV, 'Crítica ao Oportunismo e ao Subjetivismo da "União dos Brasileiros para Livrar o País da Crise, da Ditadura e da Ameaça Neocolonialista" (Dezembro 1967)', in Daniel Aarão Reis and Jair Ferreira de Sá (eds), *Imagens da Revolução: Documentos Políticos das Organizações Clandestinas de Esquerda dos Anos 1961–1971* (Rio de Janeiro: Marco Zero, 1985), pp. 118–33.

Avineri, S., 'How to Save Marx from the Alchemists of Revolution', *Political Theory* 4, no. 1 (1976): 35–44.

Aylwin, Patricio Azocar, *La transicion chilena: discursos escogidos: Marzo 1990–1992* (Santiago: Editorial Andres Bello, 1992).

Babb, Sarah, 'The Washington Consensus as Transnational Policy Paradigm: Its Origins, Trajectory and Likely Successor', *Review of International Political Economy* 20, no. 2 (2013): 268–97.

Baer, Werner, 'Import Substitution and Industrialization in Latin America: Experiences and Interpretations', *Latin American Research Review* 7, no. 1 (1972): 95–122.

Baines, Erin K., '"Today, I Want to Speak Out the Truth": Victim Agency, Responsibility, and Transitional Justice', *International Political Sociology* 9, no. 4 (2015): 316–32.

Balasco, Lauren Marie, 'Locating Transformative Justice: Prism or Schism in Transitional Justice?', *International Journal of Transitional Justice* 12, no. 2 (2018): 368–78.

Balibar, Étienne, 'Foucault's Point of Heresy: "Quasi-Transcendentals" and the Transdisciplinary Function of the Episteme', *Theory, Culture & Society* 32, no. 5–6 (2015): 45–77.

Balibar, Étienne, *Masses, Classes, Ideas* (New York: Routledge, 1994).

Balibar, Étienne, *Politics and the Other Scene* (London; New York: Verso, 2002).

Balibar, Étienne, 'Reflections on "Gewalt"', *Historical Materialism* 17, no. 1 (2009): 99–125.

Balint, Jennifer, Julie Evans and Nesam McMillan, 'Justice Claims in Colonial Contexts: Commissions of Inquiry in Historical Perspective', *Australian Feminist Law Journal* 42, no. 1 (2016): 75–96.

Balint, Jennifer, Julie Evans and Nesam McMillan, 'Rethinking Transitional Justice, Redressing Indigenous Harm: A New Conceptual Approach', *International Journal of Transitional Justice* 8, no. 2 (22 April 2014): 194–216.

Barkawi, Tarak and Mark Laffey, 'The Postcolonial Moment in Security Studies', *Review of International Studies* 32, no. 2 (2006): 329–52.

Bar-tal, Daniel, 'From Intractable Conflict through Conflict Resolution to Reconciliation: Psychological Analysis', *Political Psychology* 21, no. 2 (2000): 351–65.

Bartelson, Jens, *A Genealogy of Sovereignty* (Cambridge: Cambridge University Press, 1995).

Basham, Victoria M., 'Gender, Race, Militarism and Remembrance: The Everyday Geopolitics of the Poppy', *Gender, Place & Culture* 23, no. 6 (2016): 883–96.

Basham, Victoria M., 'Raising an Army: The Geopolitics of Militarizing the Lives of Working-Class Boys in an Age of Austerity', *International Political Sociology* 10, no. 3 (2016): 258–74.

Basham, Victoria M., Aaron Belkin and Jess Gifkins, 'What Is Critical Military Studies?', *Critical Military Studies* 1, no. 1 (2015): 1–2.

Basham, Victoria M. and Sergio Catignani, 'War Is Where the Hearth Is: Gendered Labor and the Everyday Reproduction of the Geopolitical in the Army Reserves', *International Feminist Journal of Politics* 20, no. 2 (2018): 153–71.

Bassiouni, Cherif, 'International Crimes: Jus Cogens and Obligatio Erga Omnes', *Law and Contemporary Problems* 59, no. 4 (1996): 63–74.

Bassiouni, Cherif, *The Right to Restitution, Compensation and Rehabilitation for Victims of Gross Violations of Human Rights and Fundamental Freedoms. Final Report of the Special Rapporteur, Mr. M. Cherif Bassiouni, Submitted in Accordance with Commission Resolution 1999/33*, UN Commission on Human Rights: E/CN.4/2000/62 (1999).

Basso, Luca, 'The Ambivalence of Gewalt in Marx and Engels: On Balibar's Interpretation', *Historical Materialism* 17, no. 2 (2009): 215–36.

Baudrillard, Jean, *For a Critique of the Political Economy of the Sign* (St Louis: Telos Press, 1981).

Beasley-Murray, Jon, Maxwell A. Cameron and Eric Hershberg, 'Latin America's Left Turns: An Introduction', *Third World Quarterly* 30, no. 2 (2009): 319–30.

Beitz, Charles R., 'Human Rights as Common Concern', *The American Political Science Review* 95, no. 2 (2001): 269–82.

Benjamin, Walter, 'Critique of Violence', in *Reflections: Essays, Aphorisms, Autobiographical Writings*, 277–300 (New York: Schocken Books, 1986).

Berman, Harold J., 'The Origins of Western Legal Science', *Harvard Law Review* (1977).

Bethell, Leslie, 'Politics in Brazil under the Liberal Republic, 1945–1964', in Leslie Bethell (ed.), *The Cambridge History of Latin America, vol. 9: Brazil Since 1930* (Cambridge: Cambridge University Press, 2008), pp. 87–164.

Betto, Frei, *Batismo de Sangue: Os Dominicanos e a Morte de Carlos Marighella* (Rio de Janeiro: Civilização Brasileira, 1982).

Bevernage, Berber, 'The Past Is Evil/Evil Is Past: On Retrospective Politics, Philosophy of History, and Temporal Manichaeism', *History and Theory* 54, no. 3 (2015): 333–52.

Bickford, Louis, 'The Archival Imperative : Human Rights and Historical Memory in Latin America's Southern Cone', *Human Rights Quarterly* 21, no. 4 (1999): 1–21.

Bickford, Louis, 'Unofficial Truth Projects', *Human Rights Quarterly* 29 (2007): 994–1035.

Bilbija, Ksenija and Leigh A. Payne, 'Introduction: Time Is Money – The Memory Market in Latin America', in Ksenija Bilbija and Leigh A. Payne (eds), *Accounting for Violence: Marketing Memory in Latin America* (Durham, NC; London: Duke University Press, 2011), pp. 1–40.

Björkdahl, Annika and J. M. Selimovic, 'Gendered Justice Gaps in Bosnia-Herzegovina', *Human Rights Review* 15, no. 2 (2013): 201–18.

Björkdahl, Annika and Johanna Mannergren Selimovic, 'Gendering Agency in Transitional Justice', *Security Dialogue* 46, no. 2 (2015).

Blakeley, Ruth, 'Bringing the State Back Into Terrorism Studies', *European Political Science* 6, no. 3 (September 2007): 228–35.

Boesten, J., 'Analyzing Rape Regimes at the Interface of War and Peace in Peru', *International Journal of Transitional Justice* 4, no. 1 (2010): 110–29, <https://doi.org/10.1093/ijtj/ijp029>.

Bohoslavsky, Juan Pablo and Marcelo D. Torelly, 'Financial Complicity: The Brazilian Dictatorship Under the "Macroscope"', in Dustin N. Sharp (ed.), *Justice and Economic Violence in Transition* (New York: Springer, 2014), pp. 233–62.

'Bolsonaro Attacks "putrid" Media over Marielle Franco Murder Claims', <https://www.theguardian.com/world/2019/oct/30/brazil-jair-bolsonaro-marielle-franco-murder-suspects> (accessed 8 January 2021).

'Bolsonaro Faz Piada com PIB Usando Humorista Carioca em Entrevista', <https://economia.uol.com.br/noticias/redacao/2020/03/04/apos-pib-desacelerar-bolsonaro-usa-humorista-para-evitar-assunto.htm> (accessed 8 January 2021).

Bonefeld, Werner, 'Primitive Accumulation and Capitalist Accumulation: Notes on Social Constitution and Expropriation', *Science and Society* 75, no. 3 (2011): 379–99.

Bonnin, Juan Eduardo, 'Religious and Political Discourse in Argentina: The Case of Reconciliation', *Discourse & Society* 20, no. 3 (2009): 327–43.

Borradori, Giovanna, Jacques Derrida and Jürgen Habermas, *Philosophy in a Time of Terror: Dialogues with Jurgen Habermas and Jacques Derrida* (Chicago: University of Chicago Press, 2003).

Bourdieu, Pierre and Loic Wacquant, *An Invitation to Reflexive Sociology* (Chicago: The University of Chicago Press, 1992).

Boven, Theo van, *Study Concerning the Right to Restitution, Compensation and Rehabilitation for Victims of Gross Violations of Human Rights and Fundamental Freedoms Final Report Submitted by Mr. Theo van Boven, Special Rapporteur*, UN Commission on Human Rights: E/CN.4/Sub.2/1993/8 (1993).

Brands, Hal, *Latin America's Cold War* (Cambridge, MA: Harvard University Press, 2012), <https://doi.org/1>.

Brandt, Richard B., 'The Concept of a Moral Right and Its Function', *The Journal of Philosophy* 80, no. 1 (1983): 29–45.

'Brasília Sedia Reunião Técnica sobre a Exumação de Jango', <http://www.cnv.gov.br/index.php/outros-destaques/285-brasilia-sedia-reuniao-tecnica-sobre-a-exumacao-de-jango> (accessed 9 April 2014).

'Brazil: Truth Commission Opens Route to Justice for Victims of Military Rule' (2014), <http://www.amnesty.org.uk/press-releases/brazil-truth-commission-opens-route-justice-victims-military-rule> (accessed 20 September 2021).

'Brazil Elections: Prospect of Bolsonaro Victory Stokes Fears of Return to Dictatorship', <https://www.theguardian.com/world/2018/oct/05/brazil-elections-prospect-of-bolsonaro-victory-stokes-fears-of-return-to-dicatorship> (accessed 7 August 2019).

'Brazil "Mensalao" Corruption Trial Concludes', <https://www.bbc.co.uk/news/world-latin-america-20764518> (accessed 6 August 2019).

'Brazil's Bolsonaro Claims Victory as Sinovac COVID-19 Trial Halted', <https://www.reuters.com/article/uk-health-coronavirus-brazil-sinovac/brazils-bolsonaro-claims-victory-as-sinovac-covid-19-trial-halted-idINKBN27Q1BO?edition-redirect=uk> (accessed 8 January 2021).

'Brazil's Former President Lula Walks Free from Prison after Supreme Court Ruling', <https://www.theguardian.com/world/2019/nov/08/lula-brazil-released-prison-supreme-court-ruling> (accessed 5 January 2021).

'Brazil's Leader Falsely Blames Leonardo DiCaprio for Amazon Fires', <https://www. nytimes.com/2019/11/30/world/americas/amazon-fires-dicaprio-bolsonaro. html> (accessed 8 January 2021).

'Brazilians Back Reporter Whom Bolsonaro "Felt like Punching"', <https://www.bbc. co.uk/news/world-latin-america-53887902> (accessed 8 January 2021).

Brems, E., 'Human Rights: Minimum and Maximum Perspectives', *Human Rights Law Review* 9, no. 3 (2009): 349–72.

Brito, Alexandra Barahona de, Carmen Gonzaléz-Enríquez and Paloma Aguilar, *The Politics of Memory: Transitional Justice in Democratizing Societies* (Oxford: Oxford University Press, 2001).

Brooks, Risa A., 'Integrating the Civil–Military Relations Subfield', *Annual Review of Political Science* 22 (2019): 379–98.

Brounéus, K., 'Truth-Telling as Talking Cure? Insecurity and Retraumatization in the Rwandan Gacaca Courts', *Security Dialogue* 39, no. 1 (1 March 2008): 55–76.

Brounéus, Karen, 'The Trauma of Truth Telling: Effects of Witnessing in the Rwandan Gacaca Courts on Psychological Health Karen', *Journal of Conflict Resolution* 54, no. 3 (2010): 408–37.

Brown, Chris, 'Universal Human Rights: A Critique', *The International Journal of Human Rights* 1, no. 2 (1997): 41–65.

Bruneau, Thomas C., 'Impediments to the Accurate Conceptualization of Civil–Military Relations', in Florina Cristiana Matei and Thomas C. Bruneau (eds), *The Routledge Handbook of Civil–Military Relations* (London; New York: Routledge, 2012), pp. 13–21.

Buchanan, Tom, '"The Truth Will Set You Free": The Making of Amnesty International', *Journal of Contemporary History* 37, no. 4 (2002): 575–97.

Bufacchi, Vittorio, 'Two Concepts of Violence', *Political Studies Review* 3, no. 2 (2005): 193–204.

Bulmer-Thomas, Victor, *The Economic History of Latin America Since Independence* (Cambridge: Cambridge University Press, 2014).

Cabrera, Carlos Artur Gallo, 'Do Luto à Luta : Um Estudo sobre a Comissão de Familiares de Mortos', *Anos 90* 19, no. 35 (2012): 329–61.

Caldeira, Teresa P. R., *City of Walls: Crime, Segregation, and Citizenship in Sao Paulo* (Berkeley: University of California Press, 2000).

Calmon, Francisco, personal interview, 9 July 2014.

Camacho, Fernando, 'Memorias enfrentadas : las reacciones a los informes Nunca Más de Argentina y Chile', *Persona y Sociedad* 22, no. 2 (2008): 67–99.

'Câmara Autoriza Instauração de Processo de Impeachment de Dilma com 367 Votos a Favor e 137 Contra', <http://www2.camara.leg.br/camaranoticias/noticias/ POLITICA/507325-CAMARA-AUTORIZA-INSTAURACAO-DE-PROCESSO-DE-IMPEACHMENT-DE-DILMA-COM-367-VOTOS-A-FAVOR-E-137-CONTRA.html> (accessed 18 May 2018).

Cameron, Maxwell A., 'Latin America's Left Turns: Beyond Good and Bad', *Third World Quarterly* 30, no. 2 (2009): 331–48.

'Campanha Confirma Vídeo em que Bolsonaro Fala em "Fuzilar Petralhada do Acre": "Foi Brincadeira"', <https://extra.globo.com/noticias/brasil/campanha-confirma-video-em-que-bolsonaro-fala-em-fuzilar-petralhada-do-acre-foi-brinca-deira-23033904.html> (accessed 7 August 2019).

Campbell, David, *Writing Security: United States Foreign Policy and the Politics of Identity* (Minneapolis: University of Minnesota Press, 1992).

Cannon, Barry, *The Right in Latin America: Elite Power, Hegemony and the Struggle for the State* (New York: Routledge, 2016).

Cardia, Nancy, 'Exposição à Violência : Seus Efeitos sobre Valores e Crenças em Relação a Violência, Polícia e Direitos Humanos', *Lusotopie* (2003): 299–328.

Cardia, Nancy, Sérgio Adorno and Frederico Poleto, 'Homicide Rates and Human Rights Violations', *Health and Human Rights* 6, no. 2 (2003): 3–21.

Cardoso, Fernando Henrique, 'Assinatura do Projeto de Lei sobre Desaparecidos Políticos', in *Biblioteca da Presidência da República* (Brasilia: Presidência da República, 1994), pp. 257–8.

Cardoso, Fernando Henrique and Enzo Faletto, *Dependency and Development in Latin America* (Berkeley: University of California Press, 1979).

Carneiro, Maria Luiza Tucci, 'Caixa de Pandora: O Potencial de Comunicação Museológica do Arquivo DEOPS-SP', in Marcelo Mattos Araujo and Maria Cristina Oliveira Bruno (eds), *Memorial da Resistência de São Paulo* (São Paulo: Pinacoteca do Estado, 2009), pp. 181–98.

Caruth, Cathy, 'Recapturing the Past: Introduction', in Cathy Caruth (ed.), *Trauma: Explorations in Memory* (Baltimore: The Johns Hopkins University Press, 1995), pp. 151–7.

Caruth, Cathy, *Unclaimed Experience: Trauma, Narrative and History* (Baltimore: The Johns Hopkins University Press, 1996).

Carvalho, Laura, *Valsa Brasileira: Do Boom ao Caos Econômico* (São Paulo: Todavia, 2018).

Carvalho, Maria Alice Rezende, 'Breve História do "Comunismo Democrático" no Brasil', in Jorge Ferreira and Daniel Aarão Reis (eds), *Coleção as Esquerdas no Brasil: Revolução e Democracia (1964. . .)* (Rio de Janeiro: Civilização Brasileira, 2007), pp. 261–82.

Case of Gomes Lund et al. ('Guerrilha Do Araguaia') v. Brazil. Preliminary Objections, Merits, Reparations, and Costs. Judgment of November 24, 2010. Series C No. 219. Inter-American Court of Human Rights (2010).

Castaneda, Jorge G., 'Latin America's Left Turn: There Is More Than One Pink Tide', *Foreign Affairs* (May/June 2016).

Catela, Ludmila da Silva, 'Do Segredo à Verdade . . . Processos Sociais e Políticos na Abertura dos Arquivos da Repressão no Brasil e na Argentina', in Cecília MacDowell Santos, Edison Teles and Janaína de Almeida Teles (eds), *Desarquivando a Ditadura:*

Memória e Justiça no Brasil, vol. 2 (São Paulo: Aderaldo & Rothschild Editores, 2009), pp. 444–71.

Catela, Ludmila da Silva, *Situação-Limite e Memória: A Reconstrução do Mundo dos Familiares de Desaparecidos da Argentina* (São Paulo: Hucitec, 2001).

Cavalcanti, Pedro Celso Uchôa and Jovelino Ramos, *Memórias do Exílio, Brasil 1964–19??: De Muios Caminhos* (São Paulo: Editora Arcadia, 1978).

CAVR, 'Chega!' (2005).

CEH, 'Guatemala: Memory of Silence' (1999), <https://hrdag.org/wp-content/uploads/2013/01/CEHreport-english.pdf>.

'Cemitério de Manaus Faz Hora Extra para Dar Conta de Enterros em Massa', <https://noticias.uol.com.br/cotidiano/ultimas-noticias/2020/04/28/cemiterio-de-manaus-faz-hora-extra-pra-dar-conta-de-enterros-em-massa.htm> (accessed 5 January 2021).

Chambers, J. D., 'Enclosure and Labour Supply in the Industrial Revolution', *The Economic History Review* 5, no. 3 (1953): 319–43.

Chevigny, Paul, 'The Populism of Fear', *Punishment & Society* 5, no. 1 (2003): 77–96.

Childs, Matt D., 'An Historical Critique of the Emergence and Evolution of Ernesto Che Guevara's Foco Theory', *Journal of Latin American Studies* 27, no. 3 (1995): 593–624, <https://doi.org/10.1017/S0022216X00011627>.

Chirio, Maud, *A Política nos Quartéis: Revoltas e Protestos de Oficiais na Ditadura Militar Brasileira* (Rio de Janeiro: Zahar, 2012).

Clark, Janine Natalya, 'Transitional Justice as Recognition: An Analysis of the Women's Court in Sarajevo', *International Journal of Transitional Justice* 10, no. 1 (2016): 67–87, <https://doi.org/10.1093/ijtj/ijv027>.

Clastres, Pierre, *Archéologie de la violence: La guerre dans les sociétés primitives* (La Tour-d'Aigues: Éditions de L'Aube, 2013).

'Claudio Fonteles Anucia Saída da Comissão da Verdade', Folha de São Paulo, <http://www1.folha.uol.com.br/poder/2013/06/1296999-fonteles-deixa-a-comissao-nacional-da-verdade.shtml> (accessed 11 January 2016).

'CNV, MPF-RS e SDH Conduzem Exumação dos Restos Mortais de João Goulart', <http://www.cnv.gov.br/index.php/outros-destaques/276-cnv-mpf-rs-e-sdh-conduzem-exumacao-dos-restos-mortais-de-joao-goulart> (accessed 4 September 2014).

'CNV Vai ao Chile Apurar Cooperação entre Ditaduras', <http://www.cnv.gov.br/index.php/outros-destaques/472-cnv-vai-ao-chile-apurar-cooperacao-entre-dita-duras> (accessed 9 September 2014).

CNVR, 'Informe de la comision nacional de verdad y reconciliacion' (1996).

Coatsworth, John H., 'Structures, Endowments, and Institutions in the Economic History of Latin America', *Latin American Research Review* 40, no. 3 (2005): 126–44.

Coelho, Maria José and Vera Rotta, *Caravanas da Anistia: O Brasil Pede Perdão* (Brasília: Ministério da Justiça, 2012).

Cohen, Joshua, 'Minimalism About Human Rights', *Philosophy & Political Science* 12, no. 2 (2004): 190–213.

Cohen, S., *States of Denial: Knowing About Atrocities and Suffering* (Cambridge: Polity Press, 2001).

Cohen-Almagor, R., 'Foundations of Violence, Terror and War in the Writings of Marx, Engels, and Lenin', *Terrorism and Political Violence* 3, no. 2 (1991): 1–24.

Coimbra, Cecília Maria Bouças, 'Doutrinas de Segurança Nacional: Banalizando a Violência', *Psicologia Em Estudo* 5, no. 2 (2000): 1–22.

COLINA, 'Concepção da Luta Revolucionária (Abril 1968)', in Daniel Aarão Reis and Jair Ferreira de Sá (eds), *Imagens da Revolução: Documentos Políticos das Organizações Clandestinas de Esquerda dos Anos 1961–1971* (Rio de Janeiro: Marco Zero, 1985), pp. 134–59.

Collins, C., L. Balardini and J.-M. Burt, 'Mapping Perpetrator Prosecutions in Latin America', *International Journal of Transitional Justice* 7, no. 1 (12 December 2012): 8–28.

Collins, Cath, *Post-Transitional Justice: Human Rights Trials in Chile and El Salvador* (University Park: Pennsylvania State University Press, 2010).

Collins, Randal, *Violence: A Micro-Sociological Theory* (Princeton: Princeton University Press, 2009).

Comando da Aeronáutica, 'Ofício Nº 386/GCL/7618', <http://www.cnv.gov.br/images/pdf/Sindicancia-Forca-Aerea.pdf> (accessed 22 January 2016).

Comissão Arns: Annual Report Feb 2019 – Feb 2020. Comissão de Defesa dos Direitos Humanos Dom Paulo Evaristo Arns (2020).

'Comissão da Verdade Define Estratégias de Funcionamento e Estrutura', <http://www.cnv.gov.br/index.php/outros-destaques/72-comissao-da-verdade-define-estrategias-de-funcionamento-e-estrutura> (accessed 3 September 2014).

'Comissão da Verdade Deixa Uma Grande Mágoa, Diz General', Folha de São Paulo, <http://www1.folha.uol.com.br/poder/2014/12/1564612-comissao-da-verdade-deixa-uma-grande-magoa-diz-general.shtml> (accessed 22 January 2016).

'Comissão da Verdade Deve Analisar Os Dois Lados, Diz Integrante', Folha de São Paulo, <http://www1.folha.uol.com.br/fsp/poder/42768-comissao-da-verdade-deve-analisar-os-dois-lados-diz-integrante.shtml> (accessed 19 January 2016).

'Comissão da Verdade Pede que Governo de MG Tome Medidas para Conservar Documentos da Ditadura', <http://www.cnv.gov.br/index.php/outros-destaques/97-comissao-da-verdade-pede-que-governo-de-mg-tome-medidas-para-conservar-documentos-da-ditadura> (accessed 22 January 2016).

Comissão Especial sobre Mortos e Desaparecidos Políticos, *Direito à Memória e à Verdade: Comissão Especial sobre Mortos e Desaparecidos Políticos* (Brasília: Secretaria Especial dos Direitos Humanos, 2007).

Comissão Nacional da Verdade, *Balanço Atividades: 1 Ano de Comissão Nacional da Verdade* (Brasília: CNV, 2013), <http://www.cnv.gov.br/images/pdf/balanco_1ano.pdf.>

Comissão Nacional da Verdade, 'Ofício N° 124 de, 18 de Fevereiro de 2014', <http://www.cnv.gov.br/images/pdf/OFI 124.pdf> (accessed 23 June 2016).

Comissão Nacional da Verdade, 'Ofício N° 585/2014-Cnv', <http://www.cnv.gov.br/images/pdf/OFI_2014_585.pdf> (accessed 22 January 2016).

Comissão Nacional da Verdade, *Relatório da Comissão Nacional da Verdade*, vol. 1 (Brasília: CNV, 2014).

Comissão Nacional da Verdade, *Relatório da Comissão Nacional da Verdade, vol. 2: Textos Temáticos* (Brasília: CNV, 2014).

Comissão Nacional da Verdade, *Relatório Preliminar de Pesquisa: O Caso Juscelino Kubitschek* (Brasília: CNV, 2014).

'Comissão Nacional da Verdade Entrega Relatório Final ao Arquivo Nacional', Agência Brasil, <http://www.ebc.com.br/noticias/colaborativo/2013/07/amarildo-presente> (accessed 23 July 2016).

'Comissão Nacional da Verdade Recebe Complemento de Documentação Recolhida no Rio Grande do Sul', <http://www.cnv.gov.br/index.php/outros-destaques/190-comissao-nacional-da-verdade-recebe-complemento-de-documentacao-recolhida-no-rio-grande-do-sul> (accessed 22 January 2016).

'Comitês Protocolam Demandas a Comissão Nacional da Verdade', <http://coletivorj.blogspot.co.uk/2012/08/comites-protocolam-demandas-comissao.html> (accessed 23 September 2014).

CONADEP, *Nunca Más*, edited by Eudeba, 9th ed (Buenos Aires, 1985).

Congresso Nacional, 'Diário do Congresso Nacional. Ano XIX: N. 154. Seção I. 25 de Agosto de 1964' (Brasília: Centro de Documentação e Informação. Coordenação de Relacionamento, Pesquisa e Informação, 1964).

'Coronavírus: "país de Maricas" e Outras 8 Frases de Bolsonaro sobre Pandemia que Matou 162 Mil Pessoas no Brasil', <https://www.bbc.com/portuguese/brasil-54902608> (accessed 5 January 2021).

Costa, Edmilson Silva, 'A Política Salarial no Brasil, 1964–1985: 21 Anos de Arrocho Salarial e Acumulação Predatória', Universidade Estadual de Campinas (1996).

Crenzel, Emilio, 'Argentina's National Commission on the Disappearance of Persons: Contributions to Transitional Justice', *International Journal of Transitional Justice* 2, no. 2 (1 July 2008): 173–91.

Crenzel, Emilio, 'Genesis, Uses, and Significations of the Nunca Más Report in Argentina', *Latin American Perspectives* 42, no. 3 (2015): 20–38.

'Crimes de Maio Causaram 564 Mortes em 2006; Entenda o Caso', <http://agencia-brasil.ebc.com.br/direitos-humanos/noticia/2016-05/crimes-de-maio-causaram-564-mortes-em-2006-entenda-o-caso> (accessed 23 June 2016).

D'Araujo, Maria Celina, Glaucio Ary Dillon Soares and Celso Castro, *A Volta aos Quartéis: A Memória Militar sobre a Abertura* (Rio de Janeiro: Relume-Dumará, 1995).

D'Araujo, Maria Celina, Glaucio Ary Dillon Soares and Celso Castro, *Os Anos de Chumbo: A Memória Militar sobre a Repressão* (Rio de Janeiro: Relume-Dumará, 1994).

D'Orsi, L., 'Trauma and the Politics of Memory of the Uruguayan Dictatorship', *Latin American Perspectives* 42, no. 3 (2015): 162–79.

Dahl, Robert A., 'The Concept of Power', *Behavioral Science* 2, no. 3 (1957): 201–15.

Dallari, Pedro, 'Verdade, Memória e Reconciliação', Folha de São Paulo, <http://www1.folha.uol.com.br/opiniao/2014/12/1559918-pedro-dallari-verdade-memoria-e-reconciliacao.shtml> (accessed 1 January 2015).

Dancy, Geoff and Eric Wiebelhaus-Brahm, 'Bridge to Human Development or Vehicle of Inequality? Transitional Justice and Economic Structures', *International Journal of Transitional Justice* 9, no. 1 (2015): 51–69.

Davis, Natalie Zemon and Randolph Starn, 'Introduction: Memory and Counter-Memory', *Representations* 26, no. Spring (1989): 1–6.

Debord, Guy, *The Society of the Spectacle* (New York: Zone Books, 1995).

Debray, Régis, *Révolution dans la révolution? & autres essais* (Paris: François Maspero, 1972).

Decreto-Ley 2119, de 1978 (Santiago: Diario Oficial de La República, 1978).

Derrida, Jacques, 'Force of Law: The "Mystical Foundation of Authority"', in Michel Rosenfeld, David Gray Carlson and Drucilla Cornell (eds), *Deconstruction and the Possibility of Justice* (London: Routledge, 1992).

Derrida, Jacques, *Specters of Marx: The State of the Debt, the Work of Mourning and the New International* (London: Routledge, 1994).

Derrida, Jacques, *Writing and Difference* (London: Routledge, 2001).

Diamint, Rut, 'A New Militarism in Latin America', *Journal of Democracy* 26, no. 4 (2015): 155–68.

Diário da Câmara dos Deputados. Ano LXIX – Nº 152 Quinta-Feira, 16 de Outubro de 2014 (Brasília: República Federativa do Brasil, 2014).

Diário da Câmara dos Deputados. Ano LXIX – Nº 190 Quarta-Feira, 10 de Dezembro de 2014 (Brasilia: República Federativa do Brasil, 2014).

Diário da Câmara dos Deputados. Ano LXVIII – Nº 067 Quarta-Feira, 24 de Abril de 2013 (Brasilia: República Federativa do Brasil, 2013).

Diário da Câmara dos Deputados. Ano LXVIII – Nº 088 Sexta-Feira, 24 de Maio de 2013 (Brasilia: República Federativa do Brasil, 2013).

Diário da Câmara dos Deputados. Ano LXX – Nº 049 Quarta-Feira, 1 de Abril de 2015. (Brasília: República Federativa do Brasil, 2015).

Diário da Câmara dos Deputados. Ano LXXI – Nº 056 Segunda-Feira, 18 de Abril de 2016. (Brasília: República Federativa do Brasil, 2016).

Dias, José Carlos, 'Precisamos Extirpar as Metástases Da Ditadura', <http://www.brasilpost.com.br/jose-carlos-dias/precisamos-extirpar-as-metastases-da-ditadura_b_5052473.html> (accessed 11 September 2014).

Dillon, Michael and Julian Reid, 'Global Liberal Governance: Biopolitics, Security and War', *Millennium: Journal of International Studies* 30, no. 1 (2001): 41–66.

'Dilma Deu R$ 458 Bilhões em Desonerações', <https://www1.folha.uol.com.br/mercado/2015/09/1678317-dilma-deu-r-458-bilhoes-em-desoneracoes.shtml> (accessed 6 August 2019).

Ditrych, O., 'From Discourse to Dispositif: States and Terrorism between Marseille and 9/11', *Security Dialogue* 44, no. 3 (31 May 2013): 223–40.

'Documentos Recebidos dos EUA', <http://www.cnv.gov.br/todos-volume-1/648-documentossss-eua-i-6.html> (accessed 10 December 2015).

Douzinas, Costas, *Human Rights and Empire: The Political Philosophy of Cosmopolitanism* (Abingdon: Routledge, 2007).

Douzinas, Costas, *The End of Human Rights: Critical Legal Thought at the Turn of the Century* (Portland, OR: Hart Publishing, 2000).

Doxtader, Erik, 'A Critique of Law's Violence yet (Never) to Come', in Alexander Keller Hirsch (ed.), *Theorizing Post-Conflict Reconciliation: Agonism, Restitution and Repair* (New York: Routledge, 2012), pp. 27–64.

Doxtader, Erik, 'Reconciliation – a Rhetorical Concept/Ion', *Quarterly Journal of Speech* 89, no. 4 (November 2003): 267–92.

Drake, C. J. M., 'The Role of Ideology in Terrorists' Target Selection', *Terrorism and Political Violence* 10, no. 2 (1998): 53–85.

Dunne, Tim and Nicholas J. Wheeler, '"We the Peoples": Contending Discourses of Security in Human Rights Theory and Practice', *International Relations* 18, no. 1 (2004): 9–23.

Eagle, Karen, 'A Genealogy of the Criminal Turn in Human Rights', in Karen Engle, Zinaida Miller and D. M. Davis (eds), *Anti-Impunity and the Human Rights Agenda* (Cambridge: Cambridge University Press, 2016), pp. 15–67.

Eastmond, M. and J. M. Selimovic, 'Silence as Possibility in Postwar Everyday Life', *International Journal of Transitional Justice* 6, no. 3 (12 October 2012): 502–24, <https://doi.org/10.1093/ijtj/ijs026>.

Eastwood, James, 'Rethinking Militarism as Ideology: The Critique of Violence after Security', *Security Dialogue* 49, no. 1–2 (2018): 44–56.

Edkins, Jenny, 'Ground Zero: Reflections on Trauma, in/Distinction and Response', *Journal for Cultural Research* 8, no. 3 (July 2004): 247–70.

Edkins, Jenny, *Missing: Persons and Politics* (Ithaca: Cornell University Press, 2011).

Edkins, Jenny, *Trauma and the Memory of Politics* (Cambridge: Cambridge University Press, 2003).

Eichbauer, Melodie H., 'Medieval Inquisitorial Procedure: Procedural Rights and the Question of Due Process in the 13th Century', *History Compass* 12, no. 1 (2014): 72–83.

Elster, Jon, *Closing the Books: Transitional Justice in Historical Perspective* (Cambridge: Cambridge University Press, 2004).

Encarnación, Omar G., 'The Patriarchy's Revenge: How Retro-Macho Politics Doomed Dilma Rousseff', *World Policy Journal* 34, no. 1 (2017): 82–91.

Eriksson Baaz, Maria and Judith Verweijen, 'Confronting the Colonial: The (Re) Production of "African" Exceptionalism in Critical Security and Military Studies', *Security Dialogue* 49, no. 1–2 (2018): 57–69.

Estado Maior das Forcas Armadas, 'C-85-59' (1959).

Estado Maior das Forcas Armadas, 'FA-E-01/61' (1961).

Evans, Matthew, 'Structural Violence, Socioeconomic Rights, and Transformative Justice', *Journal of Human Rights* 15, no. 1 (2016): 1–20.

Evans, Tony, 'International Human Rights Law as Power/Knowledge', *Human Rights Quarterly* 27, no. 3 (2005): 1046–68, <http://muse.jhu.edu/content/crossref/journals/human_rights_quarterly/v027/27.3evans.html>.

Exército Brasileiro, 'Ofício Nº 027-A2.2.1/A2/GaCcmtEx. EB: 64536.013874/2014-75', <http://www.cnv.gov.br/images/pdf/Sindicancia-Exercito.pdf> (accessed 22 January 2016).

'Ex-Presos Políticos Reconhecem Local de Tortura na Antiga 1ª. Cia de PE da Vila Militar', <http://www.cnv.gov.br/index.php/outros-destaques/422-ex-presos-politicos-reconhecem-local-de-tortura-na-vila-militar> (accessed 8 September 2014).

Fanon, Frantz, *The Wretched of the Earth* (New York: Grove Press, 1963).

Feaver, Peter D., 'Civil–Military Relations', *Annual Review of Political Science*, no. 2 (1999): 211–41.

Ferguson, Kathy E., 'The Sublime Object of Militarism', *New Political Science* 31, no. 4 (2009): 475–86.

Feyerabend, Paul, *Against Method* (London; New York: Verso, 1993).

Fico, Carlos, *Como Eles Agiam: Os Subterrâneos da Ditadura Militar: Espionagem e Polícia Política* (Rio de Janeiro: Editora Record, 2001).

Figueiredo, Lucas, *Ministério do Silêncio: A História do Serviço Secreto Brasileiro de Washington Luís a Lula: 1932–2005* (Rio de Janeiro: Editora Record, 2005).

Finch, Michael P. M., 'A Total War of the Mind: The French Theory of La Guerre Révolutionnaire, 1954–1958', *War in History* 25, no. 3 (2018): 410–34.

Flores-Macias, Gustavo, *After Neoliberalism? The Left and Economic Reforms in Latin America* (Oxford: Oxford University Press, 2012).

Força Naval, 'Fis Nº 260 M.Defesa/SG/SEORI/DEADI/DIPOD/PGA', <http://www.cnv.gov.br/images/pdf/Sindicancia-Marinha_volume3.pdf> (accessed 22 January 2016).

'Forças Armadas Aceitam Investigar Centros de Tortura', <http://www.cnv.gov.br/institucional-acesso-informacao/membros/index.php/outros-%0A195%0Adestaques/460-forcas-armadas-aceitam-investigar-centros-de-tortura> (accessed 22 January 2016).

Fórum Brasileiro de Segurança Pública, *Anuário do Fórum Brasileiro de Segurança Pública – 2015* (São Paulo: FBSP, 2015).

Fórum Brasileiro de Segurança Pública, *Anuário do Fórum Brasileiro de Segurança Pública – 2017* (São Paulo: FBSP, 2017).

Fórum Brasileiro de Segurança Pública, *Anuário do Fórum Brasileiro de Segurança Pública – 2018* (São Paulo: FBSP, 2018).

Foucault, Michel, *A Verdade e as Formas Jurídicas* (Rio de Janeiro: Nau Editora, 2002).

Foucault, Michel, *Archaeology of Knowledge* (London; New York: Routledge, 2002).

Foucault, Michel, *Discipline and Punish: The Birth of the Prison* (New York: Vintage Books, 1995).

Foucault, Michel, 'History, Discourse and Discontinuity', *Salmagundi*, no. 20 (1972): 225–48.

Foucault, Michel, *History of Madness*, edited by Jean Khalfa (Abingdon: Routledge, 2006).

Foucault, Michel, *Language, Counter Memory, Practice: Selected Essays and Interviews*, edited by Donald Bouchard (Ithaca: Cornell University Press, 1977).

Foucault, Michel, *Society Must Be Defended: Lectures at the Collège de France, 1975–76*, edited by Mauro Bertani, Alessandro Fontana and Francois Ewald (New York: Picador, 2003).

Foucault, Michel, *The History of Sexuality*, vol. 1: *The Will to Knowledge* (New York: Pantheon Books, 1978).

Foucault, Michel, *The Order of Things* (London; New York: Routledge, 2002).

Foucault, Michel, 'The Subject and Power', *Critical Inquiry* 8, no. 4 (1982): 777–95.

Foucault, Michel, *Wrong-Doing, Truth-Telling: The Function of Avowal in Justice*, edited by Fabienne Brion and Bernard Harcourt (Chicago: University of Chicago Press, 2014).

Foucault, Michel and Paul Rabinow, *The Foucault Reader* (New York: Pantheon Books, 1984).

Fourlas, G. N., 'No Future without Transition: A Critique of Liberal Peace', *International Journal of Transitional Justice* 9, no. 1 (28 January 2015): 109–26.

Fraher, Richard M., 'The Theoretical Justification for the New Criminal Law of the High Middle Ages: Rei Publicae Interest, Ne Crimina Remaneant Impunita', *University of Illinois Law Review* 3 (1984): 577–95.

Franco, M., 'Les exilés Argentins en France et la "découverte" des droits de l'homme dans les années 1970 et 1980', *Canadian Journal of Latin American and Caribbean Studies* 32, no. 63 (2007): 45–71.

Franco, Marielle, 'After the Take-Over: Mobilizing the Political Creativity of Brazil's Favelas', *New Left Review* 110 (March–April 2018): 135–40.

Frankel, Oz, 'Scenes of Commission : Royal Commissions of Inquiry and the Culture of Social Investigation in Early Victorian Britain', *The European Legacy* 4, no. 6 (1999): 20–41.

Frazer, E. and K. Hutchings, 'Avowing Violence: Foucault and Derrida on Politics, Discourse and Meaning', *Philosophy & Social Criticism* 37, no. 1 (18 January 2011): 3–23.

Frazer, Elizabeth and Kimberly Hutchings, 'On Politics and Violence: Arendt Contra Fanon', *Contemporary Political Theory* 7, no. 1 (February 2008): 90–108.

Freeman, Michael, 'The Philosophical Foundations of Human Rights', *Human Rights Quarterly* 16, no. 3 (2009): 491–514.

French, Brigittine M., 'Technologies of Telling: Discourse, Transparency, and Erasure in Guatemalan Truth Commission Testimony', *Journal of Human Rights* 8, no. 1 (31 March 2009): 92–109.

French, John D., 'Understanding the Politics of Latin America's Plural Lefts (Chávez/Lula): Social Democracy, Populism and Convergence on the Path to a Post-Neoliberal World', *Third World Quarterly* 30, no. 2 (2009): 349–70.

Freud, Sigmund, *The Complete Psychological Works of Sigmund Freud*, vol. 4 (London: Vintage Books, 2001).

Freud, Sigmund, *The Complete Psychological Works of Sigmund Freud*, vol. 5 (London: Vintage Books, 2001).

Fukuyama, Francis, *The End of History and the Last Man* (Harmondsworth: Penguin Books, 1992).

Furtado, Henrique Tavares, 'Confronting the Gated Community: Towards a Decolonial Critique of Violence beyond the Paradigm of War', *Review of International Studies*, no. 10 (2021): 1–20.

Furtado, Henrique Tavares, 'On Demons and Dreamers: Violence, Silence and the Politics of Impunity in the Brazilian Truth Commission', *Security Dialogue* 48, no. 4 (2017): 316–33.

Furtado, Henrique Tavares, 'When Does Repression Become Political? The Use of the Language of Trauma in the Context of Violence and Anxiety', in Emmy Eklundh, Emmanuel Pierre Guittet and Andreja Zevnik (eds), *Politics of Anxiety* (Lanham, MD: Rowman & Littlefield, 2017).

Gabeira, Fernando, *O Que é Isso, Companheiro?* 28th ed. (Rio de Janeiro: Codecri, 1981).

Galliher, John F., 'Transformative Justice: Critical and Peacemaking Themes Influenced by Richard Quinney', *Contemporary Sociology* 39, no. 1 (2010): 95–6.

Galtung, Johan, 'Violence, Peace, and Peace Research', *Journal of Peace Research* 6, no. 3 (1969): 167–91.

Galtung, Johan and Tord Hoivik, 'Structural and Direct Violence: A Note on Operationalization', *Journal of Peace Research* 8, no. 1 (1971): 73–6.

Garcia, Denise, 'Not yet a Democracy: Establishing Civilian Authority over the Security Sector in Brazil – Lessons for Other Countries in Transition', *Third World Quarterly* 35, no. 3 (15 May 2014): 487–504.

Garibian, Sévane, 'Ghosts Also Die: Resisting Disappearance through the "right to the truth" and the Juicios Por La Verdad in Argentina', *Journal of International Criminal Justice* 12, no. 3 (2014): 515–38.

Gaspari, Elio, *As Ilusões Armadas: A Ditadura Envergonhada* (São Paulo: Companhia das Letras, 2002).

Gaspari, Elio, *As Ilusões Armadas: A Ditadura Escancarada* (São Paulo: Companhia das Letras, 2002).

Gaspari, Elio, *O Sacerdote e o Feiticeiro: A Ditadura Encurralada* (São Paulo: Companhia das Letras, 2004).

Genro, Tarso and Paulo Abrão, 'Memória Histórica, Justiça de Transição e Democracia Sem Fim', in Boaventura de Sousa Santos, Paulo Abrão, Cecília MacDowell dos Santos and Marcelo D. Torelly (eds), *Repressão e Memória Política no Contexto Ibero-Brasileiro: Estudos sobre Brasil, Guatemala, Moçambique, Peru e Portugal* (Brasília; Coimbra: Ministério da Justiça; Comissão de Anistia; Centro de Estudos Sociais Universidade de Coimbra, 2010), pp. 16–24.

Gibney, M., L. Cornett, R. Wood, P. Haschke and D. Arnon, 'Database: The Political Terror Scale 1976–2015' (2015), <http://www.politicalterrorscale.org>.

Gibson, J. L., 'The Contributions of Truth to Reconciliation: Lessons from South Africa', *Journal of Conflict Resolution* 50, no. 3 (1 June 2006): 409–32.

Gibson, James, 'Overcoming Apartheid: Can Truth Reconcile a Divided Nation?' *Politikon* 31, no. 2 (1 November 2004): 129–55.

Gilbert, A., 'Salvaging Marx from Avineri', *Political Theory* 4, no. 1 (1976): 9–34.

Gilligan, George and John Pratt (eds), *Crime, Truth and Justice: Official Inquiry, Discourse, Knowledge* (Abingdon: Routledge, 2013).

Gobodo-Madikizela, Pumla, 'Transitional Justice and Truth Commissions: Exploring Narratives of Repair and Healing in the Post-Holocaust Era', *Psychology, Crime & Law* 18, no. 3 (April 2010): 275–97.

Goldman, Robert K., 'History and Action: The Inter-American Human Rights System and the Role of the Inter-American Commission on Human Rights', *Human Rights Quarterly* 31 (2009): 856–87.

Gomes, Rubinho, personal interview, 17 July 2014.

Gorender, Jacob, 'Combate nas Trevas – A Esquerda Brasileira das Ilusoes Perdidas a Luta Armada' (São Paulo: Editora Ática, 1987).

'Governo Bolsonaro mais que dobra Número de Militares em Cargos Civis, Aponta TCU', <https://g1.globo.com/politica/noticia/2020/07/17/governo-bolsonaro-tem-6157-militares-em-cargos-civis-diz-tcu.ghtml> (accessed 5 January 2021).

Grabois, Vitoria, personal interview, 22 July 2014.

Gready, P. and S. Robins, 'From Transitional to Transformative Justice: A New Agenda for Practice', *International Journal of Transitional Justice* 8, no. 3 (14 August 2014): 1–23.

Gready, Paul, *The Era of Transitional Justice:The Aftermath of the Truth and Reconciliation Commission in South Africa and Beyond* (Abingdon: Routledge, 2011).

Greco, Heloisa Amélia, '50 Anos do Golpe Militar/35 Anos da Lei de Anistia: A Longa Marcha da "Estratégia do Esquecimento"', *Cadernos de História* 15, no. 22 (2014): 160–89.

Greco, Heloisa Amélia, 'Anistia Anamnese vs Anistia Amnésia: A Dimensão Trágica da Luta pela Anistia', in Cecília MacDowell dos Santos, Edson Teles and

Janaína de Almeida Teles (eds), *Desarquivando a Ditadura: Memória e Justiça no Brasil*, vol. 2 (São Paulo: Aderaldo & Rothschild Editores, 2009), pp. 524–40.

Greco, Heloisa Amélia, 'Dimensões Fundacionais da Luta pela Anistia', Universidade Federal de Minas Gerais (2003).

Griffin, James, 'First Steps in an Account of Human Rights', *European Journal of Philosophy* 9 (2001): 306–27.

Groome, Dermot, 'The Right to Truth in the Fight against Impunity', *Berkeley Journal of International Law* 29, no. 1 (2011): 175–99.

Grugel, Jean and Pía Riggirozzi, 'Post-Neoliberalism in Latin America: Rebuilding and Reclaiming the State after Crisis', *Development and Change* 43, no. 1 (2012): 1–21.

Guevara, Ernesto, *Escritos revolucionarios* (Madrid: Catarata, 1999).

Gumieri, Julia Cerqueira, 'Espaços de Memória : Uma Luta por Memória, Verdade e Justiça no Brasil e na Argentina', *Em Tempo de Histórias* 20 (January–July 2012): 49–74.

Gumieri, Julia Cerqueira, 'O Memorial da Resistência de São Paulo: Reparação Simbólica e Ações Preservacionistas', *Histórica – Revista Eletrônica Do Arquivo Público Do Estado de São Paulo* 54 (June 2012): 1–11.

Halbwachs, Maurice, *On Collective Memory* (Chicago: University of Chicago Press, 1992).

Hall, Stuart, Chas Critcher, Tony Jefferson, John Clarke and Brian Roberts, *Policing the Crisis: Mugging, the State, and Law and Order* (London: The Macmillan Press, 1978).

Halpern, Jodi and Harvey M. Weinstein, 'Rehumanizing the Other: Empathy and Reconciliation', *Human Rights Quarterly* 26, no. 3 (2004): 561–83.

Harrison, W. C., 'Madness and Historicity: Foucault and Derrida, Artaud and Descartes', *History of the Human Sciences* 20, no. 4 (1 November 2007): 79–105.

Harvey, David, 'A Brief History of Neoliberalism' (Oxford: Oxford University Press, 2005).

Harvey, David, 'The "New" Imperialism: Accumulation by Dispossession', *Socialist Register* 40, no. 40 (2004): 63–87.

'Havendo Precedentes, Comissão da Verdade Pedirá Novas Retificações de Óbitos, Como a de Herzog, Afirma Fonteles no RJ', <http://www.cnv.gov.br/index.php/outros-destaques/103-havendo-precedentes-comissao-da-verdade-pedira-novas-retificacoes-de-obitos-como-a-de-herzog-afirma-fonteles-no-rj> (accessed 26 October 2014).

Hayner, Priscilla B., *The Peacemaker's Paradox: Pursuing Justice in the Shadow of Conflict* (Abingdon: Routledge, 2018).

Hayner, Priscilla B., *Unspeakable Truths: Transitional Justice and the Challenge of Truth Commissions* (New York: Routledge, 2011).

Henkin, Alice H., 'State Crimes: Punishment or Pardon (Conference Report)', in Neil J. Kritz (ed.), *Transitional Justice: How Emerging Democracies Reckon with Former Regimes*, vol. 1 (Washington, DC: United States Institute of Peace, 1995), pp. 184–8.

Hirsch, Marianne, 'The Generation of Postmemory', *Poetics Today* 29, no. 1 (2008): 103–28.

Hobbes, Thomas, *Leviathan* (Middlesex: Penguin Books, 1968).

Hopgood, Stephen, *Keepers of the Flame: Understanding Amnesty International* (Ithaca: Cornell University Press, 2006).

Horkheimer, Max and Theodor Adorno, *Dialectic of Enlightenment: Philosophical Fragments* (Stanford, CA: Stanford University Press, 2002).

'How a Homophobic, Misogynist, Racist "Thing" Could Be Brazil's Next President', <https://www.theguardian.com/commentisfree/2018/oct/06/homophobic-mis-mogynist-racist-brazil-jair-bolsonaro> (accessed 22 October 2018).

Howell, Alison, 'Forget "Militarization": Race, Disability and the "Martial Politics" of the Police and of the University', *International Feminist Journal of Politics* 20, no. 2 (2018): 117–36.

Huggins, Martha K., 'Legacies of Authoritarianism: Brazilian Torturers' and Murderers' Reformulation of Memory', *Latin American Perspectives* 27, no. 2 (2000): 57–78.

Human Rights Watch, *World Report 2015: Events of 2014* (Bristol: Policy Press, 2014).

Humphrey, M. and E. Valverde, 'Human Rights Politics and Injustice: Transitional Justice in Argentina and South Africa', *International Journal of Transitional Justice* 2, no. 1 (1 March 2008): 83–105.

Humphrey, Michael, 'From Terror to Trauma: Commissioning Truth for National Reconciliation', *Social Identities* 6, no. 1 (March 2000): 7–27.

Humphrey, Michael, 'From Victim to Victimhood : Truth Commissions and Trials as Rituals of Political Transition and Individual Healing', *The Australian Journal of Anthropology* 14, no. 2 (2003): 171–87.

Humphrey, Michael, *The Politics of Atrocity and Reconciliation: From Terror to Trauma* (London; New York: Routledge, 2002).

Huntington, Samuel, *The Soldier and the State: The Theory and Politics of Civil–Military Relations* (Cambridge, MA: Harvard University PRess, 1957).

Huntington, Samuel, *The Third Wave: Democratization in the Late Twentieth Century*, in Neil J. Kritz (ed.), *Transitional Justice: How Emerging Democracies Reckon with Former Regimes*, vol. 1 (Washington, DC: United States Institute of Peace, 1995), pp. 65–81.

Huysmans, Jef, 'The Jargon of Exception – On Schmitt, Agamben and the Absence of Political Society', *International Political Sociology* 2, no. 2 (2008): 165–83.

Huyssen, Andreas, *Present Past: Urban Palimpsests and the Politics of Memory* (Stanford, CA: Stanford University Press, 2003).

IBC, 'Database: Iraq Body Count: The Public Record of Violent Deaths Following the 2003 Invasion of Iraq', 2015, <https://www.iraqbodycount.org/>.

IDEA, *Reconciliation After Violent Conflict: A Handbook*, edited by David Bloomfield, Teresa Barnes and Luc Huyse (Stockholm: International Institute for Democracy and Electoral Assistance, 2003).

'IMF DATA: Primary Commodity Price System', <https://data.imf.org/?sk=471DDDF8-D8A7-499A-81BA-5B332C01F8B9> (accessed 6 August 2019).

Instituto de Estudos da Violência, *Dossiê dos Mortos e Desaparecidos Poléticos a partir de 1964* (Recife: Companhia Editora de Pernambuco, 1995).

Instituto de Pesquisa Economica Aplicada, 'Ipeadata: Dívida Externa Registrada', <http://www.ipeadata.gov.br/Default.aspx> (accessed 6 June 2019).

Instituto de Pesquisa Economica Aplicada, 'Ipeadata: Simópse Macroeconômica', <http://www.ipeadata.gov.br/Default.aspx> (accessed 5 January 2021).

Instituto de Pesquisa Economica Aplicada, 'Ipeadata: Taxa de Desocupação das Pessoas de 14 Anos ou Mais de Idade, na Semana de Referência', <http://www.ipeadata.gov.br/Default.aspx> (accessed 7 August 2019).

Instituto Nacional de Pesquisas Espaciais, Coordenação Geral de Observação da Terra, 'Programa de Monitoramento da Amazônia e Demais Biomas – Desmatamento – Amazônia Legal', <http://terrabrasilis.dpi.inpe.br/downloads> (accessed 8 January 2021).

Institutos de Estudos da Religião, *Comissão Nacional da Verdade: Balanços e Perspectivas da Finalização de Seu Processo Político-Institucional* (Rio de Janeiro: ISER, 2015).

Institutos de Estudos da Religião, 'I Relatório Semestral de Acompanhamento da Comissão Nacional da Verdade (Maio a Novembro de 2012): Documento-Base para Discussão' (Rio de Janeiro: ISER, 2012).

Institutos de Estudos da Religião, 'III Relatório de Monitoramento da Comissão Nacional da Verdade' (Rio de Janeiro: ISER, 2013).

Institutos de Estudos da Religião, *Um Ano de Comissão da Verdade: Contribuições Críticas para o Debate Público (II Relatório de Monitoramento da Comissão Nacional da Verdade)* (Rio de Janeiro: ISER, 2013).

Jabri, Vivienne, 'Michel Foucault's Analytics of War: The Social, the International, and the Racial', *International Political Sociology* 1, no. 1 (2007): 67–81.

Jabri, Vivienne, 'War, Government, Politics: A Critical Response to the Hegemony of the Liberal Peace', in *Peacebuilding: Critical Developments and Approaches* (Basingstoke: Plagrave Mackmillan, 2010), pp. 41–58.

Jackson, Richard, 'The Ghosts of State Terror: Knowledge, Politics and Terrorism Studies', *Critical Studies on Terrorism* 1, no. 3 (10 December 2008): 377–92.

Jackson, Richard, Eamon Murphy and Scott Poynting, *Contemporary State Terrorism: Theory and Practice* (New York: Routledge, 2010).

'Jair Bolsonaro é Eleito Presidente e Interrompe Série de Vitórias do PT', <https://g1.globo.com/politica/eleicoes/2018/noticia/2018/10/28/jair-bolsonaro-e-eleito-presidente-e-interrompe-serie-de-vitorias-do-pt.ghtml> (accessed 7 August 2019).

James W. Nickel, 'Rethinking Indivisibility: Towards A Theory of Supporting Relations between Human Rights', *Human Rights Quarterly* 30, no. 4 (2008): 984–1001.

JanMohamed, Abdul, 'The Economy of Manichean Allegory: The Function of Racial Difference in Colonialist Literature', *Critical Inquiry* 12, no. 1 (1985): 59–87.

Jelin, Elizabeth, 'Public Memorialization in Perspective: Truth, Justice and Memory of Past Repression in the Southern Cone of South America', *International Journal of Transitional Justice* 1, no. 1 (1 March 2007): 138–56.

Jelin, Elizabeth, *State Repression and the Labors of Memory* (Minneapolis: University of Minnesota Press, 2003).

Jinkings, Ivana, Kim Doria and Murilo Cleto (eds), *Por Que Gritamos Golpe? Para Intender o Impeachment e a Crise Política no Brasil* (São Paulo: Boitempo Editorial, 2016).

Joana, Jean and Frédéric Mérand, 'The Varieties of Liberal Militarism: A Typology', *French Politics* 12, no. 2 (2014): 177–91.

'Juscelino Kubitschek Foi Assassinado, Conclui a Comissão da Verdade de SP', Carta Capital, <http://www.cartacapital.com.br/sociedade/comissao-da-verdade-de-sp-vai-declarar-que-jk-foi-assassinado-2144.html> (accessed 11 September 2013).

Katz, P., 'A New "Normal": Political Complicity, Exclusionary Violence and the Delegation of Argentine Jewish Associations during the Argentine Dirty War', *International Journal of Transitional Justice* 5, no. 3 (19 October 2011): 366–89.

Keck, Magret and Kathryn Sikkink, *Activists beyond Borders: Advocacy Networks in International Politics* (Ithaca: Cornell University Press, 1998).

Kelly, Henry Ansgar, 'Inquisition and the Prosecution of Heresy: Misconceptions and Abuses', *Church History* 58, no. 4 (1989): 439–51.

Kennedy, David, 'The International Human Rights Movement: Part of the Problem?' *Harvard Human Rights Journal* 15 (2002): 101–26.

Kent, Michael and Peter Wade, 'Genetics against Race: Science, Politics and Affirmative Action in Brazil', *Social Studies of Science* 45, no. 6 (2015): 816–38.

Kienscherf, Markus, 'A Programme of Global Pacification: Us Counterinsurgency Doctrine and the Biopolitics of Human (in)Security', *Security Dialogue* 42, no. 6 (2011): 517–35.

Kienscherf, Markus, 'Beyond Militarization and Repression: Liberal Social Control as Pacification', *Critical Sociology* 42, no. 7–8 (2016): 1179–94.

Kritz, Neil J., 'The Dilemmas of Transitional Justice', in Neil J. Kritz (ed.), *Transitional Justice: How Emerging Democracies Reckon with Former Regimes*, vol. 1 (Washington, DC: United States Institute of Peace, 1995), pp. xix–xxx.

Krog, Antjie, *Country of My Skull* (London: Randon House, 1999).

Kuhn, Thomas, *The Structure of Scientific Revolutions* (Chicago; London: The University of Chicago Press, 1996).

LaCapra, Dominick, *Representing the Holocaust: History, Theory, Trauma* (Ithaca: Cornell University Press, 1994).

Lacerda, Tessa, '"Victim": What Is Hidden behind This Word?' *International Journal of Transitional Justice* 10, no. 1 (2016): 179–88.

Lacey, N., 'A Clear Concept of Intention: Elusive or Illusory?' *The Modern Law Review* 56, no. 5 (1993): 621–42.

Laclau, Ernesto and Chantal Mouffe, *Hegemony and Socialist Strategy* (London; New York: Verso, 1985).

Laidlaw, Zoë, 'Investigating Empire: Humanitarians, Reform and the Commission of Eastern Inquiry', *Journal of Imperial and Commonwealth History* 40, no. 5 (2012): 749–68.

Lambourne, W., 'Transitional Justice and Peacebuilding after Mass Violence', *International Journal of Transitional Justice* 3, no. 1 (26 September 2009): 28–48.

Lambourne, Wendy and Vivianna Rodriguez Carreon, 'Engendering Transitional Justice: A Transformative Approach to Building Peace and Attaining Human Rights for Women', *Human Rights Review* 17, no. 1 (2016): 71–93.

Laplante, L. J., 'Transitional Justice and Peace Building: Diagnosing and Addressing the Socioeconomic Roots of Violence through a Human Rights Framework', *International Journal of Transitional Justice* 2, no. 3 (17 October 2008): 331–55.

Laqueur, Walter, *The Age of Terrorism* (Boston, MA: Little, Brown and Company, 1987).

Lederach, John Paul, *Building Peace: Sustainable Reconciliation in Divided Societies* (Washington, DC: United States Institute of Peace Press, 1997).

Lee, Raymond M. and Elizabeth Anne Stanko (eds), *Researching Violence: Essays on Methodology and Measurement* (London: Routledge, 2003).

Leebaw, Bronwyn Anne, *Judging State-Sponsored Violence, Imagining Political Change* (New York: Cambridge University Press, 2011).

Leebaw, Bronwyn Anne, 'The Irreconcilable Goals of Transitional Justice', *Human Rights Quarterly* 30, no. 1 (2008): 95–118.

Lei No 12.528, de 18 de Novembro de 2011 (Brasília: Diário Oficial da União, 2011).

Lei Nº 12.798, de 04 de Abril de 2013 (Brasília: Diário Oficial da União, 2013).

Lei Nº 12.952, de 20 de Janeiro de 2014 (Brasília: Diário Oficial da União, 2014).

Lei Nº 13.115, de 20 de Abril de 2015 (Brasília: Diário Oficial da União, 2015).

Lei nº 4.390, de 29 de Agosto de 1964 (1964).

Lei Nº 8.159, de 8 de Janeiro de 1991 (Brasília: Diário Oficial da União, 1991).

Lessa, F., T. D. Olsen, L. A. Payne, G. Pereira and A. G. Reiter, 'Overcoming Impunity: Pathways to Accountability in Latin America', *International Journal of Transitional Justice* 8, no. 1 (30 January 2014): 75–98.

Lessa, Francesca and Vincent Druliolle, *The Memory of State Terrorism in The Southern Cone: Argentina, Chile and Uruguay* (New York: Palgrave Macmillan, 2011).

Levi, Primo, *The Drowned and the Saved* (London: Abacus, 1989).

Leys, Ruth, *Trauma: A Genealogy* (Chicago; London: University of Chicago Press, 2000).

Lijster, Thijs, '"All Reification Is a Forgetting": Benjamin, Adorno, and the Dialectic of Reification', in Samir Gandesha and Johan F. Hartle (eds), *The Spell of Capital: Reification and Spectacle* (Amsterdam: Amsterdam University Press, 2017), pp. 55–66.

'Lista de Vítimas da Esquesda Tem Ex-PM ainda Vivo', Estadão, <http://politica.estadao.com.br/noticias/geral,lista-de-vitimas-da-esquerda-tem-ex-pm-ainda-vivo-imp-,1605866> (accessed 22 January 2016).

Little, Adrian, 'Disjunctured Narratives: Rethinking Reconciliation and Conflict Transformation', *International Political Science Review* 33, no. 1 (22 June 2011): 82–98.

Loureiro, Pedro Mendes and Alfredo Saad-Filho, 'The Limits of Pragmatism: The Rise and Fall of the Brazilian Workers' Party (2002–2016)', *Latin American Perspectives*, 2016, 1–37.

Luckhurst, Roger, 'The Trauma Question' (Abingdon; New York: Routledge, 2008).

Mabee, Bryan and Srdjan Vucetic, 'Varieties of Militarism: Towards a Typology', *Security Dialogue* 49, no. 1–2 (2018): 96–108.

MacKenzie, Megan, Thomas Gregory, Nisha Shah, Tarak Barkawi, Toni Haastrup, Maya Eichler, Nicole Wegner and Alison Howell, 'Can We Really "Forget" Militarization? A Conversation on Alison Howell's Martial Politics', *International Feminist Journal of Politics* 21, no. 5 (2019): 816–36.

Maldonado-Torres, Nelson, *Against War: Views from the Underside of Modernity* (Durham, NC: Duke University Press, 2008).

Malešević, Siniša, *The Sociology of War and Violence* (New York: Cambridge University Press, 2010).

Malksoo, M., '"Memory Must Be Defended": Beyond the Politics of Mnemonical Security', *Security Dialogue* 46, no. 3 (26 February 2015): 1–17.

Mani, R., 'Rebuilding an Inclusive Political Community After War', *Security Dialogue* 36, no. 4 (1 December 2005): 511–26.

Mani, Rama, 'Balancing Peace with Justice in the Aftermath of Violent Conflict', *Development* 48, no. 3 (September 2005): 25–34.

Mann, Michael, *The Dark Side of Democracy: Explaining Ethnic Cleansing*. Cambridge: Cambridge University Press, 2005.

Mann, Michael, 'The Roots and Contradictions of Modem Militarism', *New Left Review* 162 (1987): 35–50.

Marchesi, Aldo, 'Revolution Beyond the Sierra Maestra: The Tupamaros and the Development of a Repertoire of Dissent in the Southern Cone', *The Americas* 70, no. 3 (2014): 523–53.

Marchesi, Aldo and Jaime Yaffe, 'La violencia bajo la lupa: Una revisión de la literatura sobre violencia y política en los sesenta', *Revista Uruguaya de Ciencia Política* 19, no. 1 (2010): 95–118.

'Marielle Franco: Brazil's Favelas Mourn the Death of a Champion', <https://www.theguardian.com/world/2018/mar/18/marielle-franco-brazil-favelas-mourn-death-champion> (accessed 20 May 2018).

Marighella, Carlos, *Escritos de Carlos Marighella* (São Paulo: Editorial Livramento, 1979).

Marighella, Carlos, 'Minimanual of the Urban Guerrilla', in *Terror and Urban Guerrillas: A Study of Tactics and Documents* (Coral Gables, FL: University of Miami Press, 1982).

Markarian, V., *Left in Transformation: Uruguayan Exiles and the Latin American Human Rights Networks, 1967–1984* (New York: Routledge, 2005).

Martins Filho, João Roberto, 'The War of Memory: The Brazilian Military Dictatorship According to Militants and Military Men', *Latin American Perspectives* 36, no. 5 (27 October 2009): 89–107.

Martins Filho, João Roberto, 'Tortura e Ideologia: Os Militares Brasileiros e a Doutrina da Guerre Révolutionnaire (1959–1974)', in Cecília MacDowell Santos, Edison Teles and Janaína de Almeida Teles (eds), *Desarquivando a Ditadura: Memória e Justiça no Brasil*, vol. 1 (São Paulo: Aderaldo & Rothschild Editores, 2009), pp. 179–202.

Martuccelli, Danilo, 'Reflexões sobre a Violência na Condição Moderna', *Tempo Social: Revista de Sociologia Da USP* 1, no. 1 (1999): 157–75.

Marx, Karl, *Capital: A Critique of Political Economy*, vol. 1 (London: Penguin Books, 1990).

Marx, Karl and Frederick Engels, *Collected Works*, vol. 25 (London: Lawrence and Wishart, 1987).

Mbembe, Achille, 'Necropolitics', *Public Culture* 15, no. 1 (2003): 11–40.

Mbembe, Achille, *Necropolitics* (Durham, NC: Duke University Press, 2019).

McEvoy, K. and K. McConnachie, 'Victims and Transitional Justice: Voice, Agency and Blame', *Social & Legal Studies* 22, no. 4 (11 September 2013): 489–513.

McEvoy, Kieran, 'Beyond Legalism : Towards a Thicker Understanding of Transitional Justice', *Journal of Law and Society* 34, no. 4 (2007): 411–40.

Meirelles, Renata, 'A Anistia Internacional e o Brasil: O Princípio da Não-Violência e a Defesa de Presos Políticos', *Revista Tempo e Argumento* 6, no. 11 (2014): 327–54.

Meister, Robert, *After Evil: A Politics of Human Rights* (New York: Columbia University Press, 2012).

Mendeloff, David, 'Trauma and Vengeance: Assessing the Psychological and Emotional Effects of Post-Conflict Justice', *Human Rights Quarterly* 31, no. 3 (2009): 592–623.

Mendeloff, David, 'Truth-Seeking, Truth-Telling, and Postconflict Peacebuilding: Curb the Enthusiasm?' *International Studies Review* 6 (2004): 355–80.

Menezes, Carolinie Grassi Franco de and Katia Felipini Neves, 'Rotas para um novo Destino', in Marcolo Mattos Araujo and Maria Cristina Oliveira Bruno (eds), *Memorial da Resistência de São Paulo* (São Paulo: Pinacoteca do Estado, 2009), pp. 29–39.

Mesplé, Antonio, phone interview, 6 January 2018.

Mezarobba, Glenda, 'Entre Reparações, Meias Verdades e Impunidade: O Difícil Rompimento com o Legado da Ditadura no Brasil', *Sur – Revista Internacional de Direitos Humanos* 7, no. 13 (2010): 7–26.

Mezarobba, Glenda, *Um Acerto de Contas com o Futuro: A Anistia e Suas Conseqüências: Um Estudo do Caso Brasileiro* (São Paulo: Humanitas, 2006).

Mezzadra, Sandro, 'The Topicality of Prehistory: A New Reading of Marx's Analysis of "So-called Primitive Accumulation"', *Rethinking Marxism* 23, no. 3 (2011): 302–21.

'Militarism', <https://academic.oup.com/ijtj/search-results?page=1&q=militarism&fl_SiteID=5176&SearchSourceType=1&allJournals=1> (accessed 2 June 2021).

'Militarism', <https://www.ictj.org/search-results?search=militarism> (accessed 5 June 2021).

'Militarization', <https://www.ictj.org/search-results?search=militarization> (accessed 5 June 2021).

'Military', <https://academic.oup.com/ijtj/search-results?q=military&allJournals=1&fl_SiteID=5176&page=1&qb=%7B%22q%22:%22military%22%7D> (accessed 5 June 2021).

'Military', <https://www.ictj.org/search-results?search=military> (accessed 5 June 2021).

Miller, Zinaida, '(Re)Distributing Transition', *The International Journal of Transitional Justice* 7, no. 2 (2013): 370–80.

Ministério da Defesa, 'Ofício Nº 10944/Gabinete', <http://www.cnv.gov.br/images/pdf/Defesa_FFAA_esclarecimentos_2014_09_19.pdf> (accessed 22 January 2016).

Ministério da Defesa, 'Ofício Nº 3329/MD', <http://www.cnv.gov.br/images/pdf/ofcios_MD_foras.pdf> (accessed 22 January 2016).

Ministério da Justiça, *Relatório Anual da Comissão de Anistia 2010* (Brasília: Comissão de Anistia, 2010).

Minow, Martha, 'Between Vengeance and Forgiveness : South Africa's Truth and Reconciliation Commission', *Negotiation Journal* 14, no. 4 (1998): 319–55.

Misse, Michel, 'Crime, Sujeito e Sujeição Criminal: Aspectos de Uma Contribuição Analítica sobre a Categoria "Bandido"', *Lua Nova: Revista de Cultura e Política*, no. 79 (2011): 15–38.

Misse, Michel, 'Violência, Ciminalidade e Mais-Valia', *Insight Inteligência* (Abril-Maio 2018): 65–84.

Misztal, B. A., *Theories of Social Remembering* (Maidenhead: Open University Press, 2003).

Monteiro, F. J., 'Comissão da Verdade ou Comissão do Possível?' (2012), <http://juntos.org.br/2012/05/comissao-da-verdade-ou-comissao-do-possivel/>.

Moon, Claire, 'Healing Past Violence: Traumatic Assumptions and Therapeutic Interventions in War and Reconciliation', *Journal of Human Rights* 8, no. 1 (31 March 2009): 71–91.

Moon, Claire, *Narrating Political Reconciliation: South Africa's Truth and Reconciliation Commission* (Lanham, MD: Lexington Books, 2008).

Moon, Claire, 'Narrating Political Reconciliation: Truth and Reconciliation in South Africa', *Social & Legal Studies* 15, no. 2 (1 June 2006): 257–75.

Moore, Michael S., *Placing Blame: A General Theory of the Criminal Law* (Oxford: Clarendon Press, 1997).

Morais, Lecio and Alfredo Saad-Filho, 'Neo-Developmentalism and the Challenges of Economic Policy-Making under Dilma Rousseff', *Critical Sociology* 38, no. 6 (2012): 789–98.

Motta, Rodrigo Patto Sá, *Em Guarda contra o 'Perigo Vermelho': O Anticomunismo no Brasil* (São Paulo: Editora Perspectiva, 2002).

Moyn, Samuel, 'Anti-Impunity as Deflection of Argument', in Karen Engle, Zinaida Miller and D. M. Davis (eds), *Anti-Impunity and the Human Rights Agenda* (Cambridge: Cambridge University Press, 2016), pp. 68–94.

'Na Véspera de Julgamento sobre Lula, Comandante do Exército Diz Repudiar Impunidade', <https://www1.folha.uol.com.br/poder/2018/04/na-vespera-de-julgamento-sobre-lula-comandante-do-exercito-diz-repudiar-impunidade.shtml> (accessed 8 January 2021).

Nagy, Rosemary, 'Transitional Justice as Global Project: Critical Reflections', *Third World Quarterly* 29, no. 2 (February 2008): 275–89.

'"Não São Só 20 Centavos", Dizem Manifestantes na Avenida Paulista', <https://www1.folha.uol.com.br/cotidiano/2013/06/1297985-nao-sao-so-20-centavos-dizem-manifestantes-na-avenida-paulista.shtml> (accessed 7 August 2019).

Naqvi, Yasmin, 'The Right to the Truth in International Law: Fact or Fiction?' *International Review of the Red Cross* 88, no. 862 (June 2006): 245–73.

Navarro, Marysa, 'The Personal Is Political: Las Madres de La Plaza de Mayo', in Manuel A. Garretón Merino and Susan Eckstein (eds), *Power and Popular Protest: Latin American Social Movements* (Berkeley: University of California Press, 2001), pp. 241–58.

Neal, Andrew W., 'Foucault in Guantánamo: Towards an Archaeology of the Exception', *Security Dialogue* 37, no. 1 (2006): 31–46.

Neocleous, Mark, '"A Brighter and Nicer New Life": Security as Pacification', *Social and Legal Studies* 20, no. 2 (2011): 191–208.

Neocleous, Mark, 'International Law as Primitive Accumulation; or, the Secret of Systematic Colonization', *European Journal of International Law* 23, no. 4 (2012): 941–62.

Neocleous, Mark, 'Security, Commodity, Fetishism', *Critique* 35, no. 3 (2007).

Neocleous, Mark, *The Fabrication of Social Order: A Critical Theory of Police Power* (London: Pluto Press, 2000).

Neto, Paulo de Mesquita, 'Programa Nacional de Direitos Humanos: Continuidade ou Mudança no Tratamento dos Direitos Humanos', *Revista CEJ* 1, no. 1 (1997).

'News Organizations Team up to Provide Transparency to Covid-19 Data', <https:// www1.folha.uol.com.br/internacional/en/scienceandhealth/2020/06/news- organizations-team-up-to-provide-transparency-to-covid-19-data.shtml?utm_ source=mail&utm_medium=social&utm_campaign=compmail> (accessed 8 July 2020).

Nino, Carlos, 'The Duty to Punish Past Abuses of Human Rights Put into Context: The Case of Argentina', *Yale Law Journal* 100, no. 8 (1991): 2619–40.

Nora, Pierre, 'Between Memory and History : Les Lieux de Mémoire', *Representations* 26 (Spring 1989): 7–24.

Norval, Aletta J., 'Memory, Identity and the (Im)possibility of Reconciliation: The Work of the Truth and Reconciliation Commission in South Africa', *Constellations* 5, no. 2 (June 1998): 250–65.

'Nota Oficial da CNV 50 Anos do Golpe de 64', <http://www.cnv.gov.br/index. php/outros-destaques/457-nota-da-cnv-sobre-os-50-anos-do-golpe-de- estado-de-1964> (accessed 10 April 2014).

'Nota sobre a Prorrogação do Mandato da CNV', <http://www.cnv.gov.br/textos-do- colegiado/596-nota-sobre-a-prorrogação-do-mandato-da-cnv.html> (accessed 11 January 2016).

Nunes, Felipe and Carlos Ranulfo Melo, 'Impeachment, Political Crisis and Democ- racy in Brazil', *Revista de Ciencia Política (Santiago)* 37, no. 2 (2017): 281–304.

Nwogu, N. V., 'When and Why It Started: Deconstructing Victim-Centered Truth Commissions in the Context of Ethnicity-Based Conflict', *International Journal of Transitional Justice* 4, no. 2 (4 June 2010): 275–89.

Nytagodien, Ridwan and Arthur Neal, 'Collective Trauma, Apologies, and the Politics of Memory', *Journal of Human Rights* 3, no. 4 (December 2004): 465–75.

'O Artigo em VEJA e a Prisão de Bolsonaro nos Anos 1980', <https://veja.abril. com.br/blog/reveja/o-artigo-em-veja-e-a-prisao-de-bolsonaro-nos-anos-1980/> (accessed 8 January 2021).

O'Donnell, Guillermo, 'Reflections on the Patterns of Change in the Bureaucratic- Authoritarian State', *Latin American Research Review* 13, no. 1 (1978): 3–38.

O'Donnell, Guillermo and Phillipe C. Schmitter, 'Transitions from Authoritarian Rule: Tentative Conclusions about Uncertain Democracies', in Neil J. Kritz (ed.), *Transitional Justice: How Emerging Democracies Reckon with Former Regimes*, vol. 1 (Washington, DC: United States Institute of Peace, 1995), pp. 57–64.

Obradovic-Wochnik, J., 'The "Silent Dilemma" of Transitional Justice: Silencing and Coming to Terms with the Past in Serbia', *International Journal of Transitional Justice* 7, no. 2 (16 May 2013): 328–47.

Ocampo, Joé Antonio, 'The Latin American Debt Crisis in Historical Perspective', in Joseph E. Stiglitz and Daniel Heymann (eds), *Life after Debt: The Origins and Resolutions of Debt Crisis*, International Economic Association Series (New York: Palgrave Macmillan, 2014), pp. 87–115.

Odysseos, Louiza and Anna Selmeczi, 'The Power of Human Rights/the Human Rights of Power: An Introduction', *Third World Quarterly* 36, no. 6 (2015): 1033–40.

'OHCHR Statement on Brazilian Truth Commission's Final Report', 2014, <http://acnudh.org/en/2014/12/ohchr-statement-on-brazilian-truth-commissions-final-report/>.

Oliveira, Francisco de, *Crítica à Razão Dualista/O Ornitorrinco* (São Paulo: Boitempo Editorial, 2003).

Olmeda, José A., 'Escape from Huntington's Labyrinth: Civil–Military Relations and Comparative Politics', in Florina Cristiana Matei and Thomas C. Bruneau (eds), *The Routledge Handbook of Civil–Military Relations* (London: Routledge, 2012), pp. 61–76.

'Onde Está Amarildo? Saiba quem é o Pedreiro que Desapareceu na Rocinha', <http://www.ebc.com.br/noticias/colaborativo/2013/07/amarildo-presente> (accessed 23 June 2016).

Orentlicher, Diane F., 'Settling Accounts: The Duty To Prosecute Human Rights Violations of a Prior Regime', *The Yale Law Journal* 100, no. 8 (1991): 2537–2615.

Osiel, Mark J., 'Constructing Subversion in Argentina's Dirty War', *Representations* 75, no. 1 (2001): 119–58.

'País Tem pelo menos 194 Assassinatos de Políticos ou Ativistas Sociais em 5 Anos', <https://brasil.estadao.com.br/noticias/geral,pais-tem-pelo-menos-194-assassinatos-de-politicos-ou-ativistas-sociais-em-5-anos,70002231748> (accessed 12 August 2019).

Paiva, Tatiana Moreira Campos, 'Memórias de Uma Herança: A Experiência de Filhos de Exilados Brasileiros da Ditadura Militar', in Cecília MacDowell Santos, Edison Teles and Janaína de Almeida Teles (eds), *Desarquivando a Ditadura: Memória e Justiça no Brasil*, vol. 1 (São Paulo: Aderaldo & Rothschild Editores, 2009), pp. 135–50.

Panizza, Francisco, *Contemporary Latin America: Development and Democracy beyond the Washington Consensus: The Rise of the Left* (London: Zed Books, 2009).

Panizza, Francisco and Alexandra Barahona de Brito, 'The Politics of Human Rights in Democratic Brazil: "A Lei Não Pega"', *Democratization* 5, no. 4 (1998): 20–51.

Paolantonio, Mario Di, 'Argentina After the "Dirty War": Reading the Limits of National Reconciliation', *Alternatives: Global, Local, Political* 22, no. 4 (1997): 433–65.

PCdoB-AV, 'Os Dezesseis Pontos (Novembro 1969)', in Daniel Aarão Reis and Jair Ferreira de Sá (eds), *Imagens da Revolução: Documentos Políticos das Organizações Clandestinas de Esquerda dos Anos 1961–1971* (Rio de Janeiro: Marco Zero, 1985), pp. 277–86.

PCdoB, 'Manifesto-Programa (Fevereiro 1962)', in Daniel Aarão Reis and Jair Ferreira de Sá (eds), *Imagens da Revolução: Documentos Políticos das Organizações Clandestinas de Esquerda dos Anos 1961–1971* (Rio de Janeiro: Marco Zero, 1985), pp. 4–35.

Pereira, Anthony W., 'An Ugly Democracy? State Violence and the Rule of Law in Postauthoritarian Brazil', in Peter R. Kingstone and Timothy J. Power (eds),

Democratic Brazil: Actors, Institutions, and Processes (Pittsburgh, PA: University of Pittsburgh Press, 2000), pp. 217–35.

Pereira, Anthony W., 'Continuity Is Not Lack of Change', *Critical Sociology* 38, no. 6 (2012): 777–87.

Pinheiro, Paulo Sérgio, 'Apresentação de Paulo Sérgio Pinheiro no Seminário sobre o Primeiro Ano de Trabalho da Comissão Nacional da Verdade' (2013), <http://www.cnv.gov.br/images/pdf/publicacoes/paulo_sergio/13_05_13_discurso_PSP_seminario_ONU.pdf>.

Pinheiro, Paulo Sérgio, 'Notas sobre o Futuro da Violência na Cidade Democrática', *Revista USP: Dossiê Cidades* 5 (Mar/Mai 1990): 43–6.

Pinheiro, Paulo Sérgio, Skype interview, 9 January 2018.

Pinheiro, Paulo Sérgio and Paulo de Mesquita Neto, 'Direitos Humanos no Brasil Perspectivas no Final do Século', 1995, 1–11.

Pinheiro, Paulo Sérgio and Paulo de Mesquita Neto, 'Programa Nacional de Direitos Humanos: Avaliação do Primeiro Ano e Perspectivas', *Estudos Avançados* 11, no. 3 (1997): 117–34.

Pinheiro, Paulo Sérgio and Raquel Aparecida Pereira, 'Comissão Nacional da Verdade, CNV, e os Arquivos', <http://www.cnv.gov.br/images/pdf/discurso_psp_1_abril.pdf> (accessed 12 September 2014).

Poets, Desiree, 'The Securitization of Citizenship in a "Segregated City": A Reflection on Rio's Pacifying Police Units', *Revista Brasileira de Gestão Urbana* 7, no. 2 (2015): 182–94.

Politi, Maurice, personal interview, 4 July 2014.

POLOP, 'Programa Socialista para o Brasil (Setembro 1967)', in Daniel Aarão Reis and Jair Ferreira de Sá (eds), *Imagens da Revolução: Documentos Políticos das Organizações Clandestinas de Esquerda dos Anos 1961–1971* (Rio de Janeiro: Marco Zero, 1985), pp. 89–116.

Popkin, Margaret and Naomi Roht-arriaza, 'Truth as Justice: Investigatory Commissions in Latin America', *Law & Social Inquiry* 20, no. 1 (1995): 79–116.

Popper, Karl, *The Logic of Scientific Discovery* (New York: Routledge, 2002).

'Por Motivo de Saúde, Gilson Dipp Deixa Comissão da Verdade', Folha de São Paulo, <http://www1.folha.uol.com.br/poder/2013/04/1270633-por-motivos-de-saude-gilson-dipp-deixa-comissao-da-verdade.shtml> (accessed 11 January 2016).

Portela, Fernando, *Guerra de Guerrillas no Brasil* (São Paulo: Global Editora, 1979).

'PSDB Pede Auditoria Especial do Resultado das Eleições ao TSE', <http://agenciabrasil.ebc.com.br/politica/noticia/2014-10/psdb-pede-auditoria-especial-do-resultado-das-eleicoes-ao-tse> (accessed 22 September 2018).

'Queiroz Preso: Entenda a Investigação Envolvendo o Ex-Assessor de Flávio Bolsonaro', <https://www.bbc.com/portuguese/brasil-50211661> (accessed 8 January 2021).

Quijano, Aníbal, 'El fantasma del desarrollo en América Latina', *Revista Del CESLA* 1 (1998): 38–55.

Rancière, Jacques, *Disagreement: Politics and Philosophy* (Minneapolis: University of Minnesota Press, 1998).

Rancière, Jacques, *The Emancipated Spectator* (London: Verso, 2011).

Reeves, Audrey and Charlotte Heath-Kelly, 'Curating Conflict: Political Violence in Museums, Memorials, and Exhibitions', *Critical Military Studies* 6, no. 3–4 (2020): 243–53.

Reiger, Caitlin, 'Hybrid Attempts at Accountability for Serious Crimes in Timor Leste', in *Transitional Justice in the Twenty-First Century: Beyond Truth versus Justice* (Cambridge: Cambridge University Press, 2006), pp. 143–70.

Reis, Daniel Aarão, *A Revolução Faltou ao Encontro: Os Comunistas no Brasil* (São Paulo: Brasiliense, 1990).

Reis, Daniel Aarão, 'Ditadura, Anistia e Reconciliação', *Estudos Históricos* 23, no. 45 (2010): 171–86.

Reis, Daniel Aarão, 'Ditadura e Sociedade: As Reconstrucões da Memória', in Daniel Aarão Reis, Marcelo Ridenti and Rodrigo Patto Sá Motta (eds), *O Golpe e a Ditadura Militar: Quarenta Anos Depois (1964–2004)* (Bauru, SP: Eudsc, 2004), pp. 29–52.

Reis, Daniel Aarão and Jair Ferreira de Sá, *Imagens da Revolucão: Documentos Políticos das Organizações Clandestinas de Esquerda dos Anos 1961–1971* (Rio de Janeiro: Marco Zero, 1985).

'Relator da PEC do Teto Diz que "dia do Juízo Fiscal" Virá se Projeto não for Aprovado', <https://economia.estadao.com.br/noticias/geral,relator-da-pec-do-teto-diz-que-dia-do-juizo-final-vira-se-projeto-nao-for-aprovado,10000080110> (accessed 8 January 2021).

'Relatório da Comissão Nacional da Verdade', <http://www.cnv.gov.br/> (accessed 23 June 2016).

Renner, Judith, 'The Local Roots of the Global Politics of Reconciliation: The Articulation of "Reconciliation" as an Empty Universal in the South African Transition to Democracy', *Millennium: Journal of International Studies* 42, no. 2 (2014): 263–85.

Resolução Nº 1, de 2 de Julho de 2012 (Brasília: Diário Oficial da União, 2012).

Resolução Nº 2, de 20 de Agosto de 2012 (Brasília: Diário Oficial da União, n.d.).

Resolução Nº 4, de 17 de Setembro de 2012 (Edição ext. Brasília: Diário Oficial da União, 2012).

Resolução Nº 5, de 5 de Novembro de 2012 (Brasília: Diário Oficial da União, 2012).

Resolução Nº 8, de 4 de Março de 2013 (Brasília: Diário Oficial da União, 2013).

Rezende, Claudinei Cássio de, *Suicídio Revolucionário: A Luta Armada e a Herança da Quimérica Revolução em Etapas* (São Paulo: Cultura Acadêmica, 2010).

Richmond, Oliver, *Peace in International Relations* (Abingdon: Routledge, 2008).

Richmond, Oliver P., *Peacebuilding: Critical Developments and Approaches* (Basingstoke: Palgrave Macmillan, 2010).

Richmond, Oliver P., 'The Problem of Peace: Understanding the "Liberal Peace"', *Conflict, Security & Development* 6, no. 3 (October 2006): 291–314.

Ricoeur, Paul, *Memory, History, Forgetting* (Chicago: The University of Chicago Press, 2004).

Ridenti, Marcelo, *O Fantasma da Revolução Brasileira* (São Paulo: Editora Unesp, 2005).

Roht-Arriaza, Naomi, 'Truth Commissions and Amnesties in Latin America: The Second Generation', *Proceedings of the Annual Meeting, American Society of International Law* 92 (1998): 313–16.

Roht-Arriaza, Naomi and Javier Mariezcurrena, *Transitional Justice in the Twenty-First Century: Beyond Truth versus Justice*, edited by Naomi Roht-Arriaza and Javier Mariezcurrena (Cambridge: Cambridge University Press, 2006).

Roio, José Luiz del, personal interview, 17 January 2018.

Rollemberg, Denise, 'Cultura Política Brasileira: Redefinição no Exílio (1964–1979)', *Hispanic Research Journal* 7, no. 2 (2006): 163–72.

Rollemberg, Denise, 'Esquerdas Revolucionárias e Luta Armada', in Jorge Ferreira and Lucilia de Almeida Neves Delgado (eds), *Brasil Republicano: O Tempo da Ditadura: Regime Militar e Movimentos Sociais em fins do Século XX* (Rio de Janeiro: Civilização Brasileira, 2003), pp. 43–9.

Rollemberg, Denise, 'Exílio: Refazendo Identidades', *Revista da Associação Brasileira de História Oral* 2 (January 1999): 39–73.

Rollemberg, Denise, 'Nômades, Sedentários e Metamorfoses: Trajetórias de Vidas no Exílio', in Daniel Aarão Reis, Marcelo Ridenti and Rodrigo Patto Sá Motta (eds), *O Golpe e a Ditadura Militar: Quarenta Anos Depois (1964–2004)* (Bauru, SP: Edusc, 2004), pp. 277–96.

Rollemberg, Denise, *O Apoio de Cuba à Luta Armada no Brasil: O Treinamento Guerrilheiro* (Rio de Janeiro: Maud, 2001).

Romanin, Enrique Andriotti, 'Decir la verdad, hacer justicia: los juicios por la verdad en Argentina', *Revista Europea de Estudios Latinoamericanos y Del Caribe* 94 (2013): 5–23.

Roniger, L., L. Senkman, S. Sosnowski *et al.*, *Exile, Diaspora, and Return: Changing Cultural Landscapes in Argentina, Chile, Paraguay, and Uruguay* (Oxford: Oxford University Press, 2018).

Rosenberg, Tina, 'Overcoming the Legacies of Dictatorship', *Foreign Affairs* 74, no. 3 (1995): 134–52.

Rossdale, Chris, *Resisting Militarism: Direct Action and the Politics of Subversion* (Edinburgh: Edinburgh University Press, 2019).

Rosser, E., 'Depoliticised Speech and Sexed Visibility: Women, Gender and Sexual Violence in the 1999 Guatemalan Comision Para El Esclarecimiento Historico Report', *International Journal of Transitional Justice* 1, no. 3 (2007): 391–410, <https://doi.org/10.1093/ijtj/ijm032>.

Rousseff, Dilma, 'Discurso da Presidenta da República, Dilma Rousseff, durante Entrega do Relatório Final da Comissão Nacional da Verdade' (2014), <http://www2.planalto.gov.br/acompanhe-o-planalto/discursos/discursos-da-presidenta/discurso-da-presidenta-da-republica-dilma-rousseff-durante-entrega-do-relatorio-final-da-comissao-nacional-da-verdade-brasilia-df>.

Rousseff, Dilma, 'Discurso da Presidenta da República, Dilma Rousseff, na Cerimônia de Instalação da Comissão da Verdade – Brasília/DF' (2012), <http://www2.planalto.gov.br/imprensa/discursos/discurso-da-presidenta-da-republica-dilma-rousseff-na-cerimonia-de-instalacao-da-comissao-da-verdade-brasilia-df>.

Saad-Filho, Alfredo, 'Social Policy for Neoliberalism: The Bolsa Família Programme in Brazil', *Development and Change* 46, no. 6 (2015): 1227–52.

Saad-Filho, Alfredo and Lecio Morais, 'Mass Protests: Brazilian Spring or Brazilian Malaise?' *Socialist Register* 50 (January 2014): 227–46.

Sadat, L., 'The Effect of Amnesties before Domestic and International Tribunals: Morality, Law and Politics', in Edel Hughes, Ramesh Thakur and William A. Schabas (eds), *Atrocities and International Accountability: Beyond Transitional Justice* (Tokyo: United Nations University Press, 2007), pp. 225–45.

Sales, Jean Rodrigues, 'A Ação Libertadora Nacional, a Revolução Cubana e a Luta Armada no Brasil', *Tempo* 14, no. 27 (2009): 199–217.

Santos, Cecília MacDowell dos, 'Transitional Justice from the Margins: Legal Mobilization and Memory Politics in Brazil', in Nina Schneider and Maria Esparza (eds), *Legacies of State Violence and Transitional Justice in Latin America: A Janus-Faced Paradigm?* (London: Lexington Books, 2015), pp. 37–72.

Sassen, Saskia, 'A Savage Sorting of Winners and Losers: Contemporary Versions of Primitive Accumulation', *Globalizations* 7, no. 1–2 (2010): 23–50.

Schabas, William A., 'Mens Rea and the International Criminal Tribunal for the Former Yugoslavia', *New England Law Review* 37, no. 4 (2003): 1015–36.

Schabas, William A., 'The Sierra Leone Truth and Reconciliation Commission', in Naomi Roht-Arriaza and Javier Mariezcurrena (eds), *Transitional Justice in the Twenty-First Century: Beyond Truth versus Justice* (Cambridge: Cambridge University Press, 2006), pp. 21–42.

Schick, Kate, 'Acting Out and Working Through: Trauma and (In)security', *Review of International Studies* 37, no. 04 (13 October 2011): 1837–55.

Schmid, E. and A. Nolan, '"Do No Harm"? Exploring the Scope of Economic and Social Rights in Transitional Justice', *International Journal of Transitional Justice* 8, no. 3 (14 September 2014): 362–82.

Schmitt, Carl, *Political Theology: Four Chapters on the Concept of Sovereignty* (Chicago: University of Chicago Press, 2005).

Schneider, Nina, 'Impunity in Post-Authoritarian Brazil: The Supreme Court's Recent Veredict on the Amnesty Law', *European Review of Latin American and Caribbean Studies* 90 (2011): 39–54.

Schneider, Nina, 'The Forgotten Voices of the Militares Cassados: Reconceptualising "Perpetrators" and "Victims" in Post-1985 Brazil', *Brasiliana – Journal for Brazilian Studies* 2, no. 2 (2013): 313–44.

Schwan, Gesine, 'Political Consequences of Silenced Guilt', *Constellations* 5, no. 4 (1998): 473–91.

'Secom: Comissão da Verdade', <https://www.novasb.com.br/trabalho/comissao-da-verdade/> (accessed 30 January 2021).

Secretaria de Direitos Humanos da Presidência da República, *Programa Nacional de Direitos Humanos (PNDH -3)* (Brasília: SDH/PR, 2010).

'Secretary-General's Message on the Occasion of the Presentation of the Final Report of the Brazilian National Commission of Truth' (2014), <http://www.un.org/sg/statements/index.asp?nid=8269>.

Segal, Lynne, 'Gender, War and Militarism: Making and Questioning the Links', *Feminist Review* 88, no. 1 (2008): 21–35, <https://doi.org/10.1057/palgrave.fr.9400383>.

Segato, Rita Laura, *La guerra contra las mujeres* (Madrid: Traficantes de Sueños, 2016).

Segato, Rita Laura, *Las estructuras elementares de la violencia: Ensayos sobre género entre la antropología, el psicoanálisis y los derechos humanos* (Buenos Aires: Prometeo Libros, 2010).

Seixas, Ivan and Maurice Politi, 'Os Elos que Vinculam as Vivências Encarceradas com as Perspectivas de Comunicação Museológica: O Olhar dos Ex Presos Políticos', in Marcelo Mattos Araújo and Maria Cristina Oliveira Bruno (eds), *Memorial da Resistência de São Paulo* (São Paulo: Pinacoteca do Estado, 2009), pp. 199–207.

Sharp, D. N., 'Emancipating Transitional Justice from the Bonds of the Paradigmatic Transition', *International Journal of Transitional Justice* 9, no. 1 (2 December 2014): 150–69.

Sharp, D. N. (ed.), *Justice and Economic Violence in Transition* (New York: Springer, 2014).

Sharp, Dustin, *Rethinking Transitional Justice for the Twenty-First Century: Beyond the End of History* (Cambridge: Cambridge University Press, 2018).

Sharp, Dustin N., 'Development, Human Rights and Transitional Justice: Global Projects for Global Governance', *International Journal of Transitional Justice* 9, no. 3 (2015): 517–26.

Shaw, Martin, 'Twenty-First Century Militarism: A Historical-Sociological Framework', in Anna Stavrianakis and Jan Selby (eds), *Militarism and International Relations: Political Economy, Security, Theory* (London: Routledge, 2012), pp. 19–32, <https://doi.org/10.4324/9780203101476>.

'Show de Horrores dada Surpreendente: Cientistas Políticos Analisam a Votação do Impeachment', <https://www.sul21.com.br/areazero/2016/04/show-de-horrores-nada-surpreendente-cientistas-politicos-analisam-a-votacao-do-impeachment/> (accessed 22 September 2018).

SIDA, *Reconciliation: Theory and Practice for Development Cooperation* (Stockholm: Edita Sverige AB, 2003).

Siegel, Richard Lewis, 'Transitional Justice : A Decade of Debate and Experience', *Human Rights Quarterly* 20, no. 2 (1998): 431–54.

Sikkink, K. and B. Marchesi, 'Nothing but the Truth: Brazil's Truth Commission Looks Back', *Foreign Affairs* (26 February 2015).

Silva, Luiz Ignacio Lula da, Emir Sader and Pablo Gentili, 'The Necessary, the Possible, and the Impossible: A Post-Presidential Interview with Luiz Inácio Lula Da Silva', *Latin American Perspectives* 43, no. 2 (2016): 220–37.

Silva, Nelson do Valle, 'Brazilian Society: Continuity and Change, 1930–2000', in Leslie Bethell (ed.), *The Cambridge History of Latin America, vol. 9: Brazil Since 1930* (Cambridge: Cambridge University Press, 2008), pp. 455–545.

Silva Filho, José Carlos Moreira da, 'Dever de Memória e a Construção da História Viva: A Atuação da Comissão de Anistia do Brasil na Concretização do Direito à Memória e à Verdade', in Boaventura de Sousa Santos, Paulo Abrão, Cecília MacDowell dos Santos and Marcelo D. Torelly (eds), *Repressão e Memória Política no Contexto Ibero-Brasileiro: Estudos sobre Brasil, Guatemala, Moçambique, Peru e Portugal* (Brasília; Coimbra: Ministério da Justiça; Comissão de Anistia; Centro de Estudos Sociais Universidade de Coimbra, 2010), pp. 186–227.

Silva Filho, José Carlos Moreira da, 'O Anjo da História e a Memória das Vítimas: O Caso da Ditadura Militar no Brasil', *Veritas* 53, no. 2 (2008): 150–78.

Simić, Olivera and Kathleen Daly, '"One Pair of Shoes, One Life": Steps towards Accountability for Genocide in Srebrenica', *International Journal of Transitional Justice* 5, no. 3 (2011): 477–91, <https://doi.org/10.1093/ijtj/ijr020>.

Singer, André, 'Brasil, Junho de 2013: Classes e Ideologias Cruzadas', *Novos Estudos – CEBRAP* 97 (Novembro 2013): 23–40.

Singer, André, 'Cutucando Onças com Vara Cutra: Ensaio Desenvolvimentista no Primeiro Mandato de Dilma Rousseff (2011–2014)', *Novos Estudos* 102 (2015): 43–71.

Singer, André, *Os Sentidos do Lulismo: Reforma Gradual e Pacto Conservador* (São Paulo: Companhia das Letras, 2012).

Singer, André, 'Raízes Sociais e Ideológicas do Lulismo', *Novos Estudos* 85 (2009): 83–102.

Skidmore, Thomas E., *The Politics of Military Rule in Brazil 1964–85* (New York; Oxford: Oxford University Press, 1988).

Soares, Inês Virgínia Prado and Renan Honório Quinalha, 'Lugares de Memória no Cenário Brasileiro de Justiça de Transição', *Revista Internacional de Direito e Cidadania* 10 (Junho 2011): 75–86.

Sorel, Georges, *Reflections on Violence*, edited by Jeremy Jennings (Cambridge: Cambridge University Press, 1999).

Spaulding, Norman W., 'Resistance, Countermemory, Justice', *Critical Inquiry* 41, no. 1 (2014): 132–52.

Spivak, Gayatri Chakravorty, 'Can the Subaltern Speak?' in Cary Nelson and Lawrence Grossberg (eds), *Marxism and the Interpretation of Culture* (Basingstoke: Palgrave Macmillan, 1988), pp. 271–312.

Starling, Heloisa Maria Murgel, *Os Senhores das Gerais: Os Novos Inconfidentes e o Golpe Militar de 1964*. Petrópolis: Vozes, 1986.

Stavrianakis, Anna and Jan Selby, 'Militarism and International Relations in the Twenty-First Century', in Anna Stavrianakis and Jan Selby (eds), *Militarism and International Relations: Political Economy, Security and Theory* (London and New York: Routledge, 2012), pp. 3–18.

Stavrianakis, Anna and Maria Stern, 'Militarism and Security: Dialogue, Possibilities and Limits', *Security Dialogue* 49, no. 1–2 (2018): 3–18.

Stein, Peter, *Roman Law in European History* (New York: Cambridge University Press, 1999).

Sylvester, Christine, 'Curating and Re-Curating the American War in Vietnam', *Security Dialogue* 49, no. 3 (2018): 151–64, <https://doi.org/10.1177/0967010617733851>.

Sznajder, M. and L. Roniger, *La política del destierro y el exilio en América Latina* (Mexico City: FCE, 2013).

Tatagiba, Luciana and Andreia Galvão, 'Os Protestos no Brasil em Tempos de Crise (2011–2016)', *Opinião Pública* 25, no. 1 (2019): 63–96.

'TCU Conclui Parecer sobre Contas Prestadas pela Presidente da República Referentes a 2014', <https://portal.tcu.gov.br/imprensa/noticias/tcu-conclui-parecer-sobre-contas-prestadas-pela-presidente-da-republica-referentes-a-2014.htm> (accessed 28 September 2018).

Teitel, Ruti G., *Transitional Justice* (Oxford: Oxford University Press, 2000).

Teitel, Ruti G., 'Transitional Justice as Liberal Narrative', in Ruti G. Teitel (ed.), *Globalizing Transitional Justice: Contemporary Essays* (Oxford: Oxford University Press, 2014), pp. 95–111.

Teitel, Ruti G., 'Transitional Justice Genealogy', *Harvard Human Rights Journal* 16 (2003): 69–94.

Teles, Edson, 'Políticas do Silêncio e Interditos da Memória na Transição do Consenso', in Cecília MacDowell Santos, Edison Teles and Janaína de Almeida Teles (eds), *Desarquivando a Ditadura: Memória e Justiça no Brasil*, vol. 2 (São Paulo: Aderaldo & Rothschild Editores, 2009), pp. 578–91.

Teles, Edson and Renan Quinalha, 'O Trabalho de Sísifo da Comissão Nacional da Verdade' (2013), <https://blogdaboitempo.com.br/2013/10/02/o-trabalho-se-sisifo-da-comissao-nacional-da-verdade/> (accessed 21 September 2021).

Teles, Janaína de Almeida, 'Entre o Luto e a Melancolia: A Luta dos Familiares de Mortos e Desaparecidos Políticos no Brasil', in Cecília MacDowell Santos, Edison Teles and Janaína de Almeida Teles (eds), *Desarquivando a Ditadura: Memória e Justiça no Brasil*, vol. 1 (São Paulo: Aderaldo & Rothschild Editores, 2009), pp. 151–77.

Telles, Helcimara, 'A Direita Vai às Ruas: O Antipetismo, a Corrupção e Democracia nos Protesto Antigoverno', *Ponto-e-Vírgula : Revista de Ciências Sociais* 19 (2016): 97–125.

'Textos de Claudio Fonteles: Exercitando o Diálogo', <http://www.cnv.gov.br/index.php/publicacoes/177-textos-de-claudio-fonteles> (accessed 26 October 2014).

Thompson, Edward, 'Notes on Exterminism, the Last Stage of Civilization', *New Left Review* 121 (1980): 3–31.

Tieffemberg, Silvia, 'Deber de responder. Sobre la inquisitio en América', *Anclajes* (Diciembre 2001): 71–87.

Toit, André du, 'The Moral Foundations of the South African TRC: Truth as Acknowledgment and Justice as Recognition', in Robert Rotberg and Dennis Thompson (eds), *Truth v. Justice: The Morality of Truth Commissions* (Princeton: Princeton University Press, 2000), pp. 122–40.

Torelly, Marcelo, 'Assessing a Late Truth Commission: Challenges and Achievements of the Brazilian National Truth Commission', *International Journal of Transitional Justice* 12, no. 2 (2018): 194–215.

Torre, Juan Carlos and Liliana De Riz, *Argentina since 1946: The Cambridge History of Latin America*, 1991.

'TPI Informa Avaliação Preliminar da Jurisdição do Caso contra Bolsonaro', <https://comissaoarns.org/blog/2020-12-15-tpi-informa-avaliação-preliminar-da-jurisdição-do-caso-contra-bolsonaro/> (accessed 8 January 2021).

'Trabalho Conjunto da CNV e da Petrobras Localiza Acervo na Estatal', <http://www.cnv.gov.br/index.php/outros-destaques/210-trabalho-conjunto-da-comissao-nacional-da-verdade-e-da-petrobras-localiza-acervo-na-estatal-do-petroleo> (accessed 26 October 2014).

'Transitional Justice AND Armed Forces', <https://www.lexisnexis.com/uk/legal/search/journalssubmitForm.do#0%7C%7CCOMMON-DATE,D,H,$PSEUDOLOSK,A,H%7C%7C%7C%7Carmed forces> (accessed 5 June 2021).

'Transitional Justice AND Militarism', <https://www.lexisnexis.com/uk/legal/auth/checkbrowser.do?t=1622894545819&bhcp=1&bhhash=1#0%7C%7CCOMMON-DATE,D,H,$PSEUDOLOSK,A,H%7C%7C%7C%7Cmilitarism> (accessed 5 June 2021).

TRC, 'Truth and Reconciliation Commission of South Africa Report' (1998).

TRC Sierra Leone, 'Witness to Truth: Report of the Sierra Leone Truth and Reconciliation Commission' (2004).

Tutu, Desmond, *No Future Without Forgiveness* (New York: First Image Books, 2000).

UCDP, 'Database: Uppsala Conflict Data Program (UCDP)' (2015), <http://ucdp.uu.se/#/exploratory>.

United Nations, *Agenda Item 68: Report of the Human Rights Council*, UN General Assembly: A/61/PV.82 (2006).

United Nations, 'An Agenda for Peace: Preventive Diplomacy and Related Matters', UN General Assembly: A/RES/47/1 (1992).

United Nations, 'Convention against Torture and Other Cruel, Inhuman or Degrading Treatment or Punishment', in *Treaty Series: Treaties and International Agreements Registered or Filed and Recorded with the Secretariat of the United Nations* (New York: United Nations Publications, 1996), pp. 85–209.

United Nations, 'Convention Against Torture and Other Cruel, Inhuman or Degrading Treatment or Punishment', UN General Assembly: A/RES/39/4 (1984).

United Nations, 'Convention on the Prevention and Punishment of the Crime of Genocide', General Assembly: A/RES/3/260 (1948).

United Nations, 'Declaration on the Protection of All Persons from Enforced Disappearance', UN General Assembly: A/RES/47/133 (1992).

United Nations, 'From Madness to Hope: The 12-Year War in El Salvador', UN Security Council: S/25500 (1993).

United Nations, 'Impunity: Report of the Independent Expert to Update the Set of Principles to Combat Impunity, Diane Orentlicher', UN Economic and Social Council: E/CN.4/200 (2005).

United Nations, 'Question of the Impunity of Perpetrators of Human Rights Violations (Civil and Political)', UN Economic and Social Council: E/CN.4/Sub (1997).

United Nations, *Resolution 827*, UN Security Council: S/RES/827 (1993).

United Nations, *Resolution 955*, UN Security Council: S/RES/995 (1994).

United Nations, 'Resolution Adopted by the General Assembly on 18 December 2013 68/165. Right to the Truth', UN General Assembly: A/RES/68/165 (2014).

United Nations, 'Resolution Adopted by the General Assembly on 21 December 2010 65/196. Proclamation of 24 March as the International Day for the Right to Truth Concerning Gross Human Rights Violations and for the Dignity of Victims', UN General Assembly: A/RES/65/1 (2011).

United Nations, 'Rome Statute of the International Criminal Court', United Nations Diplomatic Conference of Plenipotentiaries on the Establishment of an International Criminal Court: A/CONF.183 (1998).

United Nations, *The Administration of Justice and the Human Rights of Detainees: Question of the Impunity of Perpetrators of Human Rights Violations (Civil and Political)*, Commission on Human Rights: E/CN.4/Sub.2/1997/20 (1997).

United Nations, 'The Rule of Law and Transitional Justice in Conflict and Post-Conflict Societies', UN Security Council: S/2004/616 (2004).

United Nations, 'Universal Declaration of Human Rights', UN General Assembly: 217 A (III) (1948).

United Nations, 'Vienna Declaration and Programme of Action', UN General Assembly: A/CN.15/23 (1993).

Vagts, Alfred, *A History of Militarism: Civilian and Military* (New York: Meridian Books, 1959).

Vannuchi, Paulo, personal interview, 17 January 2018.

Vargas, João C. and Jaime A. Alves, 'Geographies of Death: An Intersectional Analysis of Police Lethality and the Racialized Regimes of Citizenship in São Paulo', *Ethnic and Racial Studies* 33, no. 4 (2010): 611–36.

Vasudevan, Alex, Colin McFarlane and Alex Jeffrey, 'Spaces of Enclosure', *Geoforum* 39, no. 5 (2008): 1641–46.

'Veja as Principais Decisões da Justiça sobre a Prisão de Lula', <https://oglobo.globo.com/brasil/veja-as-principais-decisoes-da-justica-sobre-prisao-de-lula-23755973> (accessed 7 August 2019).

Veloso, Fernando A., André Villela and Fabio Giambiagi, 'Determinantes do "Milagre" Econômico Brasileiro (1968–1973): Uma Análise Empírica', *Revista Brasileira de Economia* 62, no. 2 (2008): 221–46.

Ventura, Zuenir, *1968: O Ano que não Terminou* (São Paulo: Planeta do Brasil, 2008).

Verdeja, Ernesto, 'The Elements of Political Reconciliation', in Alexander Keller Hirsch (ed.), *Theorizing Post-Conflict Reconciliation: Agonism, Restitution and Repair* (New York: Routledge, 2012), pp. 166–81.

Verdeja, Ernesto, *Unchopping a Tree: Reconciliation in the Aftermath of Political Violence* (Philadelphia: Temple University Press, 2009).

Vezzetti, Hugo, 'Los sesenta y los setenta', *Prismas: Revista de Historia Intelectual* 15 (2011): 53–62.

Vezzetti, Hugo, *Sobre la violencia revolucionaria: Memorias y olvidos* (Buenos Aires: Siglo XXI, 2009).

Vincent, Andrew, *The Politics of Human Rights* (New York: Oxford University Press, 2010).

Waiselfisz, Julio Jacobo, *Mapa da Violencia: Os Jovens do Brasil* (Brasília: Secretaria-Geral da Presidencia da República, 2014).

Waldorf, L., 'Anticipating the Past: Transitional Justice and Socio-Economic Wrongs', *Social & Legal Studies* 21, no. 2 (30 April 2012): 171–86.

Walker, Margaret Urban, 'The Cycle of Violence', *Journal of Human Rights* 5, no. 1 (January 2006): 81–105.

Walker, Margaret Urban, 'Transformative Reparations? A Critical Look at a Current Trend in Thinking about Gender-Just Reparations', *International Journal of Transitional Justice* 10, no. 1 (2016): 108–25.

Walker, R. B. J., 'Lines of Insecurity: International, Imperial, Exceptional', *Security Dialogue* 37, no. 1 (1 March 2006): 65–82.

Weinstein, H. M., 'Editorial Note: The Myth of Closure, the Illusion of Reconciliation: Final Thoughts on Five Years as Co-Editor-in-Chief', *International Journal of Transitional Justice* 5, no. 1 (14 March 2011): 1–10.

Welland, Julia, 'Militarised Violences, Basic Training, and the Myths of Asexuality and Discipline', *Review of International Studies* 39, no. 4 (2013): 881–902.

Welland, Julia, 'Violence and the Contemporary Soldiering Body', *Security Dialogue* 48, no. 6 (2017): 524–40.

Wenar, Leif, 'On the Nature of Rights', *Philosophy & Public Affairs* 93, no. 3 (1984): 223–52.

Weschler, Lawrence, *A Miracle, A Universe: Settling Accounts with Torturers* (Chicago: The University of Chicago Press, 1990).

Westhrop, Amy Jo, Ayra Guedes Garrido, Carolina Genovez Parreira and Shana Marques Prado dos Santos, *As Recomendações da Comissão Nacional da Verdade: Balanços sobre a Sua Implementação Dois Anos depois* (Rio de Janeiro: ISER, 2016).

'Where's Amarildo? How the Disappearance of a Construction Worker Taken from His Home by Police Has Sparked Protests in Brazil', <http://www.independent.co.uk/news/world/americas/where-s-amarildo-how-the-disappearance-of-a-construction-worker-taken-from-his-home-by-police-has-8745464.html> (accessed 23 July 2016).

Wibben, Annick T. R., 'Why We Need to Study (US) Militarism: A Critical Feminist Lens', *Security Dialogue* 49, no. 1–2 (2018): 136–48.

Wieviorka, Michel, *Violence: A New Approach* (London: Sage Publications, 2009).

Williams, Randall, *The Divided World: Human Rights and Its Violence* (Minneapolis: University of Minnesota Press, 2010).

Wilson, Richard, 'Violent Truths: The Politics of Memory in Guatemala', *Negotiating Rights: The Guatemalan Peace Process* (special issue), *Accord: An International Review of Peace Initiatives* 2 (November 1997), pp. 18–27.

Wilson, Richard A., *The Politics of Truth and Reconciliation in South Africa: Legitimizing the Post-Apartheid State* (Cambridge: Cambridge University Press, 2001).

Wolfe, Patrick, 'Settler Colonialism and the Elimination of the Native', *Journal of Genocide Research* 8, no. 4 (2006): 387–409.

Wood, Ellen Meiksins, *The Origin of Capitalism* (London: Verso, 2017).

World Bank World Development Indicators, 'Urban Population (% of Total)', <https://data.worldbank.org/indicator/SP.URB.TOTL.IN.ZS?locations=BR> (accessed 30 April 2019).

World Health Organization, 'WHO Coronavirus Disease (COVID-19) Dashboard', <https://covid19.who.int/?gclid=CjwKCAiA_9r_BRBZEiwAHZ_v175MN-vbP5iTCktOsE8iSdAlU_FhJ3hZowolc3ETbUOPdmSg6cZp8hoCXw4QAvD_BwE> (accessed 5 January 2021).

Zalaquett, José, 'Balancing Ethical Imperatives and Political Constraints: The Dilemma of New Democracies Confronting Past Human Rights Violations', *Hastings Law Journal* 43 (August 1992): 1425–38.

Zaluar, Alba, 'Democratizacao Inacabada: O Fracasso da Segurança Pública', *Estudos Avancados* 21, no. 61 (2007): 31–49.

Zaluar, Alba, 'Um Debate Disperso: Violência e Crime no Brasil da Redemocratização', *São Paulo Em Perspectiva* 13, no. 3 (2005): 3–17.

Zehfuss, Maja, *Wounds of Memory: The Politics of War in Germany* (Cambridge: Cambridge University Press, 2007).

Zerbine, Therezinha, *Anistia: Semente da Liberdade* (São Paulo, Escolas Profissionais Salesianas, 1979).

Zerubavel, Eviatar, 'In the Beginning: Notes on the Social Construction of Historical Discontinuity', *Sociological Inquiry* 63, no. 4 (1993): 352–3.

Žižek, Slavoj, 'The Obscenity of Human Rights: Violence as Symptom', *Lacan.com* (2005), <http://www.lacan.com/zizviol.htm> (accessed 21 September 2021).

Žižek, Slavoj, *The Sublime Object of Ideology* (London; New York: Verso, 2008).

Žižek, Slavoj, *Violence: Six Sideways Reflections* (London: Profile Books, 2008).

INDEX